FROM MARSHALL AID
TO ATLANTIC PARTNERSHIP

FROM MARSHALL AID
TO ATLANTIC PARTNERSHIP

European Integration as a Concern
of American Foreign Policy

BY

ERNST H. VAN DER BEUGEL

WITH A FOREWORD BY
HENRY A. KISSINGER

ELSEVIER PUBLISHING COMPANY
AMSTERDAM · LONDON · NEW YORK · 1966

ELSEVIER PUBLISHING COMPANY
335 JAN VAN GALENSTRAAT, P.O.BOX 211, AMSTERDAM

ELSEVIER PUBLISHING COMPANY LTD.
RIPPLESIDE COMMERCIAL ESTATE
RIPPLE ROAD, BARKING, ESSEX

AMERICAN ELSEVIER PUBLISHING COMPANY INC.
52 VANDERBILT AVENUE, NEW YORK, N.Y. 10017

LIBRARY OF CONGRESS CATALOG CARD NUMBER 66-16277

PRINTED IN THE NETHERLANDS
BY JOH. ENSCHEDÉ EN ZONEN, HAARLEM

To the Memory of my Parents

Foreword

The most consistent and constructive American policy since the end of World War II has been the development of Atlantic relationships. Europe emerged from the second great war of this century shaken to the core. Britain had been drained by its heroic war effort. In addition, she was obliged to adjust to the loss of Empire while overcoming almost chronic economic difficulties. The Continent was shattered. Every nation had been defeated at some stage during the war. Each country either had been or was then occupied by foreign troops. Social structures were weakened. Civil government was uncertain. It would have seemed unthinkable that within fifteen years Europe would far exceed its pre-war level of economic activity, that stable governments would be constituted almost everywhere, that major advances towards European economic and political integration would be made. In the aftermath of World War II it would have seemed incredible that within two decades Atlantic relationships would be strained by the need to find a role for Europe commensurate with its political and economic resurgence.

That this has come to pass is one of the great success stories of the post-war period. The difficulties which have resulted from Europe's new-found vigor should not obscure the vision which on both sides of the Atlantic inspired the process. In the United States four Administrations have been committed to the recovery and to political integration of Europe. It was a courageous decision which ended America's isolation and committed the United States to assume its share of responsibility for the future of Western Europe. The Marshall Plan launched the United States into close cooperation with its European allies. This partnership has been strengthened with time. At first the concern was largely economic. The Korean war added the dimension of defense. In the late fifties and early sixties the debate concerned the relative weight of Europe and the United States in an Atlantic partnership. In the process, the fate of Europe and the United States has become inextricably linked.

These achievements were possible because on both sides of the Atlantic there existed a group of individuals dedicated to Atlantic partnership and aware of the fact that the future of their societies depended on their ability to give concrete expression to the interdependence which is so basic a feature of contemporary international affairs. In the United States the idealism which had led to domestic reform in the thirties was channeled into reconstruction abroad. And in Europe, the hopes which had sustained wartime suffering were embodied in the efforts of far-sighted leaders who realized that this might be the last chance to save their countries and their civilization.

Ernst H. van der Beugel belonged to this group. First as Director-General, later as Minister of State for Foreign Affairs of the Netherlands, he was intimately connected with the operation of the Marshall Plan and with the cooperative Atlantic and European efforts which grew from it. Since leaving government service, he has played a major unofficial role as European secretary of the Bilderberg meetings which bring together eminent Americans and Europeans under the chairmanship of H.R.H. Prince Bernhard of the Netherlands. In all these positions, he has rendered distinguished service to the vitality of the Western world.

Mr. van der Beugel's book entitled *From Marshall Aid to Atlantic Partnership* is the first comprehensive study of American-European post-war relations written by a European. It is extremely valuable because it shows how a good friend of the United States has viewed and reacted to American policy. It is objective and fair. His occasional criticism is gentle and always constructive. He is free of the parochialism which is the bane of so much of the trans-Atlantic debate. He writes as a citizen of a commonwealth bordering both sides of the Atlantic; he feels no need to strike poses to define his identity and he is therefore free to concentrate on the merits of an issue without regard to where in the Atlantic area it may have originated.

Perhaps the greatest service of Mr. van der Beugel's thoughtful book is the demonstration that nearly two decades of cooperative effort can be described in terms which are as valid on one side of the Atlantic as on the other. At a time when the nations bordering the Atlantic seem too often to focus their energies on their disagreements, it is well to be reminded that their achievement has been due above all to their unity. The form and nature of cooperation in the next two decades will, of course, require considerable discussion. No serious person would maintain that all the old patterns will be applicable for all eternity. Mr. van der Beugel would argue, however, that the attitudes of cooperation of nearly two decades must provide the basis of any effort to recast relationships. His book shows how much has been built, too much, in fact, for it to be hazarded by the kind of disputes which form the headlines of the day. All the realities of human aspirations and of a technology of global impact require a close association of the nations bordering the North Atlantic. But Western history is full of tragedies in which a strong community of interests has been submerged by subsidiary rivalries or insufficient understanding. If the West is to overcome its perennial problem it will be due to the actions which Mr. van der Beugel describes and to the spirit which animates his book.

August 1965   HENRY A. KISSINGER

Acknowledgements

I am greatly indebted to the Netherlands Ministry of Foreign Affairs for being allowed to study the archives on the subject of my study and especially my own papers. The staff of the archives division has been particularly kind and helpful.

In the preparatory months of my work I received valuable assistance from the United States Information Service in The Hague and the Library of the Organisation for Economic Cooperation and Development in Paris.

The hospitality and cooperation of the Center for International Affairs of Harvard University has been beyond praise.

The discussions with the Faculty Members and the assistance I received from the Staff and the Secretaries have been of great importance to my work.

I especially want to thank Dr. Robert R. Bowie and Dr. Karl Kaiser for the opportunity they gave me to discuss my problems with them.

To my friend Henry Kissinger I am not only deeply grateful for the foreword which he wrote, but also for his stimulating and penetrating comments on various parts of my study.

Without the months I spent at Harvard, this book would either not have been written or would have been delayed for many years.

The advice and comments of Dr. J. Kymmell have been as valuable for me as in the period when we both worked in the Netherlands Ministry of Foreign Affairs. I am deeply indebted to him.

Miss Eva Popper of the Carnegie Endowment for International Peace in New York, never became impatient when she received my numerous requests for books and publications.

My former and present secretaries Miss M. de Kock van Leeuwen and Miss M. van Weezenbeek have performed miracles in deciphering my handwriting and putting it into readable print.

Mr. John Rijkens checked my English with patience and understanding.

Many persons on both sides of the Atlantic have generously contributed ideas to me. A complete listing of their names would be impractical and would, in some cases, violate express wishes for anonymity.

The cheerfulness and encouragement of my wife and children have been exemplary.

July 1965   E. H. van der Beugel

Contents

CHAPTER I

Aspects of American Foreign Policy (1789–1947)

A. INTRODUCTION

On September 17, 1796, George Washington formulated his deep conviction about United States relations with the outside world.

In the field of foreign policy the outside world was Europe. There was no other source of power towards which American foreign policy could be directed.

The words of his Farewell Address[1] shaped and influenced American foreign policy for far more than a century. Other words would be used, different ideologies preached, various actions adjusted to different circumstances, but Washington's words formed the basis for the famous doctrine of isolationism which for such a long period would dominate American foreign policy. 'Europe has a set of primary interests, which to us have none, or a very remote relation. Hence she must be engaged in frequent controversies, the causes of which are essentially foreign to our concerns. Hence therefore it must be unwise in us to implicate ourselves, by artificial ties in the ordinary vicissitudes of her politics, or the ordinary combinations and collision of her friendships or enmities. Our detached and distant situation invites us to pursue a different course... It is our true policy to steer clear of permanent alliances,

1. For text of the Farewell Address: S. E. Morison, *The Oxford History of the United States 1783–1917*, (Oxford University Press, 1927), Vol. I, p. 202.

with any portion of the foreign world... Taking care always to keep ourselves, by suitable establishments, on a respectable defensive posture, we may safely trust to temporary alliances for extraordinary emergencies.'

On March 12, 1947, President Truman said: 'One of the primary objectives of the foreign policy of the United States is the creation of conditions in which we and other nations will be able to work out a way of life free from coercion...

I believe that it must be the policy of the United States to support free people, who are resisting attempted subjugation by armed minorities or by outside pressures.

I believe that we must assist free peoples to work out their own destinies in their own way...

The free people of the world look to us for support in maintaining their freedoms. If we falter in our leadership we may endanger the peace of the world – and we shall surely endanger the welfare of our nation.'[2]

Between these two addresses lies the evolution from total isolation to total and permanent involvement in world affairs.

In the context of this book it is only possible to analyze some trends and elements in the process and development of American foreign policy for this period.

Three phases can be distinguished in the evolution of this policy.

The first phase covers the period up to the attack on Pearl Harbor in December 1941. It was the first time that the United States was physically attacked. It closed a chapter of more than 150 years of foreign policy in which the threat to the national security hardly played any role in the conduct of American foreign policy. It is true that in 1939 and 1940 there was already a strong feeling amongst certain sections of the administration and of public opinion that aid to the Western democracies was closely linked to American security, but it was only at Pearl Harbor that the nineteenth century reality

2.   *Documents on American Foreign Relations,* Vol. IX, (Princeton University Press, 1949), pp. 6–7.

and the twentieth century illusion of the physical untouchability of the United States was terminated.

The second phase will briefly deal with the period of the Second World War and the American hopes, ideas, and ideals for the post-war world order.

The third period will cover the two post-war years leading to the emergence of the Truman Doctrine and the Marshall Plan. In this period the 'one world' concept definitely broke down and America learned to recognize that it had become not only the most powerful partner in a system of collective security, but the sole guardian of a free society in its struggle with the other main power in the post-war world, the Soviet-Union.

The collapse of a world system and of the power on which it rested, combined with the realization of Soviet force and ambitions, had brought the United States to a point which gave a frightening reality to the vision of Alexis de Tocqueville, that unsurpassed observer of the American scene, who wrote in 1835:

'There are, at the present time, two great nations in the world which seem to tend towards the same end, although they started from different points: I allude to the Russians and the Americans... The Anglo-American relies upon personal interest to accomplish his ends, and gives free scope to the unguided exertions and common sense of the citizens; the Russians center all the authority of society in a single arm: the principal instrument of the former is freedom; of the latter is servitude. Their starting point is different, and their courses are not the same; yet each of them seems to be marked out by the will of Heaven to sway the destinies of half the globe.'[3]

3. Alexis de Tocqueville, *De la Démocratie en Amérique*, (Paris: Librairie de Medicis, 1951), Tome Premier, pp. 623–624. Translation in John W. Spanier, *American Foreign Policy since World War II*, (New York: Praeger, 1960), p. 2.

B. SECURITY UNTIL PEARL HARBOR

The main characteristic of American foreign policy up till the Sec-- ond World War was its isolationism. This isolationism was con- sidered the best way to promote the strength and welfare of the United States and it was deeply rooted in philosophical assumptions about the nature of man and society.

Efforts have been made to explain this isolationist trend by a com- bination of geographical, economic and political facts. They try to prove that the United States is not different from other countries and that only its geographical position, combined with the state of the world outside the United States, provided America with the opportunity to be isolationist.

Without any doubt there is a great measure of truth in this kind of approach. But a real understanding of American isolationism is only possible when we do not take into account only the facts of geography, natural resources, and the outside political environ- ment. The more intangible and less concrete elements in American life, the social, moral, philosophical and political foundations of American society greatly contributed to its isolationist attitude to- wards the world around it.

As to the facts, the United States was the only power which could afford to be isolationist successfully.

During its development it was surrounded by weak northern and southern neighbors. It was protected by the Pacific and Atlantic Oceans which kept the rest of the world away. It had a phenomenal supply of raw materials within its own borders.

All this meant limitless possibilities of geographical expansion and economic development within its own territory. There was com- paratively little need to be driven overseas for trade and commerce, and in so far as commercial interests had to be protected this could be achieved without major clashes or permanent entanglements.

Apart from this, during the whole of the nineteenth century and the beginning of the twentieth century, a vital element in America's successful isolationism was the role of Great Britain.

The British system not only provided the world with the maintenance of the balance of power in Europe but above all enforced, with its naval supremacy, the Pax Brittanica and provided a shield behind which the United States could develop as a great industrial nation.

Working smoothly and without undue strains Britain provided the best possible political and economic conditions for American expansion in security.

The effective pursuit of the Monroe Doctrine was only possible because Britain firmly supported the United States policy against intervention from Europe in the Western Hemisphere.

Notwithstanding the fact that influential individuals stressed the importance of the British system for the peace and development of the United States, there was no clear and general recognition of this basic fact.

The threat to British world power undoubtedly was one of the elements which led the United States into the First World War but it was not a decisive factor. These dangers were much better understood in 1940. The real threat to British world power was, however, only fully grasped when in February 1947, Great Britain, by its intention to withdraw its commitments from Greece and Turkey, threw the full burden of world leadership on the shoulders of the United States. It was the culminating moment of a long process during which the evolution from isolationism to full leadership ran, to a great extent, parallel with the decline of British power.

However, one cannot explain and understand the roots of American isolationism merely from geographical and historical facts.

Unequalled by any other major power America sees its own society as ideal. Democracy, tolerance, and equal opportunity are cherished and incorporated in all the great documents of the Republic.

'A successful federal structure combined local loyalties and interests with the broad economic interests common to the whole area. This ideal of a more perfect union together with the inalienable rights of man to life, liberty and the pursuit of happiness came to represent in the American mind a general recipe of political salvation and at the same time an integral part of the American way of life.'[4]

Nineteenth century America was essentially a middle class society in which all men shared the same values.

'The U.S. had only a center, both intellectually and politically! This country had never experienced a feudal past and therefore possessed no large and powerful aristocratic class on the right; and because it was, by and large, an equalitarian society, it also lacked a genuine left wing movement of protest, such as Socialism or Communism.'[5]

A further reason for the lack of strong left wing tendencies was the opening of the West in combination with the high degree of mobility, which provided a constant outlet for the non-conforming elements of American society.

The philosophy of this middle class was essentially liberal. This liberal philosophy aimed at minimizing the authority and claims of the state. The power of the state was felt as an infringement of individual rights. The separation of powers was designed to keep the federal government weak. Coupled with the instinctive dislike of power politics, the American saw an essential difference between the United States and Europe. European politics were power politics because of the undemocratic nature of their regimes. America aimed at cutting itself loose from the wicked world of class conflicts and power politics. It strongly believed in its mission to spread the light of freedom to all mankind. Every immigrant added to the notion that Europe was identical with poverty, war, and unequal opportunity, while America held the torch of freedom, democracy, and unlimited possibilities for the individual. The logical consequence therefore could only be non-entanglement.

4. Barbara Ward, *The West at Bay,* (London: Allen and Unwin, 1948), p. 79.
5. John W. Spanier, *American Foreign Policy since World War II,* (New York: Praeger, 1960), p. 3.

The absence of foreign threats, the unprecedented economic development coupled with the liberal philosophy and the missionary belief in the strength and value of its own institutions made Americans strangely unaware of the role of power on the international scene.

It also brought about a legalistic approach to international relations, so ably described in George Kennan's studies.[6]

It led to undue reliance on the idea of the subordination of large number of states to an international juridical system and an underestimation of the violence of strains and discontents in the world.

It assumed the ability of each nation to solve its own internal political problems without provoking international tensions and at the same time it overestimated the possibilities of sanctions against offenders.

It inspired fights against extreme nationalism in the world but at the same time it attached an absolute value to American national sovereignty, based on the idealised notion of the United States governmental system and the structure and values of American society.

Inspite of the war fought against Spain in 1898 and the First World War there was no real adjustment to the international environments.

The war against Spain brought the United States to a certain consciousness of its power in the world. The war was not fought out of a realistic calculation of national advantage but as a crusade to free the Cubans from Spain's imperial rule. The result was on the one hand the establishment of American rule in the Philippines, Hawaii and Puerto Rico but on the other hand a deep feeling of frustation that naked power was used.

The strains between idealism and self-interest were too great.

The reluctance to recognize the facts of international power, the absence of a feeling that the national security was threat-

6. George F. Kennan, *American Diplomacy 1900–1950,* (The University of Chicago Press, 1951), and *Realities of American Foreign Policy,* (Princeton University Press, 1954).

ened and an unsolved balance between ideals and self-interest were very much apparent in the history of the entry of the United States into the First World War and the immediate post-war period.

The danger of German control of the European continent, the collapse of the British balance of power concept, and the subsequent danger of decline of British sea power were a definite threat to American security and would have justified an earlier entry into the war. But the American people fought the First World War as a crusade for freedom and democracy. No wonder that the nation after 1918 fell back into the 'normalcy' of its isolationist behavior.

Only a broader concept of self-interest, a keener realization of the power element in international intercourse and a clearer notion of the threat to national security could have prevented a relapse into the disengagement from the 'wicked' world outside.

In the inter-war years the basic formula of United States foreign policy remained the same. In the political field it relied more on giving a good example, on moral repudiation of power politics, on disarmament, and on stressing its interest in a stable world, than on active participation based on its position of power.

The outbreak of the Second World War brought about a transformation in the American outlook in a sense that for the first time, since the nation had become a world power, a great majority of the American people came to understand that America's vital interests and security were seriously affected by the events in Europe.

'For the first time the great mass of Americans reached the conclusion that the nation's vital interests could be jeopardized by shifts in the distribution of international power in foreign areas, especially in Western Europe and the North Atlantic. The chief source of this recent national awakening to the dependence of America's welfare upon events abroad has been the mounting fear since the beginning of World War II that the maintenance of America's democratic institutions and the preservation of America's territorial integrity are seriously threatened by the restless surge of agressive and anti-democratic powers outside the Western Hemisphere.'[7]

This leads to a conclusion for which Osgood's analysis is of great value.

Only at the moment that America realizes that its security is at stake, is the basis laid for America's adaptation to its role of world power and leader of the free world. But fear of national insecurity is not enough for a constructive American foreign policy.

As leader of the Western World the United States neither can nor should be solely guided by self-preservation. Realism and self-interest is compatible with allegiance to universal ideals and to a standard of values in international conduct.

Idealism and self-interest had to be combined. Idealism alone is no foundation for foreign policy. Pure self-interest would not only blur the image of the United States beyond recognition but would be self-defeating because 'it misjudges human nature and it ignores the close interdependence between principle and expedience'.[8]

The attack on Pearl Harbor in December 1941, terminated 150 years of American isolationism.

'With the death of Professor Beard isolationism lost its last trace of intellectual respectability.'[9]

It would still appear and reappear in other forms but never again in the sense of Washington's concept and never again supported by the instinctive feeling of a majority of the American people.

It would still appear at the left and at the right. It would be apparent in the blind allegiance to the United Nations, while on another issue, it would violently condemn the World Organization as standing in the way of United States independent action. It would emerge in various issues and in different forms but as a philosophy

7. Robert Endicott Osgood, *Ideals and Self-Interest in America's Foreign Relations,* (The University of Chicago Press, 1953), p. 429.
8. Osgood, *op. cit.,* p. 442.
9. Arthur Schlesinger, *The Vital Center,* (Boston: Houghton Mifflin Company, 1949), p. 219.

it had lost its cohesion, its roots, and its grip on the American minds.

In 1941 the future of the United States became inextricably bound with every other section of the globe.

C. HOPES AND IDEAS FOR THE POST-WAR WORLD (1941–1945)

United States relations with Europe should also be seen in the light of American foreign policy during the Second World War and the wartime hopes for a better future.

There is no question about the fact that in 1941 the traditional American doctrine of isolationism and neutrality had been buried. The United States knew that it could not escape involvement, that is total involvement, in world affairs. Neither was there any doubt about the major and leading role the United States should play in the establishment of a new world order. With comparatively little domestic controversy, it took leave of hundred and fifty years of mental and political isolationism. This was the great and major difference from the American approach to the First World War.

Notwithstanding the break with the past with regard to active participation in all fields of world affairs and the apparent realization and willingness to assume leadership in the post-war world, American foreign policy during the war was characterized and often dominated by some tendencies of its past convictions.

These convictions were based on a traditional reluctance to assess the nature and function of power in the conduct of foreign relations. Evidently, there was a strong and keen awareness of the power element in the conduct of the war, but the traditional depreciation of power in peacetime led to a sharp distinction between war and peace in the conduct of foreign policy; to a tendency not to relate military power to political objectives and to a divorce of force and diplomacy. As Kennan put it:[10]

10.   George Kennan, *American Diplomacy 1900–1950, op. cit.,* p. 84.

'This lends to the democratic war effort a basically punitive note, rather than one of expediency.'

The crusading character of American armed intervention, the underestimation of power in peacetime and the uncoupling of military power from political aims and objectives led to the notion of total victory and an all or nothing approach to war. 'War is thus a means employed to abolish power politics; war is conducted to end all wars.'[11]

The concept of unconditional surrender which would have such a major impact on the post-war world can be explained by this tendency.

This is reinforced by the desire of the military leaders to leave the task of military victory unaffected by diplomatic considerations and political peacetime objectives.

While in itself the concept of unconditional surrender might hardly look compatible with the general American approach to a peacetime world order, it had its deep roots in the traditional American concept of the problem of power and of the function of war.

These traditional tendencies never led to a real possibility of a relapse into isolationism. They had, however, a strong impact on interallied relations during the war and on the American ideas for the post-war order.

Another element in American foreign policy during the Second World War was the genuine belief that the rejection of the League of Nations in 1919 had been a fatal error.

The United States basically had three alternative ways to demonstrate its full participation in world affairs and to give substance to the leadership which destiny had thrown upon it.

First, it could try to force its will on the post-war world in a unilateral way. Nothing could have been more alien to its convictions and traditions.

Second, it could form alliances with other countries. This meant

11.   Spanier, *op. cit.,* p. 11.

discriminatory support of some powers in peace-time in preference
to others. At no moment during the war was there a willingness to
follow such a course. Such alliances were considered far too much
in the realm of power politics, rejected for reasons explained above.

This left the third alternative, so near to the Wilsonian tradition
and so suitable to the desire to avoid the tragedy of 1919; the
establishment of a system of collective security.

'The proposed remedy, this time was to build a better League of
Nations and to ensure the participation of the powers which had
the armed forces necessary to keep the peace.'[12]

A series of international conferences followed the adoption of
the Atlantic Charter of August 1941. United States participation in
this World War was constantly accompanied by decisions of great
political consequences and far-reaching commitments. The pledge
of United States participation in a world security organization was
a major but not the only one. There were pledges to occupy the
territory of defeated enemy states, agreements to territorial changes
in anticipation of peace settlements and the initiative to set up a
number of international organizations, intended to set the pattern
for post-war economic relations. All this was done by the United
States on the assumption of the logical transition from the wartime
alliance with Britain and the Soviet Union into a concerted post-
war action and joint world leadership.

There was a marked difference in the American and British
assessment of present and future relations with the Soviet Union.
The British and certainly Churchill had a keen awareness of power
problems in the post-war world and especially the power structure
of the European continent. They feared that the Soviet objective
was to maximize Soviet post-war territorial and political advantage.

The question of Poland formed one of the striking examples.

If Poland should pass under communist domination and become
an instrument of Soviet power, the European balance of power

12. John C. Campbell, *The U.S. in World Affairs 1945–1947,* Published for
     the Council on Foreign Relations, (New York: Harper & Brothers,
     1947), p. 26.

would be gravely affected. The competition for Germany between the two power blocs, against which the opponents of dismemberment had warned since 1942, would become inevitable. The American and British positions were based on a different philosophy. For Britain the European balance of power and the essence of victory was at stake; for the United States the issue was important but not vital.

The position paper from the Department of State prepared for the Conference of Yalta in February 1945 read: 'It now seems clear that the Soviet Union will exert predominant political influence over the areas in question. While this Government probably would not want to oppose itself to such a political configuration, neither would it desire to see American influence in this part of the world completely nullified.'[13]

On paper the British with active support of the United States got a fair degree of satisfaction on the Polish issue at the Yalta conference, but the ultimate test of strength saw the Western allies at the losing end.

Apart from the philosophical trend in United States policy towards the Soviet Union during the war, two major practical American judgments were responsible for the United States handling of its relations with the Soviet Union on the question of the post-war European structure and the approach to a world system of collective security. One was its short-term desire to avoid a lengthy and costly continuation of the war against Japan and to solicit Soviet participation in this major sector of the American war effort.

The second was Roosevelt's deep conviction that the American people would not be willing to maintain an effective armed force abroad for a substantial period after the war. There was a constant assumption of a foreseeable American withdrawal from the European area.

13. For text and analysis of this problem, W. W. Rostow, *The U.S. in the World Arena*, (New York: Harper & Brothers, 1960), p. 111 and pp. 101–119.

Both these practical judgments motivated the United States to minimize conflicts with the Soviet Union during the war and in preparation for the post-war world.[14]

In the context of the post-war construction of a collective security system, American traditional convictions of the role of power in peacetime played a predominant role.

In Soviet eyes the United Nations had a low priority compared to the more substantive post-war problems. These, in their opinion, would be governed by power relations between the Big Three. The British never approached the structure and working of the United Nations free from the balance of power problem. The United States, however, definitely saw the United Nations as a substitute for the traditionally rejected power politics.

Secretary Hull reported to Congress on the Moscow meeting of the three Foreign Ministers and the Moscow Declaration of October 1943, and stated that there would be no longer any need 'for spheres of influence, for alliances, for balance of power or any other of the special arrangements through which, in the unhappy past, the nations strove to safeguard their security or to promote their interests'.[15]

Evidently, there were dissenting voices in the United States among which Walter Lippmann's was as usual, on occasions of this magnitude, wise and penetrating. 'I do not believe that the security of the vital interests of the United States can be, should be, or will be entrusted to the collective security which a new and tentative international institution can be counted to provide. For ourselves, in the world as it is, we are certain to rely first upon our own armed power and natural strength, then upon our natural allies, and then upon a general world organization. We shall not look upon the general organization as a substitute but as a means of reinforcing them.'[16]

14. W. W. Rostow, *op. cit.*, pp. 126–127.
15. John C. Campbell, *op. cit.*, p. 28.
16. Walter Lippmann, *U.S. War Aims,* (London: Hamish Hamilton, 1944), p. 98.

And Kennan analysed the American approach as follows:

'There was no longer any question about it. Russia was no problem from the standpoint of the power relationships of the future world. The only question was one of how we were to arrange that wonderful peace time collaboration by means of which we two great continental nations... would walk hand in hand down the shining vistas of a peaceful international future.'[17]

Post-war unity between the Big Three, in the American conception, was a prerequisite for a peaceful post-war settlement. Where American policy erred was in its negation of the only possible condition for this unity: a permanent exposure of a maximum and long-term position of American unilateral strength and *de facto* power.

The diplomatic posture of the United States in the Second World War was different from its traditional policy but it still was greatly affected by basic elements of its long time history, its convictions about foreign relations and by its notion of the role of power in world affairs.

The United States came out of the Second World War as the dominant power, untouched within its borders. Its economic strength was not only intact but greatly strengthened. It was in sole possession of nuclear arms. It emerged from the war with the full realization that isolationism was no longer a possible alternative and that its future was tied to every part and section of the world. It was willing to assume leadership which it accepted, however, with reluctance and diffidence.

It came out of the war with a hope of a one-world system for which, more than any other power, it felt itself responsible. That hope was to be shattered in the two years preceding the Truman Doctrine and the Marshall Plan.

17. George Kennan, *Realities of American Foreign Policy, op. cit.,* p. 26.

D. FROM THE END OF THE WAR TO THE TRUMAN
DOCTRINE AND THE MARSHALL PLAN (1945–1947)

The policy with which the United States emerged from the war was based on the assumption that the wartime alliance between Great Britain, the Soviet Union and the United States would form the basis of the post-war order and the United Nations would be the guardian of peace.

The Teheran and Yalta Agreements would be in principle adhered to. Peace treaties would be concluded with the ex-enemy states with the aim of terminating forever the military, economic and political agressiveness of Japan and Germany.

The world economic order would be restored after a period of readjustment in which relief to the war stricken world would be mainly channelled through the United Nations Relief and Rehabilitation Administration, the Occupation Forces, or through special loans enabling especially the European countries to recover economically and politically. They could then resume there legitimate places in the world, able to sustain the United Nations in its worldwide responsibilities for a peaceful order. After this period of readjustment institutions and organizations in the economic field, notably the Bretton Wood institutions and the proposed International Trade Organization, would be instrumental in settling worldwide economic problems and in guaranteeing a free flow of trade and finance.

Stable exchange rates would be restored and the International Monetary Fund would guarantee order in the monetary field. Avoidance of undue impediments to trade would be effected through the International Trade Organization and the financing of reconstruction through the International Bank of Reconstruction and Development. The Food and Agricultural Organization would act to raise standards of nutrition throughout the world and at the same time protect and increase the incomes of the producers of food and other agricultural products.

The armed forces would be demobilized to an extent compatible with a normalized world situation.

It should be repeated that this was not an isolationist program. On the contrary, this program required full and active participation of the United States on an unprecedented scale.

Underlying this program there was an almost pathetic urge to avoid the errors of 1919 and a repetition of political and economic events leading to the Second World War. What remained, however, was the urge to return to normalcy, a different normalcy from 1919 but still normalcy. The end of the war in the American mind was still identified with the end of power politics.

'It attempted to remedy the old mistakes of 1919, rather than assess the new problems of 1945.'[18]

The lack of assessment of the new problems was twofold. First, there was an unpreparedness and unwillingness to recognize not only the intransigence of the Soviet Union but also its expansionist character and the permanence of Soviet hostility both in its Russian and in its communist policies.

Second, there was a grave underestimation of the nature and the scope of the dislocation brought about by the Second World War. The fatal weakening of the non-communist world and especially Britain and continental Europe was not realized and the vital importance of the German problem was underrated.

The political hopes of the United States were shattered by the nature of Soviet policy. The total ruin of Europe destroyed the hope of economic stability.

Jones characterizes the development leading to the situation of the post-war period as follows: 'For decades massive historical caravans had been observed moving slowly toward predictable destinations. Great Britain toward loss of Empire and inability to maintain the balance of power in Europe and order in Asia; Western continental Europe toward instability and weakness; the United States toward economic and military preeminence in

18.   Barbara Ward, *op. cit.*, p. 85.

political isolation; and the Soviet Union toward a fundamental challenge of Western civilization.'[19]

The major developments during the years from 1945 to 1947 led to the formulation of the Truman Doctrine and the Marshall Plan.

The imposition of Soviet control on the whole of Eastern Europe and the effort of the Soviet Union to break through to the Middle East led to the Truman Doctrine. The fatal weakening of Europe, its impending economic political and social collapse with its consequences for American security, together with the German problem, brought about the Marshall Plan.

It must be emphasized that the emergence of policies of this scope is a gradual process. There is no sudden transformation from weakness to strength. In the political and economic field there were already unilateral American acts and actions, during these two years, which showed an impending realization of what really was at stake. One example is the 'policy of firmness and patience' formulated by Secretary of State James Byrnes in his speech to the Overseas Press Club in New York on February 28, 1946.[20]

'But in the interest of world peace and in the interest of our common and traditional friendship we must make it plain that the United States intends to defend the Charter. We will not and cannot stand aloof if force of threat is used contrary to the purposes and principles of the Charter.'

And on March 16th, 1946, before the Society of the Friendly Sons of St. Patrick, he made another speech in New York in which he stressed the fact that the United States was 'committed to support the Charter of the United Nations. Should the occasion arise, our military strength will be used to support the purposes and principles of the Charter'.[21]

A second example was the loan to Great Britain of $3.75 billion, negotiated at the end of 1945 and approved in 1946. While the

19. Joseph M. Jones, The Fifteen Weeks, (New York: The Viking Press, 1955), p. 9.
20. Jones, op. cit., pp. 54–55.
21. Department of State, Bulletin, XIV, p. 481.

terms of the loan still reflected the traditional opinion about the post-war economic order, there was a distinct political overtone in its justification. Speaker of the House Rayburn said before the final vote was taken on July 13, 1946: 'I do not want Western Europe, England and all the rest pushed further into and towards an ideology that I despise. I fear if we do not cooperate with this great natural ally of ours, that is what will happen. If we are not allied with the great British democracy, I fear somebody will be and God pity us when we have no ally across the Atlantic Ocean...'[22]

It was also apparent in the field of foreign assistance which amounted in this period to more than $14 billion, the British loan included, of which over $6 billion was in the form of grants and $8 billion in the form of loans.

This foreign assistance, however, was not planned for the orderly transition from war to peace but had to be improvised on a bilateral basis.

Like the political actions and reactions, it was not part of a coherent over-all policy. These measures and actions were directed to particular issues and to *ad hoc* emergency situations. They were neither inspired by a basic conversion of American foreign policy nor by a fundamental change in the attitudes of American public opinion towards the world.

The imposition of communist control in the different East European countries had in every case its specific history but the result was that, often in flagrant disregard of the Yalta agreement, the Soviet Union established during these first post-war years a firm grip on the whole of Eastern Europe and the main part of the Balkans.

The painfully negotiated peace treaties with the ex-enemy states, Hungaria, Bulgaria, and Rumania, could not change this fact. Czechoslovakia was under the shadow of the Red Army and was only granted a temporary respite. Yugoslavia was under the communist regime of Marshal Tito.

22. *Congressional Record,* 79th Congr., 2nd Sess. (July, 1947), p. 681.

The case of Poland was of particular importance to the new assessment of Soviet strategy and intentions.

Without any doubt a maximum effort, short of a willingness to show and eventually use instruments of real power, was made to guarantee a democratic development of post-war Poland. The Polish question, therefore, became a test-case for Soviet willingness to adhere to the principles of Yalta and for Western preparedness to back up agreements with strength. In Poland, however, the full technique of the communist take-over method was employed. Key ministeries like Interior and Army were immediately taken over by communists; non-communists were murdered or denounced as Western agents, and the full barrage of intimidation was used. The passing of a new provisional constitution in February 1947, destroyed the hopes of the Yalta Agreement and combined with the Soviet policy in its occupation zone in Germany brought Soviet power to the Elbe.

In the meantime, Iran, Turkey and Greece became the main objects of Soviet expansion beyond regions directly under the control of the Red Army.

In the Tripartite Treaty of Alliance between Iran, the Soviet Union and Great Britain of January 1942, there was a provision that the allied forces should be withdrawn from Iranian territory not later than six months after all hostilities between the Allied Powers and Germany had been suspended by the conclusion of an armistice.

On the final date of agreed evacuation, British and American troops had already left, but Soviet troops remained. There even was a clear indication of military reinforcements.

In this specific case, through a very strong Anglo-American posture in and outside the United Nations,[23] the Iranian government became again master in its own house.

This was the first clear case where the Soviet Union showed that it did not want to risk a military showdown with the Western

23.   See the two speeches by Secretary Byrnes referred to on p. 20.

powers, but hoped to reach its objectives by different ways and means.

If Turkey and Greece would fall under Soviet control, Iran could be brought back into the Soviet-controlled area.

Soviet pressure on Turkey started in the summer of 1945 when suddenly the Soviet Union demanded the transfer of Turkish districts in the Caucasus, a revision of the Montreux Convention governing the Dardanelles Straits and the establishment of a joint Turkish-Russian control, the lease to the Soviet Union of strategic bases and the substitution of the British-Turkish association by a treaty with the Soviet Union on the lines of its treaties with the East-European countries.

In August 1946, this demand was renewed and copies of the diplomatic note were sent to the United States and British Governments.

Immediately a United States naval task force was despatched to the Mediterranean. On August 19, 1946, the United States, followed by the British Government on August 21, strongly rejected the main parts of the Soviet demands.

In Greece, Britain was the main guardian for the maintenance of its independence and a stabilizing factor in a rapidly deteriorating and chaotic situation. Soviet pressure was mainly exercised through wide scale guerilla warfare, which started in the fall of 1946.

Total economic and social dislocation aggravated the situation.

While the Iranian and Turkish problems were temporarily cured by the *ad hoc* reactions of the United States in conjunction with Great Britain, the Greek situation remained utterly precarious and an eventual collapse would inevitably lead to the outflanking of Iran and Turkey. It was at this moment, on February 21, 1947, that Britain transmitted two notes to the United States Government, one on Greece and one on Turkey. It informed the United States that for economic reasons it was unable to offer further assistance to Greece after March 31, 1947, and it hoped that the burden after April 1, 1947, would be taken over by the United States. In Turkey, Britain would be unable to provide the necessary military equipment to enable Turkey to resist an eventual armed aggression. Its program for economic development could no longer count on British assistance.

It was an established fact that Turkey could neither re-equip its military forces nor make provisions for the vital necessity of economic development without substantial outside assistance.

Under the pressure of economic and political circumstances, Britain had been compelled to a constant series of withdrawals from pre-war positions and commitments. The British system of balance of power and naval supremacy had already been most seriously affected. But the notes of February 21, 1947, were not just another event in this process of withdrawal and liquidation of the British power system.

In Washington it was immediately recognized that this was the beginning of a new era. 'Great Britain had within the hour handed the job of world leadership with all its burdens and all its glory to the United States.'[24] Spanier says:

'February 21 was thus a historic day. On that day Great Britain, the only remaining power in Europe, acknowledged her exhaustion...Now all of a sudden there was no power to protect the United States, but the United States itself; no one stood between this country and the present threat to its security. All the other major powers of the world had collapsed – except the Soviet Union which was the second most powerful nation in the world and was wedded to an expansionist ideology. The cold fact of a bipolar world suddenly faced the United States.'[25]

The emergence and formulation of a new American policy was also influenced by a variety of political pressures and opinions. There is no doubt that Winston Churchill's speech in Fulton in March 1946, made a lasting impression on the American mind.[26]

24. Joseph M. Jones, *op. cit.*, p. 7.
25. Spanier, *op. cit.*, pp. 29–30.
26. This is the so called 'Iron Curtain' speech. The expression of the Iron Curtain can already be found in a cable from Churchill to Truman in May 1945, (Rostow, *op. cit.*, p. 115).

He spoke of the indefinite expansion of Soviet power and doctrines. He concluded that the Soviet Union respected only force and he called for a close and strong political and military union of Great Britain and the United States.

The analysis of American policy by George Kennan is another example. His main thoughts were published in *Foreign Affairs* of July 1947, but his opinion was previously known in the White House and the State Department, probably as early as February 1946.[27]

It is always precarious to evaluate the impact of high officials on the formulation of policy. In this case, however, there is no question of the importance of Kennan's thoughts for the subsequent conduct of American policy.

After a penetrating analysis of the communist outlook on world affairs and the Soviet concept of the struggle with the Western world, Kennan strongly recommended a United States long-term, patient, but firm and vigilant, containment policy.

'Soviet policy cannot be effectively countered by sporadic acts which represent the momentary whims of democratic opinion, but only by intelligent long-range policies no less steady in their purpose, and no less variegated and resourceful in their application than those of the Soviet Union itself.'[28]

The political scene in Washington and especially the relation between the executive and the legislative branch of the government, so vital for the conduct of foreign policy, was hardly fitted for the requirements of the moment.

There was a Democratic non-elected President and the 80th Congress, elected in November 1946, had a Republican majority in both Houses. Historically this represented a situation which would make active and bold foreign-policy decisions extremely difficult.

The Republican party in its great majority had accepted the new role of the United States in world affairs but Congress was in a

27. Rostow, *op. cit.,* p. 199.
28. George Kennan, *American Diplomacy 1900–1950, op. cit.,* pp. 107–124.

mood for economies and substantial budget cuts. Critical voices against the structure of the new foreign economic policy embodied in the Trade Agreements program, the lending policy of the Export-Import Bank and the Bretton Woods institutions were increasing in volume and quantity. A great majority of Republicans had voted against the loan to Great Britain.

In this situation the personalities of those in position of command or of great influence becomes increasingly important. On the executive side there existed an unusually fruitful relationship between the President, Secretary of State Marshall, and Under Secretary Acheson. The Roosevelt period was not characterized by a smooth and orderly relationship between the President and his official advisers on foreign policy. The relationship between the White House and the State Department was often confused and ineffective. Under Marshall and Acheson the State Department was brought back to its full function of advising the President and executing his policy.

The personalities of Truman, Marshall and Acheson, which emerge from memoirs, biographies and writings were highly complementary and created a striking balance of courage, knowledge and orderly conduct.

In the Cabinet, people like Secretary of Defense Forrestal and Secretary of Commerce Harriman were eminently suited to support the major decisions to be taken. In addition to Acheson, the role of Under Secretary for Economic Affairs, William L. Clayton, was of great and lasting importance.

On the Congressional side, the name of the Republican Senior Senator from Michigan, Arthur H. Vandenberg, Chairman of the Senate Committee on Foreign Relations, should be mentioned. The emergence of the Truman Doctrine and the Marshall Plan, and in general the shape of post-war United States foreign policy, was to a great extent due to his role, both in the Senate and in his close and most constructive cooperation with the Administration. Both sides aimed at a bipartisan approach to the major foreign policy decisions.

The evolution of Vandenberg's thoughts on foreign policy and on the role of the United States in the world demonstrated the depth and the scope of what was happening to the country.[29]

On the basis of a joint study of the Departments of State, War and Navy, the President accepted on February 26, 1947, the recommendation to ask Congress for the authority to extend economic and military aid to Greece and Turkey. On February 27, 1947, a crucial meeting took place between the President, his advisers and the Congressional leaders. It was in this meeting that it became clear that the Administration could only win Congressional support for its request if it presented this request in a statement of global and new policy with regard to the challenge of Soviet expansion.

There is no doubt that the Administration was already deeply convinced of this necessity, but not until this meeting was the decision taken to present the policy towards Greece and Turkey in an overall doctrine.

On March 12, 1947, the President appeared in person before the joint session of Congress to deliver his Special Message. The keynotes were:

'I am fully aware of the broad implications involved if the U.S. extends assistance to Greece and Turkey... To insure the peaceful development of nations free from coercion the U.S. has taken a leading part in establishing the United Nations. The United Nations is designed to make possible lasting freedom and independence for all its members. We shall not realize our objectives, however, unless we are willing to help free peoples to maintain their free institutions and their national integrity against aggressive movements that seek to impose upon them totalitarian regimes. This is no more than a frank recognition that totalitarian regimes imposed upon free peoples, by direct or indirect aggression, undermine the foundations of international peace and hence the security of the United States... I believe that it must be the policy of the U.S. to support

29. Arthur H. Vandenberg, Jr., *The Private Papers of Senator Vandenberg*, (Boston: Houghton Mifflin Company, 1952).

free peoples who are resisting attempted subjugation by armed minorities or by outside pressures.'[30]

There is no need to go into the details of the debate in Congress and in the nation after the President's message because many of its elements will be dealt with in a later phase of this study in which the public debate following the speech of Secretary Marshall will be analyzed. The Congressional debate from March 1947, through the enactment of the European Recovery Program should be treated as a whole.

Mention should only be made of the fact that the major congressional attack came on the point of bypassing the machinery of the United Nations.

As to the relationship between the Truman Doctrine and the Marshall Plan, it is difficult to agree with Barbara Ward, who compares the 'negative and military character of the Truman Doctrine with the Marshall Plan offering an outlet for American hopes and idealism'.[31]

The Truman Doctrine and the Marshall Plan are two aspects of the same new American foreign policy. They emerge from different sources, trends and priorities, but they belong to the same concept and they aim at the same objectives. The Truman Doctrine was a policy of containment to prevent open communist aggression against states in the non-Soviet orbit. The Marshall Plan was a policy of reconstruction, aiming at the creation of sound economic conditions and the removal of the internal threat to the stability of the countries of Europe.

Before analyzing the events leading to the emergence and formulation of the Marshall Plan, attention must be given to the main facts of the German problem in the immediate post-war period.

30. For the full text see *In Quest of Peace and Security, Selected Documents on American Foreign Policy 1941–1951*, (Dep. of State Publication 4245, 1951), p. 88.
31. Barbara Ward, *op. cit.*, p. 88.

Policy towards Germany has been a major factor in United States-European relations up till today and will remain so for the foreseeable future. It has a tendency to dominate both the United States approach to the problems of its relations with Europe and its concept of European cooperation and integration. It has strongly contributed to the formulation of the European Recovery Program; it has inspired the American attitude towards the European Defense Community, the Coal and Steel Community and the European Economic Community. It has been and is today a major factor in American policy for the defense of the West and the structure of the North Atlantic Treaty Organization; it has finally been and is today a major factor in United States relations with the Soviet Union.

The declaration on 'Arrangements for Control of Germany', signed by the Commanders of the four Allied Powers on June 5, 1945, did not only fix the details of military surrender but set a pattern for civil administration under the occupation.[32]

It was an elaboration of the policy laid down at the Yalta Conference and prepared by the European Advisory Commission in London set up in 1943.

There was, however, a frightening absence of detailed agreements on political and economic policy in Germany. This was one of the main reasons for the Potsdam Conference which started on July 17, 1945.

Apart from the already accepted principles concerning disarmament and demilitarization, destruction of the Nazi and military organizations and trial of war criminals, the Potsdam Agreement mainly dealt with recommendations for the organization and principles which were to govern the occupation of each zone in Germany. These principles were to be applied by the different Occupying Powers. The Four Power Control Council in Berlin was to handle all-German issues and a Council of Foreign Ministers was created to deal mainly with German issues not resolved in Berlin and finally with the issue of German unity.

32. Department of State, *Germany 1947–1949, The Story in Documents*, (March 1950), pp. 21–23.

A second part of the agreement referred to economic policy, notably the issue of reparations. Germany was to be treated as an economic unit. A general reparation plan was to be negotiated in the Control Council within six months. Advance reparations on a limited scale were to be made, pending a general accord.

During the conference, it was already known to the Western Powers that the dismantling of industry was proceeding at an unsurpassed pace in the Soviet Zone of Germany, while current German production was being drained off to the East as well.

The Control Council hardly reached agreement on any of the major issues. In this period, Soviet and French policy towards the German problem made agreement practically impossible, were it for different reasons.

The Potsdam Agreement provided for central German agencies, but France did not sign the agreement and was not bound by it. The French did not object to economic unity, but to German unity. They went along with the idea of central administration so long as it was not in German but in Allied hands. They claimed, furthermore, the separation of the Saar, the Rhineland and the Ruhr. The Saar should be annexed, the Rhineland should be a separate state, and the Ruhr should be placed under an international regime.

The failure to achieve agreement led to different policies and priorities in the four zones of occupation and tended to create four different states with different political structures and economic and social policies.

A plan for reparations was agreed upon at the end of March 1946. It allowed Germany an industrial capacity of roughly 50 per cent of the 1938 level. Steel was the key item. Germany was allowed a capacity of 7.5 million tons and a production of 5.8 million compared to 18 million tons in 1929.

This agreement, however, was never implemented. The Western powers expected the Russians to supply food and other products to the Western zones. Not only was there no question of deliveries from the Eastern zone, but without any reference to the Allied Control Council the Russians speeded up the moving of equipment and currently produced goods to the East. This led General Clay in May 1946, to suspend the dismantling of plants in the American zone for reparation purposes. The American Administration became increasingly convinced that the economic chaos in Germany was putting an unexpected and heavy burden on the American taxpayer, but even more so that European recovery was closely linked to the German economic plight.

Gradually but unmistakably, United States policy towards Germany changed. Supreme efforts were made, however, to turn the tide of collapse of an effective Four Power policy.

In 1946, Byrnes took the unprecedented step of offering an American guarantee against German aggression for a period of 25 years. Molotov gave it a bitter reception and rejected it completely, probably on the grounds that United States presence in Europe in the form of a military guarantee for a long time was incompatible with Russian objectives.

On July 11, 1946, Byrnes made an offer at the Council of Foreign Ministers to join the American zone of occupation with any other zone. He pointed to the impossibility of administering Germany in four airtight compartments. 'The continuation of the present situation will result in inflation and economic paralysis. It will result in increased costs to the occupying powers and unnecessary suffering to the German people... We feel it our duty to exhaust every effort to secure the cooperation of the occupying powers in administering Germany as an economic unit.'[33]

Britain accepted the proposal in principle and the economic fusion of the two zones went into effect on January 1, 1947.

The French were at that stage unwilling to accept the offer. There were many motives for the French attitude, most important among them the fear of antagonizing the Soviet Union by forming a solid Western bloc.

Gradually, the major powers became aware of an element which till far in 1946 had played no role in the formulation of their policy,

33. Department of State, *Publication* 2630, (European Series 15), p. 148.

notably its impact on German public opinion.

The first clear statement of Soviet policy aimed at German public opinion was made by Molotov on July 10, 1946, at the Council of Foreign Ministers.

He lashed out against dismemberment and federalization. He stressed the necessity for a better economic life for the German people. The industries of Germany should be granted the possibility to develop beyond the level of the industry plan. In doing so, he completely reversed the Soviet stand on de-industrialization.

The courting for Germany's favor had begun and the Potsdam Agreement waned to its close.

The Molotov speech was countered by Byrnes at Stuttgart on September 6, 1946.[34] The speech initiated a new American approach to the German problem. He finally 'buried the spectre of Morgenthauism'.[35]

Without hiding the fact that the basic cause of German suffering was the war which Nazi Germany had brought upon the world, and stressing the fact that many victims of Nazi aggression were worse off than the Germans, he directed the main part of his speech to the problems of the future and notably to the economic and political reconstruction.

'It is not in the interest of the German people or in the interest of world peace that Germany should become a pawn or a partner in a military struggle for power between the East and the West.'

He admitted that the Potsdam Agreements had not been carried out and on vital questions the Allied Control Council was neither governing Germany nor allowing Germany to govern itself.

The zonal boundaries should exclusively be regarded as defining areas occupied for security reasons and not for creating separate economic and political units. If the reparation agreement resulting from the Potsdam Conference was not observed, then the level of industry plan had to be revised.

34. *Germany 1947–1949, op cit.*, pp. 3–8.
35. Max Beloff, *The United States and the Unity of Europe*, (Washington D.C.: The Brookings Institution, 1963), p. 8.

'Germany is a part of Europe and European recovery would be low indeed if Germany with her great resources... turned into a poor house.'

He pleaded for a speedy conclusion of a peace treaty. Germany should have a democratic central government which could accept its terms but not 'a strong central government dominating the German people instead of being responsible to its democratic will'.

While he did not deny the right of France to the Saar, he said that 'the United States will not support any encroachment on territory which is indisputably German or any division which is not genuinely desired by the people concerned'.

'We therefore will favor such controls over the whole of Germany, including the Ruhr and Rhineland, as may be necessary for security purposes' but not 'any controls that would subject the Ruhr and Rhineland to the political domination or manipulation of outside powers.'

The Stuttgart speech was a definite clarification of American policy towards Germany. With the intensification of the power struggle between the United States and the Soviet Union, it was inevitable to look for German support for the various positions. Hardly more than a year after the armistice, Germany started to play, still passively, its vital role in the shaping of the Western world.[36]

Before the Moscow Conference of the Council of Foreign Ministers started on March 17, 1947, John Foster Dulles, who was to accompany Secretary Marshall as special adviser, delivered a highly important speech before the National Publisher's Association in New York on January 17, 1947. There should be an economic unification of Germany, but the reason for that was also a reason for the economic unification of Europe. A German settlement should advance European unity, instead of rebuilding the 'structure of independent, unconnected sovereignties'. The industrial potential of

36. For contents and significance of the Stuttgart speech see also John Campbell, *op. cit.,* pp. 196–198, and James F. Byrnes, *Speaking frankly,* (New York: Harper & Brothers, 1947), pp. 188–191.

Western Germany should be integrated into Western Europe. It should not be left in the control of the Germans alone. A statesman-like solution of this political and economic problem providing safety against German aggression and a more stable and prosperous life for the people of Western Europe was a positive alternative to the Potsdam policy of imposed pastoralization. 'Not only Germans but neighbouring peoples will eventually rebel at trying to cover with manure the natural industrial basin of Europe.'[37]

The importance of the speech was enhanced by the fact that it had the approval of Senator Vandenberg and Governor Thomas E. Dewey of New York, leader of the Republican Party.

The fourth session of the Council of Foreign Ministers, held in Moscow in March 1947, was the real frontal confrontation of the policy of the main powers with regard to the future of Germany.

It ended in complete failure. The Russian price for German unification was a strong central government, and $10 billion of reparation payments from current German production. In pressing the issue of a strong central government it was clear that the Soviet Union aimed at domination of that government through the usual communist party tactics. They also wanted to profit not only from the productive capacity of the Soviet zone, but also from the three other zones, turning the whole of Germany into an area in which huge amounts of assistance would be poured from the West, so that they could empty it from the East.

The impact of the Moscow Conference was threefold.

It established in the minds of the American participants the certainty that the Soviet Union would only agree to a German settlement when it had the near certainty of being able to dominate the political development of Germany.

The second result was the conviction of the Americans that Dulles was right in his conception that the problem of Germany was at the heart of the problem of Europe and that it never could be settled or solved outside a European framework.

37.   John C. Campbell, op. cit., p. 471.
     Joseph M. Jones, op. cit., p. 220.

Finally, Secretary Marshall was convinced, especially after a private conversation with Stalin, that the Russians favored a delay in a German settlement.

He strongly felt that the Soviet Union would profit from the increasing chaos in Germany and from the vastly deteriorating political and economic conditions in Europe.[38] In his report to the nation on April 28, 1947,[39] Marshall said: 'The German negotiations involved not only the security of Europe and the world but the prosperity of Europe. We were faced with immediate issues which vitally concerned the impoverished and suffering people from Europe who are crying for help... We cannot ignore the factor of time involved here. The recovery of Europe has been far slower than had been expected. Disintegrating forces are becoming evident. The patient is sinking while the doctors deliberate.'

The result of and the impressions gained at the Moscow conference of March 1947, provided one of the major elements in the formulation of the Marshall Plan. Marshall's personal contribution consisted largely of his assessment of the European situation and of the Soviet attitude, acquired during this meeting of the Council of Foreign Ministers.

There were, however, other developments leading to the Harvard University speech of June 5, 1947, in which the Marshall Plan was launched.

In the beginning of 1947, it became clear that the United States and Europe had underestimated both the effects of the war on the economic situation of the European countries and the magnitude of the effort needed to put Europe back on its feet.

38. John C. Campbell, *The U.S. in World Affairs 1947–1948,* Published for the Council on Foreign Relations, (New York: Harper & Brothers, 1948), pp. 78–79.
Joseph Jones, *op. cit.,* p. 221 ff.
Harry Bayard Price, *The Marshall Plan and Its Meaning,* (Cornell University Press, 1955), p. 4 and p. 21.
39. *Germany 1947–1949, op. cit.,* p. 57.

Western Europe was losing the economic gains it had made since the end of the war. It thereby exposed itself to the disruptive political internal and outside pressures caused by stagnation, poverty and hunger. An economic collapse of Europe would not only endanger the United States goals of economic policy, aiming at the revival of economic stability in the world, but it would also destroy any possibility for a political settlement such as the United States desired to achieve in Europe. Chaos in Europe would greatly enhance the potential danger of the expansion of Soviet power.

For the Western European countries their pre-war economic position was characterized by a massive production capacity based on a high standard of efficiency in industry and agriculture. They derived, furthermore, a large income from international trade and commerce and invisible exports, such as shipping, banking, insurance and tourist trade. They held very substantial foreign investments which they had been able to make over a period of centuries.

Western Europe was, broadly speaking, an exporter of industrial goods and an importer of food and raw materials. Foodstuffs and raw materials were brought from Eastern Europe, the Far East, the Dominions and from North and South America.

In their economic relations with the United States there already existed a tendency for a dollar shortage, because of a persistent excess of imports from America over exports. This, however, was compensated by the yield of European investments in the United States, a European surplus in the field of services (mainly shipping, and insurance), and because of the large purchases of colonial products by the United States, either directly in the European Far-Eastern dependencies or through the metropolitan countries.

This pre-war European economic pattern was fundamentally changed, if not destroyed by the war:

1. Physical devastation and disruption in Western Europe and in the principal food and timber producing zones of Eastern Europe, combined with the dislocation of the European transport system,

caused a temporary paralysis of production in Western Europe.

2. War time liquidation of foreign holdings, prolonged interruption of international trade which occurred simultaneously with the loss of income from merchant fleets and foreign investments led to the exhaustion or diminution of dollar funds at a moment when many vital needs could be met only from dollar sources.

3. Human strain and exhaustion from 6 years of war and enemy occupation gravely affected the productivity of labor.

4. Internal financial disequilibrium, the inevitable result of a long war, upset the monetary stability of almost all European countries.

5. A grave shortage in the supply of food and raw materials which were vital to the European economy both for direct consumption and as earners of dollars existed in South-East Asia.

6. There was an abnormal increase in population in certain areas resulting from the war time movement of people.[40]

Most of the European countries had to start almost from scratch when the war ended.

First, recovery proceeded amazingly well. Eighteen months after the termination of the war in Europe, European industry and transport were moving again mainly as a result of the efforts of the European countries, generously assisted by substantial aid from the United States.

By the spring of 1947, the United States had provided over $11 billion to Europe in the form of grants, loans, UNRRA shipments and private contributions.

The process of recovery, however, was not maintained in the winter of 1946–1947. The European economy still in a precarious state suffered a serious set-back as a result of the continued shortage of coal, the rising prices of primary products, the prolonged world shortage of food and other essential commodities and the chaotic political situation in major parts of the former overseas dependencies. This crisis was intensified by the exceptionally cold winter of

40. Committee of European Economic Cooperation, *General Report,* (London: His Majesty's Stationery Office, 1947), Vol. I, p. 4.

1946–1947 and the drought which followed. The inability of the German economy to play its traditional role in European economic life became more and more apparent.

The credits which many countries had obtained in the post-war period were exhausted. The British loan, for instance, intended to last from three to five years, was being drawn upon at a much more rapid rate. The upsurge of recovery had used up the stocks which countries had managed to retain or acquire after the end of the war.

In order to maintain the progress which had so far been achieved, Europe was bound to maintain the volume of their imports from the American continent at increasing cost, with the consequent rapid depletion of gold and dollar reserves.

The surplus in the United States balance of payments was running at the rate of $10 billion a year. Europe was threatened with the possibility of total economic and political collapse.

Confronted with this situation, it became apparent to the United States that its interests, in the enlightened sense of the word, required continued large-scale assistance directed towards the recovery of the European nations. The magnitude of this assistance went far beyond what was planned during the war and the immediate post-war period.

Before analyzing the process within the Administration leading to the Marshall speech of June 5, 1947, mention should be made of some reactions to the European events in American public opinion.

These reactions mostly dealt with the two main elements in American policy toward Europe: the necessity of large-scale assistance and the urge for greater European cooperation. Reference has already been made to the speech of John Foster Dulles on March 17, 1947.

A major part of the influential press saw the Truman Doctrine clearly as the *Washington Post* of March 13, 1947, called a 'starter' and was deeply aware of the consequences of the British financial crisis, the failure of the Moscow Conference and the problem of Germany. There also was a deep concern about the possibility of

Soviet infiltration in Western European countries as a consequence of the threatening economic crisis.

The New York Times in the latter half of March continued to point out the interrelationship of these events.

On March 20, 1947, Walter Lippmann wrote in the *New York Herald Tribune* that there was no longer any doubt that the United States would have to make a large outlay for reconstruction and peace. He proposed that the United States make the Soviet Union an offer to invest a large sum as part of an overall political settlement. If the Soviet Union would agree to treat Europe, not just Germany, as an economic unit, the United States would find it profitable to allocate a large sum to a European Economic Union and to make a favorable loan to Russia in lieu of reparations.

On March 23, 1947, a report was released, drafted by Herbert Hoover, who at the request of the President had surveyed the economic conditions in Germany and Austria.

He concluded that 'there is only one path to recovery in Europe. That is production. The whole economy of Europe is interlinked with the German economy through the exchange of raw materials and manufactured goods. The productivity of Europe cannot be restored without the restoration of Germany as a contributor to that productivity'.[41]

On April 5, 1947, Walter Lippmann wrote a widely quoted and penetrating article in the *New York Herald Tribune*. After a clarification of his opinion that Europe was on the verge of economic collapse, his conclusion was that 'to prevent the crisis which will otherwise engulf Europe and spread chaos throughout the world our aims will have to be very large, in Europe not less than an economic union and over here no less than the equivalent of a revival of Lend Lease'.

On May 1, 1947, he followed this up by an article which contained already many important elements of the Marshall speech. Lippmann rejected the idea of allocating money to each European

41. Joseph Jones, *op. cit.*, pp. 227–228.

government separately. 'That will merely put them all on the dole, whereas what is needed is a reorganization of the bankrupt economy of Europe, and then to make the reorganization succeed, a large contribution from America of working capital.'

'So after we have discussed the separate needs of Britain, France, Italy and the rest, we should suggest to them that they meet together, agree on a general European program of production and exchange of imports and exports to the outer world, and that they arrive at an estimate of the consolidated deficit for as much of Europe as can agree to a common plan.

Such a consolidated deficit will be smaller than the sum of the separate national deficits. Moreover from our point of view it would be a refreshing innovation to make our contribution not to many separate governments but to Europe, if not to all of it at first, then at least to a very large part of it. In such way as this the contribution which we must inevitably make would serve not merely to relieve suffering but as a premium and inducement to the unification of Europe.'

After Acheson's speech[42] in Cleveland, Mississippi, on May 8, 1947, the public pressure increased mainly because some opponents of the Truman doctrine saw in Acheson's speech both a happy and welcome abandonment of what they considered the militant and military anti-communist thesis.

The introduction of more positive elements of the fight against communism through humanitarian means of aid to economic reconstruction struck a familiar note in the minds of many Americans. Among those was, for instance, former Vice-President Henry A. Wallace, a fervent opponent of the Truman Doctrine.

He made urgent appeals for a five-year world rehabilitation plan financed by the United States at a cost of about $10 billion a year of which half would be spent in the Soviet Union.

From the Republican side, Harold Stassen, in a speech in Iowa, spoke of setting aside ten percent of American production to build

42. Referred to on page 47.

worldwide peace in a program not directed against anyone.[43]

On May 25, 1947, James Reston in the *New York Times* for the first time brought out the main lines of State Department thinking. 'The old approach was to deal with the shattered economies of the several nations one at a time, lending now to Britain, then to France, then to Italy, etc. The new approach is based on the growing conviction that the problems of all these countries are interrelated and that Europe cannot recover by showing up, one at a time, the various national economies.

What is under urgent and thoughtful consideration is a proposal to call on the nations of Europe to suggest a more coordinated continental economy as a preliminary to the United States meeting them with a large-scale program of continual aid.'

Finally, mention should be made of Winston Churchill's speech on May 14, 1947, in London in which he came out strongly in favor of a united Europe and in which he pleaded for Britain to play her full part in the European family.[44]

These few quotations from many hundreds of articles and speeches demonstrate again the great influence of non-official thought on official American foreign policy.

The Marshall speech did not come as an unexpected statement. It was preceded by a public debate and influenced by the opinion of a large segment of influential commentators.

The thoughts and activities inside the Administration were a major element in the formulation of the policy leading to the Marshall speech of June 5, 1947. Jones, Beloff and Price, in their studies, have been able to quote from important internal State Department documents.

There were four main interrelated State Department activities leading to the formulation of the new policy.

1. After his return from Moscow, Marshall discussed the problem

43. Joseph Jones, *op. cit.*, pp. 233–234.
44. Text of the speech in *The New York Times*, May 15, 1947.

of Europe in relation with the Soviet attitude with George F. Kennan, Head of the State Department's newly established Policy Planning Staff and told him that he was deeply perturbed by the developments in Europe and that he wanted to take an initiative. He was in need of suggestions for such a plan.

Kennan went to work with a very small staff of Joseph E. Johnson and Carlton Savage while Jacques Reinstein joined in a later phase.

They presented their first memorandum to Secretary Marshall on May 23, 1947.

The Policy Planning Staff did not see communist activities as the root of the actual difficulties in Western Europe. It believed that the present crisis resulted in large part from the disruptive effects of the war on the economic, political and social structure of Europe. It recognized that the communists were exploiting the European crisis and that further communist successes would create a serious danger to American security. It considered, however, that an American effort in aid to Europe should be directed not to combatting communism as such, but to the restoration of the economic health and vigor of European society. It should aim to reverse the economic maladjustments which made European society vulnerable to exploitation by totalitarian movements.

It would be neither fitting nor efficacious for the United States to undertake to draw up unilaterally a program designed to place Europe on its feet economically. The formal initiative should come from Europe, the program should evolve in Europe and the Europeans should bear the basic responsibility.

The program which the United States was asked to support should be a joint one, agreed to by several European nations. The request for United States support should come as a joint request from a group of friendly nations, not as a series of isolated and individual appeals.

The program should bring Europe to a tolerable standard of living on a financially self-supporting basis. The program should give reasonable assurance that it would be the last program the United States would be asked to support in the foreseeable future.

Secret discussions with the British should be undertaken at once with respect to the general approach to this problem. Two misconceptions in respect to the Truman Doctrine should be removed. First, that the United States approach to world problems was a defensive reaction to communist pressure and that the effort to restore sound economic conditions in other countries was only a byproduct of this reaction and not something the United States would do if there were no communist menace.

Second, that the Truman Doctrine was a blank check to give economic and military aid to any area where the communists showed signs of being successful.

While the initiative should be left to Europe, the United States should undertake by the Washington agencies and through the American diplomatic missions abroad an independent study of the entire problem of rehabilitation in Europe.

As to the question of Eastern Europe, the Staff recommended that the first proposal should be one for a general European plan which should be advanced in the Economic Commission for Europe. It should be made in such a form that the Soviet satellite countries would either exclude themselves by unwillingness to accept the proposed conditions or agree to abandon the exclusive orientation of their economies. If the Russians proved able to block such a scheme in the Economic Commission for Europe, than an alternative forum would have to be found where they would not be present.

In a second memorandum, the Policy Planning Staff strongly favored the establishment of a multilateral clearing system, reduction of tariff and trade barriers, the eventual formation of a European Customs Union, the inclusion of Germany and the necessity that the plan should be in full conformity with the Charter of the United Nations in spite of its regional approach.[45]

2. On March 5, 1947, Under Secretary of State Acheson sent letters to the Secretaries of War and of the Navy in which he made refer-

45. Price, *op. cit.,* pp. 21–24.
    Beloff, *op. cit.,* pp. 14, 20–24.
    Jones, *op. cit.,* pp. 240, 249–254.

ence to the fact that aid to Greece and Turkey was only a part of a much larger problem growing out of the change in Great Britain's strength and other world circumstances. He thought it important that study be given to this wider problem. He proposed to entrust the existing State-War-Navy Coordinating Committee with this task. In order to prepare the State Department's point of view, a group was formed (the so-called Foreign Aid Committee) out of which a small group of three men, H. van B. Cleveland, Ben T. Moore and Charles Kindleberger, produced a document of great importance for the subsequent action. It was not completed till June 12, 1947, but its main ideas were circulated at an earlier date. In this document it was set out that the primary objective of United States policy towards Europe should be to bring about conditions in Europe which would cause Soviet leaders to decide that their interests were better served by negotiating a political and economic settlement and by collaborating with the United States on European matters than by continuing a policy of unilateral expansion.

A second objective should be to strengthen Western Europe and to increase its Western orientation under United States leadership, so that there would be a stronger resistance in the event of the Soviet Union declining to collaborate. It was uncertain whether the United States could attain the primary objective, this being a matter of Soviet choice, or whether the United States would have to concentrate on the secondary objective. As quickly as possible a recovery of mass living standards in non-communist countries should be brought about.

Especially in France, Italy and Germany the center groups should be prevented from drifting to the extreme Left or Right. A coordinated program assisted and planned by the United States should be designed and directed towards a strong and economically integrated Europe. The initial approach should be to the whole of Europe, in order to avoid undesirable psychological repercussions in Western Europe and to attract, if possible, Soviet participation. The Economic Commission for Europe was suggested as the agency to handle the program.

It was, however, desirable to demonstrate that the United States was both able and willing to go ahead with a consistent and adequate recovery program for non-communist Europe with or without the Soviet Union.

For this objective a purely economic program would be insufficient. Non-communist Europe should also be provided with possible goals to help fill the present ideological and moral vacuum. The only possible ideological content of such a program was European unity.

There was a possibility of developing tremendous emotional support in Western Europe behind the idea of European unity.

The immediate impact, however, of the symbol of European unity would have to be economic and not political. The United States appeal should be couched in terms of a European recovery plan which would stress the raising of European production and consumption through the economic and functional unification of Europe. In United States propaganda and diplomacy, it would be necessary to stress and even exaggerate the immediate economic benefits which would flow from the joint making of national economic policies and decisions.

The memorandum came out decisively in favor of an inclusion of the Soviet Union and Eastern Europe, mainly on the economic argument of the necessity to maintain the traditional economic intercourse between Eastern and Western Europe. There would be dangers of Soviet obstruction, but these were outweighed by the advantage of Soviet participation.

Finally, the memorandum dealt with Germany. The document said that all United States policies for German recovery should be tested not only according to their contribution to recovery in Germany and to the reduction of the United States financial burden in Germany but also to their contribution to European recovery and to the reduction of the United States burden in Europe generally.[46]

46. Jones, *op. cit.,* pp. 149–201, 243–244.
    Beloff, *op. cit.,* pp. 15–19.

3. Meanwhile the economic sections of the State Department, under the responsibility of Under Secretary Clayton, had made elaborate studies on the economic, financial, political and social situation of a dozen countries, mostly in Europe, and on estimates of how conditions would develop in the foreseeable future.

The United States balance of payments with the world and with each of the critical countries was projected through 1947, 1948 and 1949.

Studies were made about the most critical materials in relation to the reconstruction of Europe, the possibilities of the transport system and availabilities in the United States.

The problem of legislation and administrative controls was surveyed and attention was given to the issue of an eventual retention of certain domestic controls.

Claytons' judgment and personality were main factors in framing the policy leading to the speech of June 5, 1947. He returned from an extensive stay in Europe on May 19, 1947, deeply impressed by what he considered the alarming condition of Europe. He sent a memorandum to Acheson and Marshall which, according to Jones, not only influenced the content of Marshall's speech but probably induced him to make it.

He described the situation in Europe in precise economic terms. The United States had strongly underestimated the destruction of Europe's economy. The principal deficit items were coal, breadgrains, and shipping. Without substantial United States aid there would be total economic and political disintegration. Clayton suggested the appointment of a commission to study and report on the United States national ability to assist Europe. United States resources were ample. The problem was to organize United States fiscal policy and consumption so that sufficient surpluses could be made available out of the enormous production capacity. The President and the Secretary of State should make strong spiritual appeals to the American people to sacrifice a little to save Europe from starvation and chaos. He was convinced that Europe would have to be supported by grants to the amount of $6 or $7 billion for at least three years in the form of coal, food, cotton, tobacco, shipping services and other commodities. The three-year grant should be based on a European plan worked out by the United Kingdom, France and Italy and should be based on a European federation on the lines of the Benelux Customs Union. In strong verbal statements inside the Department of State and to other parts of the Administration, Clayton continuously pressed for speedy and large-scale action.[47]

4. The President had the intention of addressing the Delta Council in Cleveland, Mississippi, on May 8, 1947, but asked Under Secretary Acheson to take his place. On that occasion Acheson foreshadowed the Marshall Plan in what the President called the prologue to the European Recovery Program.[48]

The aim of the speech was to concentrate on the economic aspects of the policy as a kind of economic interpretation of the basic facts of international life with which the United States was primarily concerned in the conduct of foreign relations. The first was that most of the countries of Europe and Asia were in a state of physical destruction or economic dislocation or both. The second was that Germany and Japan had barely been able to begin the process of reconstruction. The third was that unforeseen disasters had occurred to the crops and productive capacity of Europe – severe cold, droughts, storms, and floods – slowing down the pace of reconstruction.

This had produced a staggering disparity between production in the United States and in the rest of the world.

'How are foreigners to get the dollars to cover a likely deficit of $8 billion in the next year?' Acheson asked.

47. Jones, *op. cit.*, pp. 203, 246–248.
      Beloff, *op. cit.*, pp. 19–20.
48. Harry S. Truman, *Years of Trial and Hope 1946–1953*, (Hodder & Stoughton, 1956), Vol I, p. 119.
      For text of the speech see Department of State, *Bulletin*, XVI, p. 991, and for further background Leonard Miall, 'How the Marshall Plan Started', in *The Listener*, May 4, 1961, pp. 779–780.

He described how the deficit was covered till this moment by grants, loans, liquidation of investments, remittances of private citizens and by the foreign countries drawing on their limited reserves of gold and foreign currencies. But what about the future, and what did these facts mean for the United States and its foreign policy?

It meant first, that the United States was going to have to take as large a volume of imports as possible from abroad in order to narrow the balance of payments gap between it and the rest of the world.

Second, it meant that the United States was going to have to undertake further emergency financing of foreign purchases. Further financing beyond existing congressional authorizations was an absolute necessity. No other country was able to bridge the gap in commodities or dollars.

Third, the United States should concentrate the emergency assistance on areas where it would be most effective in building world political and economic stability, in promoting human freedom and democratic institutions, in protecting liberal trading policy and in strengthening the authority of the United Nations.

Fourth, the reconstruction of Germany and Japan should be accelerated.

Fifth, the Administration would need the extension by Congress of certain executive powers, due to expire on June 30.

With specific reference to Europe, Acheson said that European recovery could not be complete until the various parts of Europe's economy were working together in a harmonious whole. 'The achievement of a coordinated European economy remains a fundamental objective of our foreign policy.'[49]

Acheson's speech was a courageous, intelligent, and extremely well-timed contribution to the development of policy in Washington.

Secretary Marshall's speech was drafted by Charles Bohlen, but altered on some points by the Secretary.

49. Jones, op. cit., pp. 24-30, 206, 211.
    Beloff, op. cit., pp. 18-19.

It was mainly based on the Kennan and Clayton memoranda with strong elements from the recommendations of the Foreign Aid Committee group and the Acheson speech of May 8, 1947.

Marshall decided personally to direct the offer of assistance to the whole of Europe, including the Soviet Union and other Eastern-European countries.

The results of all this intelligent analysis, political foresight and imagination were brought together in his address at Harvard University on June 5, 1947.[50]

'I need not tell you, gentlemen, that the world situation is very serious. That must be apparent to all intelligent people. I think one difficulty is that the problem is one of such enormous complexity that the very mass of facts presented to the public by press and radio make it exceedingly difficult for the man in the street to reach a clear appraisement of the situation. Furthermore, the people of this country are distant from the troubled areas of the earth and it is hard for them to comprehend the plight and consequent reactions of the long-suffering peoples, and the effect of those reactions on their governments in connection with our efforts to promote peace in the world.

In considering the requirements for the rehabilitation of Europe, the physical loss of life, the visible destruction of cities, factories, mines, and railroads was correctly estimated, but it has become obvious during recent months that this visible destruction was probably less serious than the dislocation of the entire fabric of European economy. For the past 10 years conditions have been highly abnormal. The feverish preparation for war and the more feverish maintenance of the war effort engulfed all aspects of national economies. Machinery has fallen into disrepair or is entirely obsolete. Under the arbitrary and destructive Nazi rule, virtually every possible enterprise was geared into the German war machine. Long-standing commercial ties, private institutions, banks, insur-

50. Text in *In Quest of Peace and Security, op. cit.*, pp. 93–95.

ance companies, and shipping companies disappeared, through loss of capital, absorption through nationalization, or by simple destruction. In many countries, confidence in the local currency has been severely shaken. The breakdown of the business structure of Europe during the war was complete. Recovery has been seriously retarded by the fact that two years after the close of hostilities a peace settlement with Germany and Austria has not been agreed upon. But even given a more prompt solution of these difficult problems, the rehabilitation of the economic structure of Europe quite evidently will require a much longer time and greater effort than had been foreseen.

There is a phase of this matter which is both interesting and serious. The farmer has always produced the foodstuffs to exchange with the city dweller for the other necessities of life. This division of labor is the basis of modern civilization. At the present time it is threatened with breakdown. The town and city industries are not producing adequate goods to exchange with the food-producing farmer. Raw materials and fuel are in short supply. Machinery is lacking or worn out. The farmer or the peasant cannot find the goods for sale which he desires to purchase. So the sale of his farm produce for money which he cannot use seems to him an unprofitable transaction. He, therefore, has withdrawn many fields from crop cultivation and is using them for grazing. He feeds more grain to stock and finds for himself and his family an ample supply of food, however short he may be on clothing and the other ordinary gadgets of civilization. Meanwhile people in the cities are short of food and fuel. So the governments are forced to use their foreign money and credits to procure these necessities abroad. This process exhausts funds which are urgently needed for reconstruction. Thus a very serious situation is rapidly developing which bodes no good for the world. The modern system of the division of labor upon which the exchange of products is based is in danger of breaking down.

The truth of the matter is that Europe's requirements for the next three or four years of foreign food and other essential products—

principally from America—are so much greater than her present ability to pay that she must have substantial additional help or face economic, social, and political deterioration of a very grave character.

The remedy lies in breaking the vicious circle and restoring the confidence of the European people in the economic future of their own countries and of Europe as a whole. The manufacturer and the farmer throughout wide areas must be able and willing to exchange their products for currencies, the continuing value of which is not open to question.

Aside from the demoralizing effect on the world at large and the possibilities of disturbances arising as a result of the desperation of the people concerned, the consequences to the economy of the United States should be apparent to all. It is logical that the United States should do whatever it is able to do to assist in the return of normal economic health in the world, without which there can be no political stability and no assured peace. Our policy is directed not against any country or doctrine but against hunger, poverty, desperation, and chaos. Its purpose should be the revival of a working economy in the world so as to permit the emergence of political and social conditions in which free institutions can exist. Such assistance, I am convinced, must not be on a piecemeal basis as various crises develop. Any assistance that this Government may render in the future should provide a cure rather than a mere palliative. Any government that is willing to assist in the task of recovery will find full cooperation, I am sure, on the part of the United States Government. Any government which maneuvers to block the recovery of other countries cannot expect help from us. Furthermore, governments, political parties, or groups which seek to perpetuate human misery in order to profit therefrom politically or otherwise will encounter the opposition of the United States.

It is already evident that, before the United States Government can proceed much further in its efforts to alleviate the situation and help start the European world on its way to recovery, there must be some agreement among the countries of Europe as to the requirements of the situation and the part those countries themselves will take in order to give proper effect to whatever action might be undertaken by this Government. It would be neither fitting nor efficacious for this Government to undertake to draw up unilaterally a program designed to place Europe on its feet economically. This is the business of the Europeans. The initiative, I think, must come from Europe. The role of this country should consist of friendly aid in the drafting of a European program and of later support of such a program so far as it may be practical for us to do so. The program should be a joint one, agreed to by a number, if not all, European nations.

An essential part of any successful action on the part of the United States is an understanding on the part of the people of America of the character of the problem and the remedies to be applied. Political passion and prejudice should have no part. With foresight, and a willingness on the part of our people to face up to the vast responsibility which history has clearly placed upon our country, the difficulties I have outlined can and will be overcome.'

CHAPTER II

The Marshall Plan and the Constitution of the Organization for European Economic Cooperation (1947–1948)

In the previous chapter an attempt was made to describe the general trends of post-war American foreign policy leading to the emergence of the Marshall Plan.

For a better understanding of the concern of United States foreign policy with the process of European integration it is necessary to give a rather detailed and chronological analysis of the first years of the Marshall Plan, mainly for three reasons.

First, the notion of Western Europe as a possible political and economic unity and of the promotion of this unity became for the first time, in a concrete way, part of American foreign policy. The vague uneasiness and even irritation about the fragmentation of the old world and the genuine desire to transplant the American image to the shattered European countries were translated into a plan and subsequent action. There was a transition from dream to reality.

It was still unclear by which methods this unity could and should be achieved.

American thinking on the subject was still in its infancy. Unity, unification, federation, integration, cooperation, self-help and mutual efforts were still different words used for the same objective. The objective, however, was there and was there to stay as an integral part of United States foreign policy.

The second reason to go into a rather detailed narrative of the events of these years lies in the possibility of seeing American influence on the process of European integration at work in a way which is far more open to examination than normally is the case in diplomatic intercourse of such a delicate character.

The third and most important reason is that this specific period has been of paramount importance for the whole post-war development and structure of the process of European integration.

The Organization for European Economic Cooperation, the North Atlantic Treaty Organization, the Western European Union, the European Coal and Steel Community, Euratom and the European Economic Community are unthinkable without the basis laid by the idea and by the implementation of the European Recovery Program. If it were only for this third reason it is worthwhile to follow closely the events since 'Mr. Marshall's Challenge'[1] and during the first period thereafter. In these days European history, to a great extent, was made in Washington D.C.

A. REACTIONS IN EUROPE

Europe's reaction was prompt. There was uncertainty and confusion about the exact scope and meaning of Marshall's words. There was, however, an instinctive feeling for the major importance of the American initiative. There is no question that Europe's reaction was inspired and motivated far more by the burning problem of the dollar shortage than by the second element of the American initiative – the call for some agreement among the countries of Europe and for a joint program.

Looking back at that period, one can hardly realize how dominating and all-absorbing the dollar problem was for the great majority of European countries. 'More and more as week succeeds week the whole of European life is being overshadowed by the great dollar

1. *The Economist,* June 14, 1947.

shortage. The margin between recovery and collapse throughout Western Europe is dependent at this moment upon massive imports from the U.S.'[2] In this remarkable *Economist* article all the elements of the Marshall speech were analyzed before it was made.

'If the dollars that are so desperately needed could somehow be represented not merely as assistance to the improvident but as the foundation of some good constructive purpose then there might be a greater chance of eliciting favourable response.'

In a warning against European laxity the article continues: 'And if the difficulties in the way are simply the unreasonable recalcitrance of the Europeans, let the United States use its great power to knock their heads together and impose agreement; there are plenty of Europeans who would welcome American dictation, if it were for a good cause. But it does not behove the Western Europeans simply to wait in attitudes of passive despair for their salvation to be thrust upon them.'

During these weeks in the spring of 1947, there was a feeling of panic in Europe about the dollar shortage and a sense of the impending *deus ex machina* in the form of American assistance.

In a country like the Netherlands, where recovery from complete wartime economic ruin was well on its way, the dilemma was clearly either to stop the progress of reconstruction or to find a solution for the dollar problem through outside assistance. In most European countries the dollar shortage was the central economic problem and at the same time the central political problem.[3]

The combination of panic about the dollar shortage and a keen awareness of impending developments in Washington after the proclamation of the Truman Doctrine created an atmosphere in Europe in which prompt reactions were to be expected.

A period of frantic diplomatic activity began.

2. *The Economist*, May 31, 1947.
3. Price, *op. cit.*, pp. 26–29.
   W. Adams Brown, Jr., and R. Opie, *American Foreign Assistance,* (Washington D.C.: The Brookings Institution, 1953), pp. 130–134.

It was logical that the initiative for a European response should fall on the two major European powers, the United Kingdom and France.

There was, however, a certain apprehension among the smaller European countries of being confronted with a *fait accompli* of the major powers, reached in consultation with the United States. There also was, during these weeks in June, a desire not to endanger an eventual participation of the Soviet Union and the other countries from Eastern Europe.

On June 13, 1947, Bevin, at a meeting of the Foreign Press Association, praised the American initiative, and in assuming the British role in a European response said with regard to an eventual Soviet participation: 'I can only say to other nations that when the United States throws a bridge to link east and west, it would be disastrous for ideological or other reasons to frustrate the United States in this great endeavour.'[4]

This, however, did not prevent him from stating in the House of Commons on June 19, 1947, that Europe should go ahead with or without the Soviet Union and that prolonged discussions should in no way delay speedy action.[5] This statement was made after Bevin's consultations in Paris where he met the French ministers in order to synchronize British and French action. This resulted in an invitation to the Soviet Union for a Three-Power Conference on June 27, 1947.

The issue of the participation of the Soviet Union confused and complicated European reactions. It was, however, resolved on July 3, 1947, when the Three-Power Conference in Paris broke down. It would be beyond the scope of this study to analyze in detail the United States approach to Soviet participation. The advantages and disadvantages of Soviet participation were fully realized. There is no reason to believe that the United States Administration was not sincere in formally extending its offer to the whole of Europe, including the countries of the Communist bloc.

4.   *The Times,* June 14, 1947.
5.   *The Times,* June 20, 1947.

Schmitt rightly says: 'Thus the Marshall Plan divided Europe after all. But evidence does not point an accusing finger at the United States. Europe needed help, and the American Government offered to supply it, secretly apprehensive perhaps of possible Russian acceptance and its effect on Congress and public opinion.'[6]

Western Europe's feelings were mixed, but there was an overtone of a genuine desire to reach agreement with the Soviet Union and a great reluctance to write off Eastern Europe before the proof was made that Soviet participation would wreck any constructive response.

The burden of handling the situation was not on the United States, but on the United Kingdom and France. There is no proof whatsoever that the United States tried to influence the two European partners to take a negative attitude.

On the one hand, there were those in Europe who clearly saw that participation of the Soviet Union would only lead to permanent obstruction.

In the previously quoted article of June 14, 1947, *The Economist* concluded: 'It follows that the attempt must necessarily be confined in the first place to Western Europe and the Mediterranean countries.' Governments, however, were far more prudent. In the back of their minds they might have been 'reconciled to the fact that any viable program would have to take place without Soviet participation',[7] but in their diplomatic actions and especially in their public behavior they did not show any sign of it. For this they had good and understandable reasons. In the United States, the transition from the 'one world' to the 'two world' concept took place only gradually. In Western Europe, the reluctance to accept the division of Europe was even greater. There was a strong feeling that active Russian opposition, aided by the strong communist movements in many Western European countries, might endanger

6. Hans A. Schmitt, *The Path to European Union,* (Louisiana State University Press, 1962), pp. 21–22.
7. David Wightman, *Economic Cooperation in Europe,* (New York: Praeger, 1956), p. 29.

the plan. Moreover the need for, and the acceptance of the Marshall proposal did not suppress the fear 'that American aid on a large scale might indeed carry with it conditions committing their governments to the support of unpredictable American policies'.[8]

In unofficial discussions during the second half of June, high officials of the Foreign Office in London made it clear to their continental partners that fundamental issues, such as liberalization of trade as part of an eventual European response, should be avoided in order not to alienate the Russians.

In welcoming Bevin's trip to Paris, for consultation with the French Government, Bidault, the French Foreign Minister, took great care to keep the Soviet Government informed and stressed that he would be ready to discuss the Marshall proposal with that government.[9] In a note which was handed to the Soviet Government on June 19, 1947, just after the Franco-British discussions, the French, in inviting Molotov to a Three-Power Conference, went out of their way to assure him first, that Marshall had not made any official proposal to the French and British Governments and second, that a joint program should be established by all the European countries which would be willing to take part in such action in close liaison with the existing United Nations agencies.[10]

The Three-Power Conference proved that nobody in the West had to take delicate and difficult decisions. Molotov made things easy for them by his completely negative attitude. In this context, out of the endless arguments used during the conference, only one should be elaborated because it showed that the Western European countries realized very clearly that the 'shopping list' approach would never be acceptable to the Americans, even though it was sometimes tempting to themselves.

This 'shopping list' approach implied that the European response

8. Price, *op. cit.,* p. 28.
9. Ministère des Affaires Etrangères, *Documents de la Conférence des Ministres des Affaires Etrangères de la France, du Royaume Uni et de l'URSS tenue à Paris du 27 juin au 3 juillet 1947,* (Paris, 1947), pp. 13–14.
10. Ministère des Affaires Etrangères, *op. cit.,* pp. 15–16.

should not go beyond the sum of the uncoordinated requirements of the individual European countries.

Especially Bevin was aware of the strong American opinion on this subject after Under Secretary Clayton's visit to London.

Clayton, during that visit, pressed for speedy action and a cooperative plan, including all European countries (with the provisional exclusion of Spain). He stressed that American aid would only be complementary to the effort of the European countries. A steering committee consisting of France, the Soviet Union, and the United Kingdom, assisted by *ad hoc* commissions, should be established to study specific commodity problems. These studies should be submitted to the United Nations Economic Commission for Europe. As for Germany, it would be impossible to envisage a European program without it, but the European report which Clayton had in mind would in no way prejudice the issues on which the Occupying Powers still had not reached agreement.

On June 28, 1947, Molotov made it quite clear that agreement was highly improbable. United States aid was welcome on a purely bilateral basis. A coordinated European program, however, in which American aid would take its place, inevitably meant interference in the affairs of sovereign states and in the existing framework of bilateral trade agreements. The main purpose of a conference should be to study the conditions attached to American aid and priority should always be given to countries formerly occupied by Germany.

This was a flat rejection of the idea of a joint approach. Only a 'shopping list' and no more was acceptable to the Russians.

On July 1, 1947, Bidault made a last and supreme effort to meet the Russian point of view. He stressed the fact that in the French proposals, which he had submitted on the previous day, nothing could be found which would affect the national sovereignty of the participating countries, nor was there any possibility of interference in their internal affairs.

Bidault, however, explicitly did not yield on the point that there should be a common European effort.

He ended with a solemn warning that not only European recovery was at stake but the whole organization of Europe. France desired a non-divided Europe.

This warm appeal met the usual cold and negative Soviet response. Threat to sovereignty, denouncement of Western policy in Germany, the danger of dividing Europe, all these arguments were again repeated. Molotov ended by solemny warning the two other governments against the consequences of the implementation of their ideas.

Bidault and Bevin announced their firm intention of pursuing the work on the European response to the Marshall proposal together with all those European countries which wanted to cooperate.

The Russian refusal had immense and lasting consequences. From that moment on Europe 'was no longer divided between allies, ex-ennemies and neutrals but into Marshall Plan countries and Iron Curtain Countries'.[11]

It was no surprise that the Soviet Union not only decided for itself but for the whole of Eastern Europe as well.

Albania, Hungary, Rumania and Yougoslavia immediately declined the Anglo-French invitation of July 4, 1947, which will be discussed later. Finland, Poland, and Czechoslovakia could not afford to act against the Soviet will, even though they were desperately in need of dollar assistance. Czechoslovakia, especially, was quite willing and even anxious to keep open the roads to the Western world but its pathetic attempts to cooperate were killed during a visit of Gottwald and Masaryk to Moscow on July 9, 1947.

In their refusal to accept the invitation, the Poles especially stressed the danger of the return of German hegemony, a theme which was to remain a permanent feature in the communist attitude towards any form of European cooperation and integration.[12]

Why did the Russians accept the Anglo-French invitation for the Three-Power Conference at all? Their motives probably were a

11.   John C. Campbell, *op. cit.,* p. 442.
12.   Statement of Jozef Cyrankiewitz, President of the Ministers Council of Poland on July 9, 1947, in *The Times,* July 11, 1947.

mixture of an effort to secure dollars on a bilateral basis, an attempt to wreck the plan from the beginning, and a desire to put the full blame of the division of Europe onto the Western Powers. This last motive was used for many years in their hostile and dangerous activities against the Recovery Plan.

The Russians used the notion of national sovereignty as a pretext to preserve the social, economic and political structure of Eastern Europe. They were deeply convinced that the United States concern for joint European action was nothing else than a pretext to dominate that part of the world.

The unsuccessful outcome of the Three-Power Conference caused the split of Europe. The notion of Western Europe was born and became the object of American policies and hopes.[13]

B. PREPARATION OF THE SIXTEEN-POWER CONFERENCE

While much of the diplomatic energy of the two major European powers was focused on the issue of Soviet participation, this by no means stopped their other activities or those of the smaller European nations in the first weeks after Marshall's speech.

The center of these actions was London rather than Paris. There,

13. For the study of the Three-Power Conference and the Russian attitude see further:
Brown and Opie, *op. cit.,* pp. 132–133.
'Molotov or Marshall', in *The Economist,* July 5, 1947.
Harry S. Truman, *op. cit.,* p. 122.
Theodore H. White, *Fire in the Ashes, Europe in Mid-Century,* (New York: William Sloane Associates, 1953), pp. 37–41.
David Wightman, *op. cit.,* pp. 25–51.
The Forrestal Diaries, edited by Walter Millis, (New York: The Viking Press, 1951), pp. 278–284.
Marshal D. Shulman, *Stalins Foreign Policy Reappraised,* (Harvard University Press, 1963), pp. 13–51.
Fred Charles Iklé, 'Der Westliche und der Sovjetische Verhandlungsstil', in *Europa Archiv,* (25. 11. 1964), pp. 837–838.

Under Secretary Clayton and Ambassador Douglas explained the preliminary views of the United States to the British Government in the last week of June 1947.

There is no evidence that the Americans had arrived at a concrete and detailed picture of the contents of a European recovery program. Nevertheless, some elements which would dominate the American policy towards the European problem for a long period, could already be traced.

First, there was a strong desire not to intervene in the internal policies of the participating countries and to cling to the notion that what was going to happen should be presented as a European initiative. This attitude was inspired by the Administration's policy, summed up in Marshall's words, that 'the role of this country should consist of friendly aid in the drafting of a European program'.

Second, the Americans insisted on the joint character of the program. From the first days on, American officials emphatically stressed the necessity of avoiding the 'shopping list' approach. There was no precision as to what this exactly meant.

The American thoughts at the outset did not go beyond a hope for some form of a multilateral clearing system, reductions of tariffs and other trade impediments, all of which eventually could lead to a customs union. In other words, while no precise plans or even objectives were available, Clayton, Douglas and many other American officials strongly suggested that a proof of the interdependence of the problems in Europe should be given. In this field there was more clarity in what should be avoided than in what should be achieved.

Third, from the beginning on there was strong American insistence on the limited period of the plan. The program should cover a period longer than one year, preferably three or four, and should be conceived and presented in such a way that at the closing of that period the aims and objectives should be achieved.

Fourth, in this preliminary phase, there were hardly any references from the American side as to the amount of available aid.

Already in this phase, the United States left no doubt that the total amount should have to be manageable for American standards.

Fifth, the German problem played a major part in United States thoughts about European recovery. One cannot stress too much the predominant place of the German problem in American post-war policy towards Europe. In this specific period, two major trends of American policy coincided. There was, in the first place, the objective of the recovery of Germany itself, or at least of the part of Germany under United States influence.

In the second place, there was the conviction that the recovery of Europe would be inconceivable without a major German contribution.

In an important directive to the Commander in Chief United States Forces of Occupation, it was stated that 'an orderly and prosperous Europe requires the economic contribution of a stable and productive Germany as well as the necessary restraints to insure that Germany is not allowed to revive its destructive militarism'.[14]

Sixth, was the problem of the role of the United Nations. The Americans were well aware of the fact that any regional approach should never be directed against the universal character of the United Nations. On the other hand, they realized that some new, probably temporary, organization was indispensable for tackling the immediate problems of European recovery. The latter opinion became much stronger after the collapse of the Three-Power Conference in Paris.

Seventh, already in their very first conversations in Europe United States officials laid much emphasis on the importance of Congressional reactions and opinions. Much of what was said or suggested by the United States Administration was openly motivated by the necessity of getting something done which would be acceptable to Congress.

Europe was for the first time fully exposed to a basic problem in

14. Directives to the Commander in Chief of U.S. Forces of Occupation regarding the Military Government of Germany, July 11, 1947, Department of State, *Press Release* 582, (July 15, 1947).

the conduct of foreign policy in the United States, caused by the very special relation between the executive and legislative branches of the Federal Government.

In the European discussions preceding the Sixteen-Power Conference, there was a sharp awareness of urgency but not a purposeful frame of constructive ideas. Anglo-Dutch discussions in the last week of June 1947, and reports from Paris revealed the decision of Britain and France to take the lead in the organization of the European response rather than in strong guidance on what really should be done and achieved.

As to ideas the role of the Benelux countries was more constructive. There were immediate consultations between the three countries leading to a common point of view and subsequent action.

A demarche was made to the United States and all other European countries in which reference was made to the Benelux Customs Union. European cooperation was stressed and attention was drawn to the Netherlands Memorandum on Germany of January 14, 1947, in which it was stated that a certain measure of German recovery was essential for the continued recovery of her neighbors. Certain difficulties could be solved only as and when German recovery progressed.

In the above mentioned Anglo-Dutch discussions, an eventual customs union was suggested by the Dutch but met with a rather reserved reaction.

In the meantime, one could not escape the conclusion that the press was more advanced in its thinking than governments.

The London *Economist*, for instance, in the already mentioned article of June 14, 1947, wrote: 'The British Government have hitherto shamefully neglected their opportunities in this direction; they have never made a sufficiently determined survey of the possibilities of a Western association. For a long time they were deterred from it by fear of offending Mr. Stalin and more recently by fear of pleasing Mr. Churchill. They will now have to work overtime if they are not to incur the charge of missing one of history's great opportunities out of mere inability to seize it.'

In the same issue the *Economist* concluded by writing: 'The statesmen of Europe would be wise not to be too practical; imaginative idealism may, in this instance, prove to be the most practical quality of all, since it may be needed to procure the dollars on which the practical calculation depend.'

On July 4, 1947, Britain and France transmitted their invitation to twenty-two European states.

'The two Governments recognize that Europe must take the initiative in the study of reconstruction and that for this purpose it is essential to draw up, as quickly as possible, a program concerning both the resources and needs of Europe. In the opinion of the two Governments a temporary organization must be set up to bring together the data on which such a program will be based. All European states, with the temporary exception of Spain are being invited to collaborate on their own free will in the work thus to be undertaken.'

A Committee of Cooperation was envisaged, which would coordinate the work of special sub-committees to deal with certain products or branches of economic activity. It should, as Secretary Marshall had suggested, seek the friendly aid of the United States in drafting the report. A meeting was convened in Paris on July 12, 1947. The report of the Committee of Cooperation was to be drawn up in time to be presented to the Government of the United States on September 1, 1947, at the latest.

Austria, Belgium, Denmark, Greece, Iceland, Ireland, Italy, Luxembourg, the Netherlands, Norway, Portugal, Sweden, Switzerland and Turkey accepted.

The other countries refused more or less as a result of Soviet pressure.

On July 4, 1947, the Soviet Union was informed and the two governments, in a last effort, expressed their hope that the Soviet Government would reverse its position.

The work could start. There was an acute dollar shortage, there was an imaginative American proposal and there were some preliminary American and European thoughts. There was, however, no blueprint, no purposeful conception on which the work could be based. Nevertheless, the conference which began on July 12, 1947, was a major step on the road to European recovery and unity.[15]

C. THE PARIS CONFERENCE OF THE COMMITTEE OF EUROPEAN ECONOMIC COOPERATION

It would be tempting for somebody who was present at the Paris Conference to give a day to day description of its work and deliberations. During this conference all the major trends in the policy of various European countries towards the problems of cooperation and integration could already be traced.

The reason why this is not attempted is twofold. In the first place, much of the material is open for study but not for publication. Second, a very detailed survey of the negotiations would go beyond the scope of this study which primarily deals with the concern of United States policy with the process of European integration.

To put the conference in the proper perspective, to understand its atmosphere and to judge its outcome, a few preliminary points should be mentioned.

1. While this was the first conference of 'Western Europe', there was in reality a wide divergence of political outlook and of economic circumstances amongst the participating countries. This was not a conference of an established group. It was rather a gathering of sovereign states, geographically close to each other, but with only one problem in common: they belonged to the non-communist world. There were members and one non-member of the

15.   John W. Spanier, op. cit., pp. 42–43.
      Barbara Ward, op. cit., pp. 113–114.

United Nations. There were ex-neutrals, ex-allies and an ex-enemy. There were countries suffering acutely from dollar shortages and on the verge of economic and social collapse and prosperous ones which were far more onlookers than real participants in the balance of payments struggle. There were participants which still were the center of large colonial or semi-colonial empires and strictly non-colonial countries; there were adherents to a strongly planned economy and strong opponents; there were major powers with a history of world leadership and small nations without strong feelings of prestige.

All of them had accepted the Anglo-French invitation, all of them wanted to participate in the European response to the American initiative, but they did so with different aims, different hopes and different needs.

2. Most of them were obsessed by the need for dollar aid and in preparing their attitude, they had given full priority to their own needs and not to the necessity of a joint European approach.

3. Neither the Americans nor the Europeans had prepared a plan. There were some very rough indications of American thinking, but even those were lacking on the European side.

Bevin's instruction to his delegation, according to his entourage, was 'you go to Paris and do your best'.[16]

4. The period, proposed for conclusion of the work in the Anglo-French invitation – July 12, 1947, till September 1, 1947 – was exceedingly short. It was rightly motivated by the threatening and rapidly deteriorating economic and political situation in most European countries and by the equally justified feeling that the Americans expected a rapid response.

But 'six weeks is a short time to outline the economy of a continent for four years'.[17]

16. Price, *op. cit.,* p. 36.
17. William Diebold, Jr., *Trade and Payments in Western Europe,* Published for the Council on Foreign Relations, (New York: Harper & Brothers, 1952), p. 5.

5. Germany was not present and, at the beginning of the conference, even not represented by the Occupation Powers.

In his opening statements of July 12, 1947, Bidault stressed the European approach more than Bevin did. While the former said that 'the hour has come to construct a Europe', the latter underlined the temporary character of the organization and the need for speedy action. 'It is a piece of *ad hoc* machinery to grapple with this special problem, and I repeat effective and quick action is required.'[18]

The conference, which was held at Ministerial level, adjourned on July 15, 1947, after having set up a Committee of Economic Cooperation under the chairmanship of Sir Oliver Franks. It further established technical committees on food and agriculture, fuel and power, iron and steel, and transport. Other committees were formed, during the course of the conference, to deal with timber, manpower and the balance of payments problem. Financial problems were referred to a Committee of Financial Experts. Out of the Committee of Economic Cooperation an Executive Committee of five was formed, (the United Kingdom, France, Italy, the Netherlands and Norway).

French ideas and British administrative technique were very important in scheduling the work of the conference. As to the organizational set-up, one fact should be specially mentioned. The governments of Belgium, Luxembourg and the Netherlands decided to act in the conference as one delegation in those committees where membership was restricted, and to present a common point of view in all matters of policy. So Dr. Hirschfeld represented Benelux in the Executive Committee. This was a unique achievement in cooperation which as such had a very beneficial influence on the development of the Benelux Economic Union.

The work of the conference can be roughly divided into two main activities. One was the work of the technical committees aimed at

18. *Documents on American Foreign Relations,* (Princeton University Press, 1949), Vol. IX, pp. 188–192.

collecting and summarizing the mass of production, consumption, export and import data, transmitted by the participating countries on the basis of agreed and lengthy questionnaires. These data were screened for inconsistencies by a central group in which Robert Marjolin, the future Secretary General of OEEC, played a major role. This work provided the nucleus of the report on the requirements for outside assistance.

The second main part of the work consisted of the preparation of the 'policy' part of the report and took place mainly in the Executive Committee, the full Committee, and last but not least, in unofficial bilateral and multilateral discussions.

In this study the second aspect of the work will be analyzed but, in judging the importance of the conference and its report, emphasis should be laid on one aspect of the technical work of the conference which was of lasting importance for European cooperation.

The collecting of national data for a common purpose was an unprecedented peacetime excercise. It brought about two elements which were of such great importance for further developments in Europe.

First, it made national governments and administrations aware of the fact that national policies, national plans, needs, and requirements were open to screening and criticism by other countries. Until this moment governmental economic activities were primarily the object of domestic policy and control. Now, for the first time, they crossed the frontier of the sovereign state and were thrown into a highly critical international environment. Those who were part of national administrations during that period realize how deeply this element began to influence policies of the national governments. While theoretically every government was aware of the impact of its own economic policy on the affairs of other countries, this theory never before was so clearly transferred into practice.

This does not imply that the Paris conference thoroughly screened the figures which were submitted by national governments. There was no time and no machinery to do this properly. When the total figures for outside assistance proved to be too high for American and even European standards, the reduction took place not by the careful screening of national data but by a change in some assumptions on which the original data were based. Nevertheless, the importance of this first excercise and its impact on national administrations was great.

It was, among other things, the first step to the division of aid by OEEC and to the Annual Review in NATO.

Second, a group of international-minded men was formed on many administrative levels. The officials in the Ministry of Transport or in the Treasury suddenly became part of a European machinery, feeling responsible for a joint venture. It was the primary school for many men who would play a major role on the post-war European scene, with additional loyalties to a broader entity than their own government. The affinity between these men who worked in Paris day and night during the summer of 1947, formed an indispensable element for future cooperation.

As to the work of the 'policy' part of the conference three subjects, relevant to this study, will be dealt with: the German problem, the discussions on European cooperation, especially the problem of a customs union and the intra-European payments arrangement, and finally the influence of the United States on the work of the conference.

1. *The Incorporation of Germany*

The issue of Germany in connection with the European Recovery Plan was mainly fought between the French and the Benelux delegations. The British took a middle of the road position and the Americans were, certainly in the first weeks of the conference, reluctant to express an outspoken point of view.

One of the issues at stake was the question whether the program, to be submitted to the United States, should be based on full utilization of existing productive capacity, the Benelux point of view, or on national plans like the Monnet plan in France.

France approached the German problem very much from the angle of security, the priority of reparations and adherence to the limitations of industry, fixed by the Four Powers in March 1946. Fear of future German competition with existing and planned French production capacity was paramount, not in the French declarations, but certainly in the background of French policy.

Benelux which had a vital stake in German rehabilitation stressed the importance of a major German contribution to the European Recovery Plan and did not object to a rise of German production levels.

Gradually, but not fundamentally, the gap between the two opinions was narrowed and a compromise solution was found and laid down in a note on 'Problems relating to Germany', attached to the Conference Report.[19]

The conference sent the same questionnaires, as were submitted to the participating countries, to the Commanders of the four zones in Germany and the three Western commanders supplied the information.

In the above-mentioned note, both Benelux and French ideas about the place of Germany in the recovery plan were incorporated. The thoughts of Benelux were expressed in a paragraph which stated that it was indispensable to take into account the future of Germany, since its economy had been in the past and by nature of things would be in the future, closely tied up with the economic system of other European countries. It was further stated that European cooperation could not be effective without fitting the German economy into the European framework.

The French school of thought found its expression in the sentence that the rate and nature of German recovery would have to be carefully controlled. The German economy could not be allowed to develop to the detriment of other European countries.

The future economic policy of Germany should remain the responsibility of the Quadrupartite Council.

19. Committee of European Economic Cooperation, *General Report, op. cit.,* p. 39.

However carefully the words were chosen, the decision to incorporate Western Germany in the plan confirmed the *de facto* partition of Germany. Western Germany would become economically a part of the new Western Europe. Inevitably too, the political future of the three Western zones would be tied to that of the Western European nations as long as Germany should remain divided.

Due to the prevailing differences of policy between the participating countries as to the future of Germany, the final result of the conference could not lay down a clear policy.

Nevertheless, what it achieved was a major step on the road to the inclusion of Western Germany into the framework of European cooperation.

2. *The Customs Union and other Cooperative Efforts*

In judging the cooperative efforts of the Paris Conference, one is tempted to belittle them by the present-day standards of cooperation and integration in Europe.

The result should be judged, however, by the possibilities and policies of that period. Customs unions nowadays might belong to the very orthodox pattern of economic cooperation. In the summer of 1947, they belonged to a very imaginative set of far-reaching ideas. The issue appeared, however, on the agenda of the conference in spite of the fact that at the outset of the conference nothing like it was contemplated.

It emerged for two reasons. One was the gradual realization that a customs union would be one of the projects which would vitalize and catch American public opinion and imagination. The second reason was that especially France and Italy took the opportunity the conference presented for endorsing a wider and lasting integration of the economies of Europe.

There was a fair measure of agreement at the conference on the necessity to lower the trade barriers as far as quota's were concerned and as far as this was in conformity with the Draft Charter for an International Trade Organization on which negotiations took place at the same time in Geneva. There also was a large measure of agreement on the Benelux scheme for a system of transferability of currencies, as proposed by the Committee of Financial Experts, and laid down in the final Report of the conference.[20]

Where opinions clashed, however, was on the idea of a customs union.

Many trends and events of the post-war economic history of Western Europe can already be traced in the discussions in Paris on that issue. The French, closely supported by the Italians, were the great protagonists of a commitment to a customs union, a commitment in principle, to be filled in subsequently. Everybody realized that it would be unacceptable to the United States and in disregard of the obligations of the International Trade Organization to form preferential tariff agreements without the ultimate objective of a customs union. There was, however, a sharp division of opinion as to the desirability of making such a commitment at this stage.

Looking at the post-war history of European cooperation and integration, it is no wonder that on this issue the French-Italian outlook was opposed by the British. The Benelux group found itself between the two schools of thought, not so much of disagreement with the French but out of fear of being locked up on the continent of Europe without British participation and without any prospect of a viable German contribution.

The French delegation vigorously took the lead but the result was rather negative. The British opposed the plan in a restrained but definite way. They were not against a study of the project but the four elements of their policy towards European integration were already apparent:

first, their fear of incompatability between their Commonwealth commitments and an eventual European customs union;

20. C.E.E.C., *op. cit.,* Appendix E, pp. 81–85.
William Diebold, Jr., *op. cit.,* pp. 21–27.

second, their fear of infraction of the national economic sovereignty and independent domestic planning;

third, their desire to maintain a special relationship with the United States in important fields of foreign policy;

fourth, their general and almost instinctive reluctance to enter into exclusive arrangements with a purely continental group of European countries.

The Benelux countries were not willing to contemplate an exclusive combination with the French and the Italians, while the Scandinavians concentrated on their own modest scheme of closer cooperation between themselves.

During informal discussions with the Americans the idea was launched of a union between the French, Italians, Benelux countries and Western Germany, but this idea was still too far from reality to have any real impact on events.

The result of all these discussions was a paragraph in the final report on the development of Benelux which at that time was the only concrete achievement in this field, a declaration of intent by the three Scandinavian countries, a very outspoken declaration of France in which it declared itself ready to enter into negotiations with all European governments sharing its views and willing to enter a customs union, a decision of France and Italy to set up a study group for a Franco-Italian customs union, and the same decision by the Greek and Turkish Governments. Last but not least, a declaration was made by thirteen of the sixteen participating countries that the decision to form a customs union could not be taken without preliminary study and that therefore the thirteen countries decided to set up a study group. The Benelux countries were going to act as sponsoring powers and arrangements were made for invitations to other states to join the group.

Even when full account is taken of the very far-reaching character of a commitment to a customs union in 1947, and of the boldness of such a step at that time, one cannot escape the conclusion that a great opportunity was lost with unforeseen but lamentable effects on post-war European history.

3. The Influence of the United States on the Proceedings of the Conference

The United States was not represented at the Paris Conference. The notion of a European initiative and the limitation of America's role to 'friendly advice' was strictly adhered to until the last period of the conference. The Europeans knew, only by instinct, what the United States expected them to do and only on a very few concrete points, like the insistence on a four-year program, was there any certainty about American reactions.

The United States Embassy in Paris, however, was extremely active in keeping informal contacts with the various delegations. Ambassador Caffery, ably assisted by Mr. Ivan White, was kept informed on every stage of the discussions. From their side they tried to clarify American thoughts, when questions were asked in the informal, mostly bilateral, meetings.

In the last days of July 1947, Under Secretary Clayton came to Paris and informal bilateral meetings between the delegates at the conference and Clayton were arranged. From these meetings it became clear that there was a marked difference between the out-spoken opinion of the Americans at the end of August 1947, and their rather vague approach during these meetings at the end of July.

The four-year period was stressed and there was a generally favorable reaction from the American side to all plans to stimulate a more liberal trade and payments system in Europe. The Americans were inclined not to be too outspoken about the German problem, probably in order not to antagonize French opinion. Strangely enough, in reply to a question on American ideas about future negotiations with the European countries, there was no positive American response to a suggestion of one of the European visitors, who expressed his worries about the prospect of sixteen competing countries engaged in bilateral discussions with the United States.

On July 31, 1947, Clayton met the members of the Executive Committee, the first official contact of the conference with the United States Administration. Clayton explained that thoughts about the recovery plan in the United States at this stage were not much further advanced than at the time of Marshall's speech. His European contacts had brought him to the conclusion that the United States had perhaps oversimplified the issues involved. His reaction to general suggestions of liberalization of trade and payments among the group of sixteen or among smaller groups was favorable, but confronted with the issue of regional arrangements, he was less outspoken.

In mentioning the importance to 'sell' the plan to the United States Congress and to public opinion, he gave more priority to the problem of the four-year period and the necessity to prove that after four years Europe would be on its feet again, than to an urgent appeal for cooperative measures.

This platonic American attitude changed markedly in the course of three weeks.

At the end of August 1947, there was a feeling in conference circles that what was achieved would not meet American approval. The Chairman, Sir Oliver Franks, went to Geneva to discuss the state of the conference with Clayton. American ideas had hardened during the last three weeks and Sir Oliver reported that the reactions of Clayton had been outspoken. First of all, the amount of total aid required should be brought within more reasonable limits than the amount of $28 billion which had emerged from the compilation of data in Paris.

Second, Clayton reproached the British that, by their negative attitude, they had wrecked the prospect of a European customs union. In response to Frank's question whether such a customs union could be considered as a condition for American aid, Clayton replied in the negative but added that such a commitment would greatly enhance the chance of Congressional approval.

Third, Clayton made it clear that the drafting of the report should not be the end of contact between the sixteen participating nations. In the report, a paragraph should be included indicating the decision of the sixteen nations to remain in contact primarily to survey the execution of the recovery plan.

On August 26, 1947, Ambassador Caffery made a more formal demarche to the chiefs of delegation in Paris. He repeated Clayton's criticism and even suggested a three or four week postponement of the final draft of the report. He announced Clayton's visit to Paris on August 28, 1947, for a meeting with the members of the Executive Committee. This meeting was postponed till August 30, 1947, because of the arrival in Paris of two high officials of the United States Administration, Kennan and Bonesteel, with news of the latest developments in Washington. This very important meeting took place on August 30, 1947, and was attended by Clayton, Caffery, Douglas, Kennan and Bonesteel on the American side and on the European side by the members of the Executive Committee. Clayton began by stating that what he had heard about the draft of the report of the conference led him to the conclusion that the whole was disappointing and would constitute a prejudice to the success of the Marshall program.

Clayton showed himself worried about the earlier mentioned amount of $28 billion. The members of the Executive Commission could explain to him that this amount had not as such been accepted by the conference but only constituted an unscreened estimate.

Then Clayton mentioned seven points which would greatly influence the ultimate draft of the report and therefore should be recapitulated.

1. Europe should prove that after the four-year's period of the plan, it should be able to live without outside assistance.

2. The deficit in the balance of payments of the participating countries to the dollar area should decrease year by year, to disappear at the end of 1951, when no further assistance could be contemplated.

There was a very strong insistence by the Americans on this point in spite of the reasonable objections by the Europeans who expressed their view that no such guarantee could be given. There existed too many factors beyond European influence, such as the situation of the overseas territories and the uncertainties about trade with Eastern Europe and South East Asia. The Americans explained that after what American public opinion considered as the failure of the loan to Britain, the United States Congress could be expected to be highly suspicious on that point. At the end of the discussion, however, the Americans were impressed by the integrity of the European reservation and were inclined to accept it.

3. During the period of American assistance the promises in the field of the European production effort should be checked and participants should give specific commitments regarding the fulfillment of the major production programs.

4. Long-term capital investments should be excluded from United States aid and should be financed preferably through the International Bank of Reconstruction and Development.

5. Participating countries should take effective steps to create internal monetary and financial stability.

6. Definite steps should be taken to diminish trade barriers leading to an eventual abolishment of all impediments to trade in conformity with the principles of the International Trade Organization.

7. For the execution of the Plan a permanent organization should be created. With great emphasis the Americans stressed the necessity of formal recognition by the participating countries of their common objectives and of joint responsibility for their attainment. All this should be embodied in a multilateral agreement. This should constitute a contractual obligation, and the organization should be set up outside the agencies of the United Nations, more specifically outside the Economic Commission for Europe.

For countries which were not willing to take part in such an organization, the situation would be as before the Marshall Plan. Each country was expected to negotiate bilaterally with the United States, but bilateral agreements would refer to the obligations under the multilateral agreement of the European nations.

After Clayton had stressed that all this should be seen in the framework of friendly advice and not considered as a dictate, the meeting came to an end.

The general impression of the European participants was favorable and the American point of view was considered very reasonable.

Weeks of feverish activity followed. A great effort was made to meet the United States point of view in spite of the great difficulties, raised by some of the participating nations.

Confusion was created by a strongly worded demarche of the United States Ambassadors in the capitals of the sixteen participating countries on September 9, 1947, in which nothing substantially was added to Clayton's remarks of August 30. There was a marked atmosphere of irritation in the American-European meeting of September 10, 1947, in which an American proposal to postpone the final draft for three or four weeks was rejected and a United States suggestion to give the report a preliminary character was accepted.

On the basis of French proposals the text was finalized and in the last meeting between the American and the European group, Clayton was able to declare that he considered the report a new page in the book of European history and perhaps of the world. He further stated that in his opinion the report would meet, to a very large extent, the views of the State Department.

In the covering letter of the final Report the participating countries wrote: 'In presenting this Report in response to Mr. Marshall's suggestion the participating countries believe that the program of concerted action, which it sets forth, marks the advent of a new state of European economic cooperation.'[21]

This is a correct statement. The basis was laid for great achievements and developments in the Western world. Opportunities were missed, but constructive planning was achieved and new elements were introduced into European cooperation which would greatly influence the process of European unity.

Diebold concludes that 'the validation of this statement in the CEEC report, rests not in the history of the Conference at

21. C.E.E.C., *op. cit.,* p. 2.

Paris, but in the events that followed and are yet to come.'[22]

The report published on September 22, 1947, might not have fired the imagination of Europe and of America, but the Paris Conference and its report formed the indispensable basis for the shape of the Western world in the years to come.[23]

D. PREPARATION AND DEBATE IN WASHINGTON

The four months which followed the completion of the Paris Report, were dominated by the preparation of the executive branch of the United States Government for the necessary legislative action by Congress.

After the strenuous effort at the Paris Conference, Europe passed through a period of non-activity in anticipation of further American action.

The process of translating the Paris Report and the views of the American Administration into legislative action in Washington was a highly complicated, time-consuming operation, requiring utmost political and administrative skill.

After transmission of the Paris Report, the European contribution to this process could only be a minor one. The Europeans could only watch and hope for the best. Their fate was totally

22.   William Diebold, Jr., *op. cit.*, p. 5.
23.   For the history of the Paris conference see further:
       Beloff, *op. cit.*, pp. 25–26.
       Brown and Opie, *op. cit.*, pp. 135–136.
       John Campbell, *op. cit.*, pp. 430–437.
       Howard S. Ellis, *The Economics of Freedom*, Published for the Council on Foreign Relations, (New York: Harper & Brothers, 1950), p. 369.
       Richard Mayne, *The Community of Europe*, (New York: Norton & Cy, 1962), pp. 76–77.
       Robert Marjolin, *Europe and the U.S. in the World Economy*, (Duke University Press, 1953), pp. 13–14.
       Price, *op. cit.*, pp. 37–39.
       Hans A. Schmitt, *op. cit.*, pp. 23–24.

involved but they could only be spectators at the scene of a major confrontation between the executive and legislative branches of the United States Government.

This period brought to Europe a keen realization of the very special features of the American system in the conduct of foreign affairs, so totally different from their own. During these crucial months, European governments learned more about the American political system than ever before.

In Europe it was and still is customary to deplore the supposedly American lack of knowledge about Europe, but at that time, there was an almost total ignorance in Europe about the political system of our greatest ally.

The speech of Secretary Marshall and the European response in the Paris Report were the indispensable prelude to what could be called 'a Marshall Plan to sell the Marshall Plan to Congress'.

In the relations between governments, the argument of the necessity for parliamentary support and approval is frequently used. In all major negotiations between European governments one should be aware of the parliamentary situation at home and abroad.

The parliamentary situation may even, at times, become a major factor in the relations and negotiations between European governments, as was the case during the negotiations for the Treaty to establish a European Defense Community and in some facets of the negotiations on the Rome Treaties.

In Europe, however, governments deal with each other and leave the care and concern for parliamentary support and eventual approval mainly to the countries in question.

The domestic political situation generally is not a preponderant factor at the negotiation table and certainly is not openly used, presented, and exposed. Agreement between governments in Europe practically always means final agreement.

In the case of required parliamentary ratification, the agreement might in very rare cases be rejected but practically never materially affected.

The very special constitutional relation between the executive and legislative branches of the Government of the United States in the field of foreign policy, for the first time, confronted the European governments with the fact that the role of Congress is, in many ways, as significant as that of the President.

It is the President, as head of the executive branch, who deals with foreign governments. These governments have no access to Congress. This leads to a situation in which foreign governments can only reach the first of the two branches in which the shaping of American foreign policy is vested, while the power of the second branch, especially in those cases where appropriation of funds is involved, is great and decisive. Under the system of the separation of powers the Constitution gives the President and Congress a joint authority in the field of foreign relations.

No one can be entirely certain how this authority is divided between the two branches of government.

Corwin remarks that 'the Constitution is an invitation to struggle for the privilege of directing American foreign policy'.[24]

Constitutionally, the United States Senate is the predominant partner of the executive branch in the conduct of foreign policy.

From the Lend Lease Act of March 1941, however, the major foreign policy decisions have required large appropriations of funds. The United States House of Representatives traditionally is the guardian of the nation's financial expenditure.

A major act of American foreign policy like the European Recovery Program, therefore, not only involves the relationship between the President and the Senate but also between the President and the House and between the Senate and the House. This, however, is not even a complete picture of the complicated process of the shaping of United States foreign policy.

In both the Senate and the House a substantial power rests in the Congressional Committees.

In the field of foreign affairs, the most powerful committee is the

24. E. S. Corwin, *The President: Office and Powers, 1787–1948,* (New York University Press, 1948), p. 208.

Senate Committee on Foreign Relations but the House Committee on Foreign Affairs certainly also is a body of considerable power and influence.

In the case of the European Recovery Program large appropriations were involved.

This implied that the Appropriation Committees of both Senate and House played an active and often decisive role. In the case of appropriations the accent of importance is on the side of the Appropriation Committee of the House.

The Senate Committee on Foreign Relations and the House Committee on Foreign Affairs, apart from their role in policy making, report on the ceiling of the financial expenditure resulting from an act of foreign policy, the so-called authorization.

The Appropriation Committees, however, report on the approval for actual expenditure, the appropriation.

This means that the policies, arising from the Foreign Relations and Foreign Affairs Committees, are filtered again through the two Appropriation Committees and often these committees view these policies from a different perspective than they were viewed when being authorized.

There is no question that this complicated system[25] resulting from

25. The subject of the role of the executive and legislative branches of the United States Government in foreign policy is very well treated in a pamphlet: *Governmental Mechanism for the Conduct of United States Foreign Relations* by the Staff of the International Group of the Brookings Institution, Washington, D.C.: 1949.
See further:
Robert A. Dahl, *Congress and Foreign Policy,* (New York: Harcourt, Brace & Co, 1950).
Daniel S. Cheever and H. Field Haviland, Jr., *American Foreign Policy and the Separation of Powers,* (Harvard University Press, 1952).
Holbert N. Caroll, *The House of Representatives and Foreign Affairs,* (University of Pittsburgh, 1958).
Ernest S. Griffith, 'The Place of Congress in Foreign Relations', in *Annals of the American Academy of Political and Social Science,* Vol. 289 (September, 1953).

the separation of powers and from the different roles of the Senate and the House of Representatives hampers from time to time the efficient handling of foreign policy problems.

The preparation for congressional approval of the Marshall Plan fully exposed this basic problem of the conduct of American foreign relations to its European partners. In this specific case it brought about the rather unique spectacle of a common effort by the executive branch of the United States Government, together with the European governments, from obtaining the cooperation and approval of the powerful third partner, the Congress of the United States.

On September 29, 1947, the British Government sent a note to the governments of the participating countries in which it said: 'Sir Oliver Franks has been asked by the United States Government to take a small group from the Committee of Cooperation to Washington for a short meeting with members of the United States Administration. The purpose of the meeting would only be to provide information on the conference report.'

Not without difficulty it was decided that Sir Oliver Franks would be accompanied by Dr Hirschfeld (Benelux), Mr. Alphand (France), Mr. Verdelis (Greece), Mr. Boland (Ireland) Mr. Campilli (Italy), Mr. Colbjaernsen (Norway), about twelve technical experts who had been instrumental in the drafting of the technical chapters of the Paris report and lastly a small so-called coordinating group consisting of Messrs. Berthoud, van der Beugel, Colonna and Marjolin.

The mission arrived in Washington on October 9, 1947, and its Atlantic crossing was not only used for frequent contact between the members, but also provided an opportunity for unofficial contact with members of the United States Congress, notably with the so-called Herter Committee of the House of Representatives.

The importance of the European mission lies less in what it achieved in practice than in the fact that it was invited to cooperate

in the preparation of the Congressional presentation of the Marshall
Plan. The group acted on behalf of the sixteen countries and was
forced to represent the European point of view and to defend
European interests. Although they had no official status and were
not even appointed mandatories, the force of events led them to
act as a group and to feel themselves responsible for the total European requirements and for the global contents of the Paris Report.
They were not supposed to plead for national interests.

The activities of the European group were only one element in one
of the most thorough and extensive preparations for congressional
action.

On June 22, 1947, that is weeks before the Paris Conference started,
President Truman set up three groups to advise him on different
aspects of the Plan. Two were drawn from official circles, while one
consisted of private persons, chaired by the Secretary of Commerce,
W. Averell Harriman. The first official group under the chairmanship of Secretary of the Interior, J. A. Krug, was charged with the
responsibility of studying the resources of the United States, with
a view to determining the nation's ability to support a program for
European recovery. The second, made up of the members of the
Council of Economic Advisers under the chairmanship of Edwin
G. Nourse, was directed to study the broad impact on the United
States economy of aid to other countries. The third committee consisted of nineteen distinguished citizens, drawn from various walks
of life. Its task was to make recommendations to the President on the
limits within which the United States could wisely and safely plan
to extend economic assistance to foreign countries, and on the relation which should exist between such assistance and the domestic
economy. It also analyzed the principles and policies which should
guide the conduct of an aid program, the needs and capacities of
the European countries, problems of finance and administration,
and last but not least, the principal reasons underlying the American
political, strategic, humanitarian, and economic interest in European
recovery.

At the same time groundwork of great importance was being laid by the Administration in support of the work of the three above-mentioned committees and for the preparation of the Administration's presentation. This work stood under the general direction of Under Secretary of State Lovett, who was assisted by an interdepartmental steering committee, chaired by Charles Bonesteel.

While the three committees and the executive agencies prepared a mass of data and opinions from the executive side, the legislative branch itself developed a great activity in studying the problem of aid to the European countries. More than two hundred members of Congress went abroad between the end of July 1947, and the calling of a Special Session of Congress on November 10, 1947 – most of them to Europe. The Congressional group whose impact on the Congressional attitude toward the Marshall Plan proved to be the most effective and far-reaching, was the Select Committee on Foreign Aid of the House of Representatives, established by the House, shortly after the appointment by the President of the Krug, Nourse, and Harriman Committees and working under the Vice Chairmanship of Representative Christian H. Herter. The Herter Committee sailed for Europe on August 28, 1947, and returned on October 10, 1947, by the same ship on which the members of the Franks mission were crossing the Atlantic. Many contacts on board the Queen Mary led to a fruitful exchange of American and European views.

The Committee published a series of valuable and penetrating reports on different aspects of the European problem and transmitted its final report, consisting mainly of the seriatim preliminary reports on May 1, 1948.

Thus, in the public sector the Congressional discussion was prepared from six mainly interdependent sources: the reports of the Krug, Nourse, and Harriman Committees, the preparatory work by the executive agencies of the Government, the studies of the Congressional committees, among which those of the Herter Committee were of major importance, and the Paris Report with the resulting discussions between government officials and the CEEC mission during its stay in Washington.

Before dealing with the European-American dialogue in Washington, a brief summary of some of the above-mentioned reports should be given.

The Krug Committee issued its report on October 19, 1947, under the title 'National Resources and Foreign Aid'. It undertook an extensive survey of the national resources of the United States and came to the conclusion that the United States economy was physically able to provide the resource requirements of a considerable program of foreign aid; that difficult supply problems existed and would continue to exist in a number of commodities, particularly wheat, steel, coal, nitrogen, fertilizers, and certain items of agricultural and industrial equipment, but that these problems could be minimized by careful screening and allocation; that urgent problems of resource conservation existed in the United States, not because of assistance to foreign countries primarily, but because of high levels of internal consumption.

The Nourse report was published on October 28, 1947.[26]
It focused its attention on the effects of exports, financed in part with government funds, on United States production, consumption and prices. It noted that previously rendered foreign aid had not prevented the American consumer from enjoying a standard of living far above any pre-war level. It regarded the price inflation already in effect as caused primarily by domestic factors, though foreign demands added to the pressures. It did not underestimate the serious effects which a foreign aid program of great magnitude would have in certain commodity fields, but the over-all effect of such a program would be smaller than that already experienced and hence manageable. 'Moreover, the industrial paralysis which could be expected to result in some other countries would have repercussions upon our own economy and upon world stability... In the

26. *The Impact of Foreign Aid upon the Domestic Economy,* A report to the President by the Council of Economic Advisors, (Washington, D.C., 1947).

longer run, the economic restoration of Europe will benefit our own economy by enabling us to obtain more goods by advantageous trade.'

The Harriman Report owes its importance and influence both to the quality of its studies and to the high standing of its members. It dealt comprehensively and specifically with the whole problem of aid to Europe, laid down the main lines of an American policy, and is widely regarded as one of the ablest reports prepared for the Government on a particular issue.

It was published on November 7, 1947.[27] While it dealt with practically all the aspects of the European Recovery Program, only its basic conclusions need to be mentioned here.

'*a*. The hope of Western Europe depends primarily on the industry and straight thinking of its own people;

b. The United States has a vital interest—humanitarian, economic, strategic, and political—in helping the participating countries to achieve economic recovery;

c. The aid which the United States gives will impose definite sacrifices on the United States;

d. The magnitude of Western Europe's deficit with the American continent in 1948 will be in the order of $7 billion, but when all possibilities of financing are taken into consideration, the approximate need for appropriations, past and future, to cover the calendar year of 1948 may be in the order of $5.75 billion;

e. The extension of such aid, now or in the future, calls for anti-inflationary policies on the part of the U.S. and for a new agency to administer the aid extended.'

The report ends with a phrase which in the present discussion of Atlantic Partnership has a strikingly familiar sound.

'Yet it is safe to say that at no time in history has there been more need for Western Europe and the United States to stand firmly together.' Barbara Ward points out that the deliberations of the

27.   *European Recovery and American Aid*, Report by the President's Committee on Foreign Aid, (Washington, D.C., 1947).

Committee were also very revealing in connection with the communist thesis, spreading also to some non-communist circles in Europe, that the Marshall plan was a last effort of American capitalism to prevent overproduction and depression in the United States by seizing markets overseas. While the non-business representatives and the Trade Union delegates on the Committee were the chief supporters of the Plan, the representatives of the business community were inclined to believe that the United States could not afford so big a program of assistance.[28]

The Herter Committee published its final report on May 1, 1948,[29] after having published an important series of studies on specific countries and problems, among which an outstanding study on Western Europe as a whole.[30] It is critical about the weaknesses of the Paris Report, notably in the field of European cooperation, and it goes far beyond the preparatory work of the executive branch in stressing the absolute necessity of greater European cooperation with specific emphasis on the importance of the German problem for European recovery.

'The essential point is not the details of the particular plan eventually adopted, but whether it accomplishes the objective to be achieved – the reintegration of Germany into the European economy. The longer a satisfactory German settlement is delayed, the longer the recovery of Europe is postponed.' In its final report the same thesis is repeated, this time, however, not on the basis of economic considerations but with strong political overtones. 'It is the belief of the Select Committee that the solution to the problem of preventing the resurgence of aggressive German nationalism is to be found within the pattern of European federation, of which a democratic Germany will be an integral but not a dominating part.'

28. Barbara Ward, *op. cit.,* pp. 135–136.
29. U.S. Select Committee on Foreign Aid, *Final Report on Foreign Aid,* House of Representatives 80th Congr. 2nd sess., 1948.
30. *What Western Europe can do for itself,* Preliminary report No. 14 of the House Select Committee on Foreign Aid, February 13, 1948.

The report deals also extensively with the role of the United Kingdom in any form of European integration and concludes that 'there is no real inconsistency between close economic cooperation with other European countries and the continuation of its simultaneous membership in the British Commonwealth of Nations. An excessive timidity toward this problem on the part of the British Government might well dampen the enthusiasm of the other nations for European economic cooperation and create an unfavorable reaction not only in the United States but in the Dominions as well. Britain alone of the sixteen nations possesses the past experience and the present economic resources and political stability necessary for bold and imaginative leadership. The success of the European effort for recovery depends in part upon the United Kingdom actively assuming the responsibility of her position.'

The report nevertheless recognizes the limitations of American possibilities to impose measures of cooperation which do not emerge from Europe itself. The preliminary report concludes with a paragraph which should be quoted as proof of the element of generosity and restraint, so symptomatic for the whole concept of the European Recovery Program.

'If we undertake the proposed European recovery program, we are in effect assuming the responsibility for the economic revival of Western Europe. Responsibility without power is a situation generally avoided by cautious people. But the alternative in terms of human lives, human misery and human slavery is perhaps too frightful to permit us the luxury of being cautious. We can only hope that the nations of Western Europe, who have the power over their own economic destinies, will themselves realize the responsibilities of their predicament and, by actively cooperating with each other, help themselves.'

The contacts and discussions of the European group were mainly with the interdepartmental Bonesteel Committee. There were conversations with Under Secretary Lovett and Clayton, many informal and formal contacts with the Harriman Committee and its individual members, but its work was mainly concentrated on further explanations of the Paris Report and on providing additional data for the benefit of the executive agencies of the Administration.

It was not a real negotiation, and the contacts with the highest level of the Administration were few. The group was, during those weeks in Washington, essentially a part of the team charged with the difficult task of making the Paris Report as attractive as possible for the presentation to Congress.

There was an inclination on the part of the Administration to change accents, to color presentations, to minimize some problems and overemphasize others, to hide existing shortcomings and to applaud practically non-existing achievements, in its efforts to win Congressional approval. All this does not imply any negative judgment on the necessity of such actions. The aim was Congressional approval for a program created solely for the benefit of the Europeans. It was no wonder, however, that the group had some difficulty, not only in adjusting itself to this situation, but suddenly becoming part of this process.

As was the case during the Paris Conference, the work of the group could be broadly divided into two major activities. The main part consisted in providing a mass of additional data and was handled by the technical experts in discussions with the competent branches of the United States Administration. Additional questionnaires were sent to the sixteen participating countries. The replies were assembled by the Washington group and transmitted to the Administration.

The other part of the work consisted of matters of policy and was discussed between the European delegates and the interdepartmental Steering Committee.

The main problems on which these discussions were concentrated were: the production program, financial policy, trade policy, the organization of the European cooperation and finally, policy questions resulting from the technical discussions.

The Americans mostly asked their questions in writing, whereupon the European delegates would draft the reply among themselves. This implied a very strict and close coordination within the European group and from time to time a real negotiation between themselves, comparable to the Paris Conference, but under greater pressure and in a more restricted circle.

In this context, it is not possible to give a detailed narrative of events. It may, however, be useful to give an example of the type of questions asked in this phase of the process.

In the field of commercial policy one of the questions was:

'Was a relaxation of barriers to intra-European trade assumed by CEEC in estimating the volume of trade between the participating countries and thus in the balance of payments position of the participating countries? If so, what was the general character of the assumption?'

On the question of the European organization, the main question was formulated by the American Administration as follows:

'Paragraph 113 of the CEEC report refers to the desirability of creating for the life of the program a continuing joint organization of the participating countries to review progress, and to ensure to the full extent possible, by joint action the realization of the economic conditions necessary to enable the general objectives to which each country has pledged itself to be effectively achieved. To what extent and through what specific types of action was it contemplated what such an organization would contribute to the success of the program?'

It will be clear that the reply to this type of questions could not go far beyond the contents of the Paris Report, first, because major changes in the Paris Report would have required major negotiations between all the participating countries and could not be left to the group in Washington, and second, because the American Administration was not in a position to commit itself to much more than the general ideas of the Marshall Plan known during the Paris Conference. A major change in European commitments and attitudes could only be possible after a further clarification of American ideas. This was not feasible before the preparatory work for Congressional action was completed and Congress had acted. There was the vicious circle of the Administration's desire to get more out of their European partners in order to convince Congress, while Europe, without more certainty about the contents of the American legislation, had already gone to its limits in drafting the Paris Report.

During these Washington discussions the emphasis, therefore, was, by necessity, more on technical clarification than on policy decisions.

An impression of the character of the group's activities can best be obtained by quoting parts of the last communication which the group sent out to the participating countries on November 7, 1947.

'As foreshadowed in earlier telegrams Committee for European Economic Cooperation group in Washington is now dispersing. The purpose of this communication is to advise you of developments and to tell you how matters stand at the end of this second phase of our work and of such arrangements as it has seemed desirable to make in Washington...

The final meeting with Mr. Lovett and his cabinet colleagues (including Mr. Harriman) took place on November 4, and was attended by all delegates. An informal aide mémoire was circulated by Mr. Lovett at the meeting and is being sent to all countries. Sir Oliver Franks expressed the hope that as this was the last meeting of its kind Mr. Lovett would be able to clarify the views of the Administration on major outstanding points of policy as far as this might be possible.

The main points made by Mr. Lovett (who emphasised that he was talking informally) were as follows.

a. The United States Administration accepted the Paris Report as a well-considered and balanced document and were broadly prepared to support it.

b. It was recognised that the European problems had a commodity and a financial aspect. Some of the supplies required from the United States should be provided without payment in dollars but even in such cases he hoped that procurement would as far as possible be kept within private trade channels. It was hoped that a large part of the aid would be in the form of grants and a smaller part by way of loans, particularly as the latter would rank ahead of loans from the International Bank. It was recognised that no transfer problem should be allowed to arise on local currency counterpart grants in the aid and that European recovery was only possible by an increase in its exports. He could not yet express any views in regard to the use of local currency but recognised that any restrictions must not interfere with financial and economic controls that must be exercised by the Government concerned.

c. The form of the United States agency to administer the proposed aid had not yet been decided but it was hoped to secure for it flexibility to allocate aid within the limits fixed by Congress and to discuss the program with individual countries; implementation would than take place through normal channels.

d. It was impossible for the United States Government to provide all the aid required to purchase the full amount of supplies from Canada and Latin America compatible with the Paris report. Some assistance must be given by these countries themselves. The question was how best to take the initiative with these countries. He thought than an initiative by the sixteen participating countries to the Pan-American Union on the one hand, and to Canada on the other, might be desirable. The United States would be prepared to play an important part in triangular discussion at a later stage but he felt that a first approach by European countries would offer the best prospects of success. Sir Oliver Franks reserved the group's position on this matter. In the discussion Mr. Lovett said that he hoped to secure the "consent" from Congress to a general formula for dealing with local currency proceeds of grants in aid within which subsequent bilateral negotiations would take place. When asked whether any conclusions had been reached as to a dollar loan for currency stabilisation, he replied that such a loan was included in their proposals but decisions had not been reached as to its size nor the time when it should be granted...

At the close of the meeting Mr. Lovett expressed his appreciation of the help afforded to the administration during the course of our visit...

Sir Oliver Franks at the last meeting of the delegates and technical Committee representatives paid tribute to the fact that the work of the CEEC group in Washington had been characterized by the same harmony and cooperation as prevailed in Paris. It had been a fruitful and indeed enjoyable period.'

The work of the European group was considered of great importance by the American officials. For the group itself – in spite of the fact that no major policy decisions were taken – the experience was most fruitful and constructive. It brought a group of Europeans, who were going to play a major role in further European developments, into the closest contact with their American opposite numbers and with the huge problems facing the American Administration in its relations with Congress. It impressed upon them the total involvement of their American colleagues in the recovery program and the necessity for enlarging the European contribution for its success.

They left Washington with many open questions as to how the Administration's program would be presented to Congress, what the amount to be requested would be, which conditions were to be attached, and how Congress would react. They went back, however, firmly convinced of the reality of the words of Under Secretary Lovett, in their last meeting with him, where he said that the real contribution of Europe could only be to abandon national beliefs and traditions in a joint approach to the recovery program.

The events in Europe, however, did not wait upon the process of planning and legislative action in Washington. The situation in France, Italy and Austria demanded relief measures before there could be a question of recovery. On October 23, 1947, President Truman issued a call for a special session of Congress for two compelling reasons, first, the continued rise in prices in the United States and second, the crisis in Western Europe. On November 10,

1947, Secretary Marshall appeared before the joint session of the Senate Committee on Foreign Relations and the House Committee on Foreign Affairs.

He announced that the President would lay before Congress the program of his Administration for aid to Europe, and he dwelt upon the basic reasons for this program. He asked for a speedy decision with regard to the interim aid program.

'I have gone at some length into the major features of the long-range program for European reconstruction and the part that the United States can prudently and wisely contribute because I fully realize that the speedy and adequate consideration of the interim aid program, which will be the first item of business presented to you, cannot be dealt with by the Congress without understanding its relationship to the program of long range reconstruction of Europe.'[31]

On November 17, 1947, the President addressed both Houses of Congress and asked them to provide emergency short-term aid of $597 million to cover urgent European needs to March 31, 1948. The emergency nature of the request was underscored by stating that the funds were not to be spent for the purposes of reconstruction and in fact, the enabling legislation was very much on the lines of the earlier UNRRA relief programs. The Authorization Act for Interim Aid was signed by the President on December 17, 1947, and soon followed by the appropriation measures. Emergency aid of $522 million was provided for France, Italy, and Austria. $18 Million was provided for China but taken from unexpended post-UNRRA sources. An additional $155 million was appropriated in March 1948.[32]

The Congressional debate on the interim aid measures forms so much an integral part with the great debate on the Marshall Plan

31.   Department of State, *Press Release,* November 10, 1947, No. 891.
32.   *Foreign Aid Act of 1947* (Public Law 389) and *Appropriations Act* (Public Law 393), 80th Congr., 1st sess. The $55 million was appropriated under Public Law 470, 80th Congr., 2nd sess.

that both debates will be treated as a whole in a further section of this chapter.

The interim aid was the final transitional step between an unplanned relief program and a planned reconstruction program.

When President Truman signed the 'Foreign Assistance Act of 1948' on April 3, 1948, one of the great debates in American history and an exhaustive three-months consideration by Congress of the European Recovery Program came to its close. Press and public opinion were deeply involved.

Many members of Congress gave expression to their awareness of its historic importance. Congressman Eaton, Chairman of the House Committee on Foreign Affairs, described it as 'the most important legislation that has come before the House in my time'.[33] It was a nation-wide debate, not merely confined to Congressional deliberations.

The debate in the nation can be followed by a study of the Committee hearings, the debate on the floor of the Senate and the House and the contents of the appendixes to the Congressional Record.[34]

In this study attention should primarily be given to that part of the debate concerning European cooperation and integration as an objective of American foreign policy in general and the European Recovery Program in particular.

The preoccupation of some members of Congress with the necessity for European unification started earlier than the debate on the European Recovery Program. It was clearly expressed during the

33. *New York Times*, Dec. 28, 1947.
34. The public hearings before the Senate Committee on Foreign Relations fill three volumes totaling 1466 pages; those before the House Committee two tomes of 2269 pages. The Senate Committee heard 9 governmental and 86 other witnesses and recorded 76 additional written statements. The House Foreign Affairs Committee heard 25 spokesmen for the Administration and received testimony from about 150 non-governmental witnesses.

debate on the aid measures for Greece and Turkey in March 1947.

On March 21, 1947, Senators William Fulbright and Elbert D. Thomas submitted the following concurrent resolution which was referred to the Committee on Foreign Relations of the Senate and accompanied by similar action in the House, where Representative Boggs was the sponsor.[35] 'Resolved by the Senate (the House of Representatives concurring) that the Congress favors the creation of a United States of Europe.'

These actions did not spring from any concrete idea as to how this objective could be achieved. Concepts like unification, unity, federalization, federation, cooperation, integration, mutual aid and self-help were used in the same speeches and articles. But in all these actions and expressions there was a still vague but deep missionary belief that, somehow, the then prevailing political and economic situation should be used to bring about something more than the restoration of a pre-war pattern.

The desire to endorse the idea of European unity was based on a great variety of motives and opinions.

There was a strong current of thought that America's power should be used to transplant to the old shattered world the ideals of federation which had brought to the United States its unique position. For many, the idea of unity was the only possibility for Europe to resist Soviet aggression. For others, it was the only way for Europe to terminate internal strife which had led the United States twice to intervene on the European scene. For others again, it was the hope of establishing in Europe the 'single market' which had been so instrumental in the development of the United States. Many felt that European unity formed the only possible solution for making Germany healthy again while avoiding the resurgence of German nationalism.

These convictions were also inspired by the disillusion with the results of the piece-meal post-war relief. In introducing his resolution in the House, Representative Boggs said: 'Already this nation

---

35. *Congressional Record*, 80th Congr., 1st sess. pp. 2418 and 2425.

has appropriated $31 billion in American money for the rehabilita-
tion of Europe and despite this fabulous sum of money the problem of Europe becomes more acute and more pressing as each day
passes.'[36]

There was a general feeling that unity in Europe was the only way
to put an end to what was feared to be a permanent American military and economic commitment.

However different the motives, however vague the constructions
and concepts were, there is no question that this urge for something new and imaginative to happen in Europe had very deep roots
in the American mind.[37]

The Congressional action in March 1948 was preceded and accompanied by a flood of editorial comments from very different sources
and milieus. A few examples might illustrate the spread of this
opinion.

The *St. Louis Post-Dispatch* of March 16, 1947, wrote:

'Like the famous advice Benjamin Franklin gave to the American
colonies for Europe it is a case of join – or die.'

Life Magazine of March 17, 1947, stated:

'To Dulles, as to more and more thinking people, our policy
should be to help the nations of Europe federate as our states
federated in 1787...Peace lies not in compromising but in invig-
orating our historic policies. The time to invigorate them is now.'

William Henry Chamberlin said in an article in the *Wallstreet
Journal* of February 3, 1947, entitled 'Europe's last chance':

'The European problem in general and the German problem in
particular may remain insoluble if they are approached on the
assumption that the continent must remain divided into completely

36. *Congressional Record,* 80th Congr., 1st sess., p. 2418.
37. George Washington wrote to General Lafayette: 'We have sowed seeds
    of liberty and union that will spring up everywhere on earth, and one
    day, taking its pattern from the United States of America, there will
    be founded the United States of Europe' (*The Writings of George
    Washington,* ed. by W. C. Ford, New York, 1889–1893, Vol. IX, p. 2847).

independent sovereign states, each with its economy in a water tight compartment.'

Sumner Welles wrote in the *Washington Post* of February 5, 1947:

'One of the most heartening developments in Europe in recent months has been the rapid increase in the popular demand of a European federation...Europe desperately needs some effective form of political and economic federation.'

Dorothy Thompson said in the *Washington Star* of February 11, 1947:

'Above all the U.S., out of her own wonderful experience of the Union of the States should support a European confederation plan. Victory must be translated into new life and that means a modern political, social and economic system.'

An editorial in the *New York Times* of April 18, 1947, stated:

'At best the federation of Europe would be a long and laborious process...But it is only too true as statesmen have said so often in one way or another that Europe must federate or perish.'

The Miami Herald of March 27, 1947, wrote:

'A United States of Europe could be the means of restoring a decent living economy to the part of Europe which represents the civilization of which we are a part. It may prove to be the only means.'

The Christian Science Monitor of April 28, 1947, concluded:

'For its part, the U.S. could hardly impose federation on Europe but it could counsel. It could call attention to its own federation. It could mold its leading and occupation policies toward upbuilding a single continental economy.'

The Memphis *Commercial Appeal* of March 23, 1947, said:

'There is no single nation in Europe that can come anywhere near sustaining itself but operating as a whole the area could do well.'

In response to Churchill's speech of May 14, 1947, in the Royal Albert Hall in London, the *Evansville (Ind) Courier and Press* of May 18, 1947, wrote:

'Only a federation holds forth hope of permanent peace and economic wellbeing for Europe.'

The *Buffalo News* of May 22, 1947, stated:
'The peoples in the ruins of Europe can take heart from the perils that beset Americans in 1787.'

On June 4, 1947, one day before his speech at Harvard, Secretary Marshall gave his reaction to the Fulbright resolution, mentioned above, in a letter to the Chairman of the Senate Committee on Foreign Relations, Arthur H. Vandenberg. The contents of this letter are of great importance because it shows the difference of approach between the Administration and the supporters of the Fulbright resolution, a difference which runs, like a continuous thread, through their dialogue about the role of the European Recovery-Program as an instrument of United States foreign policy to bring about European unity.

That difference essentially sprang from the great hesitancy on the part of the Administration to impose a certain policy on the European nations, and from its desire to leave the initiative to the Europeans. Many members of Congress, on the contrary, preferred a more active pressure from the United States. There was no difference between them as to the desirability of the ultimate objective. There was, however, a great difference in the choice of methods to be used. If Congress would have had its way, the conditions attached to the European Recovery Program, as to the pledges of cooperation between the recepients of aid, would have been very much stronger than was actually laid down in the legislation.[38]

This issue was not closed after the passing of the legislation in 1948. Every year thereafter, Congress, with increasing succes, tried to adapt the legislation to its concept.

Secretary Marshall wrote:
'I assume that the resolution has been deliberately phrased in

38. See also William Diebold, Jr., *The Schuman Plan,* Published for the Council on Foreign Relations, (New York: Praeger, 1959), pp. 551–552. Theodore Geiger and H. van B. Cleveland, *Making Western Europe Defensible,* (National Planning Association, Pamphlet No. 74, August 1951), p. 71.

general terms for the purpose of endorsing a principle without raising numerous important questions of detail.

I am deeply sympathetic toward the general objective of the resolution which is, as I understand it, to encourage the peoples of Europe to cooperate together more closely for their common good and in particular, to encourage them to cooperate together to promote the economic recovery of Europe as a whole.

Of course the United States wants a Europe which is better than that it replaces. Only as we can inspire hope of that, we expect men to endure what must be endured and make the great efforts which must be made if wars are to be avoided and civilization is to survive in Europe. But we should make clear that it is not our purpose to impose upon the peoples of Europe any particular form of political or economic association. The future organization of Europe must be determined by the peoples of Europe.

While recognizing that it is for the people of Europe to determine the kind of organized effort which may be appropriate to facilitate the peaceful development of a free Europe, the United States welcomes any initiative which may be taken by the peoples of Europe within the framework of the United Nations to insure greater cooperation among themselves, to expedite the reconstruction and restoration of the economy of Europe as a whole, to improve living standards, to strengthen the general security and to promote the general welfare.

To avoid any misunderstanding as to our purposes, I believe it desirable that some of the ideas I have expressed here to be embodied in the resolution. Perhaps the authors of the resolution might consider adding a preamble along these lines.'[39]

Senator Fulbright replied on June 13, 1947, on the floor of the Senate.

'I wish to state that I am greatly encouraged by the letter, although I think that under the circumstances as they now appear in Europe, it is unduly timid and cautious. It seems to me that some initiative

39. *Documents on American Foreign Relations,* (Princeton University Press, 1949), Vol. IX, pp. 604–605.

on the part of the United States would not be inappropriate at this juncture in our affairs. I do not agree that we should as a matter of policy always leave the initiative to other nations. Furthermore, in requesting assistance from us, as virtually every country in Western Europe has done, I think they have taken the initiative. According-ly it does not seem to me that we shall be dictating to those coun-tries or to any other country in any offensive sense if we suggest that under their present chaotic political and economic order they are no good risks either to repay loans or even to survive as demo-cratic states. I am unable to see why the suggestion that they get together and form some kind of political and economic unity as part of the bargain is dictation or undue influence.'[40]

On December 19, 1947, President Truman transmitted his Message on the European Recovery Program to Congress.[41] At the same time, the Secretary of State submitted to Congress the text of the draft bill proposed by the Department of State, together with detailed background information on the European Recovery Program.[42]

The future of Europe was now in the hands of Congress.

It became clear from the two documents that the Administration, in stressing the need for European cooperation, based itself com-pletely on the Paris Report and maintained the line that on this point the initiative should come from Europe.

The Message referred to the program of the Paris Report and stated that it rested on four basic points:

1. A strong production effort by each of the participating countries;
2. Creation of internal financial stability;
3. Maximum and continuing cooperation among the participat-ing countries;
4. An effort to increase European exports to the American continent.

40. *Congressional Record,* 80th Congr., 1st sess., pp. 6957–6958.
41. *Documents on American Foreign Relations,* Vol. IX, *op. cit.,* pp. 233–250.
42. *Outline of European Recovery Program,* 80th Congr., 1st sess., Dec. 19, 1947.

'These agreements are a source of great encouragement. When the representatives of sixteen sovereign nations, with diverse peoples, histories and institutions, jointly determine to achieve closer economic ties among themselves and to break away from the self-defeating actions of narrow nationalism, the obstacles in the way of recovery appear less formidable.'

The Administration wrote that it intended to enter into bilateral agreements with the sixteen countries in which the pledges of cooperative action among them would be included and, if possible, strengthened. 'In addition each of the countries receiving aid will be expected to enter into an agreement with the United States affirming the pledges which it has given to the other participating countries and making additional commitments.'

Notwithstanding the great importance attached by the Administration to the inclusion of Germany in the program, the Message was very cautious in its language as to the German problem.

'Every precaution must of course be taken against a resurgence of military power in Germany. The United States has made clear on many occasions its determination that Germany shall never again threaten to dominate Europe or endanger the peace of the world. The inclusion of Western Germany in the European Recovery Program will not weaken this determination.'

This was one of the few paragraphs of the Message which focused more on public opinion abroad than on congressional opinion at home.

Reference was often made to the organization of the participating countries. 'The needs of the participating countries must be reviewed in close cooperation with them and with an organization of the participating countries. In addition, I recommend that provision be made for a special United States Representative for the European Recovery Program. He would represent the United States at any continuing organization of the participating countries...'

The contents of the Message and the Outline prove that Under Secretary Clayton, in his efforts to change certain shortcomings during the original phase of the work on the Paris Report, had specifically in mind the presentation to Congress.

The debate in Congress showed that, without the changes he proposed, the legislation would hardly have passed the Congressional hurdle.

The Outline was very generous in its praise of the part of the Paris Report dealing with cooperation. 'The programs of self-help which the participating countries propose are generally sound and progressive.

The undertakings of the participating countries with respect to mutual aid and the increase of trade among themselves, as well as the generally cooperative approach to European economic problems, constitute a forward step away from the economic nationalism which had grown up in the period between the two world wars to impede economic development.' But it added that 'there are certain aspects of the program, however, with respect to which the executive branch would suggest either greater emphasis or a shift in emphasis.'

One controversial issue was disposed of even before the hearings of the Senate Committee on Foreign Relations started.

In the draft bill submitted by the Administration, there was a specific request for a $17 billion authorization, the total amount of funds estimated for the program over its entire four and a quarter year span.

On December 31, 1947, Senator Vandenberg wrote to Secretary Marshall that this should be changed into a generalized authorization for appropriations in amounts deemed necessary by the Administration and Congress until June 1952.

A Congressional authorization is a statement of the general intent of Congress with regard to spending. The specific amounts are not finally determined, and the actual money is not provided, until later appropriations are approved. Many times, the amounts actually appropriated are well below the authorized amounts.

Vandenberg realized that the huge $17 billion figure would provide a major bone of contention and an unnecessary one. It would be a point around which opposition could crystallize.

Since one Congress could not bind another on spending, it actually was the yearly cash appropriations which would provide the test. A general continuing authorization would signify Congress' intention to continue the program beyond a year.

'But to express this principle in figures, namely $17 billion, in the legislation itself may invoke a specific reliance abroad which is impossible under our constitutional procedure. Furthermore it can only be a guess of highly doubtful validity when we thus attempt to assess events for the next four years at home or abroad, and when the entire ERP enterprise is at the mercy of good or bad contingencies.'

Three days later, on January 2, 1948, Under Secretary Lovett wrote that after consultation with the President, the State Department was ready to accept Vandenberg's language. A potential stumbling block of considerable magnitude had been removed, while the principle of the four-year program was preserved.

As finally drafted, the bill referred only to 'such funds as are hereafter authorized and appropriated to carry out the provisions and accomplish the purpose of this act'.[43]

This change had a profound effect on the Congressional influence on the European Recovery Program.

Now every year a new authorization and appropriation was required. Every year hearings and debates provided the opportunity for Congress to amend the legislation and to press for certain of its points. The Congressional attitude towards the problem of European cooperation was going to be one of the main topics. 'If responsibility for the voting of the first ERP funds is on the people of the U.S. influencing Congress, responsibility for the voting of the second lot is on the people of Europe, influencing the people of the U.S.... If the ERP does not make possible a continental cooperation

43.   For this episode and the text of the exchange of letters between Vandenberg and Lovett see *The private Papers of Senator Vandenberg, op. cit.,* pp. 385–386.

which has in view this broader yield, if no larger framework becomes visible, the second appropriation for ERP is going to come hard.'[44]

On January 8, 1948, the Senate Committee on Foreign Relations opened its hearings and Secretary Marshall was the first in the parade of witnesses. In his prepared statement Marshall said:

'The initial suggestion of June 5 last, the concept of American assistance to Europe has been based on the premise that European initiative and cooperation are prerequisite to European recovery. Only the Europeans themselves can finally solve their problem.'[45]

During the lengthy dialogue between Marshall and the members of the Committee, there was an exchange of views between Senator Lodge and Secretary Marshall in which Marshall, in a very spontaneous way, gave his views on the role he saw for American foreign policy in relation to European cooperation and integration. It is a striking statement because it was unprepared, not polished by the many levels of the Department of State and impressive in its realistic recognition of the complexity of the problem.

Senator Lodge asked: 'If only we will use our good offices and promote this integration of Europe, it will be a boon to the average citizen, and a great step toward peace. Does that strike a responsive chord?'

Secretary Marshall replied: 'I like the words you used, "good offices", because that is one of the delicate phases of the problem, that we do not move in such a way as to awaken hostilities because of national pride, or that we do not offer something in a measure or form suitable for propaganda distortion by those who are trying to sabotage the program... My concern in the matter, to state it very frankly, is to get this affair going in such a way that the cooperation, the commitments which bring those countries together will in-

44. *The Economist,* Jan. 3, 1948.
45. *European Recovery Program,* Hearings before the Committee on Foreign Relations U.S. Senate, 80th Congr., 2nd sess., part I, p. 7.

crease rather than remain as they are at the time they begin to get more or less on their feet... Just how we can manage to keep the progress going toward further cooperation, toward a further consolidation of European states and a general integration, a mutual integration in relation to the economic work is a matter of great importance. I do not know just how that can be managed. I feel certain that if we had not had a tragic dilemma of vast importance we never could have gotten these agreements out of the Western nations at all. It could have been talked about and would for many, many years but like unity of command, all will agree with you in principle but they won't agree with you when you get down to business, unless it is their man that is to command, unless it is their business that is to be protected. I do not know how long the development of integration will continue. I think it will continue, if we carry out this program roughly as proposed for a period of at least four years, and would assume that a very material gain would be made during that period. And I would also assume that as a result of that gain its advantages will become so evident and we would have broken down so many of the minor oppositions which have a major effect that from there on the cause would not be quite so difficult.'[46]

As major witnesses of the Government followed Ambassador Douglas, Secretaries Harriman, Anderson, Krug, Snyder, Royall, Forrestal and the Chairman of the Board of Directors of the Export Import Bank. The importance many members attached to the idea of a customs union became apparent when Senator Lodge said while questioning Ambassador Douglas:

'Certainly you could not have a United States of Europe without having a customs union. That is the essence of the United States, isn't it?'[47]

In a very diplomatic understatement, Douglas replied that it was not the only one, though very important.

Several members found themselves more in agreement with the

46.   E. R. P. Hearings, *op. cit.*, pp. 69–70.
47.   E. R. P. Hearings, *op. cit.*, p. 89.

cautious attitude of the Administration than with their more impatient colleagues.

Senator Smith said: 'Then it is a fair statement that the act of Paris, which I look upon as a really extraordinary event, the 10 week's conference in Paris and the movement into this kind of cooperation, may well be looking toward a stronger economic federation of the countries of Europe than anything we have seen heretofore.

I think it is important for us to have that in mind, because too many people are saying: Why don't you demand the immediate setting-up of a U.S. of Europe before you do anything for them? My reply has been, that will be what we hope to see ultimately, but we are moving by this process more effectively toward that than if we demand something that cannot be accomplished overnight.'[48]

The testimony of Secretary Forrestal was highly effective. His theme was that the cost of the European Recovery Program was high but much lower than what the United States would have to spend for armaments, if it did not undertake it. Preparation to defend the United States against what might be a totalitarian world would immediately require the steep increase of military appropriations. The Marshall Plan on the other hand held out a promise of world stability that would enable the United States later to reduce its present outlay for national defense.[49]

The contributions of John J. McCloy, Bernard M. Baruch and John Foster Dulles were highly valuable.

McCloy said: 'But I do think I can say something about how the Europeans should organize. My feeling is that the more responsibility you throw on them, the better. They have a very difficult problem to achieve. It is much more difficult for an outsider nation to try to achieve it for them. You cannot devalue their currencies; you cannot balance their budgets; you cannot adjust their price systems. They have got to do it, and they have to do it themselves, and

48.   E. R. P. Hearings, *op. cit.*, p. 187.
49.   *The U.S. in World Affairs 1947–1948*, *op. cit.*, p. 503.

they have to do it with some collective consideration of the whole European problem. So I would urge strongly that they be given heavy responsibility through a European agency or group to bring about these developments, stabilization if you want to call it that; and the progress which they make toward that should be a measure of the amount of aid that is eventually given.'[50]

With great vigor, Bernard M. Baruch pleaded in point three, four and five of his eleven point program that the countries of Europe, as many as are willing, would band themselves together into a political, economic, and defense union under the United Nations. This would include the lowering of trade barriers among them. The United States and such others as would join it should mutually guarantee against aggression the nations entering into this union. 'By guarantee I mean a firm promise to go to war in joint defense if any of them are attacked; that the European nations organize to liberate and use every productive resource of the continent with those of the Ruhr regulated under priorities and international control, so as to protect the peaceful interests of Germany's neighbours.'[51]

John Foster Dulles made a very strong plea for European integration and for stronger wording of the legislation to that effect.

'It is a matter of great delicacy but the situation is ripe for a great creative act. If we do nothing and merely subsidize the continuance of the present disunity, and as you say, indicate to say to them in effect, well if you stay disunited, if you take all the perils and economic weaknesses that go with that, nevertheless we will stand behind each of you – if we say that, then the easy thing to do is to let the present situation continue.'[52]

Dulles was very outspoken in his opinion about the German problem, and the thesis he developed would form the nucleus of American foreign policy towards Europe during his tenure of office as Secretary of State.

50.   E. R. P. Hearings, *op. cit.,* part II, p. 543.
51.   E. R. P. Hearings, *op. cit.,* part II, p. 556.
52.   E. R. P. Hearings, *op. cit.,* part II, p. 605.

'Western Germany ought to be integrated into the Western economy of Europe as rapidly as possible. When I say that I do not envisage a permanent division of Germany, the only way in the world you are going to unite Germany is to create a condition in the West of Europe, which is so attractive, which sets up such an attraction on the East that the Soviet will not be able to hold out the east of Germany, then you may get Germany together again. In other words I do not reconcile myself, necessarily, to a permanent division of Germany, but I say the only way to get Germany united under conditions that will be tolerable to us and to the Western countries is to begin to integrate Western Germany into such a healthy vigorous economy of Western Europe that the people in the east of Germany will just say well, we won't go on this way any more. We are going to be part and parcel of it.'[53]

Finally, attention should be drawn to the essence of the testimony of Paul G. Hoffman, because many things he said were to become part of his policy, when he was appointed Administrator for the Economic Cooperation Administration. 'Every effort should be made to encourage the setting up and effective operation of the joint organization to review the progress achieved in the execution of the program which the governments of the sixteen participating countries have declared themselves ready to establish. Vigorous efforts should be made in the administration of the program to encourage the participating countries further to reduce trade barriers; facilitate transport between countries, increase the freedom of movement of people; develop jointly controlled resources; act as a group in determining the location and character of new basic industrial facilities; and in other ways toward a greater unity in the European economy.'[54]

He further supported Dulles' views on the necessity of making Western Germany an integral part of Western Europe.

53.   E. R. P. Hearings, *op. cit.,* part II, pp. 610–611.
54.   E. R. P. Hearings, *op. cit.,* part II, p. 848.

On February 26, 1948, the Senate Committee on Foreign Relations reported its findings and its draft bill to the Senate.[55]

'Accordingly the Committee looked with considerable satisfaction upon the far-reaching pledges, including the creation of a joint organization, which the CEEC countries voluntarily assumed at their Paris meeting. It is expected that these and other undertakings will be incorporated in multilateral pledges exchanged among the participating countries...

The present bill makes clear that the extension of aid by the U.S. results from the pledges accepted at Paris and is contingent upon the continued effort of the participating countries to accomplish a joint recovery program through multilateral undertakings and the establishment of a continuing organization...'

In stressing the importance of these obligations the Committee was sensitive to the fact that the countries of Western Europe were highly developed sovereign nations and would be properly resentful of any interference from the outside in their internal affairs. There could be no possible criticism on this score in as much as the undertakings were voluntarily assumed by the CEEC countries upon their own initiative and in no sense represented an attempt on the part of the United States to impose restrictions on the sovereign rights of the participating countries.

'While the bill provided for the economic rehabilitation of Europe, it has broader implications. Revival of the economic health of Europe combined with a development of ever closer political and economic ties among the participating countries are the main elements of peace and prosperity. It is therefore implicit in the program that at its end lies, not only in economic cooperation in the form of customs-unions and the elimination of trade and economic barriers set forth in the CEEC Report, but also in closer political and cultural bonds...Divided and engaged in nationalistic rivalries the participating countries will find it difficult to sustain their free institutions and independence and to increase their stan-

55. *Report of the Committee on Foreign Relations,* Senate 80th Congr., 2nd sess., Report no. 935, Febr. 26, 1948.

dard of living. The maintenance of their peace and genuine independence rest largely upon their mutual cooperation and sustained common effort.'

Senator Vandenberg, in a momentous speech, launched the debate on the floor of the Senate on March 1, 1948. For this speech and for his work in the Committee and on the floor, he so fully deserved the praise of the President[56] and of Paul Hoffman who said four years later, that Vandenberg had been the giant on the Congressional side. It was his leadership, both intellectually and legislatively, that led to the almost unanimous agreement given to the European Recovery Program.

On March 3, 1948, Senator Fulbright made a last effort to get the text of his resolution inserted into the bill but, after an intervention of Senator Vandenberg, he withdrew his amendment. He reached an understanding with Vandenberg that, within the near future and before the adjournment of this Congress, the Committee on Foreign Relations would hold hearings and consider Fulbright's resolution. Vandenberg said:

'I am confident that if the Committee on Foreign Relations considers the matter it will act favorably upon the expression of our approval of European Union.'[57]

On March 17, the Bill was adopted in the Senate by 69 to 17 votes.

The hearings before the Committee on Foreign Affairs of the House of Representatives[58] and the debate on the floor of the House were largely a repetition of what happened in the Senate. The emphasis on European unity was, however, greater and more outspoken.

The House passed the Bill by 329 to 74 votes on March 31, 1948. Rapidly, Senate and House conferencees agreed on a compromise text.

56. Truman, *op. cit.,* p. 125.
57. *Congressional Record,* 80th Congr., 2nd sess., p. 2286.
58. *European Recovery Program,* Hearings before the Committee on Foreign Affairs, House of Representatives 80th Congr., 1st and 2nd sess., Part 1 and Part 2.

Politically, the debate on the floor of the Senate and the House was largely a debate within the Republican Party, although the strongest attacks in the Senate came from two Democrats, O'Daniel of Texas and Taylor of Idaho.

The first was a typical representative of orthodox isolationism, the second a lonely supporter of the opposition on the left.

The debate showed a real rift between the internationalist wing and the nationalist wing of the Republican Party. The latter was basically out of sympathy with the Marshall Plan and opposed to spending such vast sums of public money for the reconstruction of foreign countries.

Max Beloff thinks that little of the debate in Congress directly concerned the possibilities that the Act would serve as an instrument for integrating Europe.[59] From the record of the discussions it becomes, however, clear that Congress definitely strengthened the hand of the Administration in its pressure for more creative acts in Europe. The debate, not only in 1948 but also in subsequent years, constituted a constant reminder for the European countries that large sums of aid required positive cooperative action on their part. The conclusion may be drawn that what has been achieved in the first four years of OEEC has been greatly influenced by the opinion of the Congress of the United States that cooperation and integration in Europe was a condition for their willingness to continue support for the European Recovery Program. In the legislation of 1948, the influence of Congress on the subject of European cooperation can best be measured by comparing the 'Findings and Declaration' in the draft legislation submitted by the Department of State with the same section in the Foreign Assistance Act of 1948.

ADMINISTRATION DRAFT DECEMBER 1947:	FOREIGN ASSISTANCE ACT 1948:
Recognizing the interdependence of the U.S. and of	Recognizing the intimate economic and other relationships

59.   Max Beloff, *op. cit.*, p. 26.

Europe, and recognizing that economic disruption remaining in the wake of war is not contained by national frontiers, the Congress finds that the existing economic situation in Europe endangers the general welfare and national interest of the U.S. and the attainment of the objectives of the United Nations. Unless normal economic conditions and stable international economic relationships are restored in Europe, it will not be possible for the countries of Europe to achieve a working economy independent of abnormal outside assistance, or maintain free institutions and national independence. Accordingly it is declared to be the policy of the U.S. that assistance be given to those countries of Europe participating in a joint European recovery program, based on self help and mutual cooperation.

between the U.S. and the nations of Europe, and recognizing that disruption following in the wake of war is not contained by national frontiers, the Congress finds that the existing situation in Europe endangers the establishment of a lasting peace, the general welfare and national interest of the U.S., and the attainment of the objectives of the United Nations. The restoration or maintenance in European countries of principles of individual liberty, free institutions and genuine independence rests largely upon the establishment of sound economic conditions, stable international economic relations and the achievement by the countries of Europe of a healthy economy independent of extraordinary outside assistance. The accomplishment of these objectives call for a plan of European recovery, open to all such nations which cooperate in such plan, based upon a strong production effort, the expansion of foreign trade, the creation and maintenance of internal financial stability, and the develop-

ment of economic coopera-
tion including all possible steps
to establish and maintain equitable rates of exchange and to
bring about the progressive
elimination of trade barriers.
Mindful of the advantages
which the U.S. has enjoyed
through the existence of a
large domestic market with
no internal trade barriers, and
believing that similar advantages can accrue to the countries of Europe, it is declared
to be the policy of the people
of the U.S. to encourage these
countries through a joint organization to exert sustained
common efforts as set forth in
the report of the CEEC signed
at Paris on Sept. 22, 1947,
which will speedily achieve
that economic cooperation in
Europe which is essential for
lasting peace and prosperity.
It is further declared to be
the policy of the people of the
U.S. to sustain and strengthen
principles of individual liberty,
free institutions and genuine
independence in Europe
through assistance to these
countries of Europe which
participate in a joint recovery
program based upon self help

and mutual cooperation. Provided, that no assistance to
the participating countries
herein contemplated shall
seriously impair the economic
stability of the U.S. It is
further declared to be the
policy of the U.S. that con-
tinuity of assistance provided
by the U.S. should at all
times be dependent upon con-
tinuity of cooperation among
countries participating in the
program.

The President signed the Foreign Assistance Act on April 3, 1948.[60]

The *Economist* wrote on April 10, 1948:
'This week it is fitting that the peoples of Western Europe should
attempt to renew their capacity for wonder, so that they can return
to the U.S. a gratitude in some way commensurate with the act
they are about to receive. For a day or two, the Marshall Plan must
be retrieved from the realm of normal day-to-day developments in
international affairs and be seen for what it is – an act without peer
in history...
  The answer lies in one thing only – the way in which the European
nations themselves go about their work of recovery... But it is not
too early to say with categorical certainty, that the success or failure
of the Plan now lies fairly and squarely with the sixteen nations.
They have been given the tools. It is now for them to finish the job.'

60. *Foreign Assistance Act of 1948*, 80th Congr., 2nd sess.

E. EUROPE AND THE CONVENTION FOR
EUROPEAN ECONOMIC COOPERATION

In deciding on the legislation before them, members of Congress were not only concerned about the issues of the recovery program, but also with what was going on in the world and especially in Europe.

Two events had a particular influence on the deliberations on the recovery program. Both strengthened in different ways the hand of the Administration and facilitated the acceptance of the legislation.

The Soviet Union foresaw that the Marshall Plan would become a reality and it made an all-out effort to strengthen its position. This, in turn, had the effect of a more intense awareness in the United States of the aggressiveness of Soviet intentions. The development reached its climax in February 1948, during the coup in Czechoslovakia.

In the beginning of February 1948, the majority of the Czech cabinet passed a resolution instructing the communist Minister of the Interior to stop turning the police force into an instrument of the Communist Party. When the resolution was ignored, the ministers of the Socialist, Populist, and Slovak Democrat parties resigned. The social democrats, who on many issues stood with the other three parties against the communists did not follow them. Gottwald demanded a new Government of communists and social democrats. President Benes had to make the crucial decision. He insisted that the old coalition should be maintained. Thereupon communist action committees assumed power throughout the country according to the classical pattern. This put Benes in the position either of accepting Gottwald's demands or facing civil war and probable Soviet intervention. This last possibility was accentuated by the presence of the Soviet Deputy Foreign Minister Zorin in Prague.

On February 25, 1948, Benes accepted Gottwald's list of new ministers. Within a matter of days, Czechoslovakia was on its way to a satellite country with all the controls firmly in communist hands.

Two weeks later, Jan Masaryk died in Prague under mysterious circumstances, a dramatic symbol of the end of freedom in his country for the second time in ten years.

The events in Prague had a tremendous effect on the West, especially on the United States.

Of course it was true that Czechoslovakia was already in the zone of Soviet control, a fact tacitly recognized by the American Administration. But the memories of 1938 and 1939 gave a special emotional touch to the American reaction and everywhere the feeling grew that the Soviet Union was preparing to take over the European countries one after the other.

Walter Lippmann wrote in the *N.Y. Herald Tribune* of March 15, 1948, that Soviet policy had reached a stage of 'strategic actions planned by military men, in anticipation of war'.[61]

The Czech situation had a major impact on the atmosphere in which Congress debated the European Recovery Program during March and speeded up the Congressional time table.

Another event, of a more constructive character, was the speech which Foreign Secretary Bevin made before the House of Commons on January 22, 1948. After describing the collapse of the one-world concept, he said, 'We have not pressed for a Western Union and I know that some of our neighbours were not desirous of pressing it, in the hope that when we got the German and Austrian peace settlement agreement between the Four Powers, this would close the breach between East and West and thus avoid the necessity of crystallizing Europe into separate blocks.'

He continued by saying that the time was ripe now for a consolidation of Western Europe and that the free nations of Europe must now draw closely together. He informed the House that in consultation with the French, talks would be proposed with the Benelux countries in the hope that treaties would be signed. 'We have then

61. For a more elaborate analysis of the events in Prague:
    The United States in World Affairs 1947–1948, op. cit., pp. 488–493,
    Harry S. Truman, *op. cit.*, p. 255.

to go beyond the circle or our immediate neighbours...and consider the question of associating other historic members of European civilization, including the new Italy, in this great conception.'[62]

There was an immediate positive reaction from the United States.

Bevin sent a message to Marshall to ask what the United States attitude would be. The President authorized Marshall to inform the British Foreign Secretary that the United States agreed with him on the urgent need for concerted action by the nations of Western Europe. The United States welcomed the European initiative and would give their undertaking wholehearted sympathy. The United States would do anything it properly could to assist the European nations to bring this or a similar project to fulfilment.[63]

The State Department endorsed Bevin's statement immediately[64] and the President in his Message to a joint session of the Congress on March 17, 1948, said in reference to the signing of the Brussels Treaty:

'This action has great significance, for this agreement was not imposed by the decree of a more powerful neighbour. It was the free choice of independent governments representing the will of their people...

Its significance goes far beyond the actual terms of the agreement itself. It is a notable step in the direction of unity in Europe for the protection and preservation of its civilization. This development deserves our full support...I am sure that the determination of the free countries of Europe to protect themselves will be matched by an equal determination on our part to help them to do so.'[65]

There is no question that Bevin's initiative was a consequence of the developments started by Marshall's speech. It was in the formal sense a European initiative. It is open to great doubt, however, whether it would have been taken without the impetus of the

62.   For the text of Bevin's speech see *Documents on Foreign Relations, Vol. X, op. cit.,* pp. 593–598.
63.   Harry S. Truman, *op. cit.,* p. 257.
64.   Department of State, *Bulletin,* XVIII, p. 138.
65.   *Documents on Foreign Relations, Vol. X., op. cit.,* p. 7.

European Recovery Program and without the full support of the United States. It was a very timely initiative because in its frantic search for proofs of European cooperation it constituted a most welcome element for the United States Administration in its dialogue with Congress.

The Brussels Treaty was signed in Brussels on March 17, 1948.

Bevin's intentions at the moment of his speech were not clear, notably not on the point whether Britain really was ready for greater political and economic integration with other European countries. The heart of the Treaty, when it was signed, proved to be the pledge of the signatories to afford all military and other aid and assistance in their power to any of them who might be the object of an armed attack in Europe.

Bevin's offer did not lead to an unorthodox and imaginative renewal of the relations between the European states.

Its importance, however, lies in other fields.

As was mentioned above, it was instrumental in the attitude of Congress towards the legislation on the European Recovery Program.

It further was the forerunner of the Council of Europe and particularly of the North Atlantic Treaty Organization. At the time of Bevin's initiative American support could not yet take the form of a military commitment. This would have required a two-third majority in the Senate and there is every reason to believe that the Congress at that moment was not ready to pledge its support for so far-reaching a commitment.

Particularly, Senator Vandenberg rejected similar proposals from some of his colleagues. Congress had first to make its decision on the European Recovery Program which was rightly considered as the foundation for every further step.

In retrospect the Brussels Organization turned out to be a useful instrument. By the accession of Italy and Germany in 1954–1955 it was transformed into the Western European Union.

The WEU would play a rather peculiar role in the field of European unity. It led and leads a life between being attacked as completely superfluous in the confusing multitude of European organizations on the one hand, and acts, on the other hand, as an indispensable framework in which, from time to time, crises in the Western world can be resolved.

Its role after the rejection of the Treaty for a European Defense Community by the French Parliament in 1954 and after the breakdown of the negotiations for Britain's entry into the European Economic Community fully justifies its existence.

During the period after the Paris Report was delivered in Washington and during the Congressional debate, there was a rising criticism in the United States and in Europe of the lack of activity of the European countries in matters of European cooperation.

On December 17, 1947, Bevin was asked in the House of Commons which steps the United Kingdom Government had taken and was going to take to stimulate European cooperation and to implement the pledges of the Paris Report.

On the point of setting up a joint organization, Bevin stated that the Governments which participated in the Paris Conference were not in a position to take steps to set up the joint organization for reviewing progress in the execution of the European Recovery Program until the means for carrying out that program were made available.

He further referred to the work of the so-called Committee on Payments Agreements, the Customs Union Study Group and the Man Power Conference to be held in January 1948, in Rome.[66]

At this point, a few comments should be made on some of these ventures which were to a great extent forerunners of the more substantial work of OEEC.

During the fall of 1947, a Committee on Payments Agreements tried to give concrete form to the Financial Expert's conclusions contained in the Paris Report.

66. *The Times*, December 18, 1947.

The Committee met in London in September 1947, and in Paris during October 1947.

On November 18, 1947, France, Italy, and the Benelux countries signed the First Agreement on Multilateral Monetary Compensation, as recommended by the Committee. Later the Bizone of Germany joined them. Eight other countries, including the United Kingdom, joined them as 'occasional members'.

Each month, the countries would report the debit and credit balances to each other and their payments agreements to a central office. The Bank for International Settlements at Basle was named as Agent.

The Agent would calculate the maximum multilateral compensations that could be made without increasing any balances. These so-called 'first category compensations' would take place automatically between the members. However, no compensation that affected an occasional member could take place without its specific consent. Before the Agent could carry out a multilateral compensation involving an increase in any balance (second category compensation), every country involved would have to agree.

The result was very limited. The eleven countries that participated in the first clearing had debts among themselves totalling $76 million. The clearing, however, amounted to only $1,7 million or about two percent of the total.

The reasons for this very low percentage were twofold.

First, certain countries were net creditors of the rest of the group as a whole and others were net debtors. It is clear that no clearing system could change this situation.

Second, practically all first category compensations involved occasional members which meant that there could not be any automatic compensation and each transaction had to be agreed upon.

This applied in still stronger form to all second category compensations. In October 1948, the agreement gave way to a more substantial one which will be discussed later and in which American aid played a major role.

The European Customs Union Study Group, the creation of which was announced in the Paris Report, met three times between November 1947, and March 1948, in plenary session while working groups met more frequently.

Its First Report contained no commitment but confined itself to a balance sheet of technical problems. Against these difficulties the report mentioned the benefits, mainly a better utilization of the various sectors of production and a wider internal market and it concluded: 'It is not practicable at this stage to pronounce definitely on the merits and disadvantages of a customs union. There is a presumption, however, that such a union would in the long run make for the greater prosperity of the countries composing it. How far it would do so, would depend on the proper solution of a great many problems and the nature of the compromise reached.'[67]

The most controversial issue in this period was whether the CEEC should be reconvened during the Congressional debate of the European Recovery Program. This should be described in some detail as a typical example of the difficulty in Europe to get accustomed to the complexities of the American conduct of foreign affairs.

During the Congressional hearing many members of Congress were critical because they felt that Europe was not doing enough to help itself.

In particular there was strong criticism because of the apparent failure to reconvene the Committee of the sixteen nations. This criticism was also voiced in the press. In a widely quoted article in the *Washington Post* of December 7, 1947, Ferdinand Kuhn Jr. wrote

67. European Customs Union Study Group, *First Report,* Brussels, March
     1948, p. 91.
     For a detailed analysis of the Payments Agreement and the European
     Customs Union Study Group see:
     William Diebold, Jr., *Trade and Payments in Western Europe,* (New
     York: Harper & Brothers, 1952), pp. 21–27 and 303–307.
     Howard S. Ellis, *op. cit.,* pp. 376–386.

under the heading 'Western Europe is not Holding up Its End of Marshall Plan': 'The sixteen nations do not even have a continuing organization, apart from a few study committees and a small staff... The British too have been holding back, perhaps because they still hope for some kind of special treatment and fear taking their place in a sixteen nation queue. But can Western Europe go on waiting for Congress and still convince Congress that it is doing everything possible for its own salvation? The European Recovery Program will mean high prices, taxes and shortages in the U.S. It will have to overcome strenuous resistance in Congress. The best way to overcome it is for Western Europe to give continuing evidence of self help.'

Embassies in Washington conveyed the same feeling to their governments. The issue was also discussed in a remarkable forum, notably during informal discussions between representatives of the Embassies of the sixteen nations in Washington who gathered every week and constituted the only opportunity for the sixteen nations to meet. The minutes of these meetings reflect extremely well the atmosphere in Washington during these weeks.

On January 5, 1948, the United States Embassies in the participating countries were instructed to approach the governments concerned to inquire what had been done since the Paris meeting and what action had been contemplated for the future, particularly regarding the continuing organization.

The United States representatives stressed the value of some action in setting up a continuing organization because it would enable the Administration to answer satisfactorily, when Congress asked them what was being done. They stressed that the amount and form of aid might well be affected in Congress by the extent of activity which was taking place in Europe.

The British Foreign Office, excelling, from time to time, in highly convincing analyses why decisions should *not* be taken, explained as its point of view that the establishment of the continuing organization would be difficult until participants knew how much aid would be voted, and more particularly what form it would take.

The British Government felt, however, sympathetic to the possibility of a short meeting, in a very near future, of the Committee of European Economic Cooperation. Indeed, a small British party was going to Paris to discuss this problem with the French.

The United States representatives seemed to feel that such a meeting would be valuable. They suggested that this meeting should have four objectives: the reaffirmation of undertakings given at Paris, the consideration of supply availabilities in the light of the Administration's bill, the conditions to be imposed on participating countries which might cause difficulties for recipients and finally, the establishment of the machinery of allocation among CEEC countries.

After Franco-British discussions in Paris from January 7–9, 1948, the participating countries were approached by the Governments of France and the United Kingdom on January 13, 1948, with a proposal to call a CEEC meeting in Paris beginning February 16, 1948. This meeting would be preceded by a rapid tour by Mr. Eric Berthoud of the Foreign Office and Mr. Robert Marjolin of France of some of the main European capitals, with a view towards reaching agreement on the agenda. It was felt useful to obtain the unofficial views of the United States Administration, particularly regarding the timing of such a meeting.

The French and British Ambassadors visited Mr. Lovett on January 14, 1948, and to their great astonishment met a negative reply.

Mr. Lovett objected in principle to the proposals, expressing the view that an early meeting would embarrass the Administration, chiefly because, in his view, it would not be possible to avoid giving the impression both of teaming up and taking aid too much for granted.

This view was publicly announced by the State Department on January 16.[68]

After the strong pressure by Congress and parts of the Administration leading to the demarche of January 5, 1948, this indeed was a

68. *New York Times*, January 16, 1948.

puzzling and confusing episode, not only for the Europeans. In its editorial of Jan. 15, 1948, the *Washington Post* wrote: 'It was dismaying to read, after the tocsin has been sounded last June 5, by Secretary Marshall himself that Mr. Lovett had put on a brake when a second meeting of the sixteen nations had been scheduled. Our policy should be to spur such a get together.'

On January 17, 1948, the participating countries were again approached by the French and United Kingdom Governments.

Keeping in mind the objections against an early meeting of the CEEC expressed by Mr. Lovett, the two Governments proposed five points:

1. Each country should publish a statement showing the progress it had achieved since the Paris Conference;

2. The Secretary General of the Paris Conference should prepare a draft progress report;

3. Consideration to preliminary steps should be taken to set up at the appropriate time a continuing organization. Such steps should include formation of a working party which would be charged with studying the constitution and functions of the future organization;

4. Consideration should be given to the commodity reports which had been tabled by the United States Administration;

5. Finally, the intention of the visit of Mr. Berthoud and Mr. Marjolin for the fairly near future was repeated.

On February 10, 1948, the Department of State communicated to the Embassies of the participating countries in Washington that the objections against the reconvening of the CEEC had been lifted. This communication was not, however, to be considered as an American proposal for such a conference. The United States would prefer to leave the initiative to the European countries. The United States suggested that at the meeting the mutual aid of the European countries and especially the establishment of a permanent organization should be dealt with. It was recommended that no discussion would take place on the conditions of aid during this specific phase of the Congressional discussions.

In the meantime the Berthoud–Marjolin mission made its round in the European capitals. They found general agreement on the necessity for establishing a working party to elaborate a draft for the charter of the permanent organization.

On February 27, 1948, the French and United Kingdom Governments proposed a short meeting of the CEEC to be held in Paris, with the following agenda:

1. Approval of the progress report of the Secretary General;

2. Reception of reports prepared by the chairmen of the Technical Committees on commodity reports tabled by the United States Administration;

3. Approval and framing of terms of reference for a working party consisting of the sixteen Governments.

The CEEC should then adjourn and agree on a further meeting to discuss and take action on proposals of the working party. This party should meet immediately after its establishment by the CEEC with the following agenda:

1. Proposals as to the continuing organization of participating countries covering functions, structure and relations to other organizations.

2. Preparation of a draft of a multilateral agreement for completion at the appropriate time.

3. Preparation for the subsequent meeting of the CEEC.

The Ministers met on March 15, 1948, under the chairmanship of Mr. Bevin. A working group of alternates under the chairmanship of Sir Oliver Franks worked out terms of reference for the working party to be charged with proposals for the charter of the new organization.

On March 18, 1948, agreement was reached on the following instructions to the working party:

1. The purposes of the organization on which the working party was to make recommendations were economic.

2. Its aim would be to promote and facilitate the realization of the economic cooperation of Europe, with the immediate task of

ensuring the success of the European Recovery Program, so that participating countries might become independent of extraordinary outside economic assistance as soon as possible.

3. The organization should consist of an assembly of representatives of all the participating countries. The Assembly should be the body from which all decisions would derive.

4. The Assembly should set up organs for the execution of its decisions including an Executive Committee and a Secretariat General. The Secretary General would be under the general instructions of the assembly whether communicated directly or by means of an Executive Committee.

5. The general business of the organization should be transacted by decisions resting on mutual agreement.

6. Subject to acceptance of the application by the Assembly, membership should be open to any country which adhered to the joint program for European Recovery based on self-help and mutual cooperation.

7. A draft multilateral agreement should be drawn up in conformity with the declarations and pledges contained in the Report of the CEEC and other relevant documents.

These terms of reference meant that the basic issues had already been decided beforehand.

A definite gain was made as to the permanence of the organization. The Paris Report of September 1947, spoke of 'an organization of a temporary character and which will cease to exist when the special aid necessary for the recovery of Europe comes to an end'. Point 2 of the terms of reference indicated a more permanent organization with objectives not focused solely on the execution of the European Recovery Program.

The issue whether the organization should have a certain autonomy and the possibility of a strong executive secretariat were prejudiced by point 4 and by point 5 of the terms of reference. Point 5 practically settled the issue whether decisions should be taken by unanimous vote.

The structure of the organization and its institutional set-up formed a point of dispute between the French and British Governments.

The French tried to introduce a certain amount of what later would be called 'supranationalism'. They pressed for a certain degree of autonomy of the organization and a strong executive board.

They also favored an international secretariat with a Secretary General entrusted with the necessary authority to coordinate the activities of the member countries and to make major policy decisions of its own. The French also suggested to give to the new organization and the Economic Cooperation Administration joint executive authority to allocate and distribute the aid granted by the United States.

The British, however, showed again their traditional dislike of strong institutions, their reluctance to relinquish national sovereignty and their preference to deal bilaterally with the United States in matters of allocation of aid. The desire of the Labor Government to remain autonomous and independent in its domestic economic planning played also a role in the British position.

The Convention which was signed on April 16, 1948, was established on the principle that the organization would be under the complete control of the participating governments. This made OEEC a pure example of intergovernmental cooperation.

At this place attention should be given to a tendency on both sides of the Ocean to give too much weight to the purely institutional aspects of international organizations.

There is no question that the concept of European integration based on supranational principles and the concept on which the OEEC was based are different.

Nevertheless, one cannot judge the performance of international organizations merely by examining their institutional set-up. An organization based on the principle of cooperation between governments might assume, in practice, autonomous functions and might even have the effect of a supranational institution, while supranational institutions might, in practice, be dominated by the most orthodox rules of power politics of national states.

During the negotiations in Paris, the United States remained in close contact with the work through Henry Labouisse and Charles Bonesteel. The American impact on the ultimate result was not very great, partly because there was a strong feeling on the American side that the establishment of the organization was a European responsibility.

American thoughts about the subject were, however, much more advanced than what came out of the negotiations between the European countries.

In a position paper on structure and functions of the continuing CEEC organization circulated within the Administration in the beginning of March 1948, the Americans attached great importance of establishing a strong and effective organization. The United States wished to see the continuing organization responsible for checking on the performance within the participating countries, for carrying out their mutual pledges and for ensuring that the most effective use would be made of American aid. It supported a strong Secretariat.

Without a strong central organization the ERP could degenerate into a competition between the participating countries for United States aid. The United States would then not only bear the burden of deciding single-handedly between competing claimants, but also of checking on the use of aid in Europe, without help from the other countries. Accordingly, the principal aim of the United States in relation to the continuing organization was to have it strong, effective and with wide responsibilities.

The paper recommended a simple majority vote for the Council and for major decisions a voting procedure based on the principle of less than unanimity.

It is obvious that the French and American concept did not prevail and that on balance the OEEC structure was greatly influenced by the British point of view.

It must be said that the reluctance to accept a strong organization was not a British monopoly. Switzerland, Ireland and the Scandinavians were definitely against an autonomous role for OEEC, and the Benelux countries were so allergic to the danger of an Anglo-French dictate that they insisted on the unanimity principle as much as the United Kingdom did. The Americans, in leaving the decision on the structure of OEEC to the Europeans, hoped that in spite of the rigidity of its character, there would in practice be sufficient flexibility in the organization to assume a constructive role in the execution of the European Recovery Program.

The judgment on the OEEC performance will be reserved for the next chapter in which its main functions and results during the first years of its existence will be analyzed.[69]

69. For the establishment of OEEC see:
Price, *op. cit.,* pp. 80–83.
European Organizations, (London: Political and Economic Planning, 1959), pp. 43–65.
Brown and Opie, *op. cit.,* pp. 155–157.
For the text of the convention:
Documents on American Foreign Relations, Volume X, op. cit., pp. 244–250.

CHAPTER III

The United States and the First Years of OEEC (1948–1950)

A. THE IMPORTANCE OF THE FIRST YEARS

The first period of OEEC, from its establishment in April 1948, till the signature of the European Payments Union in September 1950, deserves the closest attention within the framework of this study. It is in this period that the impact of the United States on every phase of European cooperation was stronger than in any other period.

In these years the United States not only possessed the monopoly of economic strength in the Western world but it used this strength to initiate and promote every step on the road to greater European unity.

The tool of dollar aid was handled by the United States Administration to achieve the double objective of economic reconstruction in the participating countries and greater European cooperation. The American concept of European cooperation changed many times in the course of these years as to its concrete form. The ultimate objective, however, remained the same and it inspired the main decisions in the use of dollar aid and the policy towards the OEEC and its member countries.

A second reason, why these two years should be treated as a whole, is the fact that the year 1950 closed the phase in which the United States gave absolute priority to economic recovery in the Western world.

That phase was characterized by the concept that recovery in Europe was a condition necessarily preceding recovery elsewhere and that no substantial resources for defense purposes were necessary nor desirable. As White wrote: 'Though the Marshall Plan continued in name down to the beginning of 1952, historically it came to its end the week the Communists attacked in Asia. It had lasted two years and had made a brave beginning; it had brought Europe to that point of convalescence where it might support the heavy charges of arms imposed by the new crises.'[1]

The third reason for the selection of this period is the fact that in May 1950, the French proposals for a joint authority to supervise the coal and steel production of France and Germany were launched. Europe of the six was born with its supranational structure and its heavy political overtones. Till that moment OEEC was the exclusive object of American foreign policy aiming at European cooperation and integration. The emergence of the Schuman Plan started a new development of integration to which American efforts in this field could be directed, a development which was more compatible with the aims and hopes of American foreign policy than the cooperative efforts of the larger and looser group of OEEC countries.

The main attention will be given to two activities of the organization in the first years of its existence.

One is its work in the field of programming and its role in the division of aid between the participating countries. The second is the field of the closely linked activities in the problems of intra-European payments and the liberalization of trade.

The selection of these two activities is not made with neglect of the other aspect of the European Recovery Program, notably the recovery in the individual countries, resulting from the invaluable support it gave to the rise in production and to monetary and financial stability. This 'bilateral' aspect of the European Recovery Program is less relevant to this study. A certain minimum of economic recovery and stability in the countries concerned was, however,

1.   Theodore H. White, *op. cit.*, p. 70.

a condition for any real achievement in European cooperation.
American policy towards the problem of European cooperation
in OEEC was based on the concept that the United States could
try to influence developments but could never achieve anything
lasting by force or coercion. In the achievements of greater European cooperation during these first years, however, American initiative played a major and decisive role.

B. PROGRAMMING AND THE DIVISION OF AID

The compromise character of the OEEC convention left a very
wide margin in which it could be decided what its real role in the
execution of the European Recovery Program would be. The
accent could lie on the strong powers of OEEC to initiate action
and make binding plans and recommendations, or on the British
concept of the primacy of self-help of national governments.

In the particular field of the procedures for determining the needs
of the participating countries for assistance or for the methods to be
used in allocating the total amount of aid available, neither the Convention for European Economic Cooperation nor the Economic
Cooperation Act of 1948, gave a clear indication.

It was an American initiative which determined the preponderant
role the OEEC would play in the programming field and particularly in the delicate question of the division of aid. 'Here, too, it was
an American initiative which provided the critical stimulus.'[2]

On April 19, 1948, a few days after the signing of the convention,
the Executive Committee of the OEEC composed a 'Note on Programming' in which it expressed its opinion that the best results for
the work of OEEC would be achieved if the organization concentrated its activities, as soon as possible, upon preparing a consolidated program for the year July 1, 1948, to June 30, 1949.

It ended its note by suggesting that a list of questions be put to the

2. Lincoln Gordon, 'The Organization for European Economic Cooperation', in *International Organization,* Vol. X, no. 11, February 1956, p. 5.

Economic Cooperation Administration. On April 23, 1948, the ECA replied in a note on 'Preliminary Views of the ECA on Programming'.

ECA stated that OEEC should have the major responsibility for coordinating and integrating the individual programs of the OEEC members.

The note further explained that at that time no official declaration could be made by the United States concerning either the amount of ECA funds which would be available for the programming activities, or how they should be allocated among the participating countries. It suggested that, for the present, OEEC and the participating countries should use the figures contained in the estimates submitted by the executive branch of the United States Government to Congress, 'Financing by Country and Commodity' (the so-called Brown Books).

From this and from conversations with American officials, especially between Henri Labouisse and the Secretary General of OEEC, Robert Marjolin, it became clear that at that moment and for the time being, it was not the intention of the United States authorities to ask OEEC to recommend a division of aid between the participating countries.

The vital and critical decision to entrust the Organization with the task of the division of aid must have been made in Washington during the month of May 1948.

In view of its great consequences for the work of the organization and its lasting impact on the development of European cooperation and integration, one is tempted to believe that this decision was carefully weighed and the consequences of it thought through on every level of the American Administration.

There is no question that at the basis of the decision was the general desire in ECA and particularly of its two leading executives, Hoffman and Harriman, to strengthen the OEEC as an institution of real European cooperation. Nevertheless, interviews with those who were active in that period on the policy-making level of ECA and State Department disclose that very pragmatic considerations also played a major role in this decision. In their opinion the decision to entrust OEEC with the task of the division of aid was much less based on a long-term view of its consequences for European integration than on a desire for 'self protection' of the State Department and ECA which gradually got tired of the endless queue of European ministers in Washington pleading their bilateral cases.

On June 5, 1948, Harriman addressed the Council of the OEEC and confronted the representatives with the *fait accompli* of the American decision.

'You will recall when I was here with you a few weeks ago, I indicated that it was the decision of the Administration of ECA to carry out the principles laid down by Secretary Marshall a year ago, to support, in every way that he could, the initiative and responsibility of your European Organization, the OEEC. That applies to your programming task as well as the other aspects of your work. It is his confident hope that you will develop a program for European Recovery which will be your program and that you will ask for the assistance of the United States Administrator within the sums available to him. In other words it is Mr. Hoffman's confident hope that just as soon as you are able to do so, you will present to him in the annual program, a program for European Recovery and will indicate the manner in which it is your judgment that the funds at his disposal can best be used. This, of course, means the division of United States aid between the different countries and in general the manner in which it can be used to make your own program effective...

It is recognized that there are great difficulties involved, but it is his confident hope that you will be able to overcome these difficulties and will be able to form the judgments through your deliberations which will make it possible for you to make the recommendations of which I have spoken. If you are able to do so, the Administration will give the greatest consideration possible to your recommendations within his responsibilities under the legislation.'[3]

3.   *OEEC Document,* C/M (48) 14, Final.

The American 'confident hope' was in reality a decision. It came as a shock to many European governments which had a genuine fear that an exercise in which the young, inexperienced organization would be responsible for a task of such complexity and delicacy might wreck its effectiveness and even its existence. At the same time there was a strong feeling in some of the participating countries that bilateral talks in Washington might produce better results for the country concerned than an unknown multilateral negotiation in Paris. This feeling was especially strong in the United Kingdom which at that time, and for many years to come, considered a special relationship with the United States as one of the cornerstones of British foreign policy and its position in the world.

Other countries, while recognizing the very heavy burden for the new organization, immediately accepted the American concept because it fitted into their ideas of the role of OEEC in European cooperation and because they realized that the 'confident hope' of the Administrator of ECA in reality was an irreversible American decision.[4]

While OEEC deliberated on the problem, the Directive for the Preparation of Programs for the year 1948/1949 nevertheless was adopted by the Council and transmitted to the participating countries. The directive laid down that each country's program should contain plans for imports, production, consumption and exports of a wide range of commodities, a forecast of the balance of payments with the dollar area, a statement of the economic policy to be followed in the year 1948–1949, the expected results of that policy, and a justification for the aid requested.

The import programs should not be limited to the imports financed by American aid but should cover total imports of the participating countries. This was a logical course: countries could only plan their American financed imports in the light of their total import programs.

4. Lincoln Gordon, *op. cit.*, p. 5.
    Baron Snoy et d'Oppuers, 'Les Etapes de la Coopération Européenne et les négotiations relatives à une zone de Libre Echange', *Chronique de Politique Etrangère*, Vol. XII, Bruxelles, 1959, pp. 575–577.

In the meantime during the month of June 1948, informal discussions were held between the European countries and with American officials about the feasibility of the division of aid exercise.

In a formal exchange of views between the Executive Committee
and Harriman, the Chairman, Sir Edmund Hall Patch, asked the
pertinent question whether, if the Organization assumed the responsibility of making proposals about the distribution of aid, it
could receive an assurance that these proposals would be accepted,
as far as possible, by the United States Administration. If this would
not be the case and the arduous work done at Paris would have to
be done again in Washington, this could ruin the very spirit of the
Organization. If the Administration should nevertheless judge it
necessary to modify substantially the Organization's proposals,
such modifications should be communicated to the Organization
in Paris and not directly to individual countries.

Harriman replied that the first thing ECA was most anxious to
avoid were 'sollicitations in Washington'. The ECA would hope and
expect that OEEC's work on the division of aid would not require
changes in Washington, provided that the job would be properly
done.

If changes would be deemed necessary by ECA, he would certainly recommend that they should be returned to OEEC.[5]

In a note to the Council of July 10, 1948, the Executive Committee
spelled out extensively the advantages and disadvantages of the
acceptance of the responsibility for the division of aid exercise. In
its conclusion, it said that after consideration of the serious issues
involved in this question, the Executive Committee recommended
that the American request should be adopted by the Council. Despite the extreme dangers and difficulties of the task, technically and
politically, of which Harriman was fully aware, the Executive
Committee considered that refusal of the American request might
involve the risk of incurring serious misunderstandings and thus
prejudice the prestige and the future of the Organization. The

5. *OEEC Document*, CE/M (48)33, Final.

Committee further considered it desirable to help the Administrator in the accomplishment of a task which was in the framework of the Organization's objectives. The Committee emphasized again, however, that this task assumed on the part of the participating countries a firm intention to agree on a program on these lines and to put the achievement of an agreed program before the immediate satisfaction of particular individual interests.

On July 16, 1948, the Council accepted the proposals and agreed on an elaborate procedure for the work to be done. In a letter of July 23, 1948, Harriman wrote to the Chairman of the Executive Committee to emphasize again the very firm opinion of Washington on the role of the Organization.

'Mr. Hoffman particularly hopes that the participating countries will resolve their problems through the mechanism of the OEEC and will not turn to him in Washington on a bilateral basis, to ask him to adjudicate their problems which are, of course, essentially European in nature.'

The stage was now set for one of the most complicated and far-reaching activities with which any international organization was ever faced.

From now on a vital issue for sovereign countries would not only be discussed, but for all practical purposes decided by a multilateral organization.

Early in July 1948, ECA gave notice to the OEEC that the amount available for allocation to the participating countries for the year 1948/1949 was $4.875 billion, which was approximately half a billion dollars short of the total which the so-called 'Brown Books' mentioned and on which the programming activities of the participating countries were based. Procedures and machinery had to be devised in order to cut down the request made by the OEEC members as a basic element of their annual programs.

At its session on July 16, 1948, the Council approved a 'Procedure for the Annual Program 1948/1949'.[6]

6.   OEEC Document, C (48) 60, Final.

'This program – and OEEC's performance on it – will also form a most important part of the material which the United States Administration will use when the time comes to ask the United States Congress for a second appropriation.'

This sentence in the Council decision was symptomatic for the relation between OEEC, its member countries, and the United States Administration. The carrot of the dollar aid was always combined with the stick of the necessary congressional approval of funds.

The note went on to say, 'The task is a difficult one. It has been made more difficult by the recent declaration to OEEC that ECA will expect this annual program to contain also a considered recommendation on the division of aid among the participating countries. The difficulties, in the way of working out a recommendation of this kind are very considerable and OEEC will have to explore them fully.'

The document then spelled out the necessity of agreement with ECA on certain basic questions. One of these was formulated as follows:

'If OEEC, in order to assist intra-European trade and to reduce as far as possible imports from the Western Hemisphere, proposes among its solution a method of intra-European payments based upon certain allocation principles for American aid, will ECA approve it in good time?'

It then formulated the answers it would like to receive from ECA. The above-mentioned problem of intra-European trade should, in the view of OEEC, receive the following reply from ECA.

'It is up to OEEC to formulate proposals. ECA is ready to accept any scheme agreed by the members which will increase intra-European trade and reduce to a minimum the import requirements from the Western Hemisphere.'

The note then made it clear that there should be first a scrutiny of programs submitted by participating countries. The vast amount of material coming into the organization by July 15, 1948, should be reduced to manageable proportions and the Secretariat General,

with the aid of such experts as it might wish to consult, would have
to prepare suitable summary tables of the balance of payments
statements, the budget programs and requirements programs, as
well as the supporting economic memoranda submitted by participating countries.

The note then continued by proposing a procedure which would
be of major importance for the future work of OEEC.

'A small group, chosen from among the Organization, shall make
an intensive study of the material prepared by the Secretariat...
The task of this group is to study the material prepared for it; to
call in such experts from the horizontal and vertical committees
as it may wish; and to put forward a preliminary proposal for the
division of aid, on the basis of data available at this stage. The group
shall also be free to call upon member's experts if it so desires, and
to refer at need to the Executive Committee and the Council...

In the working out of this preliminary distribution the group will
have to bear in mind Mr. Harriman's declaration of the kind of
program which ECA is hoping to receive from OEEC. It will
have to examine carefully the general economic conditions of the
participating countries and study their programs in the light of the
various supporting memoranda submitted.

It should by no means be impossible for such a group, with the
material at its disposal, to propose a preliminary distribution of aid
which could be used for the subsequent programming of OEEC...

The acceptance of the group's proposals by any member of the
Council shall not mean agreement at this stage to the figure put in
for that particular member country. Approval by any member of
the Council will mean only that he is prepared to treat the proposals
as a basis upon which the work can be continued.'

In agreeing to this procedure, two elements, vital for the work of
OEEC, were introduced. The first was the 'restricted committee'
principle. The agreement on the commission of four members
meant that the principle of a 'denationalized' group was accepted and
entrusted with a major and delicate responsibility. This group was
not 'supranational' in the sense that it had formal decision-making

authority independent from national governments. Its recommendations had to be approved by unanimous consent of the Council.

Essentially, however, the group had a non-national character and a non-national task. In the performance of their duty, the members of this group were not under instruction from their governments. The major result of the acceptance of the 'restricted group', dealing with matters of vital importance, was the development of an 'OEEC point of view' and the pressure this point of view would bear upon actions and policies of national governments.

In adopting this principle, every country realized that it could withhold its consent to the recommendations of the group but that this opposition would be far more difficult than in the case that the work had taken place in the group of seventeen countries. The moral pressure of a joint point of view by a 'non-national' restricted group was difficult to overcome and it put the burden of the opposition to its recommendations fully on the resisting country.

The second element, so important for the life of OEEC and subsequent developments in other Western and European organizations, was the introduction of the cross-examination of the programs submitted by the member countries, not as a rather innocent exercise, but resulting in a decision on a vital matter – the allocation of American aid.

It meant not a formal but nevertheless an essential and lasting infraction of economic sovereignty. The national administrations knew that their figures, plans and policies would be scrutinized to the fullest extent possible and every government realized that from that moment on the effect of its policy would be judged in a framework much larger than that of the national state.

National economic policy from now on was made with a keen eye on Washington, but even more so on the headquarters of OEEC.

On July 16, 1948, and after much backstage fighting, a group of four was nominated. It consisted of Guindey (France), Chairman of the Balance of Payments Committee, Roll (United Kingdom), Chairman of the Programs Committee, Spierenburg (Netherlands),

Acting Chairman of the Trade Committee, and Stoppani (Italy), Vice Chairman of the Payments Committee.

In its work, the group decided that, although the figures in the 'Brown Books' had been taken as a basis for the programs, submitted by the members, the group would examine each program on its own merits. It was faced with the formidable task of cutting the sum of all the requests for outside dollar assistance by more than one billion dollars.

Furthermore, it made the very important assumption that a system for facilitating intra-European payments would be in operation in the near future and that, therefore, no further dollar payments would be made between member countries.

In July 1948, the Council of OEEC had adopted the principles of a payments agreement. Both Europeans and Americans felt that the multilateral payments agreement of November 1947, was not adequate for increasing possibilities for intra-European trade without recourse to settlement in gold or dollars. When Marshall aid began to flow, it was clear that the United States Administration had not adopted the suggestion in the OEEC report that American dollars be allocated to a European monetary system. Only for a few months the American desire to control the use of every dollar led the United States Administration to agree to the use of ERP dollars for so-called offshore purchases in participating countries. Soon afterwards, it became apparent that the United States Administration was not willing to expand this system of the use of ERP dollars. This, combined with its negative attitude towards assigning dollars for a European clearing system, led to the system of drawing rights and conditional aid, which will be discussed later. At this place only its main features should be mentioned because it was a prerequisite to agreement on the division of aid.

The main principle was that creditor countries in Europe should receive dollar aid in the form of grants equivalent to their estimated surplus in Europe, on condition that they would contribute, in their national currencies, an amount covering that surplus from funds set aside as a counterpart to the dollar aid, the so-called local currency funds. The debtor countries, on the other hand, would be granted drawing rights against the creditor countries for the amount of their deficits, in the appropriate currency, after allowing for use of existing resources in that currency.[7]

Among the other working assumptions, the one about the level of consumption was of great importance in the exercise of the allocation of aid.

Except where a higher level could be justified by hardship or by increased employment and output, the general level of foodstuffs for human consumption and of finished and semi-finished consumer goods should in no country exceed that of 1947, if such action resulted in a reduction of the dollars available for the achievement of European recovery.

With the help of experts from other committees and from the Secretariat, the group of four spent approximately three weeks on the cross-examinations of the national programs.

Those national delegates who participated in this extraordinary exercise will remember that they entered the examination room with the special feeling of tension, so well known to anyone who has gone through examinations in private life. This feeling was intensified by the fact that, while in personal examinations, one expects a certain objectivity on the part of the examiners, in this case, there was the complication that every weakness in the program – and there were many – could lead to an increased dollar allocation for the countries of the examiners.

It is a great tribute to the system and to the behavior of the group of four that the acrimony was reduced to a minimum and that in general the examinations took place in a good atmosphere.

The questions were penetrating and covered the whole field of economic activity. This, of course, was easier for the participating countries with a certain statistical and highly developed administra-

7. OEEC, *Report to the E.C.A. on the First Annual Program,* Paris, October 1948, p. 42, and
William Diebold, Jr., *op. cit.,* pp. 34–35.

tive tradition than for other member countries for which this kind of overall economic programming activity was completely new. The main attention was given to the feasibility of the production programs, the composition and direction of the export programs, the figures about investment policy both in the agricultural and industrial sector, the possibilities of other sources for financing the program, the analysis of the consumption level and its consequences for the foreign currency position, the geographical spread of imports and exports, the position of a few key commodities like coal, timber, and steel, the balance of payments outlook in all its aspects and a detailed analysis of the program to be financed with ERP dollars. Some of the questions had to be answered with reservation, pending the elaboration of the intra-European payments system to which no concrete form was or could be given at that time.

The pressures on the individual members of the group were sometimes great and alarming. It was, for instance, extremely difficult for the Dutch member in view of the special Benelux relationship to oppose the Belgian claims. One should not be too severe in judging the many unfortunate incidents, which in spite of the generally good atmosphere took place. This was, after all, a negotiation without precedent in which the major issue in the economic life of sovereign nations was at stake.

After completing their examinations, the group of four withdrew from Paris to an unknown place in Chantilly, in order to work in an atmosphere where pressures could no longer be exercised.

On August 12, 1948, their report was transmitted to the Chairman of the Council.[8]

In its report, the group stressed that they had not divided their preliminary figures of dollar aid between conditional and unconditional aid. This division would have to take place when an intra-European payments scheme had been agreed upon and when the

8.   OEEC Document, CE (48) 65.

contributions of the individual countries to the scheme had been settled. They recommended that the provisional division of aid (which totalled $4835 million and left $40 millions to be set aside to form a fund for capital projects of general interest to European recovery) should be approved and the participating countries invited to submit, not later than September 1, 1948, revised programs based on the financial limits of this provisional division of aid.

In the meeting of the Council of August 14, 1948, pandemonium broke loose. The discussion whether the report should be discussed at all lasted for two hours.

After the first barrage was over, Guindey, on behalf of the Committee made an impressive and dignified statement:[9]

'Have these reductions been made by fair methods or not? In other words, are these sacrifices – since sacrifices there had to be – fairly divided among the various countries? Here, I can only say what we have already said yesterday. We have scrutinized the different programs. It is obvious that all these programs represented for each country something which that country legitimately regarded as a minimum. Within this minimum, we had to find imports which, while necessary, were perhaps less indispensable than others to European recovery. It was inevitable that the percentage of the imports to be sacrificed could not be exactly the same for all the countries. We have done our best, we have attempted to apply the same rules to each country. I do not think that we can make any other reply. The sacrifice had to be shared: we have divided it as best we could.' And he concluded: 'I must say that we see no reason to modify our proposals. We merely think that, as far as we may venture to make a suggestion, it may perhaps be possible in respect of certain points which I have mentioned falling within the sphere of intra-European payments to allay certain legitimate apprehensions.'

When the Chairman of the meeting asked the final verdict of the delegates, the United Kingdom, Belgium, Luxemburg, Austria,

9.   OEEC Document, CM (48) 33, Annex I.

France, Italy, Sweden, the French Zone of Germany, and the Netherlands accepted on the condition that a satisfactorily solution for the problem of intra-European payments be found.

Ireland, Iceland, Norway, Greece, Turkey, and Trieste refused, while Denmark claimed the right to go before the Council, in the course of the year, if insurmountable difficulties developed.

The sharpest disagreement was expressed by the American representative of the Bizone, Wilkinson. He enraged his colleagues by stating that a reduction of the requested amount for the Bizone would make an unfavorable impression on the United States Congress and would in all probability endanger the Congressional, authorization of the second tranche of the European Recovery Program.

In informal discussions it was agreed among the members of the Executive Committee that a solution for the problem of intra-European payments was indispensable for an agreement on the division of aid.

This would mean a highly complicated negotiation in which every intra-European bilateral debtor and creditor position would have to be negotiated.

The example of the restricted group was followed. A commission of five was suggested, consisting of England, France, Belgium, Greece and Norway.

On the night of August 15, 1948, the meeting of the Council came to the conclusion that agreement could not be reached, and it was concluded that there would be no decision on the report of the group of four. The group of five would be instructed to prepare a report for August 26, 1948, in which the intra-European debtor and creditor positions would be determined and both reports would be dealt with simultaneously. The national programming activities would be based on the figures of the group of four. If the meeting of August 26, 1948, would fundamentally change the picture, then programs could be adapted afterwards.

Only Greece and Turkey refused to accept this last point. After the meeting it became clear that if the Bizone of Germany, Greece and Turkey would maintain their point of view, other countries would reopen the issue and the total exercise would face disaster.

Pessimism about the outcome was expressed in the press which openly discussed the deadlock. In the meantime the commission of five coordinated the immensely complicated task of supervising approximately eighty sets of bilateral negotiation, in order to establish the amounts of conditional aid and corresponding drawing rights.

The gap between what the countries wanted to export under this new payments scheme and what they would like to import was revealed when the first estimates of intra-European balance of payments for the coming year were tabled in Paris. Enormous divergences appeared between the two sides of the export and import accounts. Every country naturally tried to keep its exports to other European countries to a minimum and to inflate its imports from European countries as far as decency would allow – and sometimes beyond.

This gap had to be bridged by a strenuous effort of the committee of five.

The committee was able to report to the Council on August 31, 1948. The main stumbling blocks were, again, the attitude of the Bizone, which not only objected to the figure of direct aid, but also rejected the fact that the commission of five gave it a creditor role in the intra-European payments scheme instead of the expected debtor position.

There were also fundamental disagreements about the drawing rights on Belgium and about the extreme debtor position of France. The United Kingdom was dissatisfied with its heavy creditor position. The main issue, however, was the attitude of the Bizone.

From the beginning, it was clear that the Bizone problem was essentially an intra-American one.

Since the dominant power in the bizonal economy was the American Military Government, the United States was involved in a dual capacity, as donor of dollar aid and as one of the recipients. General Clay took the position that no foreign organization could assume the right to apportion American dollars to an agency of the United States Government.[10]

The question was whether ECA was in a position to overrule the United States Military Administration in Germany. This was not the case. It became apparent that Harriman, to a great extent, had to accept the position of the Bizonal authorities. What made this attitude even more difficult to accept was the fact that the United Kingdom Government was hardly consulted on this issue.

After hectic and high level consultations between Spaak, Cripps, Harriman, and many others, a decision was reached in which the claims of the United States military authorities in Germany were almost totally accepted. The United States attitude was a regrettable blot on its very clean record in the division of aid exercise. A critical editiorial in the *Washington Post* of September 9, 1948, said: 'We sympathize with the Europeans to the extent that Mr. Lawrence Wilkinson, General Clay's representative had no business trying to stage a hold up in the OEEC by saying that Congress would see that the Bizone got adequate treatment, if the OEEC failed to provide it. That is not the way to behave in a community exercise.' *The Economist* wrote: 'On two important points of principle decisions have been taken and it is difficult to avoid the conclusion that both decisions are wrong.

In the first place, the allocation of aid between the European nations, which was, on the strongest American insistence, to have been a purely European responsibility has been drastically modified by direct American intervention... After a prolonged deadlock, Mr. Harriman intervened on the side of the American Military Government... Thus the Europeans were deprived of their full responsibility and in the event a direct American fiat took the place of European agreement.

10. See also John C. Campbell, *The United States in World Affairs 1948–1949*, Published for the Council on Foreign Relations, (New York: Harper & Brothers, 1949), pp. 184–185.

The second point of principle is even more unfortunate. Nothing will so discourage Europe...than the belief that the United States intends to rebuild Western Germany at the expense, if necessary, of everybody else. Yet what other conclusion can be drawn from a decision which treats Bizonia as a most favoured child and releases the Germans from obligations of mutual help imposed on their neighbours.'[11]

The Council accepted the proposals on September 11, 1948, reservations being maintained by Greece and Turkey.

After some further minor changes the report was transmitted to Harriman at a Ministral Meeting of the Council on October 16, 1948. On the same day the Intra-European Payments System was signed.

The ultimate division of aid and European contributions was as shown in the table on p. 156.

As becomes clear from the events mentioned above, the division of aid exercise was not performed without serious difficulties and disagreements. It definitely was not a pure example of a cooperative effort, if indeed such examples exist at all in international intercourse. The question how the objective was achieved is irrelevant, however, compared to the fact that it was achieved at all.

Spaak, the Chairman of the Council, in transmitting the report, said with justified pride:

'The distribution among the European nations, so cruelly tried by the war, faced with the satisfaction of so many essential needs, possessed of different economic systems and sometimes opposed interests, of the large sums which America has generously placed at the disposal of Europe was no easy task. I repeat, that to succeed in sharing these sums in good will and in mutual understanding was no light undertaking...'

And after describing the double significance of the day on which the Intra-European Payments Agreement also was to be signed, he concluded:

11. *The Economist,* September 11, 1948.

Direct Aid and European contributions
(in Million Dollars)

	Direct Dollar Aid	Intra-European contributions (—) or receipts (+)	Net Aid
United Kingdom	1.263	—282	981
France	989	+323.3	1.312.3
Italy	601	— 20.3	580.7
Netherlands	496	+ 71.7	567.7
Bizone	414	— 10.2	403.8
Belgium-Luxemburg	250	—207.5	42.5
Austria	217	+ 63.5	280.5
Greece	146	+ 66.8	212.8
Denmark	110	+ 6.8	116.8
French Zone	100	+ 0.8	100.8
Norway	84	+ 31.8	115.8
Eire	79	—	79
Turkey	50	— 19.7	30.3
Sweden	47	— 25	22
Trieste	18	—	18
Iceland	11	—	11
Total	4.875	—	4.875

Note: Contributions and receipts shown in column 2 are dollar equivalents of local currency surpluses and deficits.

'It is a step, not only towards cooperation between the European nations, but also between Europe and the United States.'

Harriman, in accepting the report, said:

'In receiving the first annual program of the OEEC, I permit myself to share with you in the pride that comes from a great accomplishment in a new area.'[12]

And finally, Hoffman, in announcing that he had received the first annual program prepared by the OEEC, called the preparation an unprecedented achievement. 'This is the first time in history that

12.   OEEC Document, CM (48) 46.

the free peoples of Europe have cooperated in the preparation of an economic program embracing nineteen separate political units and covering the efforts of two hundred and seventy millions of inhabitants.'[13]

Even taking into account the slight inflation of words, usual at these kind of events, the judgment was essentially right. It should, however, not be forgotten that both the carrot and the stick were at that time in full operation.

There was a fundamental difference between the programming activity for the 1949/50 program and the activities for the 1948/49 program described above.

The national programs, the division of aid and the monetary arrangements were treated as a whole in the Report to the Economic Cooperation Administration on the First Annual Program adopted in October 1948.

For the following year, these three activities were treated separately. The Report to the Economic Cooperation Administration on the 1949–1950 Program was finalized and adopted in the last days of 1948, while the decision on the division of aid and the amended monetary arrangements took place late in 1949.

The problems which had to be faced for 1949/50, as far as the technique of programming was concerned, were different from those which had to be coped with in the first annual report. In the first place, there was a tendency to consider the 1949/50 program part of the long-term program on which an interim report was drawn up at the same time and which contained information not available when the 48/49 report had been written.[14]

In the second place, it was not known, as in July 1948, what amount of aid was available for the participating countries during the fiscal year under consideration.

In the third place, while the 1948/49 program was being prepared, the year to which that program related had already begun. This

13. *ECA Bulletin,* No. 232, October 18, 1948.
14. The long-term program will be discussed later.

time the Organization was trying to forecast the economic lives of participating countries for a period which would begin only six months after the adoption of the report.[15]

The work, therefore, had to be provisional and a more detailed and elaborate program would have to be drawn up at a later stage when more accurate forecasts could be made especially with the knowledge of the available amount of ERP aid.

The primary importance of the plans for 1949/50 was that they had to provide the ECA with sufficient information to show the United States Congress how much aid the participating countries would need in the second year in order to sustain another twelve months of the European Recovery Program.

A dilemma, ably described in the Report, arose from the fact that on the one hand the time for drawing up the program was unfavorable but that on the other hand it was necessary to provide ECA with material for the Congressional considerations.[16]

'The OEEC has no wish to forward national programs for 1949/1950 to the ECA without any combined comment. On the other hand, it is neither possible nor reasonable to expect that comment could now, in December 1948, be detailed and precise, and in particular be quantitative as far as individual countries are concerned. In the first place, many questions have been thrown up as a result of the study of the Long-Term Programs which will require thorough and intensive study in the months to come. Out of that study will emerge comments on individual countries' intentions, as well as on their bearing on the intention of other countries. In the second place even for the practical operations of the year 1949/1950 itself, it is too early to be definite... On the one hand, the Organization is aware of weaknesses in individual countries programs, it is conscious of doubts which the combined intentions must raise. On the other hand, it is not today in a position to ask countries to consent here and now to a modification of their plans in this or that respect.

15.   OEEC, *Report to the Economic Cooperation Administration on the 1949–1950 Program,* Vol. I, p. 9.
16.   OEEC, *op. cit.,* pp. 11–18.

...In the light of the *prima facie* comments on individual countries which can be made, it must be ensured that for all countries taken together the total sum of aid is not in excess of an amount which could reasonably be regarded as sufficient for the job.

This is no easy task. What it involves is devising some method of overall screening which results in a figure of total aid which is the minimum considered necessary and which shows the figure into which it is believed the sum total of individual countries' needs could be compressed if that amount of aid were made available.'

Then, rather casually, the Report suddenly pointed out the basic weakness of this kind of exercise and the dangers of the fiction that at that time Western Europe could be treated as an economic unit.

'The dangers of such a method are very great. It is above all open to serious misunderstanding and misapplication. Essentially, what it means is to imagine that the whole of the participating countries are one single economic unit with the same currency, the same commercial system, the same methods of government and administration, the same statistical apparatus and with as high a degree of interchangeability of factors of production and products as a single national unit can be said to possess. Now it is clear that this is not the case with the countries participating in the Organization. There is therefore a serious danger that every time a global comment is made it may lead the unwary to apply it to any one individual country with the most disastrous consequences. However, the Organization feels its right to take this risk, confident that executive agencies of the United States Administration and the people of the United States will understand the reason which led to the adoption of this particular method of dealing with the aggregation of national programs at the present time.'

The programs were submitted to close and detailed scrutiny. The method of the 'cross-examination', which had such a beneficial influence on the life of the Organization and on the awareness of national governments, was maintained and refined. On the one hand, the examinations lacked the tension and the penetrating analysis of the previous year, because the allocation of dollar aid was not the purpose of the exercise, on the other hand, however, this fact brought about a greater objectivity in the deliberations.

Six national delegations, acting as a working party, were responsible for making the detailed examination of the submitted programs. Within this working group, pairs of delegates were nominated to make special studies of each program.

After each pair of delegates had completed their studies, they discussed their views with the delegation of the country concerned. When this had been done, each program was examined in the Programs Committee composed of representatives of all delegations, with the two delegates, in charge of making a special study of the program, taking the lead in the cross-examinations.

On the basis of these discussions, each pair of delegations prepared a report on the program for which it was responsible. These reports were accepted by each interested country as a fair statement of the problems raised by its program. Evidently, this acceptance was obtained only after fierce negotiation and pressure, and it was not to be assumed that any country whose program was reported upon necessarily agreed with the criticism expressed in the statements.

In the request to present their national plans, OEEC called the attention of the participating governments to the fact that, since less American aid would probably be available, most countries would have to get along with fewer ECA dollars in 1949/1950 than in the preceding year. Ten countries and the French Zone of Germany, however, asked for more aid than they had received in the previous year, national requests adding up to approximately $4,700 million.

By a global method this amount was reduced to $4,350 million.

The Chairmen of the Executive Committee and the Council, Sir Edmund Hall Patch and Baron Jean Charles Snoy, together with the Secretary General of OEEC, Robert Marjolin, went to Washington in the early days of January 1949, to help ECA with the preparation of material for the Congressional presentation.

This presentation fell into two parts, reports of a general nature and detailed studies of the programs of individual countries. So far as the latter were concerned, the group of three had made it clear that they could accept no responsibility and could express no opinions. The degree of confidence from the member countries in the non-national point of view of the top officers of their organization had not matured enough to accept them as mandatories.

The group did not neglect its public relations activities and held a widely published press conference on January 12, 1948,[17] in which it explained the working of the Organization and the progress made in the field of European cooperation. As in October 1947, the United States Administration highly valued the participation of European officials in its difficult task of convincing Congress and American public opinion of the need of such large scale aid to Europe.

The months of June through August 1949, were the most critical in OEEC's history. When one reads through the minutes and the reports of that period one can only conclude that it was almost a miracle that OEEC survived.

The concentration of seemingly insoluble issues, the complexity of the problems, the fact that eventual solutions of extremely difficult issues was dependent on the solution of even more complicated ones, the frequency of meetings on ministerial and official levels and the growing irritations and tensions led to a situation in which a breakdown of the still fragile organization could be expected.

There were four main reasons for this state of affairs.

1. While the definite amount of congressional appropriations for the fiscal year 1949/1950 was not yet established, it was certain that it would not exceed $3750 million which already meant a substantial cut in the aid requested by the participating countries and on which their national programs had been based.

2. There was a definite need for a revision of the first Payments Agreement of October 1948, and the issue of the multilateralization of drawing rights had to be decided.

17.   OEEC Information Dept., *Press Communique,* C (49) 5, January 19, 1949.

Belgium as the main creditor country in Europe, played a major role in this respect and its attitude caused a round of negotiations, which itself would have been enough to exhaust the Organization and its negotiators. In the meeting of the so-called Consultative Group of Ministers held on June 29–30, 1949, an agreement was reached on the Belgian issue and on the main principles of a partial multilateralization of drawing rights.

Before any division of aid was made, Belgium was assured of $312,5 million conditional aid and was obliged to give $87,5 million in loans.

It was further decided that in principle the drawing rights would be multilateralized for twenty-five percent and would remain bilateral for seventy-five percent.

3. In that same meeting Harriman informed the Council that ECA wanted to reserve, out of the appropriations for the year 1949/50, a fund of $150 million to promote the most rapid possible liberalization of intra-European trade and payments, by providing safeguards against unforeseeable risks involved in measures of liberalization. The interesting aspect of this proposal was not the scope of the amount, nor the clarity with which the United States officials explained what they exactly had in mind, but the fact that for the first time the criterion of need on which the dollar allocations were based was supplemented by the criterion of merit.

In view of the vagueness of the American plan and of the already existing necessity of drastically cutting the requests for aid, this American proposal was most unwelcome to the majority of participating countries.

4. The most serious reason for the long and bitter struggle of these months was the fact that the rapidly deteriorating balance of payments position of the United Kingdom, particularly towards the dollar area, led this country to submit to the Programs Committee a memorandum in which the prospective sterling area dollar deficit, estimated in December 1948, for the year 1949/50, at $940 million, was increased to more than $1500 million. This meant that agreement in the Programs Committee on the division of aid, al-

ready improbable before the British memorandum, would now become impossible.

The Organization was confronted with a complete deadlock and with the prospect of not being able to recommend anything concrete to the United States Administration. It should not be forgotten that, at that moment, the Congressional debate on the 1949/50 appropriations was still in a very difficult phase. In the meeting of July 29, 1949, it was decided that the Programs Committee, under these circumstances, could not be requested to propose a division of aid. The Council itself was the only body to face this impossible task.

The Programs Committee therefore should confine itself to a technical screening. Relieved from its heavy and highly disagreeable responsibility, it chose a procedure in which the country whose request for aid was discussed should not be present. When the Committee reported to the Council on August 19, 1949, no single country, with the exception of Belgium, could agree to its recommendation. On August 16, 1949, Hoffman arrived in Paris and explained that after his already difficult defense of the request for new funds before Congress, open disagreement among the participating countries about the division of aid would make an extremely unfavorable impression on Congressional and public opinion in the United States.

In the night of August 30, 1949, the exhausted and desperate Council took a wise decision. It entrusted Marjolin and Snoy to have conversations with all the delegations of the participating countries and to try to recommend a solution.

Everybody realized, that this was the last chance for agreement. Snoy recalls[18] how he and his colleague had to go through many crises of conscience for eight days and nights. After having made some working assumptions, the two men separated and when they met again they discovered that their individual efforts came to similar results. This gave them courage to face a hostile Council.

18.   Baron Snoy et d'Oppuers, *op. cit.,* pp. 576–577.

After long and bitter discussions, the realization that refusal of the recommendations would lead to the breakdown of OEEC ultimately led to an agreement.[19]

The Council decided to approve the recommendations and to transmit the report to the United States Special Representative in Europe for consideration by the ECA.

In mid-September 1949, Hoffman sent his very important reply to OEEC. His answer implied the end of this procedure of allocating aid by the OEEC.

'The Economic Cooperation Administration is gratified that through the OEEC the participating countries have made their recommendations for the division of aid for the year 1949/1950. Obviously no definite position can be taken by the ECA, until the Congress has determined the appropriation. It should also be pointed out that the recommendations have made no allowances for the general reserve fund which the ECA proposes to establish primarily to facilitate measures for the liberalization of trade within Europe. Subject to these considerations, it can be said that the OEEC recommendations will be taken as the pattern for the allocations of aid during the first six months of the 1949/50 fiscal year, and that these allocations will be kept under review during this period and if necessary adjusted from time to time in the light of actual developments.

The decision of the ECA on the use of the balances of the current fiscal year will be *directly related to the performance of the participating countries, acting both individually and collectively through the OEEC in effectively using the aid and realizing the objectives of the convention for European Economic Cooperation and the Economic Cooperation Act.*'[20]

In view of this major policy decision and of the suggestion by the

19. The solution recommended by Snoy and Marjolin included the use of the $150 million reserve fund. The ECA insisted, however, on maintaining this separate fund and realized its objective by a four percent cut, across the board, in the country allocations.

20. Italics mine.

Snoy-Marjolin group after the accomplishment of their difficult task, the Council decided in November 1949, that for the two remaining years, programming should be based on American assistance, divided proportionately as established in the division of aid during the year 1949/50. The assumption should be that the amount available in the year 1950/51 would be seventy five percent of the previous year and in 1951/52, fifty percent.

Hoffman's speech in October 1949, which will be dealt with later, brought OEEC a new major activity after the energy it had spent on the programming and division of aid activities.

Lincoln Gordon is right when he describes the OEEC activities on the division of aid as follows: 'This episode has recently been described as an OEEC failure, but in view of the pressures at the time, the extraordinary fact is that the second division of aid effort did not break down completely. In a sense, the very resourcefulness of OEEC in improving special machinery to deal with a crisis was a sign of its resilience and vitality as a corporate institution. In this as in many other OEEC crises when the chips were down, responsible European ministers felt that they simply could not afford to carry disagreement to an ultimate breaking point.

There was a certain fear for the future of OEEC because many felt that the division of aid had been the main source of life and vigour for the OEEC as an institution. The organization had gone through two real trials by fire and it had emerged not only intact but stronger.'[21]

It was therefore so important that the Hoffman speech of October 1949, analyzed below, gave OEEC a new and wider field of activity.

Diebold is also aware of the lasting importance of the role of OEEC in the division of aid.

'Less clearly visible then these measures was a third major accomplishment. In connection with the allocation of American aid, the annual review of each other's economy, national policies and performance were exposed to close criticism from other countries and

21.   Lincoln Gordon, *op. cit.,* pp. 5–7.

from the OEEC secretariat under Robert Marjolin. These confrontations did much to develop the practice of economic cooperation and the sense of common interests and standards. By creating the need to "think multilaterally" as one regular participant put it, this process made an important contribution to integration.'[22]

C. THE FOUR-YEAR PROGRAM

The objective of the European Recovery Program, as it was initially conceived, was to make the participating countries independent of outside financial assistance within a period of four years. From the beginning, this concept had many arbitrary elements.

The choice of a period of four years was more a political decision, than that it was based on concrete economic data and plans. The group of participating countries was not selected as a coherent economic region but was formed on the basis of purely political considerations. The Paris Report of 1947 was not a cohesive integrated plan. The notion of the four-year period was not a result of the Paris Report. This report was written on the basis of an earlier American decision that four years was the maximum period to which the United States Administration could commit itself for extending financial assistance, and even that was only accepted in principle by Congress and not by a commitment on appropriations. It was to be expected that the ECA, soon after the creation of OEEC, wanted to stress the necessity of a four-year program which was compatible with its own concept of the European Recovery Program and which it needed for its future presentations to Congress.

This process was initiated by a speech of Paul Hoffman, before the Council of OEEC, on July 25, 1948.

He started by expressing his view that the support of the American people for the European Recovery Program stemmed from their

22.   William Diebold, Jr., 'The Process of European Integration', in *Current History*, Vol. 42, March, 1962, p. 130.

belief in the pledges of the participating countries both to combine their economic strength, to make the fullest collective use of their individual capacities and potentialities and to undertake the elaboration and execution of a joint recovery program.

He then called for a master plan of action, aimed at the full recovery of the European economy by June 30, 1952, when American aid would terminate. This master program would, of course, be a composite of programs developed by the participating countries. He made it clear that what he had in mind was a program of action, not a rigid plan.

The four-year program of action, which he envisaged would in part be stated in terms of production in agriculture and key industries, in part in terms of exports and imports of key commodities.

It would also include programs in such fields as monetary, financial and trade policies, where governments and governments only could take action. In addition to the programs for each of the countries, the OEEC should have a four-year plan of action of its own, calling for specific accomplishments in the direction of making free the movement of goods, services and peoples among the nations.

From this speech it is already apparent that the adoption of a real integrated master plan for European recovery would be a difficult, if not an impossible task. The plan could only be based on plans and forecasts of the individual participating countries. These countries varied widely in the capability to control their total economic life in a four-year period. Even the most organized and most centrally controlled nation among the group only had a real grip on imports and a much more indirect influence on other important facets of its economic life.

The member countries were not chosen because their economies were complimentary, nor because they constituted a natural and self-evident single economic region.

There was a huge discrepancy between the fiction that there could be an economic plan for the whole of Western Europe and the fact that what could be available, at the maximum, were plans of individual and sovereign countries which even lacked the authority to control their own economy for a four-year period.

OEEC was not a central authority with powers comparable to those of the national state and even these powers were insufficient for the exercise in question.

Such an authority was a condition for a real four-year plan for Western Europe as a whole but was at the same time an unrealistic notion in this period of European cooperation.

It could be argued that by using its immensely powerful leverage of dollar aid, the United States Administration could have forced upon the participating countries the revolutionary political and economic decisions necessary to draw up and implement a coordinated, cohesive and purposeful plan of action.

Senator Fulbright had this in mind when he said to Hoffman: 'You are trying to make these countries prosperous, are you not? Are you not in effect destroying in a way, the real incentive to bring about a union by being so successful in this recovery?'[23]

Even if the Administration had firmly intended to use all its power to bring about this fundamental change in the method of cooperation between the participating countries, it is open to very serious doubt whether it could have succeeded in view of the circumstances prevailing in Europe. But it did not have this intention. As Beloff says:

'As was already the case from the first days of the Marshall Plan there was a deep conviction in the Administration that, as a matter of policy, movements toward the reshaping of Europe must come from Europeans... and that American pressure should be limited to supporting such initiatives. The Administration was reluctant to appear to be dictating to sovereign European governments and was at most willing to use its influence to try and bring recalcitrant countries into line with the majority of OEEC members.'[24]

23. *Extension of European Recovery Plan*, Hearings on S 833, 81st Congr., 1st sess., p. 48.
24. Beloff, *op. cit.*, p. 36.

All this does not imply that the exercise on the four-year program was a useless one.

On August 7, 1948, the Council adopted the directive for the long-term program, and national administrations went to work. In November 1948, the headquarters of OEEC was the center of a series of critical examinations of the national programs. The highly effective method of examination by a small group of experts from designated countries was maintained.

The very useful 'confrontation' technique fully worked.

But it was asking too much of OEEC to weld these varied documents, realistic and unrealistic, detailed and highly generalized, and representing conflicting economic outlooks, into a coherent whole.

There were wide divergences between the sums the ERP nations proposed to sell among themselves and the total they intended to buy.

Great Britain, the Netherlands, and the Scandinavian countries based their plans on extensive control of their internal economies and their external trade. France, Belgium, and Italy were attempting to achieve the same results by more liberal methods and by a much lesser degree of control over the economic life of their countries.

In the view of most countries, it was a strange paradox that the United States, which did not itself believe in such detailed planning, was pressing European countries to adopt planning techniques that required stringent governmental controls.[25]

As to the balance of payments with the outside world, the national programs of imports and exports showed that Western Europe in 1952, would still have a deficit of $800 million. OEEC, however, stated that it was more realistic to estimate this deficit at approximately $3000 million.

Late in 1948, OEEC came to the conclusion that the publication of a long-term program would be virtually impossible and would, if pushed through, weaken the position of OEEC and its image in

25.   Brown and Opie, *op. cit.,* p. 201.

the United States. Instead, it published on December 30, 1948, the Interim Report on the European Recovery Program.[26]

The first volume contained the Report of the Council of OEEC to the Economic Cooperation Administration and dealt with the first stages of the ERP.

Its importance and its limitations are very ably expressed. The second volume contained the integral text of the national programs of the member countries for the recovery period ending June 30, 1952, submitted to the OEEC.

'It should be stressed that this report is not a joint European recovery program. Nevertheless there lies behind it a period of cooperative activity unlike anything hitherto known in the economic relations between any group of independent states. The national programs presented to the Organization give a more complete picture of national plans, intentions and forecasts than has ever before been available. Each of these national programs has been considered in great detail by the various committees of the Organization. Searching questions, going to the heart of national economic policy, have been put to the national representatives by their colleagues. As a result of this cross-examination the Organization has come to apprehend more fully than ever before what are the vital European problems. It is in consequence far better fitted for the task which it now has immediately before it, the construction of a joint European recovery program.'[27]

The Interim Report was not to be followed by a final report.

'It was now evident that some approach other than the coordination of national plans would have to be adopted in the joint recovery effort. The ECA indicated that what should be attempted was agreement on the general lines of policy, with particular reference to policies or sectors of economies that were amenable to

26.   OEEC, *Interim Report on the European Recovery Program*, (Paris: December 1948).

27.   *Interim Report, op. cit.,* Vol. I, p. 14.

government control. The concept of an integrated long-term program for Europe slipped quietly out of sight.'[28]

Patterson believes that the Administration abandoned its previous concept of the four-year program because it realized the danger that the plans of the individual nations appeared to develop along lines of national autarchy, resulting in a Europe less rather than more economically unified.[29]

This certainly was an important element in the changing attitude of the ECA. The compelling reason for this change was, however, the realization that the task, as originally planned, was an impossible one.

In his assessment of the report, Harriman stated that its significance lay in the fact that it was a realistic definition of the work to be done.

'Anyone who thought that the seperate programs developed by nineteen different political units would not contain inconsistencies, one with another, did not understand what was involved.'[30]

The problem, however, was not that there were inconsistencies. The problem was, that there was no possibility and no authority to overcome them.

Instead of facing the too heavy task of continuation of the work of the four-year program, the Organization adopted in March 1948, a Plan of Action of which the main elements were:

1. Financial and monetary stabilization in all participating countries during the 1949/1950 period;

2. The rapid increase in exports;

3. Curtailment of non-essential dollar imports;

4. Elimination of internal disequilibrium, leading to a healthy expansion of trade in Europe;

5. Concerted action in the investment for the modernization of production;

28. Brown and Opie, *op. cit.,* p. 201.
29. Gardner Patterson, *Survey of United States International Finance,* (Princeton University Press, 1950), p. 135.
30. ECA, *Press Release,* January 14, 1949, Paris.

6. Exchange of information and decisions necessary to coordinate investments;

7. An attack on the problems of surplus manpower in some participating countries.

Thus, the attempt to force Europe into a real integrated program slipped into the more realistic and orthodox approach of economic cooperation between sovereign nations in sectors of their economic life over which they had a certain measure of authority.

D. THE CONGRESSIONAL DEBATE IN 1949

We have already stressed the importance of the fact that, during the first Congressional debate on the European Recovery Program, Congress refused a four year's authorization and insisted on a yearly decision for both authorization and appropriation. The European Recovery Program was therefore debated six times in Congress before it was merged with military assistance in the Mutual Security legislation.

The importance of these debates stems not from fundamental changes Congress made in the proposals of the executive branch of the United States Government, but much more from the pressures resulting from the fact that the debate would take place at all.

The activities of the Economic Cooperation Administrator and OEEC were, for a substantial part, geared to the necessity of presenting to Congress a program demonstrating that real progress had been made in Europe. The unification of Europe remained one of the constant and permanent themes of the Congressional deliberations. As was the case in the executive branch of the government, the meaning of unification was left undefined. Only Senator Fulbright was explicit in his drive for specific political unification. On the floor of the Senate, he complained that for more than two years he had urged the government to encourage frankly and positively the political unification of Europe, but that the Government had not seen fit to do so. He rejected the idea that his thesis was open to a charge of imperialism. Imperialism, he said, would mean dividing Europe, whereas he asked for the encouragement of its unification. He called the sharp distinction between economic and political affairs a basic fallacy of the policy-makers in the State Department and in ECA, and he thought that the executive branch attached undue significance to economic cooperation and recovery which, in his opinion, would not itself be sufficient to aid the process of integration.[31]

Fulbright was at the extreme wing of those who thought that the European Recovery Program should be used as an instrument of European political unification. There was, however, a general concensus of Congressional opinion that more should be done to foster and promote European cooperation and integration.

The executive branch of the United States Government was at all stages of the ERP impressed by this very outspoken element in Congressional opinion.

In its report of January 10, 1949, the joint Committee for Economic Cooperation (the so-called watchdog committee) wrote:

'To what extent the OEEC organization and accomplishments so far represent a real unification of Western Europe is difficult to determine. Mr. Hoffman has emphasized the significance of the fact that representatives of the participating countries have worked together over a period of months debating controversial issues and reaching solutions which it was possible for them to agree upon in most instances.'

After having noted the charges against the United Kingdom's reluctant attitude towards European cooperation and integration and the structural weakness of the French position, the report continued by saying: 'As a consequence of these doubts it apparently remains to be determined whether the OEEC is to fill the role of the organization established by the nations of Western Europe to further economic unification, whatever sacrifice to their own national prestige may be necessary or whether on the other hand the OEEC exists merely because it is necessary to have such an

31. *Congressional Record*, 81th Congr., 1st sess., pp. 3960–3970.

organization if the countries of Europe are to receive the aid made available under the ECA Act of 1948.'[32]

In quoting this report, a word should be said about the documentation and information of members of the United States Congress.

Compared to the work which parliaments in Europe undertake, the very high quality of the studies performed for members of the United States Congress by the executive branch and by the staffs of the various Congressional committees is most impressive. Apart from the extensive way in which Congress is informed by the Administration, it is further supported in its work by a multitude of reports and excellent research by the staffs of the committees or by outside expert advice.

As a result of this the United States Congress is by far the best documented, informed and staffed parliament in the world.

The only problem which arises is whether this amount of documentation really can be digested.

The documentation for the European Recovery Program, when it was first debated in 1948, required a solid reading period, excluding every other activity, of four to five months.[33]

On February 8, 1949, Hoffman, Acheson, and Harriman testified before a joint session of the Senate Foreign Relations Committee and the House Foreign Affairs Committee.[34] The general trend of their statements was one of pride in the achievements and of prudent confidence in the future of European cooperation.

Hoffman said:

'From the ECA point of view, the real proving period lies ahead and it lies immediately ahead. We can now say with assurance that Europe is through the first phase of its economic recovery. In the

32. *Report on Progress of the Economic Cooperation Administration,* (Report of the joint Committee for Economic Cooperation, Jan. 10, 1949), pp. 11–12.
33. Robert A. Dahl, *op. cit.,* pp. 128–130.
34. *Extension of European Recovery Program,* Hearings before the Committee on Foreign Affairs, 81st Congr., 1st sess., pp. 1–28.

months ahead Europe must tackle the more difficult problem of making major readjustments which break away from its traditional and now inadequate ways of paying its way in the world. In the months ahead the Governments of Europe face some tough decisions, decisions which must be made and carried out if Europe is to stand on its own feet...

This is the time to hit hard for European recovery – time for the Europeans to take the drastic steps necessary for real recovery.'

Acheson, in expressing his views on European unification, said:
'I believe that we have recognized here from the very beginning and so have the participating countries, that the greater the unity, both economic and political, among the free nations of Europe, the greater the progress toward the restoration of those conditions of economic health, social tranquillity, political freedom and security which represents our common goal...

The form and nature of these developments along economic and political lines must, if they are to be strong and lasting, come from the people of Europe themselves. Only they themselves can work out their salvation through their own efforts. Our role, as the Congress has already determined, must be to encourage and support these efforts.'

Harriman concluded his statement by emphasizing that the program of economic cooperation in Europe stood out as one of the most constructive and hopeful efforts among nations.

The reaction of Congress to the achievements and future of European cooperation was more cautious and skeptical than the statements of the executive branch. There was a sharp clash of opinion between Acheson and Fulbright on February 11, 1949, about the necessity of political unification.

Acheson emphasized that there had to be more progress on an economic level before true political integration could be achieved. He was strongly supported by Senator Connally, Chairman of the Senate Foreign Relations Committee, who even went so far as to say that he would be prepared to take action against any Economic

Cooperation Administration official who went outside the proper field of economic assistance into the political sphere.[35]

During the Committee hearings, there was no disagreement in Congress about the absolute necessity of greater cooperation and integration in Europe. The issues at stake were the role of the United States and, more specifically, whether the dollar aid should be made conditional on a clear performance of greater cooperation and integration in Europe.

This latter view was successfully opposed by the Administration on the ground that undue pressure would not produce the desired results.

On March 8, 1949, the Senate Committee reported its findings to the full Senate.[36]

'The Committee examined carefully the progress made during the year among the ERP countries toward economic and political integration. The voluntary steps taken over the past year, such as the Brussels Treaty, the work of OEEC and the Council of Europe, clearly indicate that the Economic Cooperation Act has created an unusual opportunity for advance in this direction. In order to express its approval of these developments the Committee adopted an amendment to the statement of policy in the preamble of the Act by inserting the words "to encourage the unification of Europe."

This objective of encouraging European unification is thus declared to be the desire of the people of the United States. Nevertheless the Committee feels strongly that the impetus toward unification must come from the European peoples themselves without interference or dictation from the outside.'

The House Committee, reporting to the House of Representatives on March 25, 1949, stated:

'At the same time the participating nations have moved toward stronger and wider cooperation. The only question in the Com-

35. *The Times,* February 12, 1949.
36. *Extension of the European Recovery Program,* Report of the Committee of Foreign Relations U.S. Senate on S 1209, March 8, 1949.

mittee's mind was this: Is the rate of development rapid enough?'[37]

In the preamble of the Authorization Act, the words 'it is further the policy of the United States to encourage the unification of Europe' were inserted.

The debates on the appropriations were not only lengthy but far more difficult for the Administration. Much of the discontent about the rate and intensity of European cooperation and integration, already apparent in the debates on the Authorization Bill, were repeated in a more outspoken and rather irritated way. This was undoubtedly caused, among other things, by the record of OEEC in the first half of 1949, which had not been impressive.

This impatience and irritation on the side of Congress was one of the causes of the Hoffman speech of October 1949. In the hearings Hoffman stated that he intended to go to Europe to deliver as strong a message as possible on the necessity for a more promising attitude of the European countries towards European cooperation and integration. The Appropriation Act was not signed until October 6, 1949, after lengthy arguments between the conferencees of the House and Senate about the size of the appropriations.

In the next year, attempts were again made to insert into the legislation a fixed schedule of accomplishment in the field of unification as a condition of continuing aid, but as in previous years, these attempts were defeated on the ground that it was not the appropriate role of the United States Government to force solutions on Western Europe through its financial assistance.

Much more important, however, was the fact that in February 1950, the Economic Cooperation Administrator requested to withhold $600 million of the authorization applied for, in order to encourage the pursuit of a program of liberalization of trade and payments in Europe.

At that time the negotiations on a European Payments Union clearly showed that its success depended mainly on an American financial contribution.

37. *Extension of the European Recovery Program,* Report of the House Committee on Foreign Affairs on H.R. 3748, March 25, 1949.

The six congressional debates on the legislation of the European Recovery Program have been one of the most, if not the most, important influence from the other side of the Ocean on the development of European cooperation and integration.

E. THE HOFFMAN SPEECH OF OCTOBER 1949

The speech, which Hoffman made for the Ministerial Council of OEEC on October 31, 1949, was the result of a variety of factors and developments.

OEEC was in a period of great difficulties and even crises.

The four-year program – the attempt at an integrated recovery program – led only to the Interim Report of December 1948, and was soon abandoned as the focal point of OEEC activities.

The division of aid exercise, which twice had been the primary source of life and vigor for OEEC, was substituted by the decision that subsequent instalments of aid, which were in any case to decrease rapidly, be divided in the same ratio as the Snoy-Marjolin formula. The ECA had decided to bring the element of merit into the allocation of dollar aid, which meant more emphasis on unilateral American decisions.

The OEEC Plan of Action, which replaced the long-term program in the spring of 1949, was definitely not the kind of activity which either could inspire a real imaginative effort or provide even a minimum basis for the aims and objectives of the European Recovery Program.

The negotiations on the revision of the Payments Agreement in the summer of 1949, were difficult, sometimes frustrating, and at no time led to a real break through the still prevailing bilateralism of the European trade and payments pattern. The devaluation of sterling on September 19, 1949, followed by most of the currencies of other OEEC countries, was welcomed as a contribution to a better balance between the dollar area and the European monetary spheres, but was on the other hand resented because there had not been even the beginning of European consultation in the framework of OEEC.

There was also a keen realization that the European Recovery Program approached its half way mark, and only two years of outside financial assistance remained. There was no indication whatsoever that at the end of the road Western Europe would really be able to pay its own way.

Last, but not least, the Congressional debates on the extension of the Economic Cooperation Act had proved that there was disillusion and even irritation, on the other side of the Ocean, about the performance of the participating countries in the field of European cooperation and integration. There was a general feeling that a third authorization and appropriation would run into grave difficulties if nothing substantial happened in the Paris headquarters.

Against the background of these events and circumstances, it seemed logical and obvious that the time was ripe for a new impetus and initiative from the Economic Cooperation Administration.

Both Beloff and Price have studied the staffwork of ECA in preparation for the Hoffman speech. As was the case with the speech of Secretary Marshall in June 1947, Hoffman's speech was a condensation of a variety of thoughts and concepts of his collaborators.

The groundwork was, according to Beloff, laid down in two documents.[38]

One was prepared by Theodore Geiger, H. van Buren Cleveland, and John Hully, and consisted of three sections.

The first analyzed the reasons why the industrial revolution in Europe had failed to have the same far-reaching effects as was the case in the United States.

To the authors, it seemed that now a new opportunity existed, partially because some of the social stratifications and traditional patterns of consumption, which had hampered economic growth in Europe, had been swept away as a result of the war and occupation, and partly because the desire for higher standards of living was

38. Beloff, *op. cit.,* pp. 38–44.

being accelerated by the increasing knowledge of the American standard. They were, however, firmly convinced that the new goals could only be attained by fundamental alterations in the economic structure as a whole.

In the second section, the authors went into Europe's problems in terms of economic theory, explaining economic growth primarily in terms of a widening market which would permit the maximum advantages to be obtained from a division of labor.

Pointing to the small size of the European markets, they thought that this was the main reason for the limitation of the intensity and the spirit of competition.

What was required was something basically different, notably the formation of a single pervasive and highly competitive domestic market in Western Europe of sufficient size and scope to support mass production for mass consumption. This required the elimination of barriers to the free movement of goods, persons, and ultimately capital.

The basic disparity in Western Europe was the fact that the particular size of the unit necessary for its continued, successful existence in the world economy was, in their opinion, larger than the actual size of the existing political units.

The third section of the document discussed the obstacles to action and the first steps that needed to be taken. It also dealt with possible institutional arrangements. What the authors suggested was the establishment of an Intra-European Commerce Commission, modeled on the United States Interstate Commerce and Federal Trade Commissions and having, like its American counterpart, quasi-executive and judicial powers.

Quite apart from what might be done by such a commission, a high degree of coordination of national economic policies would have to be undertaken. Insuperable obstacles might arise because of the unwillingness of participating countries to open up their economies to unpredictable impacts generated by their neighbor's actions, particularly in the field of money and prices. The proposed removal of economic barriers between the countries of Western

Europe might create a need for the coordination of their policies. This process was beyond the capacities of normal diplomacy or of intergovernmental committee procedures such as those of OEEC.

This document was followed by another paper by the first two authors entitled: 'The Economic Integration of Western Europe'. Part of this paper is quoted by Price.[39]

The German problem was brought into the picture. What solution, asked the authors, is there to the German problem, outside of membership in a Western European Union? Membership in a union might well be the one method for making Europeans out of the Germans and for harnessing their talents for management and production for a better cause than German nationalism.

The authors concluded by saying that this was the historical moment to act. Promised improvements in general conditions had appeared. Most countries found themselves in a condition of rapidly increasing welfare. At the same time ECA still disposed of sufficient funds to assist in overcoming dislocation which might arise from the eliminations of barriers to trade. After 1952, however, and progressively from then on, these factors would be dissipated.

Persons most familiar with the attitudes of Congress were afraid that a continuation of ERP at the minimum necessary level of aid could not be expected unless Western European countries clearly embarked on a course of economic unity.[40]

It is quite understandable that Hoffman did not, in his speech, accept the full range of the far-reaching concept of these working papers. He did not, for instance, propose any institutional change, nor did he give his statement the political overtones proposed to him. He concentrated mainly on the second section of the first paper quoted above. This came also nearest to his own concept. Hoffman was moved and inspired by the advantages of the great

39. Price, *op. cit.,* pp. 120–121.
40. Both documents have not been available to the author. The quoted texts have been taken verbally from the studies of Beloff and Price.

single market and he was deeply convinced that Europe should, assisted by dollar aid, aim at something which would be comparable to the size of the United States economy. Educated in a branch of industry which flourished because of its huge market possibilities and its highly competitive character, he sought with great vigor and conviction to transplant the notion of a large single market economy to the other side of the Ocean.

His philosophy can very well be traced in his book: 'Peace Can be Won' and particularly in the seventh chapter.[41]

In speeches before the American Federation of Labor in St. Paul, Minnesota, on October 5, 1949, and before the Canadian Chamber of Commerce on October 27,1949, in Montreal, Hoffman announced the main theme of his forthcoming Paris speech.[42] On October 31, 1949, he addressed the Council in Paris with a statement of which Stebbins said, 'Seldom if ever had an American representative spoken more bluntly to a European official audience'.[43]

'We must now devote our fullest energies to two major tasks. These tasks are: first to balance Europe's dollar accounts so that Europe can buy the raw materials and other items which mean employment and better living. The second – and to say this is why I am here – is to move ahead on a far-reaching program to build in Western Europe a more dynamic, expanding economy which will promise steady improvement in the conditions of life for all its people.

This I believe means nothing less than an integration of the Western European Economy.'[44]

41. Paul G. Hoffman, *Peace Can be Won,* (New York: Doubleday & Co., 1951).
42. Published by ECA Information Service on the same dates.
43. Richard P. Stebbins, *The U.S. in World Affairs 1949–1950,* Published for the Council on Foreign Relations, (New York: Harper & Brothers, 1950), p. 131.
44. This is practically the first time that Hoffman uses the word 'integration' without, however, precisely defining it. What he means probably comes close to Marjolin's analysis on page 41 of his *'Europe and the U.S. in the world Economy'* (Duke University Press, 1953).
   He defines integration as meaning all the steps taken to the objective of

He then described shortly what had to be done in order to achieve the first of these tasks – a sound domestic fiscal policy and provisions for direct incentives to private exporters. Then he came to his real message:

'Urgent as I regard the first major task – that of balancing Europe's trade with the dollar area – its performance will not be meaningful unless we have come to grips with our second task – the building of an expanding economy in Western Europe through economic integration. The substance of such integration would be the formation of a single large market within which quantitative restrictions on the movement of goods, monetary barriers to the flow of payments, and eventually, all tariffs are permanently swept away. The fact that we have in the United States a single market of 150 million consumers has been indispensable to the strength and efficiency of our economy. The creation of a permanent, freely trading area, comprising 270 million consumers in Western Europe would have a multitude of helpful consequences. It would accelerate the development of large scale, low cost production industries. It would make the effective use of all resources easier, the stifling of healthy competition more difficult.

Obviously, such a step would not change the physical structure of European industry, or vastly increase productivity overnight, but the massive change in the economic environment would, I am convinced, set in motion a rapid growth in productivity. This would make it possible for Europe to improve its competitive position in the world and thus more nearly satisfy the expectations and needs of its peoples. This is a vital objective. It was to this that secretary Marshall pointed in the speech which sparked Europe to new hope and new endeavour. It was on this promise that the Congress of the United States enacted the ECA Act. This goal is embodied in the Convention of the OEEC.

I know that the difficulties which stand in the way of its achievement will spring all too readily to mind, but before integration is

 complete unification, even though they may fall short of the final objective.

dismissed as a merely romantic possibility, too remote to have any bearing on practical, immediate decisions, I invite you to weigh the alternative.

Even assuming brilliant success in overcoming the dollar deficit in the next two years, the end of ERP in 1952, will at best leave Europe in only a precarious balance with the dollar area. Monetary reserves will be inadequate, and it is plain that dollar shortages will recur in one country or another the first time the European economy is subjected to serious pressure. In the absence of integration, nations would each separately try to protect their dollar reserves. They would attempt to earn dollars from each other by restricting imports. The vicious cycle of economic nationalism would again be set in motion...

This is why integration is not just an ideal, it is a practical necessity. This being so, it is your job to devise and put into effect your own program to accomplish this purpose – just as it was your responsibility, which you carried out so ably, to take secretary Marshall's original suggestion and give it life and breath.

In a program designed to accomplish effective and lasting integration, certain fundamental requirements suggest themselves. First, means must be found to bring about a substantial measure of coordination of national fiscal and monetary policies. Trade and payments cannot long continue free among countries in which there are widely divergent degrees of inflationary, or de-flationary, pressure. The development of such differences in financial pressures among different countries will inevitably force the re-imposition of restrictive controls. Unless individual countries accept the necessity for some co-ordination of domestic financial policies the prospects for eliminating even the most restrictive types of controls over international trade will be dim indeed. Co-ordination of these vital national policies need not result in identity of policy...

Even when effective means are found to co-ordinate financial policies and to promote needed exchange-rate changes there are still bound to be temporary disturbances in the flow of trade and payments between countries. Their whole impact should not be allowed to fall upon the gold and dollar reserves of the individual countries. I believe, therefore, that a third essential of any plan you devise must be a means to cushion the effect of those inevitable temporary disturbances.

Means must be found to insure that severe strains are not imposed upon the maintenance of integration through conflicting commercial policies and practices. Such strains might arise from disguised barriers to trade within an area or from radically divergent policies toward external trade.

This brings me to our final suggestion, which has to do with the path by which this goal of integration may be reached. I have repeatedly referred to the creation of a single European market. Many of the immediate steps that need to be taken toward this goal can, and will, involve the whole group of the participating countries. But there are other arrangements, some already in prospect, involving smaller groups of countries which, I am convinced, will also turn out to be steps toward the same objective. I do not believe that any path toward integration should be left unexplored. It seems to me absolutely essential that arrangements arrived at within groups of two, three, or more countries should be in harmony with wider possibilities of European unity and should, under no circumstance involve the raising of new or higher barriers to trade within Europe than already exist...

I have made a number of references to the urgency of starting immediately on this programme of integration. My conviction on this point is based, in the first place, on the acute realisation of the very short time still remaining during which American aid will be available to cushion the inevitable short run dislocations which a programme of integration will involve.

There is another very important reason for speed. The people and the Congress of the United States, and, I am sure, a great majority of the people of Europe have instinctively felt that economic integration is essential if there is to be an end to Europe's recurring economic crises. A European programme to this end – one which showed real promise of taking this great forward step successfully –

would, I strongly believe, give new impetus to American support for carrying through into 1952 our joint effort towards lasting European recovery.

For all these reasons – but particularly because of the urgency of the need – I do make this considered request: that you have ready early in 1950 a record of accomplishment and a programme, which together, will take Europe well along the road toward economic integration...

The immediate goal is a solidly based prosperity for an economically unified Western Europe – a goal which President Truman reaffirmed to me just before I left Washington. Beyond that lies what has been the hope of all men of good will during your lifetime and mine, an enduring peace founded on justice and freedom. That high hope can be realised if we, the people of the free world, continue to work together and stick together.'[45]

The speech can be interpreted in different ways. There definitely was not a clear or precise concept of what was meant by integration. While there were parts of the speech, which could lead to the belief that integration in the political and institutional sense was the ultimate aim, it is more probable that Hoffman, in his speech, made the creation of a single integrated market practically identical with the more orthodox concept of liberalization of trade and payments.

In a highly critical comment on Hoffman's speech, *The Economist* wrote on November 5, 1949:

'In short, America has the power, if it will be patient to impel Europe along the road to real integration but it must recognize the fact that it may take a generation of planning and adaptation to reach the stage at which it brings real economic benefits to the Continent. It has also the power to persuade Europe to take all the risks involved in quickly creating a free market – if it will underwrite the venture. What is not possible, what might indeed shatter the Marshall Plan and frustrate the whole purpose of American

45.   Full text of Hoffman's speech in *O.E.E.C. Document,* C (49) 176.

policy is a spectacular attempt to combine short-term recovery with a long-term reorganization of Europe, to telescope into one great act of policy a process which took over three generations to complete in the free industrial United States.'

The reaction in OEEC was mixed. It was obvious that Hoffman's reference to the possibility of closer cooperation between smaller groups was taken up immediately by the French to push their ideas about European continental cooperation with the Italians and the Benelux. Sir Stafford Cripps declined flatly to enter into any form of real integration that would prejudice Britain's relation with what he called the already 'well integrated' sterling area.

Harold Callender, the *New York Times* correspondent in Paris, whose coverage of the first years of the Marshall Plan was an example of well informed and intelligent journalism, said to the author of this study after the meeting with Hoffman: 'This is a simple matter. The British got American aid already before the Marshall Plan started and if necessary they will get it afterwards. You on the continent will have a hard job.'

The immediate response to Hoffman's speech was disappointing. It was mainly the United Kingdom which failed to give guidance to a more positive European response. After a few days, the Council adopted a resolution accepting Hoffman's ideas in principle but no decision on real implementation was reached, except on a further reduction of import quotas.

But in spite of different interpretations and dogmatic controversies about the speech, and in spite of the first discouraging reactions, the Hoffman intervention was the beginning of the second major achievement of OEEC – the creation of a program of intra-European trade liberalization and of European currency transferability through the creation of a European Payments Union.

The main features of these developments will be analyzed in the next section. The criticism of Hoffman's speech cannot conceal the basic fact that it was again American and not European initiative which pushed Western Europe further on the road to greater cooperation and integration.

F. THE LIBERALIZATION OF INTRA-EUROPEAN
PAYMENTS AND TRADE

Hoffman's speech of October 1949, gave a new impetus to the movement to liberalize trade and payments between the member countries of OEEC.

In view of the fact that, after the division of aid for the fiscal year 1949/1950, the role of OEEC in the allocation of dollars for further reconstruction became a limited one, it was a natural development that its main activities were concentrated on the closely linked problems of trade and payments.

These activities have not led ultimately to the establishment of a really integrated market, nor to an OEEC customs union or free trade area.

Nevertheless they were a constructive contribution to further recovery in Europe and they laid the basis for all future attempts to achieve economic integration.

1. *Liberalization of Payments and the European Payments Union*

In the description of the first division of aid exercise, mention was made of the introduction of the conditional aid and the resulting system of drawing rights laid down in the First Agreement for Intra-European Payments and Compensations, signed by the Council on October 16, 1948.

This scheme was only a limited step on the road to the multilateral use of European currencies and did not go further than the then prevailing circumstances permitted. It was recognized that the free transferability of European currencies could only be reached in phases. In view of the widely different internal positions of the participating countries and of the highly vulnerable state of the monetary reserves in many countries, this transferability could not be achieved in one bold stroke.

Apart from the more objective reasons for a limited approach to the problem of the liberalization of intra-European payments, there were also differences in policy.

Belgium had, since 1947, pleaded the cause of greater flexibility and transferability of European currencies in the settlement of intra-European indebtedness. It was the United Kingdom, at the other extreme of opinion, which violently opposed any provisions under which continental holders of sterling could transfer sterling to other countries in settlement of their debts.

The first payments scheme was probably not an important factor in increasing intra-European trade. The increase was mainly due to the rise in production in the participating countries. It nevertheless is clear that the system of conditional aid, drawing rights and compensations assisted the expansion of trade. During the first six months of its operation from October 1948, to March 1949, about one-half of the intra-European trade deficits were financed by this system.

Nevertheless, there were three main objections against the scheme.

First, the scheme offered no effective incentive to the debtor countries to get on their feet again. The bigger their prospective deficits, the larger the amount of aid they could claim from the other OEEC countries.

This argument could of course be used against the whole European Recovery Program. But in the intra-European payments agreement the surpluses and deficits and the corresponding contributions and drawing rights were further removed from supervision by ECA than were the direct grants. Effective control and the possibilities of sanctions were much more remote.

Second, there was a certain rigidity and artificiality in the trade patterns envisaged by the system under discussion.

They were based on estimates of intra-European payments over a period of twelve months. These estimates were made, as was mentioned earlier, in a very short period of time and they were liable to a wide margin of error. They were based on forecasts of foreign trade. The possibility of error grew if the attempt was made to forecast not only a country's foreign trade in general but its precise interchange of goods with a great number of particular countries.

The bias toward error was further increased by the counter-incentives stressed under the first point.

When it became evident that surpluses arising from intra-European trade would have to be given away as contributions and that deficits would be met by gifts under the guise of drawing rights, a number of countries hastily recast their balance of payments expectations.

Four months after the estimates had been made, it was already evident that they were badly astray. For instance, neither Italy nor the Bizone had yet used any of the sterling drawing rights which were allotted to them in October 1948.

In many cases, however, countries tended to use drawing rights even if it meant paying higher prices for imports than would be paid if they were bought elsewhere. Considerations of price were of secondary importance, since the debtor could freely obtain goods from a country on which it had drawing rights.

The payments agreement was therefore tying European trade in a straight jacket, the rigidity of which was increased by the fact that drawing rights were not transferable.

A third objection against the scheme was that the rigid bilateral pattern of European trade which it encouraged was in turn dependent on an essentially transient factor, notably the dollar-aid under the European Recovery Program of which the conditional aid formed a part. The reconstruction of European trade was therefore being built on a foundation which itself would be removed, at the latest, in 1952. The structure of European trade would then be poised in mid-air without support from the conditional grants which at that time carried its weight.

The weaknesses of the first payments agreement soon led to strong pressures to change the system. These pressures originated mainly on the American side, but Belgium and Switzerland too, continued their fight in favor of liberalizing the plan. The ECA was strongly in favor of revision and it made it abundantly clear that it was not prepared to give its consent to the continuation of a scheme which used American funds to finance European trade on such a rigid bilateral basis. During April 1949, the ECA proposed that in the new agreement, drawing rights should be transferable among OEEC members. It also proposed the possibility of converting drawing rights into dollars.

The aim of ECA was to bring down European prices and costs and to give creditors a stronger incentive to compete with other exporters, including the United States. Debtors should have the possibility of a wider choice for their purchases.

Total transferability, however, might create a situation in which holdings of one currency by another country might be raised above the agreed point and would lead to conversion into gold or dollars.

The second division of aid, described in an earlier section, and the fight over the issue of the revision of the Payments Agreement would throw OEEC into the most serious crisis of its existence.

The British took the lead in the fight against the American objectives. For them, the easing of trade between OEEC countries was a praiseworthy objective, provided there was no risk involved for further dollar losses. The idea of an eventual transferability of drawing rights into dollars was particularly objected to because the British were convinced that the time had not yet come to let American competition in on equal terms. They were still haunted by the convertibility clause of the United Kingdom–United States loan agreement of 1945, with its obligation for sterling convertibility. What made things worse was that the negotiations on the revision of the payments agreement was accompanied by a steady drain on Britain's gold and dollar reserves, which fell below what was considered the danger mark.

The other OEEC countries were, according to their specific economic positions, lining up in the fight which was considered mainly a British-American controversy.

The net debtors favored the American plan, because it gave them a wider choice among suppliers. On the other hand, they had some reason to fear for their exports in a European trade system which was very competitive.

Belgium and Switzerland supported the American plan because they were competitive and relied on the acquisition of additional dollars. Britain was supported by the Scandinavian countries and France was still unsure where the greatest benefits were to be obtained and therefore acted as the author of compromise plans.

The fight in OEEC was interpreted by many in dogmatic terms. The *Neue Zürcher Zeitung* of June 2, 1949, wrote that 'behind the technical questions was the decision whether the European economy was to take a step toward a free-market-oriented structure, or whether it was to remain stuck in the swamp of planned economy measures.' This opinion was more than matched by *The New Statesman and Nation* of July 2, 1949, which wrote: 'Because free enterprise is now the mode in Western Europe, Sir Stafford Cripps has found himself fighting an insular battle for survival, and is naturally accused of sabotaging European unity. His reply must be that Britain refuses point-blank to sacrifice fair shares for all and planned recovery for the sake of unity with the bankers whose policies now dominate Western Europe. For the end result of such European unity would be to destroy the bulwark against communism which it was the whole purpose of Marshall Aid to create.'

There was also a feeling in the United Kingdom Government that the American insistence on transferability was a subtle pressure for devaluation of sterling.

The whole issue tended to become intertwined with problems going far beyond the necessity of making a short-term practical decision on the revision of the scheme.

Countless suggestions were made, and the *Economist* wrote on July 2, 1949, that these displayed a wealth of ingenuity which could usefully have been applied to more constructive and important spheres of economic endeavor.

While these alternative plans were discussed at the expert level, the real negotiations took place between Harriman, Cripps, Spaak, and Petsche in the last week of June 1949, in Brussels. Belgium proposed only a fifty percent transferability, and the French wanted to compromise on a 40–60 basis. It was during this week, that Harriman reluctantly dropped the suggestion for convertibility of drawing rights into dollars and cleared the path for agreement. But Cripps still would not agree. The Americans made it very clear that they would not support a payments plan they could not approve.

Callender wrote in the *New York Times* of July 1, 1949, that never before, not even during the difficult battle over the division of aid, had Harriman and his staff taken such a direct and active part in a decision under the Marshall Plan that the European leaders were obliged to make.

On June 29, 1949, the Council of OEEC met and negotiated for two long days and nights. Early in the morning of July 1, the compromise was found and agreement was reached on the principle of transferability of drawing rights up to twenty-five percent, while a special scheme was accepted for the Belgian position. On July 7, 1949, Hoffman accepted it for ECA.

At that time, however, the exact amount of dollar aid, which was an indispensable element in the determination of drawing rights was not yet established because of the long Congressional debate. It was therefore necessary to continue the terms of the old agreement till September 7, 1949, when the new agreement was signed.[46]

The four main features of the agreement were the partial transferability of drawing rights, the provisions dealing with the special position of Belgium, the provisions intending to make the agreement more flexible than the first agreement and the efforts to overcome the distortion of incentives that had drawn so much criticism.

Three quarters of the drawing rights to which debtor countries were entitled were divided among the contributing countries. These rights were bilateral and not transferable. The remaining twenty-five percent was earmarked for the debtor country but

46. OEEC, *Agreement for Intra-European Payments and Compensations for 1949–1950,* Paris, September 7, 1949.

were not assigned to any particular creditor country. These multilateral drawing rights could be used to finance trade deficits with
any other participating country, with the exception of Switzerland.

Apart from the multilateralization of twenty-five percent of the
drawing rights, the payments agreement contained provisions to
secure a greater flexibility in the course of its term.

A clause was included in which it was stipulated that the OEEC
should carry out comprehensive reviews of the operation of the
agreement at least twice during the year ending June 30, 1950.

ECA felt that these reviews were necessary in order to ensure that
countries did not gain dollars from the pool of drawing rights by
holding down their imports from other European countries.

'It is the Administrations' understanding that the Organization's
periodic review of the working of the Plan will be searching and
that action will be taken to correct defects and weaknesses that may
appear.'[47]

As to the issue of the false incentives of the first agreement a
clause was inserted which stated that creditors were permitted to
complain to OEEC against the abnormal use of the multilateral
drawing rights established in favor of any of its debtors. Debtors
could complain if they were hindered in using their bilateral
drawing rights or if they found their deficits being artificially maintained or increased by the action of another party to the agreement.

The devaluations in the fall of 1949, and other important events
led to very substantial revisions of drawing rights during the term
of the agreement. The French balance of payments position improved dramatically. Germany was running a far larger deficit than
expected.

In general, as the second Report of the OEEC stated, 'one of the
outstanding features of recent months has been a movement towards balance in intra-European trade. France, for example, which
previously has had a deficit with almost every country has in the
second half of 1949, been in overall surplus with the other partici-

47. ECA, *Press Release,* July 8, 1949.

pants. Belgium, whose intra-European surplus had been about twice her dollar deficit, now has a much reduced surplus. The United Kingdom, which previously had been a net exporter to the Continent, has become during the past year a moderate net importer from the other participating countries.'[48]

The movement toward balance meant that drawing rights were able to cover a larger part of the deficits than in the previous year, but above all, it had great importance as a pre-condition for a new and better kind of payments agreement.

Although the second agreement retained the main defects of the first one, it performed a useful and unavoidable function in the process which led to the greatest achievement of European cooperation in that period, the European Payments Union.[49]

Already, during the final phase of the negotiations on the revision of the intra-European payments scheme, there was a widespread feeling in the Economic Cooperation Administration and in OEEC that an entirely new approach to the problem of intra-European payments was necessary and that the payment schemes for 1948/1949 and 1949/1950 should be regarded as merely temporary arrangements on the road to a more basic and lasting solution of the problem. Currency devaluations in the fall of 1949, the trend toward equilibrium in intra-European trade for many participating countries and the new American drive for further European cooperation and integration stimulated this process. There was a growing conviction on both sides of the ocean that arrangements based on estimates of future bilateral payments deficits were far too rigid and that the stimulus of competition was lacking as long as only part of the drawing rights were transferable. There was no real incentive for the debtors and creditors to improve their overall balance of payments position. Finally, it became increasingly clear that the bilateral overtones of the payment agreements till now

48. OEEC, *European Recovery Program, Second Report*, Paris, 1950, p. 18.
49. Diebold analyses the second Payments Agreement in great detail on pp. 64–87 of his study on European Trade and Payments.

had barred a real attack on the removal of quantitative restrictions in intra-European trade. Both ECA and OEEC were rightly considering the problem of intra-European trade and payments as one whole. A payments scheme never should be an end in itself but solely a means to achieve a greater amount of freer trade. As Marjolin wrote:

'The second principle was to link together the efforts to free trade and the efforts to make currencies convertible. What really mattered was that there should be free movement of goods and services. A payments system had to be created which would make it possible for Europe to reach that objective. In other words, the EPU was primarily an instrument for the expansion of trade.'[50]

According to Price, work on this issue within the Economic Cooperation Administration had already begun in the summer of 1949. A working committee of ECA elaborated a proposal in which a clearing union was envisaged, with machinery for full multilateral payments that would obviate the need for bilateral balancing between countries and might be based on a new European currency system, fully backed by gold, but convertible into gold only in case of large multilateral inbalances. Incentives were to be provided for both creditors and debtors.

Richard Bissell of ECA discussed the proposal in Paris, and after his return to Washington, a more formal message was sent to Harriman's office, amending and elaborating the proposal for presentation to the governments of OEEC.[51]

At the same time, OEEC was preoccupied with the problem, and there were constant informal contacts between the experts of ECA, the various Treasury and Central Bank authorities, and the secretariat of OEEC.

On November 2, 1949, the Council of OEEC adopted a resolution regarding further measures of cooperation in response to the above mentioned speech of Hoffman.

50. Robert Marjolin, *Europe and the United States in the World Economy*, (Duke University Press, 1953), pp. 64–65.
51. Price, *op. cit.*, p. 125.

After the decision to adopt the objective of removing quantitative restrictions before December 15, 1949, at latest, on at least fifty percent of their total imports on private account from the other member countries as a group, the Council dealt further with the problem of intra-European payments.

In December 1949, the American proposals were distributed among the member countries of OEEC.

This Draft Working Paper on Intra-European Currency Transferability and Liberalization of Trade of December 9, 1949, stated: 'The participating countries should set into operation before the end of the current program year 1949/50 a system of full intra-European currency transferability providing freedom of intra-European payments on current account, the rapid elimination of quantitative trade restrictions, and the maximum possible freedom of invisible transactions. The system should be so designed as to foster the creation and maintenance of intra-European payments equilibrium. While some volume of ECA dollars in declining amounts may be utilized in the system during the remainder of the ERP period, provision should be made for a gradual and orderly transition to a system ensuring the maintenance of free intra-European payments and unrestricted trade after ECA aid is no longer available.'

The link with the program of liberalization of trade was laid by the following paragraph:

'Achievement of full transferability for current account transactions should eliminate the need among the members for bilateral trade restrictions, all of which should be removed upon the coming into effect of the system of transferability. Remaining quantitative restrictions on trade should be multilateral in character, should be rapidly reduced, and by the end of 1950 should be substantially eliminated. Any other restrictions on current account payments remaining during the ERP period should likewise be progressively reduced and should be on a multilateral basis applied equally to all participating countries.'

In accordance with the emphasis on closer cooperation between smaller groups of countries in the Hoffman speech of October 1949, the working paper stated:

'Arrangements of the kind described below which would be appropriate for all or most of the participating countries and the sterling area are not, of course, inconsistent with closer associations among smaller groups of participating countries which would go much further toward the objective of economic integration. In fact, such developments would mutually strengthen each other.'

The paper then continued with a precise description of the working of the system. It specifically mentioned the use of ECA dollars to back up the system. In a section on administrative adjustments, the paper dealt with the necessity for continuing review and consultation:

'The system should provide for continuing review and consultation on the actual position of each member and the national policies affecting the payments balance, and should provide for recommendations on possible means of restoring equilibrium.

When a member's deficit or surplus position passes beyond some specified percentage of its quota, its position should be specially reviewed. It should be made possible within limits for the clearing union to provide, for appropriate time periods, facilities (perhaps in the form of loans) beyond those established under the automatic operation, on condition that specified remedial action be taken by the country in the form either of modifications of internal economic policies or of exchange rate adjustments, or both. During such limited periods, when the specified remedial measures are taking effect, countries in extreme debtor positions might be authorized to protect their reserves through temporary, multilaterally applied restrictions affecting current payments.'

Finally, it dealt with the institutional aspects:

'Operation of the clearing union along the lines previously described will require continuous guidance by a body of the highest competence. It is suggested that this central guidance be provided by a supervisory board acting within the framework of the OEEC, consisting of permanent representatives of the principal participating countries and rotating representatives of other participating countries. Decisions should not require unanimity.'

There seems to have been a certain controversy between the Treasury and the State Department on one side, and ECA on the other side, whether this concept of a European payments system would not contribute to the formation of a permanent soft-currency area in Western Europe and thus frustrate the long-term objectives of United States foreign economic policy. Would it not conflict with the rules and objectives of the International Monetary Fund? Would it not freeze discrimination against dollar imports and would it not delay and hamper the efforts for full convertibility in some of the participating countries? This fear found its expression in the semi-annual Report to the President and the Congress by the National Advisory Council on International Monetary and Financial Problems, for the period October 1, 1949–March 31, 1950.

'The operation of the proposed EPU should not conflict with obligations undertaken by the United States and other member governments to the International Monetary Fund...The establishment of the Union on the regional basis proposed should not prevent anyone of the participating country or group of participating countries from moving as rapidly as possible toward currency convertibility and economic integration independently of the rate of progress of other members of the proposed Union.'

It was a great disillusion to ECA that OEEC failed to reach agreement on the new plan in its session of late January 1950. The Council approved, instead, a statement of broad principles to be inserted in its Second Report to ECA.[52]

Two points of this elaborate statement should be mentioned.

It contained the elements of the ECA plan but the main area of disagreement was compressed in the sentence that the new system

52.   OECC, Second Report, *op. cit.,* pp. 228–232.

would have to be reconciled with whatever bilateral payments agreements remained in force and with the working of the sterling area.

Months of strenuous negotiations followed. The main obstacle to agreement was the British attitude, this time aggravated by the fact that British elections were to be held in February 1950. The British would not commit themselves on the Payments Union before that crucial date in their political life.

Their basic objection to the agreement was the inclusion of sterling on the same basis as other European currencies, in view of the substantial part sterling played in world trade and other international transactions. They considered continuation of British bilateral payments agreements essential to the continued functioning of the sterling area and to the gradual expansion of multilateral facilities offered within the sterling area. The United Kingdom reaffirmed, that its policy was to extend the area, over which sterling could be used multilaterally, by gradually liberalizing the regulations governing the use of sterling but it refused to accept complete transferability through the new system from one European country to another. It demanded safeguards against interference with its bilateral agreements and against the possibility of supplying gold and dollars to the Union.

After top level negotiations a compromise was reached. Creditor countries of the Union had a right to choose whether they would hold their credits in sterling or in monetary units of the Union.

A special guarantee of $150 million was given to the United Kingdom to cover the contingency of large gold or dollar payments to the new Union.

The British arguments were as usual, to a certain extent, technically and economically valid and they were presented and negotiated with a remarkable administrative and technical skill. But there was an equally remarkable lack of political instinct and sense of direction.

It was as if time and time again the British were unable to grasp the basic trend of events and were blind to the opportunities for giving real political leadership on this side of the Ocean, a leadership everybody was still waiting for.

After having again dealt with specific Belgian difficulties, the Council of OEEC agreed on the terms of EPU on July 7, 1950.

It took a few months to translate these terms into formal documents and to wait for the Congressional appropriations which this time included $500 million solely to support a program for liberalizing trade and payments in Europe.

On August 18, 1950, the Council adopted the Treaty establishing EPU, and the Treaty was formally signed on September 19, 1950.[53]

In view of its importance for the work of OEEC and its role in the development of European cooperation and integration, its complicated contents should be briefly described.

The agreement provided for a fully automatic multilateral system that would permit each participant to offset its deficit with any member against its surplus with other members, so that each country would need to be concerned only with its balance of payments with the rest of Europe as a whole, and not its balance with any single member of the Union.

Each member country was assigned a 'quota' equal to 15 percent of its intra-European exports, imports, and invisible transactions in 1949. The quotas totaled 3950 million units of account – a unit being defined as an amount of gold equal to the current gold content of the American dollar. This aggregate determined the maximum cumulative deficit or surplus which might be financed through the EPU. Six countries which were expected to run deficits in their intra-European trade that could not be covered under the system or repaid in the foreseeable future were given initial credit balances totaling 314 million units of account. Three prospective creditors – the United Kingdom, Belgium-Luxemburg, and Sweden – were assigned initial debit balances totaling 215 million units; these balances represented, in effect, transfers by the prospective surplus

53. Text in *O.E.E.C. Document*, C/M (50) 24, and in O.E.E.C., *A European Payments Union and the Rules of Commercial Policy to be followed by Member Countries*, Paris, 1950.

countries to the EPU, for which they would receive equivalent amounts of 'conditional aid' as part of their ECA dollar allocations. Arrangements were made for the Bank for International Settlements to serve as agent for the EPU in calculating the net surplus or deficit position of each country.

The ECA provided $350 million as an initial working capital fund, since it was probable that gold payments by the Union would exceed those to the Union.

In each monthly clearing operation, the relationship of each country's balance to its respective quota determined the proportion of credit and gold payment required for settlement with the EPU. For both creditors and debtors, the first 20 percent of their quotas involved no transfer of gold. For clearances exceeding this percentage, creditor countries extended to the EPU credits equaling 50 percent of the settlement and received from the Union an equivalent amount in gold. For debtors, the amount of gold required for settlement with the EPU increased on a progressive scale. These arrangements were intended to stimulate member countries to avoid excessive surpluses or deficits and to encourage them to make basic shifts in their production, trade and invisible transactions.

The agreement provided for the establishment of a Managing Board, charged with the supervision of EPU operations. This body consisted of seven members appointed for a one year term by the Council.

A representative of the United States could attend the meetings of the Managing Board with the right to participate in discussions but not in decisions.

Decisions were to be taken by less than unanimity, notably by a majority of at least four of its members.

To follow the history of EPU would be beyond the scope of this book.

In assessing its importance, it should be stated that it made a unique contribution to the expansion of intra-European trade by breaking through the system of bilateral payment agreements. It played an indispensable role in the development of trade liberalization through the large new source of intra-European credit it created.

The EPU strengthened the confrontation techniques developed in OEEC.

The consultations between the Managing Board of EPU and the participating countries became an important element in the conduct of monetary and fiscal policy of the participating countries. They clearly influenced and sometimes even guided these policies.

In launching the idea of EPU and in allocating funds to it, much against the original provisions of the European Recovery Program, the United States was highly instrumental in its creation and functioning.

The original apprehension that EPU would freeze Europe into a permanent soft currency area proved to be incorrect.

On the contrary, the European Payments Union proved to be an indispensable step on the road to total convertibility of the major European currencies.

The EPU helped to re-establish competition in Europe. It developed a sense of collective responsibility for financial stability. It never pretended to be the ultimate goal in the monetary field. That goal could only be total convertibility.

It was, however, an instrument of major importance in the achievement of two objectives, both so warmly supported and stimulated by United States foreign policy, European integration and the full convertibility of currencies.

2. *Liberalization of Trade*

In both the Report of the Committee of European Economic Cooperation of September 1947, and the Convention establishing OEEC, the need for the removal of barriers on trade between the countries of Western Europe was stressed as a main element of European recovery and cooperation.

From the Interim Report of December 1948, it became clear,

however, that there was no agreement on how this should be achieved. The tone of the Report with regard to this problem was cautious if not overcautious.

'The objectives towards which the participating countries intend to move during the coming years are transferability of currencies and the maximum practicable freedom of intra-European trade. But there are a number of steps to be taken before these objectives can be reached. It is indispensable that the recovery of Europe should be built on solid foundations; the participating countries must work together, stage by stage, for it would be disastrous if they were to proceed without sufficient preparation and with undue haste, only to be faced with a precipitate return to chaotic conditions.'

If any criticism can be made of the liberalization program in OEEC, it is certainly not that it was drawn up with undue haste.

The Report mentioned a variety of conditions which had to be fulfilled before intra-European trade could be really liberalized. While these conditions, like suppression of inflation and steps toward balancing the area's dollar accounts, were in themselves not illogical, a word should be said about the concept that a multitude of conditions should be fulfilled before a real liberalization of trade could take place. This approach to the problem is heard in every negotiation about free trade. It has the appearence of economic soundness, but it is basically a typical protectionist argument in defense of the *status quo*.

If too many conditions have to be fulfilled prior to a liberalization of trade, the result will always be that nothing happens at all.

This concept is blind for the effects of trade liberalization itself on the conditions which the protagonists of this school want to fulfil before the liberalization measures are put into effect.

One of the best examples is the history of Benelux. Those in Benelux who at the beginning of its development were reluctant to accept free trade between the three countries used the difference in the balance of payments positions and the difference in wage levels as arguments against removal of trade barriers. What happened, in practice, was that the removal of trade barriers helped to solve both problems.

The first moment OEEC became seriously involved in the trade liberalization issue was in the spring of 1949, when it adopted the Plan of Action mentioned above.

During the negotiations on the payments agreement in June 1949, the British proposed a program for the removal of part of the quantitative restrictions in intra-European trade.

Cripps qualified his plan by stating that removal of quota's should not lead to the loss of gold or dollars. The climate in which Cripps made his proposals was such that the other participating countries were not inclined to believe in his sincerity. There was suspicion that his suggestions were merely a tactical move in the British fight against multilateralization of drawing rights.

The exclusion of state trading in the British approach to the removal of quantative restrictions was a further reason for continental disbelief in Britain's intentions. Nevertheless, the British proposal led to the adoption of a program of liberalization by OEEC at the end of June 1949.

In October 1949, the participating countries had removed quotas on approximately thirty percent of their private trade with each other. The percentages of the different countries varied, however, from eighty percent in Belgium to zero in Greece.

Every country chose the range of products for which quotas were to be removed in such a way that the least harm was done to national interests.

Most of the quantitative restrictions were removed on raw materials and other essential supplies or in fields where quotas did not restrict imports anyhow. There was discrimination between participating countries in the sense that quotas were not removed *vis-à-vis* creditor countries.

It was also in this field that Hoffman's speech of October 1949, worked as a warning and a stimulus.

In the Council meeting of November 2, 1949, the Council of OEEC decided that by December 15, 1949, each member country was to remove quotas on at least fifty percent of its 1948 private imports from the rest of the group. For the first time, the principle was adopted that the percentage of liberalization was to be reached in each major category of imports, *i.e.* food, raw materials and manufactured goods.

A five-man Central Group was appointed to establish equitable standards and to report to the Council on the progress of the program.

The fifty percent exercise could not be considered as a major achievement. Denmark, Germany, Iceland, Norway, and Turkey did not meet the requirements set by the Council and the Central Group. The fifty percent was applied to sectors where little or no resistance could be expected. Even ECA which had the understandable tendency to overemphasize the achievements of OEEC in its relations to Congress, said in its Eighth Report: 'It is now well recognized that the removal of the first fifty percent of import restrictions, once the idea had been accepted, was not too difficult, except for a few countries. Further steps will touch vested interests and will hit the use of import quotas which have been used as protective devices by some countries in lieu of high tariffs and other restricted practices.'[54]

The step from fifty percent to sixty percent liberalization was decided upon in January 1950. It fell again short of American expectations.

Because this step was conditioned on further elaboration of the payments issue, the obligation to remove quotas on sixty percent of trade did not become effective until early October 1950.

Because so many of the impediments to European trade were rooted in currency difficulties, the creation of EPU was of great importance in the development of the intra-European trade scheme.

54.   ECA, *Eighth Report to Congress,* covering the quarter ended March 31, 1950, p. 10.

The OEEC, in endorsing EPU, also laid down objectives and methods in the field of further trade liberalization.

These rules were first adopted in the agreement on EPU, approved by the Council in July 1950, and laid down in the so-called Code of Liberalization, adopted on August 18, 1950. The Code came into effect on September 19, 1950, at the same time as the EPU agreement.

One of its main achievements was that it put an end to discrimination among the OEEC countries.

As soon as EPU came into effect all liberalization measures were to be non-discriminatory.

By the end of 1950, all existing liberalization measures were to be applied equally to imports from all member countries, or else they were to be withdrawn.

After February 1, 1951, all imports from member countries had to be treated equally, whether subject to quota or not. OEEC had to decide what constituted equality in the administration of quotas.

As to the exceptions, there were five main categories:

a. A country could discriminate in its non-liberalized trade against another participating country which was posing to its exports obstacles which frustrated the general objective of liberalization and the development of multilateral trade and which was thus prevented from securing the benefits it could reasonably expect.

b. If a country that had liberalized eighty-five percent or more of its imports found that serious and unnecessary damage was being done to its economy, because its exports of commodities of special importance suffered exceptionally severe consequences from the failure of another country to liberalize imports of these commodities, it could discriminate against the offending country in the importation of products not liberalized.

c. A similar exception was provided for countries with a few staple exports not included in the liberalization measures of other countries.

d. A government could also take measures against dumping.

e. Countries being part of a special customs or monetary system could in addition to carrying out their general obligations in the field of liberalization remove additional quotas in trade between themselves.

The Code specified procedures how exceptions would be agreed upon. If countries could not reach agreement in bilateral negotiations, OEEC procedures, in some cases leading to a decision whether exceptions were justified, were set in motion.

Agreement on these principles marked an important step in Western European economic cooperation. In so far as the principles were applied, they would remove a major element of distortion from intra-European trade. EPU removed the justification for any discrimination on balance of payments grounds but the trade rules went further and called for an end to discrimination on any basis except in the cases sanctioned by the Code.

Diebold concluded:

'In addition to their immediate importance the rules for trade equality, coupled with the EPU gave some meaning to the concept of Western-Europe as a trading area. Discrimination within the group was rejected, at least in principle. By virtue of this decision and those removing quotas, countries in the OEEC assumed certain obligations to other members (and got certain rights against them) that were different from their rights and obligations in dealing with countries outside the organization. Previously each country could treat other members of the OEEC differently; now in important commercial matters it is obliged to treat them all equally.'[55]

On October 27, 1950, the Council of OEEC adopted a resolution which obligated participating countries to liberalize quotas up to seventy-five percent of their private trade with other OEEC countries. In view of the specific agricultural difficulties, the seventy-five percent would apply to total imports and not to the three abovementioned categories. It lasted till the summer of 1951, till substantial progress in this phase could be registered.

55. William Diebold, *op. cit.*, pp. 175–176.

This line of liberalization was pursued until 1955, when ninety percent of the quantitative restrictions were abolished.

Before terminating this section on the liberalization of trade and payments in OEEC, a few specific issues in this field must be briefly mentioned.

In the period that imports were totally subject to a system of quantitative restrictions, the role of tariffs in intra-European trade was negligible.

The notion that quotas were worse trade barriers than tariffs also helped to play down the importance of tariffs.

This notion is true to the extent that tariffs can be overcome by a better cost structure and price, while a quota is a definite barrier.

Tariffs still permit some link between foreign and domestic prices. Quotas cut that link.

The difference, however, must not be exaggerated. Tariffs can be prohibitive, and there is certainly no economic foundation for the view, which at that time in Europe prevailed in some quarters, that when quantitative restrictions were abolished, something like a 'single market' would be already achieved. Nevertheless, the quantitative restrictions were the logical field wherein to start the process of trade liberalization in Western Europe but gradually it became clear that the more successful OEEC was in the elimination of quantitative restrictions the more tariffs became the main obstacle, not only to freer trade but to a real integration effort in Europe.

It would be beyond the scope of this book to go into details of the continuous attempts to bring the issue of lowering tariff walls into the program of OEEC. It was natural that this attempt was mainly made by those participating countries which had a relatively low tariff structure. They stood to lose most by eliminating quantitative restrictions when other member countries abandoned their quotas but retained their high tariff walls.

OEEC did not go further than recognizing that the problem existed, which it had already registered in the CEEC report of 1947.

It is beyond doubt that the failure of OEEC to bring the lowering of tariff walls within its orbit would have grave consequences for the future of European cooperation and integration in the wider Western European framework. It also is indisputable that the main reason for this failure was the policy pursued by the United Kingdom.

It should, however, also be noted that the attitude of the United States Government towards this problem was not very clear. The United States was torn between the universalist economic policy for global trade liberalization and the support for regional cooperation.

American pressure and initiative, so dominant in practically all efforts for greater European cooperation and integration, was practically non-existent in the attempts to bring OEEC to deal with the tariff problem. In this case, British reluctance was not compensated or overcompensated by American firmness.

This American attitude was already expressed by Clayton during the Paris Conference, when he made it clear that the creation of preferential tariff groups, without a definite undertaking to form a customs union, would not be in agreement with principles of American foreign economic policy.

The main power of making decisions in economic policy towards Europe was vested in the Economic Cooperation Administration. On this point, however, the more global and universalist attitude of the Treasury and parts of the State Department, notably the priority they gave to GATT and other world wide solutions, could not be overcome by the more 'regionalist' approach of ECA.

The priority of GATT in the tariff field had always been a keystone of British economic policy as well. The decision to take special action in OEEC in the tariff field could, according to their view, only be made if reductions of intra-European tariffs formed a phase in the establishment of a customs union. Britain was not willing to consider such a course for reasons already explained in a previous chapter.

The British attitude could be summarized as follows: No preferential tariff arrangement without the prospect of a customs union and no customs union because of the Commonwealth preferences.

Gaitskell said in the House of Commons on November 16, 1950: 'The question of tariffs affects a much wider area than the European Payments Union area...it is no use to deal with it in the European framework alone. That is the line we have always adopted in OEEC and on the whole, I think it has been accepted.'[56]

This last sentence of Gaitskell's remarks proved to be a wrong assessment of the feeling of many other European countries. The British view was not only not accepted, it was bitterly resented as a proof of the negative British attitude towards a basic problem of European integration. There was at that time a real problem of reconciling the provisions of GATT with a preferential tariff system in Western Europe. With American aid and British political backing, however, a solution for this dilemma could have been found.

The process of integration between the six countries of continental Europe, which were going to form the Coal and Steel Community and the Common Market had very strong political overtones and motivations. In the purely economic sphere, the split in Europe, one of the most harmful developments in the post-war era, was partly due to the refusal of the United Kingdom to deal seriously with the tariff problem in OEEC.

Another specific issue is the history of the Customs Union Study Group mentioned in Chapter II.

It can best be characterized by Diebold's description that it has been pretty much a backwater of European economic cooperation.[57]

While it did some useful work on nomenclature and valuation, both preliminaries to the eventual formation of a Western European customs union, the formation of such a union could only spring from the political will of the participating countries. This will was lacking. The Study Group whose establishment, at the

56. *The Times,* November 17, 1950.
57. William Diebold, *op. cit.,* p. 317.

time of the Paris Report of 1947, was hailed as a token of the positive attitude of the European countries towards European cooperation and integration, was apart from some technical achievements condemned to sterility.

A third specific issue is the formation of smaller units in the field of European cooperation.

In his speech of October 1949, Hoffman emphasized the possibility of the so called 'sub-regional' approach.

After launching the idea of the smaller groups within OEEC, he tempered it with the caution that it seemed absolutely essential to him that arrangements arrived at within groups of two, three, or more countries should be in harmony with wider possibilities of European unity and should, under no circumstances, involve the raising of new or higher barriers to trade in Europe than already existed.

In a further paragraph, he stressed that the broader objectives of economic integration of all the participating countries should not prevent efforts towards establishment of close economic arrangements within one or more smaller groups of countries.

Before the Common Market came into being, only the Benelux achievements were a real step forward in the sub-regional field of closer economic cooperation.

In general Benelux is underestimated in the literature on European cooperation. Perfect economic union was not achieved mainly because of difficulties in the agricultural sector. But the fact that three countries established a full customs union with a near perfect common tariff, a near total free circulation of goods between them, and a joint foreign economic policy operated by mixed delegations in trade negotiations, should be considered as a major achievement in the field of European cooperation and integration.

Its development is now overtaken by the dynamism of the Common Market. But in the early hours of post-war European cooperation, the Benelux development stood out as an imaginative and bold undertaking.

The same cannot be said of the plans to form a Scandinavian customs union between Norway, Sweden, and Denmark, and the French-Italian customs union, both announced in the Paris Report of September 1947.

Negotiations between France and Italy led to a treaty which was signed in Paris on March 26, 1949, but was never ratified by either parliaments. Negotiations on the European Payments Union and subsequent developments in the integration effort of the six European countries overtook its eventual development.

While special cooperation and consultation between the Scandinavian countries was and still is a permanent feature of the European scene, this did not lead to the formation of a customs union. The plans for a Nordic Union were overtaken by the Free Trade Area discussions.

Efforts to bring about closer cooperation between France, Italy, and the Benelux countries were a permanent and major objective of French foreign and foreign economic policy.

As was mentioned above, the efforts to reach such agreement were already apparent in the French attitude during the Paris Conference in 1947. The proposed customs union between France and Italy was always considered, especially by the French, as a step toward a construction among the five countries, a construction which would find its place in post-war European economic history under the unfortunate name of Fritalux or Finebel.

The resentment against the lack of consultation prior to the devaluation of sterling[58] and the Hoffman speech of October 1949, gave a new impetus to these plans.

The French pressed for a further liberalization among the five countries than in the larger OEEC framework and a higher degree of convertibility of their currencies, assisted by some kind of central monetary fund.

There is no question that these French thoughts were more mo-

58. There is a legitimate question whether devaluation of a currency can be effected otherwise than in the strictest secrecy.

tivated by the political desire to lead a continental European grouping than by an urgent desire for a really liberal economic policy.

It was mainly Dutch resistance which delayed action on this plan. This resistance sprang generally from a basic lack of confidence in the French intentions. In the beginning, the Dutch insisted very much on inclusion of the United Kingdom in any scheme of closer European cooperation and integration. When it became clear that the desire for British participation was not answered on the other side of the Channel, Dutch insistence centered on the inclusion of Germany.

In a remarkable set of conversations in Paris, during December 1949, a compromise between the French and Dutch points was materializing. While negotiations should take place between France, Italy and the Benelux countries because French public opinion would not accept direct participation of Germany, it was agreed that putting eventual agreement into operation would wait till Germany could be included.

Before any definite commitments could be made, the negotiations for the European Payments Union and the launching of the Schuman Plan overtook the developments towards a Finebel-Fritalux construction.

Three plans, which also were overtaken by subsequent developments, should finally be mentioned, the Stikker, Pella and Petsche plans.

Two features of the Stikker Plan are worth mentioning because for the first time two ideas were launched which would be instrumental in the further efforts for European integration.

One was the sector approach of integration which was accepted in the Schuman Plan leading to the Coal and Steel Community.

The other was the notion that total liberalization of trade, which took away from national governments the traditional weapons of economic defense, should be accompanied by measures which would compensate for the eventual harm done to certain economic activities in the participating countries.

This notion was also accepted in the philosophy of the Coal and Steel Community and the Common Market.

In conclusion, it must be said that it was especially in the field of trade liberalization that the limitations and weaknesses of OEEC have been most apparent.

G. CONCLUSION

What has been achieved under the European Recovery Program and notably in the field of European cooperation and integration, sprang from American initiative and assistance. From the moment of the launching of the Marshall Plan, it became apparent that European integration was a major objective of American foreign policy. In 1947, American foreign policy pursued the objective of an integrated community of free nations, economically and politically strong enough to resist 'piecemeal or wholesale absorption by the Soviet Union'.[59] It pursued this aim primarily within the framework of its stand against communist aggression. Gradually, European integration became an objective which American foreign policy tried to achieve for its own sake. While the aims and objectives of the European Recovery Program were confined to the field of economic integration, there was always a strong political element in the United States concept of European integration.

Its main origin was the widely held view in the United States and among the average citizen that the principles of the United States Constitution, which had been so successful in solving economic and political problems on their own continent, should likewise be applied to Western Europe.

However imperfect the analogy may be, the argument contains an instinctive feeling or intuitive judgment that concerted action and some form of integration was essential to cure European ills.

59. *Major Problems of United States Foreign Policy 1949–1950,* (Washington, D.C.: The Brookings Institution, 1949), p. 406.

This instinctive feeling was best expressed in the continuous efforts of Congress to make the objective of greater European unification a condition for American assistance. In trying to assess the success of American efforts in this field, two things should be kept in mind.

The first is that, while there can be no disagreement on the basic objective of American foreign policy, the notion of European integration had been neither really thought through nor clearly defined.

It ranged from ideas like federal union, European federation, the United States of Europe, confederation, customs union, an integrated four-year recovery program, the concept of the single market, investment coordination and integrated planning to very practical measures of trade liberalization and payments agreements.

The only common denominator of all these ideas was the conviction that in Europe the nation state was too small a unit to solve the economic and political problems with which the Western world was confronted and that joint action was imperative. The precise form of joint action, however, remained undefined in the formulation of American policy.

The second element to be noted was the strong conviction on the other side of the Atlantic Ocean, that in making European cooperation and integration a vital objective in its foreign policy, the initiative as to how this integration should be achieved was primarily a European responsibility. While there was American pressure on specific points in the execution of the Marshall Plan, it was a basic feature of American policy to consider the promotion of unity and integration a matter for the Europeans themselves.

The concept of 'friendly aid' from the speech of Secretary Marshall remained predominant in American thinking.

The most immediate needs in the first phase of the European Recovery Program were the restoration of basic industrial and agricultural production and the creation of internal financial stability, both primarily national problems. Very soon, however, European economic integration became a major objective of American policy in the framework of the European Recovery Program. The attempt to create an integrated four-year program failed in the beginning of 1949. Thereafter, the most concrete form to the idea of European integration was given in the Hoffman speech of October 1949.

Lincoln Gordon writes about this phase:

'It should be noted that even at this stage there was no overt appeal for supranationality or federation. There should also be noted the distinction drawn between the short run goal of abolishing quantitative restrictions and monetary barriers and the eventual goal of a European customs union.'[60]

At that time, it became clear that the most concrete form the United States was going to give to its notion of European integration was the concept of the single market as formulated by Hoffman.

'Obviously the greatest single contribution the ECA would make to Europe's enduring prosperity was to help it toward economic integration. I wish I could say that this has been done, that as a result of ECA activities all sections of the European economy have been welded into a single market as unencumbered by trade impediments as our own American market. Unfortunately that is not true. Europe is still plagued with tariffs, which slow down the exchange of goods and services among the countries. Nevertheless enough progress has been made to enable me to say definitely that the trend toward autarchy has been reversed.'[61]

With his speech in October 1949, the stage was set for the two major accomplishments of OEEC since 1950, the abolishment of quantitative restrictions to trade and the mutual convertibility of European currencies.

At the same time, it must be said that OEEC's intra-European trade and payments program fell short of the common or single market ideal for which Hoffman had appealed. Achievement and limitation of OEEC was determined by this program.

---

60. Lincoln Gordon, 'Myth and Reality of European Integration', in *Yale Review*, Volume 45, September, 1950, pp. 80–103.
61. Paul G. Hoffman, *op. cit.*, p. 125.

The achievements of the European Recovery Program and OEEC for European cooperation and integration were judged with rather negative conclusions by a number of observers.

Spinelli wrote for example: 'The money which the Americans thought they were going to help the Europeans to overcome economic nationalism served only to reconstitute the old national economies instead of creating one market and one European economy.'[62]

Florinsky said, in analyzing the results of ERP and OEEC: 'Their greatest achievement is the allocation of American aid, which powerfully contributed to the economic rehabilitation of Europe. Yet, granted that the OEEC and the EPU have performed and are performing useful functions, it would be unreasonable to claim that they have brought appreciably nearer the economic integration of Europe as defined earlier in this chapter.'[63]

Rostow, in discussing the limits and achievements of the Marshall Plan, acknowledges the fact that the concept of unity was advanced by the Marshall Plan experience but says: 'On the American side initial thought about how to use the Marshall Plan as an instrument for European unity was relatively shallow. The European Recovery Plan presented at the end of the summer of 1947 was, at American insistence, overlaid with pious but not profoundly felt statements of intent to proceed with customs unions and other enterprises looking toward European unity. The one serious common function allocated to the OEEC in the first instance was the responsibility for making a united allocation of American funds; and even though the allocation of other people's resources is the easiest issue on which to get international agreement, the United States had to take an increasing hand even in that process as time went on. On the whole therefore – because the British opposed it, because the economic

62. A. Spinelli, 'The Growth of the European Movement since World War II', in *European Integration,* ed. by C. Grove Haines, (Baltimore: The Johns Hopkins Press, 1957), p. 54.

63. Michael T. Florinsky, *Integrated Europe,* (New York: The Macmillan Company, 1955), p. 56.

requirements of unity did not converge with requirements for prompt recovery, and because the United States was unclear as to how its influence should be applied – the Marshall Plan did not succeed in moving Western Europe radically towards unity.'[64]

Schmitt states: 'As long as the governments remained sole masters of their economies, one danger would be tackled by sixteen unrelated partial cures. The fact remained that after lip services had been paid to the truth of international economic inter-dependence, each nation returned to the assiduous fattening of domestic herd ... But the intimate union of economies which had been expected on both sides of the Ocean, had not materialized under the OEEC.'[65]

And Ernst Haas, in his momentous study about the process of the uniting of Europe, concludes:

'Apart from its initial activity in "slicing up the pie" of Marshall Plan funds amongst the sixteen recepient countries, the basic fact concerning OEEC activity is its failure to contribute to long-term integration.'[66]

Ellis follows a different line in his critical remarks, because much more than the previous authors, he stressed the point that European cooperation and integration would not solve Europe's problems, unless its economic relations with the rest of the world could be greatly improved.

Unless this happens, 'Western Europe is in danger of becoming an inefficient economic entity, a high cost area chronically dependent on subsidies from the rest of the world to maintain its standard of living. This could happen with or without the integration of Europe; integration alone cannot prevent it.'

This conclusion was preceded by the author's opinion that there was a danger that cooperation would become an uncritical catchall.

'What action is likely to produce the best result in each set of

64. W. W. Rostow, *op. cit.*, p. 216.
65. Hans A. Schmitt, *op. cit.*, pp. 28–30.
66. Ernst B. Haas, *The Uniting of Europe,* (London: Stevens & Sons Ltd., 1958), p. 520.

circumstances, fits no simple formula. Not all cooperation is good cooperation.'[67]

This study concludes with a more positive evaluation of the work done by OEEC and the impact of the European Recovery Program on European integration. As to the above mentioned opinions about the inadequacy of American policy, it is true that American ideas about the necessity for European cooperation and integration lacked precision and were often based more on political and economic instinct than on a balanced and matured analysis of what was possible and attainable in a limited period of time.

It is equally true that the emphasis on specific forms of cooperation and integration changed many times during the four years of the European Recovery Program.

But given the fact that there was a definite reluctance on the American side to enforce solutions which were not acceptable to all or some of the major participants in the European Recovery Program, tribute should be paid to the policy of the United States Government and especially to ECA for its permanent and imaginative stimulation of various forms of European cooperation and integration.

What may be challenged, however, is the American reluctance to use the dollar aid of the European Recovery Program to impose measures of cooperation and integration in Europe, a move for which the European situation rightly or wrongly (and in some important cases wrongly) was not yet considered ripe by some of the European countries.

In evaluating this reluctance, the conclusion must be that on balance it was a wise policy.

In dealing with sovereign states, even if these states are impoverished and politically and economically impotent, as was the case in Europe during the first years of the Marshall Plan, there is a limit beyond which even a country of the unique power of the United

67. Howard S. Ellis, op. cit., pp. 444–445.

States cannot go in imposing far-reaching measures such as those leading to European integration. A viable integration cannot be imposed externally, because the essence of its viability is the will of the people primarily involved. Perhaps on points of detail a certain criticism is justified regarding the use the United States made of its power to use dollar aid as an instrument to stimulate European co-operation and integration. However, the basic policy decision not to impose far-reaching measures was an admirable act of stateman-ship of the United States Administration and it was even more admirable in the light of the constant and persistent Congressional pressures.

As far as the critical judgment concerns the results of OEEC it-self, those whose judgment on balance is more positive than what was quoted above, deserve attention and agreement.

Not closing their eyes for the serious limitations and missed oppor-tunities during the first years of OEEC, Price, Diebold, Marjolin, and Lincoln Gordon attach great importance to the achievement of OEEC in the process of European cooperation and integra-tion.[68]

OEEC lacked the authority of a unified, central institution with directive and decisive powers. It failed to coordinate investments and to siphon funds to European underdeveloped areas and to modernization of industries on a continental scale. It failed also to take decisive steps to form an irrevocable single market, were it only for its impotence to deal with the important problem of tariffs.

But it brought intra-European economic cooperation to an un-precedented level in an extremely short span of time.

It should not be forgotten that a start had to be made in a situation

68. Price, *op. cit.,* p. 356 and pp. 406–412.
Marjolin, *op. cit.,* pp. 40–59.
William Diebold, Jr., 'The Process of European Integration', in *Current History,* Vol. 42, March, 1962, p. 130.
Lincoln Gordon, 'Myth and Reality in European Integration', *op. cit.,* and 'The Organization for European Economic Cooperation', *op. cit.*

in which impoverished, war-stricken countries, with a very strong tradition of complete economic sovereignty, were brought together, not because their economies were complimentary but solely because they belonged to the part of the world which cherished freedom and democracy.

In judging the achievement of OEEC, its work should not be considered as a final step. The positive judgment grows when it is recognized that its accomplishment paved the way for what was to follow in the field of European integration and cooperation.

Should a unified Europe emerge as the result of a long historical process, the Marshall Plan and the work of OEEC have made an indispensable contribution, even if the immediate results of their work were disappointing against the light of initial expectations.

While the European Payments Union eased the way for European integration and, at the same time, was a most important step on the road to full convertibility of currencies, the trade liberalization program, limited in scope and execution, was a vital link in the chain of events leading to the Common Market.

As already was indicated in previous sections, great importance should be attached to the fact that through the exercise of the division of aid, the examination of the annual programs and the working of the restricted groups like the Managing Board and the Steering Board for Trade, national policies and performance were exposed to close criticism from other countries and from the Secretariat. These confrontations were instrumental in making the practice of economic cooperation a reality in European life. They developed and stimulated a sense of common interest and standards.

Eric Roll, who played such an important part in this field, wrote in the April 1958 issue of *Lloyds Bank Review*:

'The technique of the questionnaire and the mutual analysis of replies, the crossexamination of one's expectations and plans by one's peers, have had a powerful effect in moulding national policies. At the very least, they have created a general readiness to "look over one's shoulder" before taking any major step in economic policy, of asking what consequences it might have for one's partners, and how any adverse results might be mitigated. Subtler in its working, often as powerful, and sometimes even more so, than more rigorous constitutional obligations, this habit of consultation and cooperation has resulted in a real limitation of national sovereignty in economic matters.

The thousands of European officials, involved in the work of Marshall Plan and OEEC, became extremely sophisticated in the problems of each other's economies and politics. They began to think in European terms.'

The practice of confrontation of national policies and the procedures which were developed during that process cannot be overestimated for its importance to further developments in European integration.

Finally, in assessing the importance of this period, one fact of major importance should be mentioned. It was in the framework of the European Recovery Program and OEEC that Germany was brought back as a partner at the conference table of Western Europe.

On October 31, 1949, the delegates of the Federal Republic of Germany took their place in the Council of OEEC. This process took place without undue political tension.

The problem of Germany has formed since 1947 a major, if not the major, element in the policy of the United States toward the process of European cooperation and integration. In assessing the importance of the Marshall Plan and OEEC, the fact that Germany, for the first time since the war, took part in the councils of Western Europe should get all the attention it deserves.

The fact that, in spite of all these major accomplishments, OEEC has not lived up to many hopes and expectations is partly due to the intrinsic difficulty of bringing together seventeen war-stricken, economically and politically widely different sovereign nations in a very limited period of time, but is also, to a great extent, due to the attitudes and policies of member countries.

The United Kingdom and France both bear a great share of responsibility.

In France, it was not so much a lack of imagination and genuine desire for further integration as the basic political instability and economic weakness which went a long way in excluding energetic collective measures. And where the imagination and desire for further integration was present, it did not inspire enough confidence because of the suspicion that the French tended to subordinate the ideals of integration to a desire to play a dominant role on the continent of Europe.

As for the United Kingdom, it gave to OEEC a highly valuable contribution in administrative skill. Without the contribution of the British Civil Service, OEEC would never have been able to meet successfully the immense task with which it was faced.

In the field of policy, however, no single fact has been so harmful to the possibility of the development of OEEC as an instrument for integration as the British refusal to commit itself to full partnership with the continent of Europe.

Lack of imagination, the desire to single itself out in a special relationship to the United States, the obsession with the idea that more loyalty to Europe would mean less loyalty to the Commonwealth, and the high priority the Labor government gave to an undisturbed domestic economic planning prevented the United Kingdom from playing the role that only Britain, in this field, could have played. It was the role to lead the European nations into a real effort for economic integration.

There are many extenuating circumstances for this attitude. Acquittal, however, is not possible.

The work of OEEC will again be mentioned in the next part of this study when its role during the negotiations in the Free Trade Area and its conversion into the Organization for Economic Cooperation and Development will be discussed.

Until that moment, it led a relatively quiet life, mostly concentrating on the refining of the rules for the liberalization of trade and payments. Military cooperation and above all the emergence of the Europe of the Six replaced it on the stage of Western cooperation.

Price's final verdict is that if integration is defined as synonymous with unification, OEEC did not realize it. But if integration is understood to mean a dynamic process of joint efforts to deal with joint problems then OEEC was instrumental in bringing this new reality to the European scene.

There is every reason to share this judgment.

CHAPTER IV

United States Policy towards Europe until the Rejection of the European Defense Community (1950–1954)

As has already been explained, there were specific reasons for following chronologically the development of United States policy towards European cooperation and integration during the emergence of the Marshall Plan and the first years of OEEC.

The following part of this study deals with the period starting in 1950, the year in which the Schuman initiative leading to the European Coal and Steel Community was taken and the war in Korea brought about a much more pronounced emphasis on the strengthening of the defense of Western Europe.

Until now an attempt was made to follow American actions and reactions to the process of European cooperation and integration, not only on a chronological basis, but also to give a description which was as complete as possible.

In both aspects the structure of the second half of this study will be different.

There will of course be some chronological system but the emphasis will be much more on a topical approach. There will be fewer facts and more emphasis on trends.

In view of the vastness of the subject, the complexity of the problems, the mountains of published material and of the fact that many documents, relevant to the study are not yet available for publication, completeness will not be attempted.

In selecting trends and subjects, one runs the risk of neglecting developments and policies which for an ultimate judgment of the period might be highly relevant. If, for example, developments in NATO are dealt with rather briefly, this in no way means that either NATO as an instrument of Western cooperation is under-estimated or that United States policy towards NATO is not linked in the closest possible way to the problem of its policy to-wards European cooperation and integration.

For the above mentioned reasons, to which should be added the necessity of limitation of a study of this kind, a selection should be made, in the hope that it will be adequate for following the main trends of United States foreign policy towards Europe in the period under review.

A. THE UNITED STATES AND THE SCHUMAN PLAN

Approximately at the time of the signing of the European Payments Union, the crowning achievement of OEEC, this organization ceased to be the major object of American foreign policy towards European cooperation and integration. Two major developments brought about a change in American policy towards Europe.

One was the Schuman initiative of May 1950, with its immense consequences for the cause of European unification. The other was the Korean war which brought to a definite end the priority of economic recovery in Europe as an objective of American foreign policy. It added to this policy, as an equally and even more impor-tant aim, the further strengthening of the defense of America's European partners and the necessity of a German defense contri-bution.

In the first chapter of this study, it was mentioned how strongly the development of European cooperation and integration was due to American initiative. There was no question of imposing upon the European countries a certain particular structure of unification, but there was a persistent effort to use the Marshall Plan as an in-strument for closer European cooperation and integration.

This by no means implies that European unity was exclusively an

American concern. Broad sections of European official and non-official opinion and activities were concentrated on the same aims and objectives.

This study deals with the American side of the process of European unity and it would be beyond its scope to describe the development of the ideas about European unity in Europe itself.

Amongst other things these European endeavors led to the creation of the Western Union Treaty in March 1948, and the signing of the statute of the Council of Europe in May 1949. Behind these formal expressions and results, there was a growing and deeply felt conviction in Europe that the period of the supremacy of the nation-state was over. The discussion about the new organization of Europe occupied the minds of uncounted Europeans.[1]

To abstain from describing these developments does not intend to underestimate their importance nor to suggest that they had no vital bearing upon the emergence of the new forms of European organization.

Up till 1950, however, with the exception of the creation of the Council of Europe and Benelux, there was a causal link between American foreign policy and the concrete and practical forms of European cooperation and integration. Power and initiative for shaping the Western world were, for all practical purposes, vested in America. While the monopoly of power remained on the American

1. There is a mass of literature about these early years of the movement to greater European unity. See amongst many other studies:
    'Political and Economic Planning', in *European Organizations, op. cit.*
    Richard Mayne, *The Community of Europe, op. cit.*
    Ben T. Moore, *NATO and the Future of Europe,* (New York: Harper & Brothers, 1958).
    Mary Margaret Ball, *NATO and the European Union Movement,* (London: Stevens & Sons, Ltd., 1959).
    Arnold J. Zurcher, *The Struggle to Unite Europe 1940–1958,* (N.Y. University Press, 1958).
    Hans A. Schmitt, *op. cit.*
    F. S. C. Northrop, *European Union and United States Foreign Policy,* (New York: The Macmillan Company, 1954).

side of the Ocean, with the announcement of the Schuman Plan, the initiative for a concrete and major step on the road to European unity shifted to Europe.

The Schuman Plan was the result of European initiative. Amongst the many reasons for the strong and unequivocal support it received from the United States, not the least was the feeling that at last the policy which aimed at European responsibility for the organization of Europe began to bear fruit.

The main elements of the Schuman Declaration in May 1950, were particularly suited to gain full American support.[2]

The major motives for American stimulation of European integration corresponded with the key elements of the Schuman announcement. The statement first said: 'The movement of coal and steel between member countries will immediatedly be freed of all customs duty; it will not be permissible to set up differential transport rates for them. Conditions will gradually be created which will spontaneously provide for the more rational distribution of production at the highest level of productivity. The proposed organization – in contrast to international cartels, which tend to impose restrictive practices on distribution and the exploitation of national markets and to maintain high profits – will ensure the fusion of markets and the expansion of production.'

This idea directly corresponded with one of the main objectives of the Marshall Plan – the creation of a single market. The fact that this single market was confined to only two major products did not prevent the United States from considering this part as a direct response to American policy followed during the first years of the Marshall Plan and based on the firm belief that the full economic potentialities of Europe could only be developed on the basis of a spacious and highly competitive market.

In the preceding section, we have seen that this strong American

2.   Text in *Documents on American Foreign Relations,* (Princeton University Press, 1951), Vol. XII, p. 85.

belief found its major expression in the October 1949 speech of
Paul Hoffman before the Council of OEEC.

This does not mean, however, that the American Administration
in general and the Economic Cooperation Administration in
particular had anything in mind that should lead to the precise
form of the Schuman declaration. Lincoln Gordon wrote:

'It will be noted that even at this stage there was no direct appeal
for supranationality or federation. There should also be noted the
distinction drawn between the short run goal of abolishing quantitative restrictions and monetary barriers and the "eventual" goal
of a European customs union.'[3]

Indeed, the American Administration thought in terms of liberalization of trade and payments. It is significant that when the
Schuman Plan was first mentioned in the official report of the
ECA to Congress, it formed a subsection of the chapter Liberalization of intra-European Trade.[4]

Paul Hoffman confirmed this opinion in an article in the *New York
Times Magazine* of May 21, 1950, in which he wrote about
Schuman: 'He, a European, goes much further than any American
would have dared to propose at this time.'

There is no question that part of the Schuman Declaration was
understood in the United States as a contribution toward the eventual realization of a single European market.

There neither is any doubt that what had been achieved in OEEC
cooperation, laid important economic foundations on which structures like the Schuman Plan could be built. Delouvrier wrote:

'If the system of the European Payments Union which was built
up through the efforts of the OEEC, had not existed, I do not know
how the ECSC could have worked properly. On the other hand,
the OEEC, in developing the liberalization of trade, in having the
quota system abandoned, made it possible for the ECSC to work,

3. Lincoln Gordon, 'Myth and Reality in European Integration', in *Yale
    Review*, Vol. 45, no. 1, Sept. 1955.
4. Economic Cooperation Administration, *Ninth Report to Congress for the
    Quarter ended June 30, 1950*, (Washington D.C., 1950).

and prevented its irrational nature – in having cut off coal and steel from everything else – from giving rise to difficulties of too serious a nature.[5]

But many other factors were involved which prompted the United States to welcome, wholeheartedly, the Schuman initiative. Its positive attitude was only motivated in part by the policy in favor of the economic unification of Europe, in the sense of a common European market.[6]

The Schuman Declaration continued:

'In taking upon herself for more than twenty years the role of champion of a United Europe, France has always had as her essential aim the service of peace. A united Europe was not achieved and we had war... The gathering together of the nations of Europe requires the elimination of the age-old opposition of France and Germany... The solidarity in production thus established will make it plain that any war between France and Germany becomes not merely unthinkable, but materially impossible.'

These key sentences from the Schuman Declaration corresponded with the political preoccupation of the United States Government with the problems both of Germany itself and the relation of Germany to the issue of European integration. As was mentioned in the first chapters of this study, it was already apparent in the beginning of 1947, that the notion that the German problem could not be solved outside the framework of a stronger European structure, became a cornerstone of the European policy of the United States.

In 1963, former Secretary of State Dean Acheson summarized this permanent factor in United States foreign policy in a speech at the

5. Paul Delouvrier, 'Problems and Possibilities in European Integration', in *European Integration,* ed. by C. Grove Haines, (Baltimore: The Johns Hopkins Press, 1957), p. 117.
6. Milton Katz, 'The Community of Europe and American policy', in *The United States and the Western Community,* ed. by H. Field Havilland, Jr., (Haverford College Press, 1957), p. 7.

University of Connecticut: 'My thesis is that in making political and military judgments affecting Europe a major – often the major – consideration should be their effect on the German people and the German Government...

The reason for urging this priority can be stated briefly. Germany is the point of contact between the Atlantic Alliance and the Soviet Bloc. The division of Germany and the continued occupation of Eastern Germany by Soviet troops... is for the purpose of bringing all Germany under Soviet influence. Such a result would... make Russia's will dominant in Europe...

Germany's geographical position and strength make that country indispensable to the existence of both a united Europe and a European defense. Germany has surpassed all other large European countries in steadfast support of the principles and institutions of a united Europe...

Germany is the most sensitive and responsive of all European countries to American actions, whether or not we wish it, and for good or ill...

Germany not only is the most sensitive of the large countries, and reacts more vigorously to American action, but Germany's reactions are important, far-reaching and decisive. The other large countries either do not reach, or reach less, or their reactions have less effect than Germany's.'[7]

And in a speech on the objectives of American policy towards European unity and Atlantic Partnership at the University of Dayton, on September 18, 1963, W. W. Rostow, Counselor and Chairman of the Policy Planning Staff, said:

'Germany is located astride the balance of power in Europe. It represents a critically important area, population and concentration of resources between the East and the West.'[8]

To all these rational factors should be added a less rational one, the undeniable natural affinity between large segments of American public opinion and the German people. In looking towards the

7. *The New York Times Magazine*, December 21, 1963.
8. Department of State, *Press Release*, No. 475, Sept. 17, 1963.

different European powers, many Americans are greatly impressed by the energy, industry and hard working efficiency of the German people, even to a point where other allies of the United States wonder whether too much concentration on Germany could not lead to a certain lack of balance in American policy.

The above mentioned quotations of Acheson and Rostow do not imply that in the beginning of 1950, all these elements were clearly established as American policy.

There is some truth in Beloff's statement that 'it was not at this time possible to say that the Americans had a coherent German policy.'[9]

Nevertheless, the basic elements of United States policy towards the German problem gradually emerged. The United States had a direct if partial responsibility for the domestic and foreign policy of the West-German State. A decision to make Germany a viable entity was not only pressed by the American occupation authorities under the powerful and vigorous leadership of General Clay but was also desired by Congress in order to lessen the financial burden of the American engagement in Europe. The East-West struggle for political control of Germany and the wish to avoid any authoritarian political tendencies there, led with the aforementioned factors to the objective of the establishment of a viable German entity and the restoration of German sovereignty in a larger European framework. In this respect nothing could fit American policy better than the initiative of the French Foreign Minister.

The element of Franco-German rapprochement in Schumans declaration was also particulary welcome to the policy makers in Washington. A Congressional Staff study[10] stated:

'The U.S. Government, although it played no direct role in the conception and establishment of the ECSC, has on the whole

9.   Max Beloff, op. cit., p. 54.
10.   U.S. Foreign Policy: Western Europe, a Study prepared at the request of the Committee on Foreign Relations U.S. Senate by the Foreign Policy Research Institute of Pennsylvania, October 15, 1959.

regarded it favorably from the beginning, particularly because it
fostered Franco-German cooperation.'

In a conference, at Haverford College, during the spring of 1956,
former United States Special Representative in Europe, Milton
Katz, that wise and experienced observer of the European scene,
said:

'I would go further and say, if France and Germany really wanted
Franco-German unity, then, apart from the special range of problems which we touched on when we spoke of the possible conflicts
about German unification, that would be the kind of unity which
could be harmonized reasonably easily within the larger scope of
American policy. To me the European Coal and Steel Community
...is primarily significant as a means for bringing about Franco-
German unity.'[11]

There was a widespread realization in the United States that twice
in this century it had gone to war, costly in human lives and financial resources because of intra-European rivalry, mainly caused by
Franco-German antagonism.

American policy towards a speedy restoration of German viability
and sovereignty was slowed down and often prevented by French
distrust of Germany, French apprehensions of the growing political
and economic effectiveness of the emerging new West-German
State and French insistence on the priority of reparations and security guarantees.

The Saar problem also remained one of the stumbling blocks for
any real European solution.

There was a strong feeling in the United States that the central
problem of European unity was, to find a solution for Franco-
German rapprochement, but that it was beyond the power and
possibilities of American foreign policy to force such solution.

The French initiative which offered the hope for a new basis for
Franco-German cooperation could not but deeply impress the
United States Government and American public opinion.

Diebold in his momentous study of the Schuman Plan writes:

11.   *The United States and the Western Community, op. cit.,* p. 115.

'American policy had played a part in bringing European and German affairs to a point at which Schuman was moved to take his initiative. He knew that his bold move was bound to be welcomed in the United States and would almost certainly win strong support from the American Government... American opposition might have been fatal; American support could not guarantee success. French and German interests were bound to be controlling.'[12]

Finally, the Schuman Declaration said: 'The pooling of coal and steel production should immediately provide for the setting up of common foundations for economic development as a first step in the federation of Europe...

By pooling basic production and by instituting a new higher authority, whose decisions will bind France, Germany and other member countries, these proposals will build the first concrete foundation of the European federation which is indispensable to the preservation of peace.'

It was emphasized earlier that while the urge for greater European unity was a prominent element in the formulation and execution of American foreign policy, the precise structure and form of this unity was not thought through, neither was it the intention of the American Government to impose upon its European partners specific solutions.

However, American opinion about European integration was tempted to draw an analogy with the history of the United States. This was true with regard to the single market concept and to the principle of federation as well.

Often these analogies ignored the immense differences in national origins and economic, political and historical developments. Nevertheless, one cannot explain the American concern for European cooperation and integration without realizing how strong the urge

12. William Diebold, Jr., *The Schuman Plan: A Study in Economic Cooperation 1950–1959*, Published for the Council on Foreign Relations, (New York: Praeger, 1959), p. 46.

was in the United States to transfer to other areas the blessings of the single market concept and the federal principle which were considered as the main causes for the unique position, it had achieved in the world.

The part of Schuman's Declaration in which the federal principle for Europe was announced was warmly welcomed in the United States because it struck this note of analogy with United States history.[13]

In a pamphlet of the National Planning Association which, not least because of the caliber and position of its authors, had a great impact on American thinking, the principle of the necessity for an authority with powers beyond those of the national state was strongly endorsed.[14]

'Western Europe's dependence on American aid and its military and political weakness were all related to its subdivision into small and mutually isolated economic compartments – hence that a breakdown of this compartmentalization was a necessary precondition of real and lasting European recovery. However, the method chosen to realize this objective – 'liberalization' by mutual consent of restrictions on trade and payments among the European countries – proved to be quite inadequate. It soon appeared that fully sovereign governments would not, indeed could not, go very far in reducing their trade barriers against each other and that the effective unification of national economies involved far more than mere liberalization of trade and payments.

The problem of creating a single market out of a group of separate national economies is not simply a matter of international agreement to remove barriers to trade and payments. It also requires some kind of central authority which either directly or through an appropriate mechanism... can effectively ensure that the national

13. For an illuminating analysis of the problem of American federation as a pattern for Europe see Henry Steele Commager, 'The U.S. and the Integration of Europe', in *European Integration, op. cit.,* p. 262–278.

14. Theodore Geiger and H. van B. Cleveland, *Making Western Europe Defensible,* prepared for the N.P.A. Committee on International Policy, Planning Pamphlet, no. 74, August, 1951, pp. 20–21.

economic conditions will be mutually consistent and harmonious.'

In its Conference Report on the Economic Cooperation Act of 1950, Congress noted that 'The freedom of trade necessary for a truly unified market can exist only if such agreements are effectively – and that means politically enforceable.'[15]

Thus, the Schuman Plan met four policy objectives of the United States at the same time, the formation of a large single market in Europe, the inclusion of the new sovereign West German State into a Europe on the way towards unity, the establishment of peace between France and Germany and the emergence of the federal principle in the process of European unification.

The idea of some merger of the coal and steel industries in that part of Western Europe was much older than even the immediate post-war period.

In his attack on the Treaty of Versailles, Keynes pleaded for a revision of the Treaty and a restoration of the natural links between the iron and coal producing regions of Western Europe.[16]

Diebold and Schmitt quote Adenauer who during the Ruhr occupation after the First World War stated that 'a lasting peace between France and Germany can only be attained through the establishment of a community of economic interests between the two countries.'[17]

Rathenau, Loucheur, Reynaud, Hugo Stinnes, Stresemann and others broached similar ideas during the period between the two world wars. After 1945, Churchill, André Philip and especially Karl Arnold, Minister-President of North-Rhine Westphalia adapted these ideas in some way or another to the post-war situation of

15. *Conference Report on the Economic Cooperation Act of 1950,* May 19, 1950, p. 18.
16. John Maynard Keynes C. B., *The Economic Consequences of the Peace,* (London: Macmillan Cy., 1920), pp. 90–93.
17. William Diebold, Jr., *op. cit.,* p. 43.
     Hans A. Schmitt, *op. cit.,* pp. 53–54.

Europe in general and Germany in particular. Arnold, already in 1948, and repeating the theme in the following years pleaded for a substitution of the one-sided international control of Germany's heavy industry by an international coal and steel industry of the whole Western European region.[18]

The United States became activily involved in this problem because of its position as Occupying Power in Germany and not less by its special role in the process of European reconstruction and cooperation.

A special status for the Ruhr became part of American policy during the course of 1947, mainly as a counter-move against French insistence on separation of the Ruhr from Germany.[19]

In his speech in Stuttgart on September 6, 1946, Secretary of State Byrnes said about the Ruhr problem:

'The United States will favor such control over the whole of Germany, including the Ruhr and Rhineland, as may be necessary for security purposes. It will help to enforce those controls. But it will not favor any controls that would subject the Ruhr and the Rhineland to political domination or manipulation of outside powers.'[20]

Just before the London Conference of Foreign Ministers in 1947, Secretary of State Marshall said: 'The United States believes that safeguards must be set up to insure that the resources and industrial potential of the Ruhr, particularly in respect of coal and steel, should not be left under the exclusive control of any future German

18. Karl Arnold, *Deutsche Beitrage zur Verwirklichung der Europa Idee*, (Politeia, Bonner Universitätsreden zu öffentlichen Fragen, I).
19. 'Authoritive French policy statements zigzagged between separation and some form of international control that would leave the territory in Germany'. (William Diebold, Jr., *op. cit.,* p. 30).
   For the French 'separation' policy see a.o. Louis F. Aubert, *Securité de l'Occident, Ruhr-Rhin*, (Paris: Librarie Armand Colin, 1946), and especially the summary on page 138. 'La Ruhr et la rive gauche du Rhin doivent être détachées de la souveraineté allemande. C'est la condition indispensable d'une solution assez large et assez souple pour être juste....'
20. *Germany 1947–1949, The Story in Documents, op. cit.,* p. 8.

Government but should be used for the benefit of the European community as a whole.'[21]

In this point of view, Marshall was strongly supported and probably strongly influenced by John Foster Dulles who at that time acted as one of his main advisers.

During the London Conference, Marshall concluded his statement on economic and security questions posed by the Ruhr issue by saying: 'What is required in the view of the United States delegation, is a mechanism which permits the various interests to be resolved when they come in conflict, rather than to have one dominated by the other. What is required, in other words, is a European solution in a Europe which includes Germany.'[22]

The text of a Draft Agreement on the Establishment of the International Authority of the Ruhr was signed on December 28, 1948, by the representatives of Belgium, France, Luxemburg, the Netherlands, the United Kingdom and the United States.[23]

There were during these years influential American voices pleading for extension of international control of the heavy industries to other than German regions. One of these was Lewis Douglas, the chief American negotiator during the conference on the International Authority of the Ruhr. Both as President of the International Bank and as American High Commissioner in Germany, John McCloy expressed a keen interest in the idea of a European solution for the problem of the Ruhr and Jean Monnet, undoubtedly the principal power behind the idea of the Schuman Plan, considers Clayton as one of the men who helped to clarify his ideas which resulted in the Coal and Steel Community.

'It was in my talks with Mr. Clayton that the germ of the idea developed that Ruhr production should contribute to the production of the whole of Europe.'[24]

21. Department of State, *Bulletin,* November 30, 1947, p. 1028.
22. *Germany 1947–1949, op. cit.,* p. 330.
23. Text of the draft agreement in *Germany 1947–1949, op. cit.,* p. 332.
24. Ellen Clayton Garwood, *Will Clayton: A Short Biography,* (University of Texas Press, 1958), p. 33.

All this does not mean that the United States inspired the Schuman Declaration. It only means that the Schuman Declaration had many sources, amongst which were the opinions of highly influential Americans.

At this place, it should be noted how vital the opinion and influence of a few men like Douglas, McCloy and Clayton has been on the formulation of American policy towards the European issues.

They, like Lovett, Hoffman and Harriman, have served their country in many functions, without belonging to the career diplomats. Neither were they prominent in party politics. They had great experience in private enterprise, mostly in banking. They were dedicated internationalists and recognized, in a progressive way, the problems with which the United States were faced as the leading power of the Western world after the Second World War. Time and time again, their service was required even after they went back into private business.

The United States Government is unique in the sense that it draws so much talent from the non-governmental spheres.

The United States and Europe have immensely benefited from the wisdom, the knowledge, the open-mindedness and the willingness to serve of these men.

After the Schuman Declaration on May 9, 1950, the official United States support immediately proved that the basic elements of the plan met the main trend of its policy in Europe.

On May 7, 1950, Acheson was informed in Paris by Schuman, even before the latter had informed his cabinet colleagues. His reaction was positive but in view of the unexpectedness and boldness of the plan rather reserved.[25] But before leaving Paris for London he expressed a far stronger endorsement:

'We welcome the bold and imaginative proposal announced by

25. *The New York Times,* May 11, 1950.

Mr. Schuman on behalf of the French Government, which should be a very real contribution, not only to the strengthening of relations between France and Germany, but to the integration and expansion of the European economy.'[26]

From then on, strong support for the Schuman Plan became a permanent feature of practically all United States actions and statements with regard to Europe. President Truman called it 'an act of constructive statemanship in the great French tradition' on May 19, 1950.[27]

Support came from Paul Hoffman and Averell Harriman during the Foreign Aid hearings in Congress in June 1950.

Congress endorsed the idea to such an extent that the Administration had to fight against Congressional attempts to cut off all aid to the United Kingdom because it did not participate in the Plan.

In the Mutual Security Act of 1951, Congress provided the necessary authority for transfers of funds directly to the Community. And when the High Authority took office in the fall of 1952, an Ambassador – David Bruce – was accredited to the new Community. A loan agreement of $100 million was negotiated in August 1954, between the United States and the Community. In his testimony before the House Committee on Foreign Affairs the Assistant Secretary of State, Livingston Merchant declared that the loan was based on straight political considerations.[28]

Although there was no official American involvement in the negotiations of the Schuman Plan, some American officials played a very significant role. An elaborated account of that role is given in Diebold's study.[29]

Monnet established a close relationship with the United States

---

26. Department of State, *Bulletin,* May 27, 1950, p. 383. For an account of Acheson's conversations in Paris see his spirited and human *Sketches from Life,* (New York: Harpers & Brothers, 1959), pp. 33-35.
27. Department of State, *Bulletin,* May 29, 1950, p. 828.
28. *Hearings on The Mutual Security Act of 1954* before the House Committee on Foreign Affairs, 83rd Congr., 2nd sess., 1954, p. 683.
29. William Diebold, Jr., *op. cit.,* pp. 551-564.

Embassy in Paris, where Ambassador Bruce and especially William Tomlinson gave valuable advice.

In Germany, the activity of the High Commissioner John McCloy and his General Counsel Robert Bowie was of critical importance in convincing the Germans of the necessity of accepting certain provisions of the Treaty which they were reluctant to support. This applied in particular to the acceptance of deconcentration measures which were necessary to meet the conditions of the French Government.

Great support was given by the United States during the negotiations in the framework of the General Agreement on Tariffs and Trade in Geneva during 1952, when the new Community asked for a waiver from the most-favored nation treatment and other specific departures from established rules.

In doing so, the United States had to reconcile the two classical trends in its own Administration – unconditional support of European regional integration and concern for the furthering and the maintenance of a global multilateral trade liberalization.

At this place, attention should be given to two closely related phenomena without which American policy towards European cooperation and integration cannot be fruitfully analyzed. One is the position and influence of Jean Monnet, the other the fact that in spite of broad and often rather instinctive support, real policy-making in connection with the problem of European integration on the American side has been in the hands of remarkably few persons in the executive branch of the United States Government.

Not only has Monnet been the auctor intellectualis of many steps on the road to European unification, he has also been a driving force in the execution of existing plans.

His most remarkable capacity has been his great influence on the formulation of United States policy towards Europe.

He exercised this influence through a network of close friendships and relationships, some of them going back to the pre-war period.

He had two characteristics of unusual importance for the conduct of his work. His presentation was always highly effective and he was independent in his judgment.

He influenced American statesmen and American officials and used this influence on European statesmen and politicians.

His relationship with people like Eisenhower, Dulles, David Bruce, McCloy, Douglas Dillon, Tomlinson, Butterworth, Bowie, George Ball, Stanley Cleveland, Robert Schaetzel and a few others is unique in the sense of how one individual from a foreign country can influence leading statesmen and officials of a very powerful and in many aspects decisive nation.

There cannot be a formal proof of this great and permanent influence. The history of American policy towards the process of European unification cannot, however, be explained without recognition of Monnet's influence on the formulation of that policy.

This fact in no way implies agreement on all points with Monnet's opinion and activities. It does imply, however, recognition of his unique stature and his impact on American official thinking.

The fact that this influence could be effective brings to the foreground the second element mentioned above. In spite of the immense influence on a wide range of American interests, the formulation of the policy towards European unification was in the hands of a remarkably small group of men, mainly in the Department of State. This certainly was true in the period when Dulles headed the Department. There was a very thin line of communication in matters of formulation of European policy, which ran either from Monnet through the Paris Embassy or the United States Representatives in Brussels and Luxemburg through one or two officials in Washington, directly to Dillon or the Secretary of State and through them to the President, or it originated in the State Department – mainly in the Policy Planning division – and followed the same direct and short road.

Under the Kennedy and Johnson Administration, Under Secretary George Ball served as a direct link between Monnet and the top of the American Administration.

Only during the last years and as a consequence of the realization that the process of European integration might, under certain circumstances, be harmful to United States interests and the cohesion of the Atlantic cooperation, the group of those in Washington who are concerned with policy towards Europe has been broadened.

The analysis of the process of European unification and the American concern with that process proves the great importance of the personal element in the formulation of policy.

History cannot only be explained by objective developments and facts. Without the simultaneous tenure of office by Schuman, de Gasperi and Adenauer, all three coming from border regions in their respective countries and inspired by the same religious background, the process of European integration would have taken a different course. Without Monnet and his unusual influence on the small group of policy-makers in Washington, the course of events in this field would also have been different.

It is natural that the form of European integration, symbolized by the Schuman Plan, raised next to the overwhelming support, also some doubts in the United States. The fear of cartellization and the permanent opposition of the defenders of the multilateral worldwide system of trade were apparent but never effective in diminishing the strong official line of support.

What is more remarkable, however, is that voices which doubted the absolute certainty that this kind of continental integration might in the long run contain elements which would threaten American interests and the strength and cohesion of the Atlantic association, were so weak at that time.

As will be described later, these doubts would become somewhat stronger at the end of the fifties and in the beginning of the new decade. At the time of the Schuman Plan, however, they were hardly expressed.

To prove that they were not completely absent, two examples might be given.

In a minority opinion in the pamphlet of the National Planning Association Committee on International Policy, Osborne writes:

'But I do not believe that a purely European or Continental Union would be inclusive enough to solve Western Europe's fundamental problems.'[30]

And more basically, Diebold states in a remarkable article of October 1950:

'Many Americans who have welcomed the Schuman Plan have assumed it would tie Germany effectively to the West. It may, but the possibility exists that it may strengthen the forces making for a Europe that tries to be neutral in the struggle between the United States and Russia.

At this stage the issue cannot be judged with finality. The subject is a tricky one, especially for an American observer. The evidence is opaque; developments are likely to be ambiguous. There is often no sharp distinction between steps toward the desirable end of strengthening Europe, materially, politically and spiritually, and measures which increase the possibility that Western Europeans may try, however, futilely, to disengage themselves from the main currents of world politics.'[31]

B. THE UNITED STATES AND THE EUROPEAN DEFENSE COMMUNITY

Northrop[32] wrote:

'The foreign policy of the United States since 1949, of both the Truman and the Eisenhower Administration, has rested on the re-arming of the Germans inside the European Defense Community.

30.   Theodore Geiger and H. van B. Cleveland, *op. cit.,* p. VIII.
31.   William Diebold, Jr., 'Imponderables of the Schuman Plan', in *Foreign Affairs,* October 1950, p. 120.
32.   F. S. C. Northrop, *op. cit.,* p. 13.

This establishes an essential tie between Continental European Union and United States foreign policy.'

The real situation was considerably more complicated than this statement suggests.

The period between the American initiative for a German defense contribution in NATO in September 1950, and the rejection of the Treaty to establish a European Defense Community by the French Assembly in August 1954, is characterized by an evolution of American foreign policy which deserves attention in the framework of this study.

While it is true that American foreign policy towards Europe in these four years had as one of its primary objectives the inclusion of German military strength in the defense of the West, it is equally true that, certainly in the first year of this period, agreement on the framework in which this contribution could best be embodied, was a matter of controversy and not an established and accepted objective of American foreign policy in the same sense as the re-armament of Western Germany undoubtedly was.

American policy in these years evolved, through the issue of German rearmament, from a policy of general support for European cooperation and integration into a specific support for a specific form of European integration – the supranational union of the six countries of continental Europe.

Northrops' thesis is valid for the period when Dulles took over the Department of State under the Eisenhower Administration but not for the last years of the Truman Administration.

Since the last part of 1951, American policy accepted the fact that German rearmament seemed only possible through the structure of the European Defense Community, but at that time the EDC was basically the means through which the primary objective of German rearmament could be achieved. Only in the course of 1952, but much more pronounced after the change of Administration, did the EDC become for American policy an end in itself as a definite step on the road to supranational continental European integration.

The outbreak of the Korean War on June 25, 1950, led to the belief in the United States that the Soviet Union might now embark upon a course of overt military aggression against the Western world.

'The attack upon Korea makes it plain beyond all doubt that Communism has passed beyond the use of subversion to conquer independent nations and will now use armed invasion and war.'[33]

In retrosprect one might question the analogy between the communist attack in Korea – an area from which the United States had withdrawn her troops and which it had publicly excluded from her 'defensive perimeter'[34] – and a possible attack on the NATO area. But at that time there was a definite feeling that the Korean War could be a preliminary and diversionary movement to a military showdown with the West.[35]

With the outbreak of the Korean War, the emphasis of American policy towards Europe gradually shifted from recovery to rearmament. The main issues, emerging from this process, were closely interwoven. They were the strengthening of the military potential of NATO and as a consequence of this policy the rearmament of Western Germany.[36]

It would fall outside the scope of this study to analyze the situation out of which the North Atlantic Treaty Organization emerged or to follow in detail the problems of its very first period.

Nevertheless, there are a few facts and trends which are relevant for the better understanding of the United States attitude towards German rearmament in general and the European Defense Community in particular.

33. Statement of President Truman on June 27, 1950, Department of State, *Bulletin*, July 3, 1950.
34. Robert Endicott Osgood, *NATO, The Entangling Alliance*, (The University of Chicago Press, 1962), pp. 68–69.
35. W. W. Rostow, *The U.S. in the World Arena, op. cit.*, pp. 218–219.
36. See also Richard P. Stebbins, *The U.S. in World Affairs 1950, op. cit.*, pp. 257–259.

On March 17, 1948, the Brussels Treaty was signed by the United Kingdom, France and the Benelux countries.

The United States attitude towards this development was expressed by President Truman in his address to a joint session of Congress on the same day.

'This development deserves our full support. I am confident that the U.S. will by appropriate means, extend to the free nations the support which the situation requires. I am sure that the determination of the free countries of Europe to protect themselves will be matched by an equal determination on our part to help them to protect themselves.'[37]

Already in January 1948, Foreign Secretary Bevin had approached the American Government in order to get its reaction on his intention to transform the Dunkirk Treaty into a more extensive defense arrangement. Authorized by the President, Marshall informed his British colleague that the United States would do anything it properly could do to assist the European nations to bring this or a similar project to fulfilment.

No formal commitment could be taken. The steering of the European Recovery Program through Congress had absolute priority and a combination of the extension of substantial economic aid with military guarantees at that time most certainly would have jeopardized the success of the Marshall Plan.

Nevertheless, the development towards an Atlantic defense arrangement was on its way.

On April 29, 1948, the Canadian Prime Minister suggested[38] in the Canadian House of Commons a collective security league, com-

37. Harry S. Truman, *Years of Trial and Hope, op. cit.* p. 256, and *Congressional Record,* 80 Congr., 2nd sess., pp. 2996–98.
38. *'Proposed North Atlantic Treaty',* External Affairs, Vol. I, No. A, November 1948, p. 4.
    It is generally assumed that the Canadian Prime Minister at that date proposed the outline of the North Atlantic Treaty Organization. It was only in a speech in the Canadian House of Commons on June 19, 1948, that he became more specific about the desirability of a regional defense pact between the United States, Canada and Western Europe.

posed of states which were willing to accept more specific obligations than those contained in the Charter of the United Nations and
went on to say that such a collective security league might grow
out of the plans for Western Union.

In September 1948, the Brussels Treaty Powers decided to form a
Western Union Defense Organization with a Defense Committee,
assisted by joint chiefs of staff of which Field Marshal Lord Mont-
gomery was appointed Chairman.

In the United States, the clear intentions of the executive branch of
the government needed some form of Congressional support before
it could lead to a formal commitment of such wide implications as
would be embodied in the NATO Treaty arrangement.

By an unusual close cooperation between Under Secretary of
State Lovett and Senator Vandenberg the foundation of such support was laid.[39]

An important step was reached when the so called Vandenberg
resolution was passed by the Senate on June 11, 1948.[40] Its contents
were characterized by the formulation of Vandenberg in describing his objectives: 'Within the Charter of the United Nations but
outside the veto.'

After dealing with the use of the veto in the United Nations, the
Resolution laid down in general terms the American approach to
the problem of security in Europe. The United States government
should further promote 'the progressive development of regional
and other collective arrangements for individual and collective
self-defense in accordance with the purposes, principles and provisions of the Charter.' It should make clear its own determination
to exercise the right of individual or collective self-defense under

39. The best source for this development is *The Private Papers of Senator
Vandenberg, op. cit.,* pp. 399–421.
40. *Senate Resolution 239,* Reaffirming the Policy of the United States to
achieve International Peace and Security through the United Nations
and Indicating Certain Objectives to be Pursued, 80th Congr., 2nd
sess., May 19, 1948.

Article 51, should any armed attack occur affecting its national security. Finally, it should promote 'association of the U.S. by constitutional process, with such regional and other collective arrangements as are based on continuous and effective self-help and mutual aid, and as affect its national security.'

Although the Vandenberg Resolution left considerable uncertainty as to the nature and scope of United States support, its adoption constituted a landmark on the path to the conclusion of the North Atlantic Treaty.

In July 1948, during the Berlin blockade, it was announced that United States and Canadian representatives were participating in the activities of the Brussels Treaty Defense Committee and since then, for all practical purposes, took full part in the security functions of the organization.

In Washington, secret conversations took place between the seven powers concerned.

In the beginning of 1949, Denmark, Iceland, Italy, Norway and Portugal accepted the invitation to join and on April 4, 1949, the North Atlantic Treaty was signed by the twelve countries.

In accepting the principle of Article 5 of the Treaty, in which the parties agree that an armed attack against one or more of them in Europe or North America shall be considered an attack against them all, the United States took upon itself an unprecedented commitment which constituted, and still constitutes to-day, the essence of the North Atlantic Alliance.

On February 20, 1949, Reston wrote in the *New York Times* that there existed two conceptions of the Alliance. 'One is that we were trying to create a military combination so strong, so well armed and so well supplied with actual and potential bases, within striking distance of the Soviet Union that the Politburo would not dare to risk aggression. The other conception is that we were trying to create an institution that would make it clear to everybody concerned that certain areas of Europe were vital to our security and provide the machinery for planning the defense of the North Atlantic area'.

There were important bodies of opinion, certainly in military circles, who aimed at the first concept and basically saw the Alliance as a means of redressing the military unbalance of the European continent through the construction of a full-scale integrated defense of Europe.

The political approach, however, was undoubtedly based on the second concept and in spite of many seemingly contradictory and sometimes confusing words and actions, should be accepted as the then prevailing trend in American thinking and policy.

In its initial phase NATO was essentially what Osgood calls a 'guarantee pact'[41] designed to enhance the credibility of America's commitment to the defense of Europe. It was far more an extension of the Monroe doctrine to Europe than the determination to build up, with American support, an integrated Atlantic defense system.

As Secretary Acheson said in a broadcasted speech on March 19, 1949: 'The control of Europe by a single aggressive, unfriendly power would constitute an intolerable threat to the national security of the United States.'[42]

For psychological reasons, the alliance declared itself bound to the objective of local defense, but for practical political and economic reasons, it really relied upon America's threat of nuclear retaliation.

Vandenberg, who in Congress did more than anybody else to prepare and defend the North Atlantic Treaty, was quite emphatic on the point of stressing the guarantee character of the Pact. On December 9, 1948, he wrote: 'There is no proposal to put a joint military machine into present physical being, if I understand the matter, except at a planning and equipment level. The purpose is to provide available potentialities.'

And in the Senate he said on July 6, 1949: 'In my view its invincible power for peace is the awesome fact that any aggressor upon the North Atlantic Community knows in advance that from the very moment he launches his conquest he will forthwith face what-

41.   R. E. Osgood, *op. cit.*, p. 35.
42.   Department of State, *Bulletin*, March 27, 1949, p. 385.

ever cumulative opposition these United Allies deem necessary . . . to restore peace and security. It is not the military forces-in-being which measure the impact of this knock-out admonition, important though they are.

It is the potential which counts, and any aggressor knows that he forthwith faces this potential from the moment he attacks.'[43]

George Kennan, who at that time occupied the chairmanship of the State Department's Policy Planning Staff, wrote that he considered the alliance in 1948 and 1949, simply as the means of restoring Western Europe's self-confidence and providing a modest military shield behind which the West could proceed with the prior task of economic reconstruction.

He never supposed that the alliance was intended to redress the military balance in the face of any imminent danger.

'The central agency in our concept was not NATO but the European Recovery Program, and none of us dreamed at that time that the constructive impulses of this enterprise, which looked to everyone so hopeful in those days, would be overtaken and swallowed-up in the space of a mere two or three years by programs of military assistance based on a wholly different concept of the Soviet threat and of Europe's needs.'[44]

In the hearings before the Senate Committee on Foreign Relations on the North Atlantic Treaty, the Administration denied that it implied the obligation to extend large-scale military aid and it stated that rearmament would be limited to strengthening Europe's small existing forces. It denied that substantial numbers of American troops would be stationed in Europe or that Germany would be permitted to remilitarize, or contribute to allied forces.[45]

The issue became more obscured during the debate on the Mutual Defense Assistance Act which President Truman sent to Congress

43. *The Private Papers of Senator Vandenberg, op. cit.,* p. 419 and pp. 495–496.
44. George F. Kennan, *Russia, the Atoms and the West,* (New York: Harper & Bros, 1957), pp. 88–91.
45. *Hearings on the North Atlantic Treaty,* Senate Committee on Foreign Relations, 81st Congr., 1st sess., pp. 12–57.

on July 25, 1949, the day he signed the instrument of ratification of the North Atlantic Treaty.

In spite of the fact that during the hearings on that important legislation the staggering fact of the Soviet explosion of an atomic device in August 1949, was known, Secretary Acheson declared that 'we do not believe that to discourage military aggression it is necessary to create Western European defense forces which are by virtue of their size capable of successfully resisting an all-out attack. What is required, is, rather sufficient strength to make it impossible for an aggressor to achieve a quick and easy victory.[46] There is truth in Osgood's comment that the Administration had failed to acknowledge or resolve the contradictions between declared strategic objectives, war plans, and actual capabilities.[47]

In summary, in the pre-Korean period of NATO, the trend in the United States concept of NATO was that overt military Soviet aggression in Europe was highly improbable and that the basic function of NATO was not the urgent build-up of adequate military strength in Europe. It was rather a combination of two major notions.

One, that is best described as an extension of the Monroe Doctrine to the Atlantic area, in the hope that this would be a clear indication of where the United States would stand in the event of any further Russian expansion in Europe, the second, the strong feeling in the United States and in Europe that a complete economic recovery in Europe would not be possible without a political addition to the large-scale economic aid. Only the formal United States commitment embodied in the North Atlantic Treaty could take away Europe's basic sense of insecurity and thus contribute to the original objectives of the European Recovery Program.

Finally, attention should be given to one aspect of the United States approach to the problem of NATO. It is generally accepted that the

46. *Hearings on the Military Assistance Program of 1949,* 81st Congr., 1st sess., p. 27.
47. R. E. Osgood, *op. cit.,* p. 45.

European Recovery Program and the North Atlantic Treaty belong to the same basic concept of American foreign policy. While this is undoubtedly true, yet there was one important difference in the approach to the economic and the political-military aspects of this policy.

In the economic field the philosophy of American policy was based on the notion that temporary United States aid would restore Europe's economic and social health and make it independent from further American assistance. This implied first, a strong emphasis on European cooperation and integration and second, an organization of European countries in which the United States did not participate as a member and where its role was confined to 'friendly advice'.

From the beginning of NATO, the United States chose to build up a new organization on an Atlantic basis in which it would participate as a full member. 'Under the North Atlantic Treaty the United States accepted a permanent obligation to bear its share of the burden of mutual defense, rather than formulating a temporary program of military assistance aimed at building up an integrated European defense which would eventually be independent of a continuing American subsidy. Instead of backing Western Union, we overshadowed it with the far more imposing NATO structure.'[48]

It is of course possible to explain this difference by the mere fact that real European independence in the political-military sector, certainly at that time, was inconceivable. But the rejection of the notion of a military self-supporting and independent Europe still could leave open the option of an Atlantic structure based upon strong European cooperation and integration, as had been the objective in the economic field.

It is remarkable, however, that in the first years of NATO the United States did hardly discuss this possibility.

Although Congress continued in the same period its insistence that the European Recovery Program should be used as an instrument to promote European unity, there was no similar pressure to

48.   Ben T. Moore, *op. cit.,* p. 25.

use American military commitments and assistance for the same purpose.

In the hearings during the congressional considerations of the North Atlantic Treaty, Senator Fulbright was a lonely voice when he said:

'I have felt that as a practical matter the political federation of Europe is within the realm of possibility, providing this country might give a little leadership and a little encouragement and we have the instrumentality to give it through, particularly the ECA and now with this American military guarantees and aid. But if our policy is negative in that respect, we just fail to get one of the principal, if not the principal advantages of these efforts.'[49]

The rest of the Senate was satisfied with the very platonic expression that the North Atlantic Pact created a favorable climate for further steps toward progressively close European integration.[50] Moore is right when he concludes that in that period for purposes of defense, the idea of European union was replaced by that of a North Atlantic community.

The post-Korean years would fundamentally affect these trends in American thinking about the defense of Europe.

The outbreak of the Korean War brought into focus a multitude of problems which were already in existence but the solution of which either was delayed by another set of priorities or by the understandable desire of governments not to embrace at the same time too many issues of a highly controversial and complex nature.

European recovery was well on its way, although the process was slower than was expected, most certainly in the field of European unification. OEEC had, however, adopted a program for liberalization of trade and payments and the introduction of the Schuman Plan opened a perspective for a common European market and eventually a true European federation.

49.   *Hearings on the North Atlantic Treaty*, 81st Congr., 1st sess., p. 369.
50.   *North Atlantic Treaty*, Report of the U.S. Senate Committee on Foreign Affairs, 81st Congr., 1st sess., p. 25.

NATO fulfilled its role as a formal American commitment to the military security of Western Europe. Joint military planning was slowly started and a modest beginning was made with the equipment of the European defense forces.

Germany was gradually drawn into the economic organization of Europe by its membership of OEEC and into the political framework by its membership of the Council of Europe. The Schuman Plan could provide the basis of a more solid inclusion of Germany into a European continental union. And while there was no relaxation in the basic elements of the East-West struggle, the possibility of an overt Soviet military aggression in Europe was considered as remote. Moore wrote:

'It seemed as if for the first time since the war these matters could now be discussed in leisurely and rational fashion...and fresh decisions could be taken after careful thought rather than in hectic response to the pressure of crises. Like the dream, three and a half years earlier, of an approaching era of relaxation, this vision was to be shattered this time by the fire of communist forces advancing southward in Korea.'[51]

There was undoubtedly a difference in appreciation of the implications of the Korean War between the United States and Europe, which by itself created new problems and reciprocal irritations. The feeling that Korea meant a definite turn in Soviet policy in the sense that military aggression everywhere became a much stronger possibility, was more deeply felt in the United States than in Europe. This gave rise to European reactions, fearing that the United States military and economic potential from now on would be more concentrated on non-European areas, while in the United States the inadequacy of European sacrifices for its own organization and defense became more pronounced.

The issue of priority of European recovery over rearmament, the exact nature and extent of United States military assistance in the field both of aid and of commitment of forces to Europe, the trans-

51.   Ben T. Moore, *op. cit.,* p. 34.

formation of NATO from a guarantee pact with a rather weak military structure and potentiality into a powerful and integrated organization, the removing of the barriers to the use of German armed forces and the question whether this should take place in an Atlantic rather than a European framework, all this – it was felt in the United States – had to be dealt with under a great sense of urgency and without delay.

The effort to cope with these issues and problems dominated the scene of the second half of 1950 and the subsequent years.

The main issues involved were discussed in September 1950, when first the British, French and United States Foreign Ministers met and afterwards, the North Atlantic Council assembled in New York.

On September 9, 1950, President Truman prepared the ground for these meetings in a radio address in which he announced not only a greatly enlarged defense program but added, in an effort both to allay European doubts about American intentions and to bolster greater European efforts, that 'on the basis of recommendations of the Joint Chiefs of Staff, concurred in by the Secretaries of State and Defense, I have to day approved substantial increases in the strength of the U.S. forces to be stationed in Western Europe in the interest of the defense of that area...

A basic element in the implementation of this decision is the degree to which our friends match our actions in this regard. Firm programs for the development of their forces will be expected to keep full step with the dispatch of additional United States forces to Europe. Our plans are based on the sincere expectations that our efforts will be met with similar action on their part.'[52]

The United States entered the negotiations in September 1950, with a concept in which the problem of strengthening the Atlantic Alliance by all possible means, including unprecedented American commitments, was intimately linked with the problem of German rearmament.

As to the first part of its program aiming at transforming NATO

52. Department of State, *Bulletin,* September 17, 1950, p. 458.

into an effective military organization designed to redress the military unbalance of the continent it was not too difficult to convince its European partners, the more so after the revelation that the Soviet Union possessed the atomic bomb.

Preliminary decisions on this point had been taken at the meeting of the twelve NATO Ministers in May 1950, in London in which the principle of 'balanced collective forces' was accepted.[53] In the meetings of the North Atlantic Deputies in late July and August 1950, it was recognized that economic requirements would henceforth be subordinated to the overriding needs of the military program and even more stress was laid on the collective character of the forces to be developed.

At the September meeting in New York, it was decided to establish, at the earliest possible date, an integrated force under centralized command which should be adequate to deter aggression and to ensure the defense of the West. The centralized force was to be organized under the North Atlantic Treaty Organization which would be responsible for its political and strategic guidance. Its Supreme Commander would have sufficient delegated authority to ensure that national units allocated to his command were organized and trained into an effective force in time of peace as well as in the event of war.[54]

In sharp contradiction to the smooth acceptance of these principles stood the violent opposition, particularly from the French, to the second element of the American proposals – the rearmament of Germany.

It is extremely difficult to establish exactly when and how the decision to rearm the Germans was made in the United States.

53. Department of State, *Bulletin*, May 29, 1950, p. 830.
   The principle of balanced collective forces implied the decision to abandon the attempt to build up self-sufficient national defense establishments, but in stead gear their expansion entirely to the collective requirements established by the appropriate Treaty authority.
54. *Documents on American Foreign Relations, Vol. XII, 1950, op. cit.*, p. 213.

It is undoubtedly true that the military advisers of the United States Government, already before the outbreak of the Korean War, stressed the necessity of a German defense contribution as a condition to a real possibility of a so-called forward strategy in Europe, but the background and timing of the political decision is still untraceable.

What is relevant, however, is that in September 1950, it was official American policy. Truman who had the unusual capacity to reduce complicated issues to their simplest and basic form, justified the decision in the following words:

'The German people, divided between East and West, were still under occupation following the defeat and destruction of Hitler. But the land they inhabit is the very core of Europe, and the people who live in it have proved over the centuries that they have the will and the ability to defend it. Without Germany, the defense of Europe was a rearguard action on the shores of the Atlantic Ocean. With Germany there could be a defense in depth, powerful enough to offer effective resistance to aggression from the East... Any map will show it, and a little arithmetic will prove what the addition of German manpower means to the strength of the joint defense of Europe.'[55]

This conviction led to the proposal of Acheson, first to Bevin and Schuman and later to the North Atlantic Council, to decide then and there on the formation of German military contingents. Ten divisions should be placed under the operational command of the North Atlantic Treaty Commander-in-Chief. The German units would not constitute a German army or require the reestablishment of a German general staff. They would form part of the new integrated North Atlantic defense force and their equipment needs would not be allowed to interfere with the prior requirements of the North Atlantic Treaty countries.

This proposal, although it took already into account expected French objections, was still far beyond what the French were willing to accept. There certainly was no enthusiastic welcome of the

55. Harry S. Truman, *op. cit.*, p. 268.

American proposals from the other NATO partners but without the French they would have probably been accepted as a counterpart of America's intention to station additional forces in Europe and to assume the Supreme Command of the integrated defense force. The French opposition, however, was impossible to surmount.

The Tripartite Communiqué issued in New York on September 14, 1950, could, in connection with this problem, only state that 'to make the protection of the German Federal Republic and the Western sectors of Berlin more effective they will increase and reinforce their forces in Germany. They will treat any attack against the Federal Republic or Berlin from any quarters as an attack upon themselves.'[56]

As to the problem of German rearmament the Communiqué continued:

'The Ministers are fully agreed that the re-creation of a German national army would not serve the best interests of Germany and Europe. They also believe that this is the view of the great majority of the German people. The Ministers have taken note, however, of sentiments recently expressed in Germany and elsewhere in favor of German participation in an integrated force for the defense of European freedom. The questions raised by the problem of the participation of the German Federal Republic in the common defense of Europe are at present the subject of study and exchange of views.'[57]

In view of the basic disagreement between the three Occupying Powers, it was no wonder that the North Atlantic Council had to confine its conclusions, with regard to this matter, to an agreement that Germany should be enabled to contribute to the build-up of the defense of Western Europe and to note that the Occupying Powers were studying the matter to make recommendations, at

56. Stebbins rightly concluded from this statement that Germany was admitted to the benifits of the North Atlantic Treaty without as yet imposing any corresponding obligation on the government of the Federal Republic, *op. cit.,* p. 270.
57. Department of State, *Bulletin,* October 2, 1950, pp. 530–531.

the earliest possible date, as to the methods by which Germany could most usefully make its contribution.[58]

The American reaction to the failure to reach agreement was best expressed in a melancholic despatch from Acheson to the President, dated September 15, 1950. He told how he had explained to his British and French colleagues that the administration had been able to bring about a complete revolution in American policy by being prepared to place substantial forces in Europe, to put these forces into an integrated force for the defense of Europe, to agree to a command structure, to agree to a supreme commander, to join in a program for integrating European production and to take far-reaching steps in the financial field and that this scheme involved a defense as far to the east as possible, but that this was inconceivable without facing squarely the question of German participation. He concluded by stating that the discussions proved that his colleagues were prepared to accept what the United States offered, but were not prepared to accept what the United States had asked.[59]

Before an analysis of the period following the September 1950, meetings in New York is made, two aspects of the situation should be mentioned.

One is the unmistakable trend in the United States Government, in that period, to be less interested in promoting European unity than in the priority of building up overall defense capabilities with the inclusion of German defense forces.

The Truman-Acheson approach was an Atlantic approach and did not contemplate a solution of the German defense problem within a European framework. Till well into 1950, the pressure for European integration in the executive branch of the United States Government mainly sprang from the activities of the top of the Economic Cooperation Administration and notably from Hoffman and Bissell. There certainly was strong support in some sec-

58. *Documents on American Foreign Relations, Vol. VII, 1950, op. cit.,* pp. 213–214.
59. Harry S. Truman, *op. cit.,* pp. 269–270.

tions of the State Department and from American officials abroad but the inspiration for a policy of European integration came mainly from the ECA.

The second aspect relates to the question whether the insistence on German rearmament by the United States in September 1950, was a right policy decision.

Looking at the history of German rearmament after 1950, one cannot escape the conclusion that the American decision to push German rearmament in the framework of NATO was premature.

More than five years after the American proposal, not a single German soldier was in uniform or contributed to the defense of the West. In the meantime French and German domestic policies were embittered to the extreme by this problem. Anglo-American relations were heavily burdened by the same issue. American policy towards Europe came to a point where the United States Secretary of State spoke of an 'agonizing reappraisal'. Every action in the Atlantic world for years to come would be overshadowed and, from time to time, distorted because of this issue. These prices were high and probably too high in the light of the ultimate results. This was not at all due to American policy alone. But to assess rightly probable reactions in the political life of its allies and the consequences of these reactions for the working of the alliance and the relations between its members, is one of the ungrateful tasks of the leader of that alliance.

The American decision of September 1950, did not meet that test.

The year that followed the NATO meeting of September 1950, was characterized by a multitude of trends and events, none of which led to a definite solution of what now had become the crucial problem of the Western alliance – the rearmament of Germany – but all of which were somehow related to this issue. It affected relations between the United States and its European allies, the relations between the major European countries, the domestic political situation, especially in France and Germany, and the United States attitude towards the development of European unification.

It was a year of uneasy suspense in which forces were stirred up which put a serious strain on the alliance.

The New York meetings of 1950, had made it clear that the American proposal to put German forces directly under the operational command of the North Atlantic Commander in Chief was unacceptable to the French.

But it was generally accepted – also by France – that some form of remilitarization of Germany could not be blocked indefinitely. As to Germany, there are indications that, during the meeting in September, the German Chancellor sent a message indicating that German participation in the defense of the West should be based on equal status for the German forces.

The French Government tried to counteract the American proposals by two main devices. One was a delaying tactic in order to reach a situation in which a stronger Western force would already be established before German units would actually be formed. The second was an effort to keep German forces as small as possible, without operational autonomy and completely integrated into larger international units. In short, they aimed at the impossibility for German forces to be an instrument of German policy.

There were, however, also more positive elements at work in France who, reluctantly accepting the United States insistence on German rearmament, tried to use it as an instrument in furthering the development of Franco-German rapprochement and European integration in the process which had been started by the launching of the Schuman Plan.

Acheson was already informed in September that Monnet was working on a plan in accordance with this line.[60]

The idea of a European army was first launched by Churchill, prior to the September meetings, during the August session of 1950 of the Consultative Assembly of the Council of Europe in Strasbourg.

On August 11, 1950, the Assembly adopted a resolution calling for

60.   Dean Acheson, *Sketches from Life, op. cit.,* p. 42.

the immediate creation of a united European army, under the authority of a European Minister of Defense, subject to proper democratic control and acting in full cooperation with the United States and Canada.[61]

While this resolution had no visible impact on the deliberations of the Ministers of the North Atlantic Council in New York in September, it certainly had a bearing on the official French counter-proposals to the American initiative, which were formulated by the French Premier Pleven in the French National Assembly on October 24, 1950. He suggested that Western Germany, although not to be admitted to NATO, should nevertheless contribute to the defense of Europe through its participation in a European army. Such a European army would form part of the eventual North Atlantic Force but would be responsible in the first instance to a European defense ministry and an appropriate European political authority. It would work on the basis of a common budget and it would realize, within the bounds of possibility, the complete integration of all human elements and material, under a unified European authority, political and military. The national contingents would be integrated at the lowest practicable level, that of combat teams of 3–4000 men. German units would be admitted, provided that the Schuman Plan was first accepted and the European Defense Minister and Political Authority had been chosen.[62]

The Western alliance was now confronted with two alternative plans, both providing for a German defense contribution. One aimed at direct participation in NATO of German military units in the shortest possible time. The other provided for a European defense structure which, apart from the doubt about its military feasibility, would in all circumstances delay German remilitarization for a prolonged period. No wonder that the meeting of the Defense

61. *Summary of Debates,* Consultative Assembly, Second Ordinary Session, August 7–11, 1950, pp. 59–71.
62. For the text of Pleven's address see *Chronique de Politique Etrangère,* Bruxelles, Vol. V, Sept.–Nov., 1952, pp. 588–591.

Ministers of NATO in Washington, at the end of October 1950, in which the French Defense Minister, Jules Moch, explained and defended the French plan, did not come to an agreement.

An uneasy compromise between these two concepts was found at the North Atlantic Council meeting in Brussels in December 1950.

The French got a silent endorsement to go on with the exploration of the possibilities of the Pleven Plan.

Apart from completing the arrangements for the establishment in Europe of an integrated force under centralized control and command and a request to President Truman to designate General Eisenhower as Supreme Allied Commander in Europe, the main decision of the Council was embodied in the final Communiqué as follows. 'The Council also reached unanimous agreement regarding the part which Germany might assume in the common defense. The German participation would strengthen the defense of Europe without altering in any way the purely defensive character of the North Atlantic Treaty Organization. The Council invited the Governments of France, the United Kingdom and the United States to explore the matter with the Government of the German Federal Republic.'[63]

These phrases sounded very promising. In the first place, however, referring the negotiations to the Bonn Government and the three Occupying Powers did not solve the problem but only delayed its solution and shifted the basic issue from NATO to the negotiations in Germany. In the second place, the NATO meeting in Brussels started two parallel sets of discussions, one in Germany and one in Paris – the latter on the basis of the Pleven Plan. Theodore White said that they 'went their separate ways, like a two-ring circus with spectators bobbing their heads back and forth to find out what was going on.'[64]

In the following months there was a multitude of forces at work, often pulling in different directions and making the picture of Western cooperation confused and unclear.

63. *Documents on American Foreign Policy, Vol. XII, 1950, op. cit.*, p. 215.
64. Theodore White, *op. cit.*, p. 269.

The negotiations between the three Occupying Powers and the Federal Government – the so-called Petersberg negotiations – proceeded in the military field, and by the end of March there was agreement on a technical military level.

This agreement contained an authorization to the Federal Republic to establish four army corps, consisting of 12 divisions, with a peacetime strength of 15,000 and a war strength of 18,000. This force was envisaged, however, without a general staff and with Germany's war production closely tied in with that of the Western world.[65]

The Petersberg negotiations led an isolated life from the political facts which ultimately would determine what was really going to happen. They could not be harmonized neither with German policy, nor with French policy and the broad tendencies in other parts of Europe.

This study does not provide the space to describe in detail the German reactions to the problem of its rearmament and the method by which this rearmament could best be achieved.

There are, however, a few trends which should be mentioned for a better understanding of the problem.

An important part of German public and political opinion rejected the concept of rearmament under all circumstances. The motives for this attitude were varied and complex. There was a genuine feeling that in view of the violent Soviet opposition against any form of German rearmament, the prospects for German reunification would be reduced to zero by a remilitarization.

Under the post-war generation there was a strong feeling of reluctance to take up arms again. Illusions of a possible neutrality and a genuine feeling of alarm at the prospect of militarism, which twice had brought total ruin for Germany, were important elements in that school of thought which was apparent not only in the Social

65. Richard B. Stebbins, *The U.S. in World Affairs 1951,* Published for the Council on Foreign Relations, (New York: Harper & Brothers, 1951), p. 64.

Democratic Party but also in important segments of the Protestant Church.

On the other side, there was a strong tendency only to accept rearmament when two conditions were fulfilled. First, equality in the status of the German forces with other comparable allies and a minimum of discriminatory provisions in any settlement to this effect, second, the restoration of full sovereignty of the Federal Republic with a maximum abolition of the still existing restrictive provision in the relation between the Federal Goverment and the Occupying Powers.

There is no doubt that Adenauer adhered to this last school but – and this cannot be overestimated – in combination with a continuation of what should be called the Schuman Plan approach. For Adenauer this meant interlocking Germany's destiny to the Western world with the main emphasis on Franco-German rapprochement, in a framework which would go beyond the orthodox alliance and which would embody the germs for a federated European structure.

To all this was added a general feeling that the risks of German rearmament were too great, should the Allied forces in Germany remain as they were at that moment. In order to lift the basic feeling of insecurity and to get the Germans to accept the risks of rearmament against the threatening Soviet policy, allied forces in Germany had to be strengthened.[66]

In spite of their cooperation on the purely military level, leading to the deceptive Petersberg Agreement, the French never had abandoned their ideas expressed by Pleven in October 1950.

Rejection of any form of a German national army with direct admittance to NATO, delegation of national sovereignty to a common defense authority along the institutional lines of the Schu-

66. R. E. Osgood, *op. cit.,* p. 82.
Gordon A. Cray, 'Germany and NATO: The Rearmament Debate 1950–1958', in *NATO and American Security,* ed. by Klaus Knorr, (Princeton University Press, 1959), pp. 236–261.

man Plan, ratification of the Schuman Plan and a minimum size of contributing German units, remained the basis of French policy and provided the main elements of the negotiations in Paris between France, Germany, Italy, Belgium and Luxemburg (initially the Dutch acted only as observers) in February 1951.

The only development in the French attitude consisted in the acceptance of more German equality and more understanding for the necessity that basic national units had to be larger than the Pleven Plan originally had envisaged.

From these German and French positions it became clear that the United States was confronted with a highly complicated political situation in which a formula had to be found under which the prime objective of the German defense contribution could be reconciled with the prevailing policies of the major European allies.

Gradually, the conviction emerged from the American side that the greatest common divisor, in order to achieve German rearmament, had to be a combination of the non-discriminatory inclusion of workable German military units in a supranational European framework, the simultaneous restoration of full sovereignty to the German Federal Republic and a substantial formal and material commitment of American forces to the European continent.

The uncertain character of United States policy towards the methods of German rearmament continued during the first half of 1951. Secretary of State Acheson gave a qualified support to the negotiations in Paris which started in February 1951,[67] but the real turn in American policy had to wait till General Eisenhower, the newly appointed Supreme Allied Commander, embraced the project of the European Army. After a first brief visit to his new command area, Eisenhower reported to the President and to Congress. In his speech to Congress on February 1, 1951, Eisenhower said:

'There has to be a political platform achieved, an understanding that will contemplate an effectual and an earned equality on the

---

67. Department of State, *Bulletin*, Febr. 19, p. 287.

part of Germany, before we should start to talk about including units of Germans in any kind of army.'[68]

There is no doubt that Eisenhower first considered the European Army Plan as contrary to sound military organization. But during the first months of his new office, he became convinced of its double significance, as the only avenue open to German rearmament and as an instrument for European integration.

The insistence on German rearmament in the form of direct admittance to NATO, at this particular moment, had been considered by the most important American representatives in Europe as at least unfortunately timed. Men like McCloy and David Bruce and the staff of the Paris Embassy were in the closest possible contact with Monnet, working on the realization of the Schuman Plan and supporting Monnet's ideas on the European Army project. They arranged meetings between Eisenhower and Monnet and it is highly probable that the links between a small group of American diplomatic representatives, Monnet and Eisenhower brought about the latter's conversion to full support of the basic ideas of the European Army plan. He gave public expression to his ideas in a speech before the English Speaking Union in London on July 3, 1951, in which he came out in full support of a workable European federation[69] which was understood to imply the notion of an integrated European defense force. There is every indication that in his communications to Washington, Eisenhower was emphatic on the point that the project to recruit Germans forthwith and admit Germany to NATO had to be abandoned and that the European Army project had to be accepted.

Eisenhower, Gruenther and Bruce voiced the same idea to the Subcommittee of the Senate Committee on Foreign Relations which held hearings in Europe during July 1951. Eisenhower in particular said:

'I believe in it this much – when I came over here I disliked the whole idea of a European Army and I had enough troubles without

68.   *The New York Times,* February 2, 1951.
69.   *The New York Times,* July 4, 1951.

it. However, I have decided that it offers another chance for bringing another link in here, so I made up my mind to go into the thing with both feet... So I am going to try to help, and I realize that a lot of my professional associates are going to think that I am crazy. But I am going to tell you that joining Europe together is the key to the whole question.'[70]

The policy of exclusive support for the Schuman-Monnet concept of European integration became more and more apparent, when Ambassador Bruce was transferred to Washington in 1952, to assume the office of Under Secretary of State and it became completely established after Dulles took over the State Department.

Nevertheless Acheson states that 'in the summer of 1951, as the European Defense Community took form, my first impression grew to a conviction that the United States should plump for this solution and do what could wisely be done to help it on... The President's approval made support of the EDC official U.S. policy.'[71]

From the summer of 1951 on, the European Army Plan was accepted and supported by official United States policy, primarily as the only avenue open to German rearmament but gradually in 1952, and especially since the Eisenhower Administration took office, this plan became an end itself, as the symbol of progress in the process of European integration.

The rigid approach to continental European integration was very clearly and purely exposed in the pamphlet, already mentioned, which Theodore Geiger and H. van B. Cleveland wrote for the National Planning Association in August 1951.

Their strong argument for continental integration in the economic, political and military field was based on the concept of the consolidation of NATO into three component member units – the United States, the United Kingdom and the Commonwealth, and

70. Max Beloff, *op. cit.*, pp. 78–79.
71. Dean Acheson, *op. cit.*, p. 44.

the continental countries represented as a group through their supranational agencies.

In the chapter on military integration it is stated that only the United States and the United Kingdom were economically and politically strong enough to be able to work on an intergovernmental basis. Each could afford fully balanced national military establishments, generally capable of defending its own borders. Each had a powerful and diversified industrial economy. None of them was affected by the feeling that conditions in the modern world had proven the inadequacy of the nation state and neither of the two had any psychological sense of need for a tight form of supranational organization – nor did they need it. In contrast to these two nations, the continental countries were weak – economically, politically and militarily. No continental country, not even Western Germany, had the economic capability to equip its forces rapidly.

There was no question about the adequacy of the morale of American and British forces, because they were citizens of strong nations which never had yet lost a major war.

The continental countries, on the contrary, could only contribute forces to NATO as a loose assortment of small, unspecialized national units, each supplied separately and inadequately from its own small, unspecialized arms industry.

Continental soldiers and citizens felt themselves members of small, weak countries quite incapable of defending themselves.

The average continental was by no means convinced that the separate national state could be made defensible. The only possibility in the military field for a solution of the German problem and for the issue of a worthwhile defense contribution of the continental European countries was through a supranational continental military organization, whose relationship to the United States and the United Kingdom was analogous to that which existed between the two English speaking countries.

In consequence, the French plan for a European Army was far from being a maneuver. In fact it provided the only promise of both an effective and safe German rearmament and an adequate continental defense contribution to the collective NATO efforts.[72]

The pamphlet is an interesting one and proved to be very influential. It summed up the reasons and motives of American support for a specific kind of European integration – the continental supranational structure based on Franco-German friendship. It was at the same time visionary, and rigid in the choice of the means for obtaining certain ends. It was symptomatic for American policy to be followed in a long period after 1951.

What is striking in the pamphlet is its choice for continental European integration and the exclusion of the United Kingdom from this process. It placed the United Kingdom in another category of strength and possibilities than the European continental countries, thereby at the same time overestimating the potentialities of post-war Britain and underestimating the potential strength of the major continental countries.

This point of view never was accepted to that extreme in official United States policy. At that moment and also in subsequent periods, United States foreign policy was disappointed at the British attitude towards European integration and blamed a major part of the slowness of this process on British reluctance to declare itself a part of Europe. This opinion was especially strong in the legislative branch of the United States Government.

On the other hand, however, there is no doubt that also in official United States policy, the United Kingdom was not placed in the same category as the continental allies. Britain remained a special case, a partner more intact and stronger than the countries on the continent. At that time, there still was an American attitude on which the United Kingdom could base its policy of a special Anglo-American relationship.

In the history of the European Defense Community, this tendency was also apparent. While Churchill's interventions in Strasbourg and the attitude of the Conservative Party in opposition led many to believe that a change of Government in the United Kingdom

72. Theodore Geiger and H. van B. Cleveland, *op. cit.,* p. VI and pp. 31–41.

might bring about a more positive policy towards the problem of European integration – a belief shared by important segments of the American Administration – it soon became clear after the Conservatives assumed power in October 1951, that this was not the case.

There was a stronger interest in the EDC than in the Schuman Plan, because of its major importance for the defense posture of the Western world. Sir David Maxwell Fyfe, on November 28, 1951, before the Strasbourg Council of Europe, made it clear, however, that there was no question of an impending British participation.[73]

Signs of real United States pressure on the United Kingdom in this problem can hardly be found.

On the contrary, already in his abovementioned speech in July 1951 before the English-Speaking Union, Eisenhower concluded by saying: 'We, the peoples of the British Commonwealth and of the United States have profited by unity at home. If, with our moral and material assistance, the free European nations could attain a similar integration, our friends would be strengthened, our own economies improved and the laborious NATO machinery of mutual defense vastly simplified.'

This was a clear indication that in Eisenhowers view Britain should remain outside the integration process at that time.

In his memoirs, Eden is even more specific. During the NATO conference in Rome, in November 1951, he sent a personal message to the Prime Minister in which he said: 'I met General Eisenhower on the morning of November 27th. The General volunteered his opinion on the question whether any offer on our part to participate

---

73. Council of Europe, Assembly, *Official Report,* 3rd sess., 1951, p. 514. See for this episode amongst others:
    H. J. Heiser, *British policy with regard to the unification efforts on the European Continent,* (Leiden: A. W. Sijthoff, 1959), pp. 57–59.
    Anthony Nutting, *Europe will not wait,* (London: Hollis & Carter, 1960), pp. 40–42.
    H. C. Allen, *The Anglo-American Predicament,* (London: Mac Millan & Cy., 1960), pp. 57–59.

in the European army would be decisive for the success of the project. He said that he was convinced that such an offer now would be a mistake...He confirmed that this was a definite conclusion which had not been lightly arrived at...In his view, we and the United States could be more effective as elements supporting the European Army within the Atlantic Organization...It might be no bad thing if the Europeans could stand on their own.' And from this Eden concluded: 'This conversation was important. The United States Government had previously been inclined to favour our entry into the Defense Community. It was now clear that the policy which we preferred could be pursued in full accord with them.'

During his visit with the Prime Minister to Washington in January 1952, this impression was confirmed by Acheson who told him that the Americans had no wish to urge the United Kingdom to join EDC.[74]

Before proceeding with the analysis of the United States attitude towards the European Army Plan, the scene in Washington and especially the Congressional atmosphere should be briefly reviewed.

In spite of the uncertain attitude of the Administration with regard to the framework in which the German rearmament problem should be solved and in spite of the fact that in the period, immediately following the outbreak of the Korean War, the problem of European economic integration and political unification seemed somewhat obsolete in the light of the pressing problems of strengthening NATO and the defense of the West, the objective of European cooperation and integration remained an unspecified but deeply felt concern of Congressional opinion. During the hearings and debates of the Mutual Security Act 1951, there was no congressional pressure on this point, comparable with what had happened in earlier years. Congress, nevertheless, strengthened the expression of its intentions by writing into the Act as an objective of American policy 'the economic unification and *political* integration of

74. *The Memoirs of Sir Anthony Eden: Full Circle,* (London: Cassell & Cy., 1960), pp. 32–35.

Europe.'[75] In the Mutual Security Act of 1952, Congress was even more emphatic:

'The Congress welcomes the recent progress in political federation, military integration, and economic unification in Europe and reaffirms its belief in the necessity of further vigorous efforts toward these ends as a means of building strength, establishing security and peace in the North Atlantic area. In order to provide further encouragement to such efforts, the Congress believes it essential that this Act should be so administered as to support concrete measures for political federation, military integration and economic unification in Europe.'

And while the Administration had asked for a general authorization along these lines, Congress was more specific and only authorized transfer of funds to 'A. The North Atlantic Treaty Organization; B. the European Coal and Steel Community; C. the organization which may evolve from current international discussions concerning a European Defense Community.'[76]

Very revealing for the mood of Congress was a meeting between a delegation of American Congressmen and a delegation from the Consultative Assembly of the Council of Europe in Strasbourg from November 19–23, 1951.[77]

The American interventions were a series of emotional appeals for European integration with constant reference to the federal development of the United States. Representative O'Toole for instance concluded his remarks as follows:

'In conclusion, let me say that if you do not do something about this problem – if you do not something about the United States of Europe and a Common Army – then you are not here as delegates to the Council of Europe, you are here as official death watchers at the death of a civilization.'

75. *Hearings on Mutual Security Act of 1951*, 82nd Congr., 1st sess.
    Mutual Security Act of 1951, 82nd Congr., 1st sess.
76. *Mutual Security Act of 1952*, 82nd Congr., 2nd sess.
77. Conference of Strasbourg, Nov. 19th–23rd, 1951, *Official Record of Debates*, issued by the Secretariat of the Council of Europe, 1951.

In their report to Congress, the delegation reported about the confusion in Europe as to ways, means and tempo of European unification.

'To some extent this confusion may be attributable to lack of clarity as to the policies of both the United States and Great Britain.'

After criticizing the United Kingdom attitude, the report concludes that the failure of Western Europe to make more realistic progress toward European unification resulted in large part from a tendency to overemphasize the difficulties of unification and to underestimate the dangers that will inevitably flow from failure to unify. And it sadly recorded that past United States legislative references to economic and political integration had not brought about the positive achievements which many members of Congress expected to flow from such reference and that other means might need to be chosen to achieve those results.[78]

Finally, mention should be made of the debate in Congress in the first months of 1951, on the issue of sending additional United States troops to the European area. The debate was initiated by former President Hoover in December 1950, who urged an alternative world policy based upon withdrawal from Europe and concentration on the Western Hemisphere.[79] The protagonists of this policy based their arguments on two main points. First, a deep mistrust in the willingness of the European allies to defend themselves and to bring adequate sacrifices for a reasonable defense contribution. Second, a conviction that NATO ground forces were and would be inadequate compared to the overwhelming forces of the Soviet Union. The United States should defend Europe by pre-

78. *The Union of Europe: its Progress, Problems, Prospects and Place in the Western World,* Senate Document, No. 90, 82nd Congr., 2nd sess., 1952, pp. 18–19.
79. See for the debate:
Ben T. Moore, *op cit.,* pp. 40–43, and
Assignment of Ground Forces of the United States to Duty in the European Area, Hearings on Sen. Con. Res. 8, 82nd Congr., 1st sess., 1951.

paring to use overwhelming air and sea power instead of what seemed to them a useless sacrifice of American lives in Europe, in the event of actual war. Anyhow, before the United States should send more troops to Europe, the Europeans should prove that they were willing to defend themselves.

After long hearings and debates in which the Administration's case was ably defended by Eisenhower, Acheson, Bradley and Marshall, the Senate adopted a resolution on April 4, 1951, in which it declared among other things that 'the security of the United States and its citizens is involved with the security of its partners under the North Atlantic Treaty, and the commitments of that Treaty are therefore an essential part of the foreign policy of the United States.'

It further approved the President's appointment of General Eisenhower, the placing of American armed forces under his command, and the plan to send four additional divisions to Western Europe. But it added that the major contribution to the ground forces under General Eisenhower's command should be made by the European members of the North Atlantic Treaty and that no ground troops in addition to such four divisions should be sent to Western Europe without further Congressional approval.[80]

In the debates, no specific mention was made about the European Army Plan. But what became very clear was that in the opinion of Congress, American commitments were stretched to the extreme, or even beyond it, in the light of what they considered as an inadequate response from Europe.

In the latter half of 1951, the process was set in motion whereby United States foreign policy towards Europe became gradually but increasingly linked with the success or failure of the European Defense Community. Not only its policy towards Western Europe

80. *Senate Resolution 99, 82nd Congr., 1st sess., April 4, 1951, and Assignment of Ground Forces of the U.S. to duty in the European Area,* Report of the Senate Committee on Foreign Relations and Committee on Armed Services, 82nd Congr., 1st sess., 1951.

as a whole, and the individual European countries, became intimately interwoven with the fate of EDC, but its NATO policy was
dominated, not only by the problem of German rearmament, but
by the specific solution of this problem through the European
Defense Community. It was as if highly complicated problems like
the structure and strength of NATO, the problem of European
unity, the German problem, the relation of European unity to the
Atlantic Alliance, the basic relation of the United States toward
Europe and NATO, were all reduced to one single problem – the
fate of the European Army project. 'Washington having cold-
shouldered the Pleven proposal, later shifted to the opposite extreme, and came to look upon EDC as the corner-stone of America's European policy.'[81]
Every major meeting of Western statesmen and organizations
became involved in this issue as a matter of prime importance.

The negotiations in Paris between France, Italy, Germany and the
Benelux countries (the Netherlands changed its status from observer to full participant in October 1951) received a strong impetus
from the unqualified United States support. The delegations presented an Interim Report to their respective Governments on July
24, 1951, in which the broad outlines of the European Army project were sketched. It became clear that ultimate success of the plan
depended on many elements which could not be negotiated in the
framework of the Paris discussions. The ratification of the Schuman
Plan, the relations between EDC and NATO, additional guarantees from the United States and the United Kingdom and above all
the replacement of the occupation statute for Germany of 1949, by
a new status for the Federal Republic were some of the important
matters to be considered. They implied a technically and politically
highly complicated set of negotiations.
As to the new status of Germany, the Three Foreign Ministers,
during their meeting in Washington in September 1951, had

81. Michael T. Florinsky, op. cit., p. 104.

agreed that the participation of Germany in the common defense should 'naturally be attended by the replacement of the present occupation statute by a new relationship between the three Governments and the German Federal Republic.'

Germany's new European position in a European framework would be 'inconsistent with the retention in future of an occupation status or of the power to interfere in the Federal Republic's domestic affairs.' All this should lead to 'the inclusion of a democratic Germany, on the basis of equality, in a Continental European Community, which itself will form a part of a constantly developing Atlantic Community.'[82]

At the meeting of NATO in Rome, in November 1951, Eisenhower made a strong and emotional plea for the European Army Plan and the six EDC powers presented a report in which they set out that they had reached agreement on the rapid creation of a European defense force to be placed under the command of Eisenhower. The force would consist of 43 national combat teams and supporting groups, totaling roughly 1,300,000 men. The basic national unit would be approximately 13,000 men and international command would only take place at the corps and army level.

From this, it became clear that the French had gone a long way to meet the original German and American objections against too small a size of the national units and integration at too low a level to be militarily effective.

But Acheson did not succeed in convincing the North Atlantic Council to put an unqualified acceptance and endorsement of EDC in its final communiqué.

France and Germany, particularly, claimed more certainty about the additional British and United States guarantees and a stronger formal link between NATO and EDC, while the Benelux countries felt that this kind of emergency decision would not contribute to the ultimate success of the Plan.

The Communiqué only stated that there should be prompt dis-

82. Tripartite Declaration and Communiqué, September 14, 1951, in Department of State, *Bulletin,* September 24, 1951, pp. 485-486.

cussions with the Paris conference of the EDC powers about the problem of 'correlating the obligations and relations of the European Defense Community with those of the North Atlantic Treaty.'[83]

Hectic activities in Paris, Bonn and London led to substantial progress, and in the final communiqué of the Ninth Session of the North Atlantic Council, held at Lisbon on February 20–25, 1952, it could be said that:

'The Council took note of a report of the Paris Conference on the EDC and a report by the Occupying Powers on the proposed contractual arrangements with the German Federal Republic. The Council found that the principles underlying the Treaty to establish the EDC conformed to the interests of the parties to the North Atlantic Treaty... The North Atlantic Council agreed to propose to its members and to the EDC reciprocal security undertakings between the members of the two organizations. All these decisions are inspired by the conviction that the NATO and the EDC have a common objective, to strengthen the defense of the North Atlantic Area, and that the development of the EDC should be carried forward in this spirit...'[84]

Under very high pressure and often under great difficulties the work on this extremely complicated series of documents, treaties and protocols was finished in the course of May and the scene was set for the signing of the documents. On May 26, 1952, the Convention on Relations between the Three Powers and the Federal Republic of Germany was formally signed. It brought full sovereignty to Germany, but this full sovereignty was intimately linked with the acceptance by Germany of the concept of European unification.

'The Three Powers and the Federal Republic recognize that both the new relationship to be established between them by the present convention and its related Conventions and the Treaties for the

---

83.   Department of State, *Bulletin,* December 10, 1951, p. 952.
84.   *Documents on American Foreign Relations 1952,* Published for the Council on Foreign Relations, (New York: Harper & Brothers, 1953), pp. 170–171.

creation of an integrated European Community, in particular the Treaty on the Establishment of the European Community for Coal and Steel and the Treaty on the Establishment of the European Defense Community, are essential steps to the achievement of their common aim for a unified Germany integrated within the European Community.'[85]

In Paris, on May 27, 1952, a multitude of documents were signed, among which the most important were the Treaty constituting the European Defense Community, three Protocols defining the relations between the EDC and NATO, a Tripartite Declaration by the Foreign Ministers of the United States, the United Kingdom and France, and a Treaty of Guarantee between the members of the EDC and Great Britain.

In the EDC Treaty, it was stipulated that West Germany was to receive full sovereignty in the sense of the above mentioned Convention, when all signatories had ratified the Treaty.

Only a few elements of the EDC Treaty should be mentioned. It followed the political and institutional lines of the Schuman Plan. Its Assembly was instructed to submit plans for a definite organization with a permanent elected assembly on a democratic basis. The permanent organization was to be so conceived that it could constitute one of the elements of an ultimate federal or confederal structure, based upon the principle of the seperation of powers. This implied the conviction of the signatories that European unity in the defense field implied European political unity. Discrimination against Germany was minimized but it was still there, were it only for the fact that Germany would not become a member of NATO.

The protocols defining the relations between EDC and NATO provided for an undertaking of the EDC countries to regard any armed attack on one or more of the NATO countries in Europe or North America as an attack against themselves and a reciprocal commitment of all the NATO countries with regard to any armed

85.   *Documents on American Foreign Policy 1952, op. cit.,* pp. 232–233.

attack against the territory of any EDC member, or on the European Defense forces.

The Tripartite Declaration contained a pledge, particularly of the United States and the United Kingdom, to regard any action threatening the integrity or unity of the Community as a threat to their own security and their resolution to station such forces on the continent of Europe, including the Federal Republic of Germany, as they deemed necessary and appropriate to contribute to the joint defense of the North Atlantic Treaty area.

The Treaty of Guarantee between the EDC and Great Britain pledged the parties to render all military aid and other aid and assistance in case of an armed aggression and as such went further than the corresponding pledge incorporated in the North Atlantic Treaty.[86]

The formal machinery to achieve at the same time the strengthening of NATO, the sovereignty of Germany and its inclusion into a framework of an integrated continental Europe was established and with it the primary aim of United States foreign policy seemed to be attained.

At the signing ceremony, Acheson expressed his 'profound conviction that what we have witnessed today may well prove to be one of the most important and most far-reaching events of our life-time...We have seen the beginning of the realization of an ancient dream – the unity of the people of Western Europe.'[87]

86. For text of the documents see:
   Documents on American Foreign Policy 1952, op. cit., pp. 211–248.
   For an analysis of the different treaties, protocols and declarations see among others:
   F. S. C. Northrop, *op. cit.,* pp. 16–19.
   Arnold J. Zurcher, *op cit.,* pp. 84–94.
   Richard P. Stebbins, *The United States in World Affairs 1952,* Published for the Council on Foreign Relations, (New York: Harper & Brothers, 1953), pp. 150–170.
   R. E. Osgood, *op. cit.,* pp. 91–93.
87. Department of State, *Bulletin,* June 9, 1952, p. 897.

Under Secretary of State David Bruce said somewhat later:
'I myself feel that this creation of a European Defense Community
is the most significant thing that has happened in Western civilization, not in my time, not in our time, but for a period of hundreds
of years.'[88]
These profound but exalted expressions could not stop the development of the next two years in which it became clear that the
French Parliament failed to accept the concept which was mainly
conceived by the French Government, while the United States
became exclusively committed to a scheme which it originally had
opposed.

When the Eisenhower Administration assumed office in January
1953, it was confronted with a situation in which the United States
in its conduct of foreign policy was totally committed to a successful conclusion of the procedures leading to ratification of the EDC.
In Europe and especially in France, rather more than less obstacles
existed on the road to ratification than at the moment of the signing
of the Treaty in May 1952.

The Pinay-Schuman Government in France had resigned in
December 1952, and in his inaugural address on January 6, 1953, the
new Prime Minister René Mayer announced that the EDC Treaty
would be submitted to Parliament at an early date, but that the
French Government would seek certain modifications which could
be eventually laid down in additional protocols.[89]

Furthermore, he committed himself to a further effort to associate
Great Britain more intimately with the EDC, and finally he made
it clear that Germany had to renounce its contention that the Saar
was German territory.

The protocols were also intended to give France a special status,
mainly with regard to the French forces committed to EDC.

88.   Senate Committee on Foreign Relations, *Hearings, Convention on Relations
      with the Federal Republic of Germany,* 82nd Congr., 2nd sess. p. 64.
89.   Richard P. Stebbins, *The United States in World Affairs, 1953,* Published
      for the Council on Foreign Relations, (New York: Harper & Brothers,
      1954), pp. 159-160.

When the Treaty was formally presented to the French National
Assembly on January 29, 1953, the Foreign and Defense Ministers
Bidault and Pleven repeated the pledge, made by their Prime
Minister in his inaugural declaration, that the French Government
wanted to make the treaties more precise on certain points through
accompanying protocols which should be discussed by the signatory states and brought to the attention of the Parliament.[90]

While the situation in the other five countries was not without
complications – certainly not in Germany where an important section of public and parliamentary opinion remained violently opposed to the EDC concept – it became clearer every day that the
ultimate fate of EDC would be decided by the French parliament.[91]

In the last year of the Truman-Acheson period, there had been
genuine support for the EDC but, as was mentioned above, primarily as a means for expediting the German defense contribution.
The proposed community seemed to be the only form in which a
German defense participation could be accepted by all the parties
concerned.

When Eisenhower and Dulles assumed office, the President and his
Secretary of State not only continued this policy of support but
mainly because of the personality and convictions of Dulles, EDC

90. For the text of their declarations see:
     Documents on American Foreign Relations 1953, Published for the Council on
     Foreign Relations, (New York: Harper & Brothers, 1954), pp. 257–269.
91. For background and facts of the French political and parliamentary
     situation with regard to the European Defense Community there are
     two indispensable publications:
     La Querelle de la CED, Recueil publié sous la direction de Raymond
     Aron et Daniel Lerner avec la collaboration de J. Fauvet, St. Hoffmann,
     A. Grosser, J. J. Marchand, J. Stoetzel et J. Vernant, Cahiers de la
     Fondation Nationale des Sciences Politiques, No. 80, (Paris: Librairie
     Armand Colin, 1956), and
     Nathan Leites and Christian de la Malène, *Paris from EDC to WEU,*
     Research Memorandum of the Rand Corporation of March, 1956,
     R.M.–1668–R.C.

became the 'panacae for Europe's difficulties, a symbol of its regeneration and a touchstone of its future.'[92]

To the arguments from the Truman-Acheson period, the deeply rooted belief of Dulles was added that the future of Europe, Europe's place in the East-West ideological and politico-military struggle, the strength of the Atlantic Alliance, and the problem of Germany, could only be solved in the framework of a supranational European construction along the lines of the Schuman Plan and the European Defense Community.

The United States policy towards these problems was dominated for the years to come by the personality and convictions of Dulles. The adherence of the United States to this specific form of European cooperation, with the practical exclusion of real and genuine support for any other form or organization of Western cooperation, became a cornerstone of American foreign policy, led and inspired by this forceful Secretary of State.

Long ago he had called Europe 'historically the world's worst fire hazard'.

On February 10, 1947, he summarized his ideas of European unity, the problem of Germany and the policy, which the United States should follow toward these issues in a way which was so typical for his later policy as Secretary of State: 'Of course increased unity in Europe depends primarily upon the continental peoples themselves. But the United States has there both moral rights and political power. Formerly Europe could have its wars without involving us. Now American blood, shed in two European wars, gives us the right to speak. Our position in Germany gives us a special claim to be heard, for what is done with that power will either promote unity in Europe or perpetuate disunity. We have a responsibility that is inescapable.'[93]

In his *War or Peace* he had already written: 'We cannot risk a

92. Richard P. Stebbins, *The United States in World Affairs 1953, op. cit.,* p. 154.
93. See for the text of Dulles February 1947, speech:
     Beloff, *op. cit.,* p. 80.

German national army. We might risk having Germans individually as part of a European army, along with French and Belgians, under non-German command and stationed anywhere in Western Europe, preferably not in Germany.'[94]

His friendship with Monnet was extremely close and strong and lasted during a period of four decades. There is no doubt that of all the foreign statesmen, he met during his tenure of office, he felt closest to Adenauer. No comparable link existed between Dulles and any British statesman. The Europe, he tried to promote was Monnet's and Adenauer's Europe. His close relationship with the President and the strong and sometimes authoritarian way in which he governed the Department of State led to a United States foreign policy which carried his very strong and personal mark.

In the more than six years of his tenure of office, United States policy towards Europe and European integration was the policy of Dulles.[95]

No wonder that United States policy and United States prestige became increasingly identified with the ratification of the EDC Treaty.

In his Inaugural Address, President Eisenhower specifically asked for progress on the deadlock on EDC and he urged that the enlightened and inspired leaders of the Western nations try with renewed

94. John Foster Dulles, *War or Peace,* (New York: Macmillan & Cy., 1950), p. 218.
95. For a description of his personality, policy, modus operandi and relation to the President:
Hans J. Morgenthau, 'John Foster Dulles', in *An Uncertain Tradition,* ed. by Norman A. Graebner, (New York: McGraw-Hill Book Cy., 1961), pp. 289–309.
Emmet John Hughes, *The Ordeal of Power,* (New York: Atheneum, 1963).
Roscoe Drummond and Gaston Coblentz, *Duel at the Brink,* (New York: Doubleday, 1960).
Richard Goold-Adams, *The Time of Power,* (London: Weidenfeld and Nicolson, 1962).

vigour to make the unity of their peoples a reality. He repeated this plea in his State of the Union Address on February 2, 1953.[96]

Dulles brought one new element in United States policy with respect to EDC. From the beginning of his taking over the Department of State, he used the threat of a reversal of America's European policy if EDC would fail.

A week after taking, office he made a broadcast to the nation in which he said that the United States had made a big investment in Western Europe on the theory that there could be unity there.

'If, however, there were no chance, and that I just refuse to believe, but if it appeared, there were no chance of getting effective unity, and if in particular France, Germany, and England should go their separate ways, then certainly it would be necessary to give a little rethinking to America's own foreign policy, in relation to Western Europe.'[97]

The first elements of the 'agonizing reappraisal' threat were already apparent.

After a bitter debate, the West-German Bundestag gave final approval to the EDC Treaty on March 14, 1953, and thereby the first step on the road to ratification in Europe was set. The visit of Adenauer to Washington, in the beginning of April, stressed the importance of this step and the United States showed its appreciation by concessions in many fields, like a pledge for granting substantial military aid to the German contingents, economic aid to Berlin, assistance in the question of resettlement of the German refugees, reconsideration of the status of war criminals and many other issues.[98]

During the eleventh meeting of the North Atlantic Council in Paris, held from April 23–25, 1953, Dulles proposed and introduced a special resolution regarding the EDC. The Council declared that

96. Text in *Documents on American Foreign Relations 1953, op. cit.,* p. 21.
97. Richard P. Stebbins, *The U.S. in World Affairs, 1953, op. cit.,* p. 21, and Richard Goold-Adams, *op. cit.,* p. 79.
98. *Documents on American Foreign Relations 1953, op. cit.,* pp. 278–282.

it attached paramount importance to the rapid entry into force of the Treaty establishing the EDC and consequently to its ratification by all signatories.[99]

In the meantime, American pressure mounted and every act of American diplomacy towards the European countries was inspired and dominated by the issue of the ratification of EDC. During the enactment of the Mutual Security Act 1953, Dulles indicated that American investments in Western Europe might depend upon Europe's unity in accordance with the defense treaty.[100]

Congress underlined this policy by the so-called Richards Amendment to the Mutual Security Program appropriation for 1953–1954, which stipulated that half of the funds provided for European military aid could be made available only to the European Defense Community or to its member countries. If the Community failed to come into existence, the funds could not be made available by the executive branch unless Congress changed this provision on recommendation of the President.[101]

In its policy toward the signatories of the Treaty, the Administration concentrated on the five partners of France, in order to present France with the *fait accompli* of ratification by its partners, thereby making a French refusal even more embarrassing and disruptive. American diplomacy was furthermore active in assuring compliance by the five with the additional French requests, mentioned above.

In spite of the fact that indications for French ratification were at the least doubtful, there is every reason to believe that the United States representatives abroad were instructed to refuse any discussion of alternatives to the EDC.

The atmosphere of American policy was expressed by Northrop, a faithful adherent of the Dulles concept, when he wrote:

'If EDC in Continental European Union fails, the foreign policy

99.   *Documents on American Foreign Relations 1953, op. cit.,* p. 207.
100. Department of State, *Bulletin,* February 23, 1953, pp. 287–290.
101. *Congressional Record,* 83nd Congr., 1st sess., p. 8683, and *Mutual Security Act of 1953,* Section 101.

of the U.S....with respect to Communist expansion in Europe fails also.'[102]

In his visit to the capitals of the EDC countries in March and April 1953, Ambassador Bruce stressed the link between speedy ratification of EDC and the decisions by Congress and the Administration in the field of military aid. His theme was that for the United States, the political, military and economic unification of Western Europe had become an end in itself and was no longer a means. Without such unity America might turn away from Europe.

At the conference between France, the United States and the United Kingdom at Bermuda from December 4–8, 1953, it seems that Dulles prepared his colleagues in a very brusque way for the policy which would culminate a few weeks later in his 'agonizing reappraisal' speech.

Dulles told them that the United States was in a mood in which, unless there was some positive action towards European unity in the next two or three months, its foreign aid appropriations would be so rigid and so qualified that there would be very serious repercussions on the NATO programs. He could not take the responsibility for saying that Congress would continue their firm and loyal support of NATO, or pursue the creation of a strong economic and military body on the continent of Europe, if this situation were to drag on much longer.[103]

The American pressure found its culmination at the Paris meeting of the North Atlantic Council on December 14–16, 1953.

The text of Dulles' statement at the Council was slightly altered and handed to the press. Europe had to move on to more complete and organic forms of union. Treaties between sovereign states were not enough. He emphasized that the establishment of EDC would ensure intimate and durable cooperation between the United Kingdom and United States forces and the forces of the EDC on the

102. F. S. C. Northrop, *op. cit.*, p. 22.
103. *The Memoirs of Sir Anthony Eden, Full Circle, op. cit.*, p. 55. For text of the Bermuda Communiqué see *Documents on American Foreign Relations, 1953, op. cit.*, p. 216.

European continent. 'If, however, the European Defense Community should not become effective; if France and Germany remain apart, so that they would again be potential enemies, then indeed there would be grave doubt whether continental Europe could be made a place of safety. This would compel an agonizing reappraisal of basic United States policy...It may never again be possible for integration to occur in freedom, although it might be that Western Europe would be unified, as East Europe has been unified, in defeat and servitude.'[104]

And to take away any impression that his speech for the NATO Council might be considered as an emotional outburst, he underlined his arguments, the next day, in a press conference. 'The United States was not at the moment making any plans on the supposition that EDC would fail. If it did fail it would call for a fundamental reappraisal of United States policy.

The United States is not interested primarily in the EDC as a means of getting any fixed number of German divisions. At present, it is interested in trying to create a situation so that the Western countries will not commit suicide. If they decide to commit suicide, they may have to commit it alone. If events compelled the United States to an agonizing reappraisal, one of the elements in that reappraisal would be the disposition of United States forces.'[105]

After his return from Paris, he told the National Press Club on December 22, 1953, that rejection of EDC would mean a reexamination of the so called forward strategy in Western Europe which he defined as a plan to defend the entire area of the prospective EDC countries, rather than to contemplate from the beginning the abandonment of advanced positions in Germany which might make the rest of Europe untenable.[106]

To prove that this unprecedented bluntness in the intercourse between allied nations was not Dulles' policy but United States policy,

104. *The New York Times,* December 15, 1953.
105. *The New York Times,* December 15, 1953.
106. Department of State, *Bulletin,* Jan. 4, 1954, pp. 3–7.

the White House released on December 23, 1953, the opinion of the President.

'The President was informed concerning the prospects of bringing into being the European Defense Community, a matter which has long been of deep concern to him. He considers this the only practical proposal for ending permanently the recurrent strife between France and Germany, provoked twice in our own generation by German militarism, and of creating a solid core at the center of the NATO structure. The President shares the view which had been expressed to the Council by Secretary Dulles that failure soon to consummate the EDC would confront the United States with the necessity of reappraising its basic policies as regards Europe.'[107]

From all these statements it becomes clear that for United States policy the EDC far exceeded the issue of German rearmament. The issue was now presented in terms of the broadest political ideology and had elements of an almost theological dispute.

From a conversation with Eden, it becomes clear that Dulles, apart from his deeper political and ideological convictions, based his policy of intentional brusqueness on the hope that it would be effective. He wanted to give French public opinion a jolt because he thought the French were not aware of the very grave consequences upon American policy if the hopes of a European arrangement, which would unite France and Germany, were to be dashed. Monnet's opinion was that it was not possible to find a French Government which could put through EDC and govern France, since the majorities required for those purposes were different. Therefore, Dulles intended to wait for a French Government which could take office solely for the purpose of putting through EDC.

He further warned Eden that the United States and Britain were approaching a parting of the ways with regard to European policy. If things went wrong, the United States might swing over to a policy of Western Hemisphere defense, with the emphasis on the Far East. Moreover he was afraid that if EDC were not ratified in the

107. Department of State, *Bulletin,* January 4, 1954, p. 7.

spring, the Germans would become disillusioned with the European idea and would press strongly to be released from the present allied restrictions.

He expressed the hope that Britain might find an occasion to underline his warnings and also make some appeal to France.[108]

Stebbins wrote: 'Few periods of recent history have tested the solidarity of the Western world more severely than the late spring and summer of 1954.'[109]

The months till August 1954, were characterized by frantic efforts to save EDC from collapse.

Germany, the Netherlands, Belgium and Luxemburg had ratified the Treaty and no major difficulty was expected in Italy.

Parliamentary and extra-parliamentary agitation in France increased. The Laniel Government itself was divided. On April 7, 1954, General de Gaulle denounced the EDC project and urged upon France to become independent, both from the United States and the Soviet Union.

The interpretive protocols, proposed earlier by France had been reluctantly accepted by the other signatories already in June 1953.

Now French policy was directed to obtain additional guarantees from the United States and the United Kingdom.

These new French desires were satisfied to a large extent by an Association Agreement between the United Kingdom and the proposed European Defense Community, signed at Paris on April 13, 1954, and by a message from President Eisenhower to the Premiers of the Six European Defense Community nations on April 16, 1954. After consultation with congressional leaders of both parties the United States, like the United Kingdom, pledged the maintenance in Europe of its fair share of the forces needed for the joint defense of the North Atlantic area.

And like the United Kingdom, the message implied that the

108. *The Memoirs of Sir Anthony Eden, Full Circle, op. cit.*, pp. 57–58.
109. Richard P. Stebbins, *The United States in World Affairs, 1954,* Published for the Council on Foreign Relations, (New York: Harper & Brothers, 1955), p. 132.

United States commitment was not looked upon as something that would automatically lapse after twenty years. (The French had always been concerned about the difference of the treaty-period between NATO and EDC.)[110]

On June 17, 1954, Mendes France declared in his investiture speech that he would submit new proposals regarding the EDC. Dulles continued his 'agonizing reappraisal' line in different speeches and declarations. From June 25–29, 1954, the Americans and the British met on the highest level in Washington.

As to EDC, the conversations showed again that both were deeply concerned about the establishment of an effective defensive force on the continent of Europe and the inclusion of Germany in that defense. The main difference remained that the British by no means were as committed as the Americans to a specific concept of the German participation.

This led to a Communiqué in which a strong endorsement of EDC and an appeal for speedy ratification and support for the American concept of European continental union was, for the first time, combined with the possibility of an alternative solution for a German defense contribution. A working party was set up in London to consider what might be done if the EDC Treaty would not materialize.[111]

In Congress, the Senate Foreign Relations Committee approved an amendment to the Mutual Security Act 1954, calling for the cessation of all United States aid to countries which failed to ratify the EDC Treaty or an acceptable alternative by December 31, 1954.

On July 12, 1954, Dulles wrote a letter to the Chairmen of the Senate Foreign Relations Committee and the House Foreign Affairs Committee in which he wrote:

110.   For text of the Association Agreement with the United Kingdom and the Presidential Message see:
   Documents on American Foreign Relations 1954, Published for the Council on Foreign Relations, (New York: Harper & Brothers, 1955), pp. 82 and 85.
111.   *Documents on American Foreign Relations 1954, op. cit.,* p. 62.

'As a result of these talks with the British Government it has been recommended on both sides that, if the French Assembly adjourns without taking action on the EDC Treaty, the French Government should, as a first step, be asked to join with the United States, the United Kingdom and the Federal Republic in bringing the Bonn conventions into force in the absence of the Treaty...

This would afford an opportunity to complete arrangements for a German defense contribution.'[112]

The Senate promptly adopted a resolution encouraging the President to take any steps that might become necessary, during the coming months, to restore sovereignty in Germany and to enable her to contribute to the maintenance of peace and security.[113]

On August 19, 1954, Mendes France put his proposals for modification of the EDC Treaty before his five colleagues at a conference in Brussels. These proposals would have emptied the Treaty of its basic political meaning, because every trace of supranationalism was to be either deleted or delayed.

He met a solid front of refusal. At a certain moment, he created the impression that his proposal had the support of the American Government and it took an urgent trip of Ambassador Bruce to Brussels to rectify that impression in the strongest possible form.

On August 30, 1954, the French Assembly, voting not on the Treaty itself but on a Gaullist motion to remove the Treaty from the agenda and pass to other business, rejected the Treaty by 319 against 264 votes with 43 abstentions, among which there were the members of the Government. The analysis of the vote reflected the often opposite motives among the advocates and opponents of the Treaty. The communists and Gaullists were solidly against while the M.R.P. unitedly supported the Treaty. The Radical-Socialists, the Independents and the Socialists, however, were completely split.

Immediately after the rejection, Dulles called it a tragedy and

112. Text of the letter in *Documents on American Foreign Relations 1954, op. cit.,* pp. 104–106.
113. *Senate Resolution 295,* 83rd Congr., 2nd sess., July 30, 1954.

issued a bitterly worded statement. But the Western alliance did not collapse. The agonizing reappraisal did not take place. The fact that the United States had been so exclusively and totally committed to the EDC project made it impossible for it to take a new initiative. In view of the dramatic development of the last few years, it seemed natural and appropriate that the new initiative should come from the partner in the Western alliance which was least involved in the EDC history. Eden immediately took the initiative to probe an alternative solution. His conversations led to a period of frantic diplomatic activity, culminating in the London Conference of September 1954.

The old Brussels Treaty was revived into a Western European Union, expanded to include Germany and Italy and linked with NATO.

Germany was to become a member of NATO after all signatories had ratified the new Brussels Treaty and a convention providing for the continued stationing of allied forces in West-Germany, subject to German consent, was signed. All allied forces on the continent were placed under the Supreme Allied Commander in Europe. The new organization was, among other things, empowered to fix the maximum force levels of its members on the recommendation of NATO's military authorities.

Germany declared unilaterally not to manufacture atomic, chemical or biological weapons and other specific war material except on the request of SACEUR and approved by a two-thirds majority of the Council of WEU. In return for accepting these restraints the Federal Republic gained the full authority of a sovereign state over its internal and external affairs, a national military establishment and through its membership of NATO a full and major voice in the councils of the Western alliance.

Great Britain promised to continue to maintain on the continent the four divisions and the tactical air units, already assigned to SACEUR, and not to withdraw them against the wishes of the Brussels Powers.

The United States made an important contribution to the success of the conference by renewing the pledge which the President had given on April 16, 1954, in connection with the European Defense Community. The treaties and protocols which were initiated at the London Conference were signed in Paris during the Conference on October 19–23, 1954.[114]

On December 28, 29 and 30, 1954, the French Assembly ratified the various treaties and protocols and in May 1955, over four and a half years after the NATO members had accepted a German contribution in principle, the Federal Republic joined NATO on terms far more similar to the original United States proposals of September 1950, than to the EDC concept.

In the relations between the United States and Europe and in the concern for European integration of United States foreign policy, the history and fate of German rearmament and the EDC Treaty have been of immense importance.

There is reason to doubt the wisdom of certain aspects of American policy during this period. The dogmatic character of this policy, the refusal to consider alternatives, the confusion between means and ends and the unprecedented pressure to obtain a specific solution for a problem over which the United States had no ultimate control, led to a situation in which the strain on the Western alliance was increased instead of mitigated. In these kind of circumstances, the leader of the alliance should have more maturity and wisdom, should act less dogmatically and should not commit its power and prestige to a case, of which the success was so much in doubt.

On the other hand, however, it was a reasonable assumption al-

114. For a detailed analysis of the history of the conferences see among others:
Robert E. Osgood, *op. cit.*, pp. 95–98.
Richard P. Stebbins, *The United States in World Affairs 1954, op. cit.,* p. 150–167.
Richard Goold-Adams, *op. cit.*, pp. 162–168.
The Memoirs of Sir Anthony Eden, Full Circle, op. cit., pp. 146–174.
For the text of the formidable array of protocols and documents:
Documents on American Foreign Policy 1954, op. cit., pp. 106–184.

ready in 1950, that the objective of German rearmament could only be attained by some unorthodox form of cooperation and not by the traditional form of an alliance. At that time, it was difficult to foresee that the French would ultimately reject their own concept and accept a construction to which they were so violently opposed. In retrospect, the decision to propose the German rearmament issue in 1950, seems more detrimental to the harmonious development of the Western Alliance than the support for EDC after that premature and untimely proposal had been made.

There is wide spread criticism about the pressure which the United States exercised on its European partners and which culminated in the 'agonizing reappraisal' policy.

In general, the prestige of a major power is not increased when after continuous threats of reversal of policy, this policy is not changed, when the issue arises for which this reappraisal was prepared. One should also recognize how much irritation was caused by the brusqueness of Dulles' policy. His action, however, ultimately had the beneficial effect that the British Government immediately proposed an alternative for EDC and became actively and completely involved in the pursuit of a successful solution and further that the French Assembly in December 1954, accepted this solution. Dulles' policy had made it clear to the French that a second refusal would have meant either a German rearmament without French consent, or a possible basic change in the American commitment to Europe.

The validity of the thesis that American pressure was partly responsible for the French rejection of EDC is open to grave doubt. It caused irritation and it was used by French elements which would have rejected EDC anyhow. With or without American pressure, the vote of August 1954, would, in the then prevailing circumstances, have been negative for purely domestic French reasons.

The United States would, however, have been more helpful if it would have tried in an inconspicuous way to put EDC in the right limited perspective and would not have given it this fierce ideological and dogmatic mark.

With the failure of EDC, it seemed as if the post-war movement for this specific form of European integration had come to an end and United States policy in support of this concept had to be transformed. Neither was true, as will be discussed in the following chapter of this study.

The United States, quite naturally, remained much more in the background with regard to the problem of European integration than had been the case during the EDC period.

But as soon as the concept of European unity along the lines of the Schuman Plan was revived at the Conference of Messina in June 1955, it became apparent that the support for this policy in the United States had not died with EDC but had become a basic and constant element in the formulation and conduct of its foreign policy.

CHAPTER V

The United States and European Integration (1954–1961)

A. INTRODUCTION

During the years 1950–1954, and more specifically since the Eisenhower-Dulles Administration, the support for the supranational form of continental European integration became a firmly embedded, unchangeable and permanent part of American foreign policy.

Even in the most recent years in which fundamental assumptions in the relation between the United States and Europe and the structure of the North Atlantic Alliance have been challenged, one cannot say that this has basically altered or affected the conviction of the United States that European integration was and is in the best interests of the United States and per definition a strengthening factor of the North Atlantic Alliance.

Inevitably, in recent times more doubts are expressed, more question marks put, more emphasis laid on certain aspects of specific American interests, but the policy toward the integration of Europe has remained constant in its broad lines.

Support of the European Economic Community, support of Euratom, reluctance towards the European Free Trade Area and finally, President Kennedy's concept of the Atlantic Partnership, on the basis of equality between the United States and Europe, constitute the practical policy, resulting from this permanent conviction.

The policy of the United States towards the problem of European unity had of course to adjust itself to a set of new circumstances. The growing strength and unity of the European countries, individually and collectively, posed many complicated and often agonizing problems. The deterioration of the United States balance of payments since 1958, the problems of defense, notably the nuclear dilemma, the trade problems between the United States and the EEC and the challenge of Gaullist France to the notion of Atlantic cooperation as well as to the concept of European integration, confronted the United States with the necessity of choice and decisions in its European policy. But even these often drastic changes and challenges did not shake, and one is inclined to say, strangely enough, the approach to European integration which emerged in the years between 1950 and 1954.

The collapse of the European Defense Community affected the tactics of United States policy towards Europe but not its strategy. The latter remained the same, notably support for supranational continental European integration.

The only surviving institute, the Coal and Steel Community, was constantly supported by American diplomacy and policies.

When the High Authority was established in Luxemburg, the United States was one of the first countries to send a permanent mission to the High Authority, led by one of its highest ranking ambassadors, David Bruce.

In April 1954, a $100 million loan agreement to the Community was signed.

In its presentation to Congress the Administration left no doubt that this was primarily done on political grounds.

Assistant Secretary of State Livingston T. Merchant declared during the hearings that the loan was largely granted on 'straight political justifications'.[1]

After the rejection of the EDC Treaty, the United States supported the establishment of the Western European Union but dur-

---

1. *The Mutual Security Act of 1954*, Hearings before the House Committee on Foreign Affairs, 83rd Congr., 2nd sess., April 5, 1954, p. 683.

ing these trying months, a certain nostalgia was apparent with regard to what the United States considered the pure form of European integration.

The subsequent Paris Conference of October 1954, finally settled the burning problem of the German defense contribution and the membership of the sovereign German Federal Republic of NATO, both vital aims of American foreign policy.

During these intricate negotiations the United States role was helpful but not inspiring, in spite of the warm message of March 10, 1955, sent by the President to the Prime Ministers of the seven countries signatory to the Western European Union Treaty[2] and the message of congratulation which Dulles sent to the Western powers, when finally agreement on the treaties was reached and in which he called this event 'a shining chapter in history'.[3]

The United States also put maximum diplomatic pressure on France, when again at the end of 1954, the French Assembly hesitated to ratify the treaties mentioned above.

In the United States, however, the feeling prevailed that the Western European Union 'had possibly saved an alliance but that the principle of European Union continued to be in jeopardy.'[4]

An example of this nostalgia was provided by the unexpected and sudden visit of Dulles to Bonn on September 16, 1954, which rather upset the delicate negotiations that the British Foreign Secretary was conducting on the continent of Europe.

In the Communiqué issued in Bonn on September 17, 1954, the German Federal Chancellor and the American Secretary of State declared that 'there was complete agreement that European integration was so vital to peace and security that efforts to achieve it should be resolutely pursued and that this great goal should not be abandoned because of a single set-back.'[5]

On September 15, 1954, Dulles sent a message to Eden with severe

2. Department of State, *Bulletin*, March 21, 1955, pp. 461–465.
3. Drummond and Coblentz, *op. cit.*, p. 110.
4. Hans A. Schmitt, *op. cit.*, p. 231.
5. Department of State, *Bulletin*, Deptember 27, 1954, p. 434.

criticism about the proposed Western European Union Treaty because it was not supranational. He repeated this during his subsequent talks with the British leaders in London. He told them that 'it was really immaterial whether a NATO plus Brussels solution was better or worse than EDC. Congress had been "sold" on the latter as the means of uniting Europe which would then be capable of standing on its own feet without American help ... He emphasized the importance of keeping alive the idea of real integration in Europe. Dr. Adenauer had expressed qualms that it might be difficult to make further progress in that direction through the Brussels Treaty Organization because of British membership and he, Mr. Dulles, hoped that some means could be devised which would enable the others to go ahead if they so desired, without the United Kingdom, in fields extending further than Brussels.'[6]

This was said after the complete collapse of EDC and even before the alternative arrangement of the WEU Treaties was accepted. Is there better proof where the heart of United States foreign policy toward Europe really was?

In all public speeches, communiqué's and congressional documents, the Administration continued to stress this element of its policy.

Where strategy remained unaltered, tactics, however, had to change.

The opinion that undue United States pressure on the EDC had created adverse effects left its mark on American policy.

The period of American initiatives with regard to European integration changed into support and help for what now was considered primarily a European initiative.

The whole machinery of American diplomacy was put at the disposal of every movement in that direction and countless contacts between the possible sources of new European initiatives – especially Monnet and the groups around him – were established and strengthened.

6. *The Memoirs of Sir Anthony Eden, Full Circle, op. cit.,* pp. 158–164.

The emphasis, however, had shifted to the other side of the Ocean.

The emergence of the European Economic Community and Euratom during 1955 and 1956, would provide United States foreign policy with a new object on which it could concentrate its concern with the process of European integration.

B. THE UNITED STATES AND THE
EUROPEAN ECONOMIC COMMUNITY

The main characteristic of American policy towards the two new emerging instruments of European integration – the European Economic Community and Euratom – was the primacy of foreign policy considerations over all others.

In its policy towards the European Defense Community it was logical that United States support for a political aim was rooted in political considerations.

What was striking in its endorsement of the new economic structures, was the fact that its approach to it was primarily inspired by non-economic motives.

There was no American initiative. There was even, what Beloff calls, the tendency 'to avoid the appearance of any undue interest when things in Europe began to go ahead again with the Messina Conference of June 1955.'[7]

But there was the strong desire of the American Government to be as helpful as possible in the achievement of further progress along the lines of the Schuman Plan. Above all, there was the use of American influence through public and through diplomatic and semi-diplomatic action.

There was also a strong element of protection of American interests. This element, as will be demonstrated later, grew much stronger around 1959 and in the years thereafter.

7.   Max Beloff, *op. cit.,* p. 89.

With regard to the Common Market development, there was some tension between the political approach to European unity on the one hand and on the other, the trend in American economic policy which aimed at a non-discriminatory global system of trade and payments. In his thorough analysis of commercial policy, Isaiah Frank compares the support of OEEC with the United States endorsement of the Common Market:

'The OEEC system derived its principal *rationale* from the fact that it was established at a time when the alternative to regionalism in Europe was bilateralism, not multilateralism. In considering the implications of the Common Market for third countries, it must be remembered that this new preferential arrangement is coming into effect at a time when the currencies of the major trading nations of the world are externally convertible and when the alternative to preferences is full non-discrimination.'[8]

All this required a strong political lead from the President and the Department of State in order to maintain the priority of broad foreign policy considerations over often valid economic objections. This lead was amply provided, especially by Secretary Dulles and the top echelon of his Department.[9]

In publications and comments about the new developments in Europe, there was a broad consensus of agreement with United States official support for the European initiatives. But even when the support was qualified, all studies came to the same conclusion as to the analysis of the Administration's attitude. It was United States policy to subordinate economic hesitations to its belief 'that

8. Isaiah Frank, *The European Common Market,* (New York: Praeger, 1961), p. 293.
9. 'Mit der Ausschlüsslichkeit, die ein Kennzeichen seines Stiles war, lehnte es Dulles ab, seine Unterstützung der Europäischen Wirtschaftsgemeinschaft auf Grund anderer Erwägungen einzuschränken.' See
    Raymond Vernon, 'Die Vereinigte Staaten und die europäischen Handelsblöcke', in *Europa-Archiv,* Folge 17/1960, p. 541.
    Sydney Dell, *Trade Blocs and Common Markets,* (London: Constable, 1963), p. 43.

a strong, prosperous and more unified Western Europe was in the best interest of the United States.'[10]

The Conference of Messina of June 1955, between the Ministers of Foreign Affairs of the member states of the European Coal and Steel Community, became identified with the 'relaunching' of Europe.

The period between the rejection of the European Defense Comminuty and the Messina Conference was characterized by the efforts to ensure the parliamentary ratifications of the Western European Union Treaty and to give new impetus to the ideas of European integration along the Schuman-Monnet lines.

Messina was a result of different forces at the end of a period which Mayne calls the period of 'constructive opportunism'.[11]

10. Miriam Camps, *The European Common Market and American Foreign Policy*, Memorandum No. 11, (Center of International Studies, Princeton University, November 1956).

See among many publications:

The European Common Market and its Meaning to the United States, A Statement on National Policy by the Research and Policy Committee of the Committee for Economic Development, May 1959.

Emile Benoit, 'The United States and a United Europe', in *Current History*, Vol. 42, No. 247, March 1962, pp. 172–179.

Henry Tasca, 'Die Vereinigten Staaten, Westeuropa und die Entwicklungsländer', in *Europa Archiv*, Folge 5, 1960, pp. 143–154.

A Study of European Economic Regionalism. A new Era in Free World Economic Politics, Report of a Special Study Mission of the Subcommittee on Europe of the Committee on Foreign Affairs, House of Representatives, 86th Congr., 2nd sess., No. 48971, January 1960, p. 87.

United States Foreign Policy – Western Europe, A study prepared at the request of the Committee on Foreign Relations U.S. Senate, 86th Congr., 1st sess., No. 46478, October 1959, p. 8.

The European Economic Community and the United States, Subcommittee on Foreign Economic Policy of the Joint Economic Committee, 87th Congr., 1st sess., No. 76810, November 1961.

In his highly critical analysis of U.S. policy towards European regionalism Reuss stresses also the unqualified support which the Eisenhower Administration gave to the new European treaties. Henry S. Reuss, *The Critical Decade*, (New York: McGraw-Hill Book Co., 1964), pp. 34–35.

11. Richard Mayne, *op. cit.*, p. 116.

One of these forces undoubtedly was the Common Assembly of the Coal and Steel Community. In their resolutions of May 1955, they pressed for studies and conferences to find ways of extending the powers of the Community and preparing treaties aiming at the next stage in the process of European integration.[12]

A substantial contribution to the new initiatives was made by the Benelux countries. In these smaller European countries, the deception at what seemed to be the end of the Schuman-Monnet concept was very great indeed.

Their adherence to the supranational form of international organization was not only rooted in their easy acceptance of the limited function of national sovereignty in a modern world but also in their conviction that their interests would be better guaranteed by independent institutions.

Certainly in the Netherlands, this attitude became a dogma of Dutch foreign policy and was defended with a nearly religious zeal. In the Netherlands and to a lesser degree in Belgium, there was a strong feeling that the ultimate aim of political unity in Europe had to be achieved through phases of economic integration. In their view, a political structure would collapse if it was not built on the fusion of economic interests. This approach strongly coloured their attitude in the negotiations on the European Political Community which, not to their regret, collapsed together with the European Defense Community.

The ideas of the Netherlands about economic integration found their first expression in the earlier mentioned Stikker Plan which was presented to OEEC in June 1950.[13]

It aimed at trade liberalization by removing all barriers, including

---

12. A. H. Robertson, *European Institutions,* (London: Stevens & Sons Ltd., 1959), p. 27.
   For text of resolutions:
   Annuaire de l'Assemblée Commune, pp. 397–399 and 407.
13. *The Netherlands Government's Plan of Action for European Integration,* June 1950, distributed in the U.S. by the Netherlands Information Bureau.

all tariffs, to intra-European trade. It thought to achieve these aims by an industry-wise approach, and its most imaginative part was the proposal for a European Integration Fund. This gave expression to the notion that complete elimination of trade barriers would create economic and social problems which could only be solved by a joint responsibility.

The Dutch thoughts after the Schuman Plan developed into a concept of the creation of a general customs union. They were discussed in 1953, on the basis of the so-called Beyen Plan and were merged with the Belgian ideas of extension of the powers of the Coal and Steel Community to other sectors.

Out of the confrontation between the thorough Dutch work and the greater political experience and ingenuity of the Belgians, a Benelux Memorandum was born which, on May 20, 1955, was presented to the other member governments of the ECSC.[14]

In taking their initiative, the Benelux countries were not without fear of being dominated by a Franco-German arrangement, resulting from a meeting between Adenauer and the French Foreign Minister, which took place at the same time.

The Communiqué of this meeting announced that the two governments had agreed that the time had come for a new impulse to European cooperation and mentioned specifically transport, air-navigation, aeronautical construction, and above all, research regarding atomic energy and its use for peaceful purposes.[15] Like in the Benelux Memorandum the word 'supranational' was carefully avoided.

The Benelux Memorandum, however, was very clear on the point that what should be done in Europe, implied the establishment of a common authority 'endowed with the powers necessary to the realisation of the agreed objectives'.

These objectives were integration in three specific sectors, trans-

14. French text in *Chronique de Politique Etrangère*, Institut des Relations Internationales, 1955, pp. 523–526.
15. Miriam Camps, *Britain and the European Community 1955–1963*, (London: Oxford University Press, 1964), p. 22.

port, electricity and nuclear energy and the creation of a general common market.[16]

The Germans and the Italians circulated a memorandum in response to the Benelux proposals. The German Memorandum reflected the deep division in the Federal Government between the 'supranationalists' led by Adenauer and the 'multilateralists' who found their inspiration in Dr. Erhard.[17] This division which influenced the German attitude in the coming negotiations, never affected the ultimate results which always bore the stamp of Adenauer's approval.

The Italian Memorandum dealt mainly with social and economic development aspects of new efforts for integration.

A third and very effective source of the new initiatives was Jean Monnet, the President of the High Authority of the ECSC, and the small group of his close collaborators.

In November 1954, Monnet informed the member governments of the ECSC that he was not available for reelection as President of the High Authority on the end of his term in February 1955. As the reason for his decision, he stated that he wanted to be completely free to work for the establishment of a United States of Europe.[18]

The Benelux Memorandum and the general feeling that the worst effects of the EDC defeat were over, moved him to write to the six governments, just before the Messina Conference, that he was, willing to reconsider his decision.[19]

16. See also the account of one of the best informed insiders of this period. Baron Snoy et d'Oppuers, *Les Etapes de la Coopération Européenne et les négotiations relatives à une Zone de Libre Echange, op. cit.,* pp. 588–593.
17. Karl Kaiser, *EWG und Freihandelszone,* (Leiden: Sijthof, 1963), pp. 8–10.
18. Institut des Relations Internationales, *Chronique de Politique Etrangère,* Vol. VIII, No. 5, p. 505.
    He repeated his decision and the motives for it during the Session of the Common Assembly in Strasbourg on November 30 (*Débats de l'Assemblée Commune,* no. 7, Luxembourg, 1955, p. 21).
19. *Chronique de Politique Etrangère, op. cit.,* pp. 510–511.

The French Government, however, as usual divided over the European issue, decided to put up the name of René Mayer for election. On June 10, 1955, Monnet published an article in the London *Times* in which he restated his objectives for European unity.[20]

Of great and lasting influence was his decision to form a new organization – the Action Committee for the United States of Europe. For the first time, a highly powerful pressure group was formed on a European scale.

Its membership consisted of the leading parliamentarians and trade-unionists of the six countries with the exclusion of the extreme right and left.[21]

The first aim of the Committee was to see that the decision of the Messina Conference would be translated into action and results. Membership of the Committee implied support for the Schuman-Monnet concept of European integration.[22]

The inclusion of the German social democrats in this group was a striking achievement in view of the recent attitude of that party towards the issue of European integration.

It was financed by the participating organizations and supported by funds from United States foundations. The Action Committee met for the first time on January 18, 1956, and endorsed the Messina Communiqué with special emphasis on the necessity for establishing a European Atomic Energy Authority which could handle the critical energy deficit on a supranational basis.[23]

This reflected Monnet's preoccupation with the problem of nuclear energy, to which he gave greater priority, at that moment, than to the idea of a common market.

The great influence of Monnet on the thoughts and actions of the United States Government was analyzed in the previous chapter.

20. *The Times,* June 10, 1955.
21. For a list of its founding members see Hans A. Schmitt, *op. cit.,* p. 234.
22. *The New York Times,* October 14, 1955.
23. *Action Committee for a United States of Europe,* First Session, Meeting of January 17 and 18, 1956, pp. 3–9.

Here, it is necessary to describe briefly the influence of his Committee on the events in Europe.

A new technique of parliamentary pressure on governments was initiated. As soon as the Action Committee agreed on a certain issue or line of action, the governments were, in view of the composition of the Monnet group, confronted with a solid front, the attitude of which they were forced to take into account. These attitudes were not only moulded during sessions of the Action Committee. If for instance, the Netherlands Government took a position during the negotiations, which in the eyes of Monnet was detrimental to the outcome, the Dutch members of the group were mobilized to put pressure on the Netherlands Government to yield a point or to take action or initiatives which, by itself, it would not have undertaken. This, sometimes, severely limited the possibilities of negotiation for the governments and it often subjected them to a force which did not originate in the political life of their own countries.

The method worked to a great extent in the Benelux countries, Germany and Italy. In France, the parliamentary situation was so complicated that it was impossible to control or influence the French position through the French members of the Action Committee. But even in France its action was not without effect.

Criticism about the action of the Committee must be expressed on one vital point. Monnet was so obsessed by the necessity of obtaining concrete results that he and his Committee tended to lend a willing ear to the most difficult partner in the negotiations – France. Thereby, it often lost its indispensable objectivity and sometimes, unwillingly, became an instrument of French demands and negotiating positions.

The Conference between the six powers was held at Messina on June 1 and 2, 1955. Snoy describes the incidental factors which led to its success and which had so much to do with atmosphere and personalities.[24] Miriam Camps is right in saying that 'in retrospect

24.   Baron Snoy et d'Oppuers, *op. cit.*, p. 590.

the Messina Conference appears to have been a turning point –
although at the time reluctance to undertake precise commitments
was more evident than zeal for making Europe.'[25]

The Communiqué stated that the time had come to make a fresh
advance towards the building of Europe.

Thereafter, it singled out as objectives the sectors of transport,
energy and especially atomic energy for peaceful purposes. In the
second section of the Communiqué the governments recognized
that the establishment of a European market, free from all custom
duties and all quantitative restrictions, was the objective of their
action in the field of economic policy. This market should be
achieved in phases and a list of questions followed, which required
study. The system of these questions can be refound in the ultimate
treaties. Undoubtedly the main achievement of Messina was in the
field of procedure. It was decided that conferences should be called
to work out treaties or other arrangements concerning the questions under consideration.[26, 27]

Furthermore, it was decided, that a political personality would
preside over a Committee of Governmental Representatives. A
month later, Spaak was chosen for this function and it is no ex-
aggeration to say that without his political drive the Treaties of

25. Miriam Camps, *The European Common Market and American Policy,*
op. cit., p. 4.
26. French text of the Messina Resolution in *Chronique de Politique Etrangère,*
op. cit., pp. 519–546. English text in '*White Paper*', July, 1955, pp. 7–9.
27. For the Messina Conference see further:
P.E.P., *European Organisations, op. cit.,* pp. 295–296.
U. W. Kitzinger, 'Europe: The Six and the Seven', in *International
Organization,* Vol. XIV, Number 1, 1960, p. 25.
U. W. Kitzinger, *The Challenge of the Common Market,* (Oxford:
Blackwell, 1962), pp. 13–14.
Walter Hallstein, *United Europe,* (Harvard University Press, 1962),
pp. 16–17.
Emile Benoit, *Europe at Sixes and Sevens,* (Columbia University Press,
1961), pp. 3–4.
George Lichtheim, *The New Europe, Today and Tomorrow,* (New York:
Praeger, 1963), pp. 47–48.

Rome would either not have been established at all or subjected to endless delays.

Eden, with a certain resignation, remarked after his visit to Washington in 1956, that 'the U.S. Government entertained for the proposals resulting from the Messina Conference the same enthusiasm as they had shown towards the ill-fated European Defense Community.'[28]

The United States showed this support in two ways. One was the public and constant support for the new initiatives by the American Administration. Equally important was a second element. The American diplomatic machinery was, as it were, put at the disposal of the efforts to translate the Messina initiatives into concrete results.

The public announcements were numerous. In December 1955, Dulles said at a press conference, that the West should go ahead with the plans for the development of integration and unity of Europe. 'I am not thinking in terms of the military unification, although that is important. I am thinking more in terms of the general development of the European idea and moving toward a United States of Europe in terms of economic and political unity.'[29]

In an address in Chicago on December 8, 1955, he stated:

'But there is also need for unity on a more intimate basis among the continental European nations themselves. The six nations... have begun to create common institutions, notably the Coal and Steel Community. I was glad to find on my last visit to Europe that the movement to develop along these lines is taking on new vitality. That movement must obtain its strength primarily from the peoples concerned. It is, however, a development in which the United States has a deep interest and which it is prepared to support if opportunity offers.'[30]

In a speech on NATO in New York on April 23, 1956, the Secretary said:

'We believe in the closer integration of some Western European

28. The Memoirs of Sir Anthony Eden, Full Circle, op. cit., p. 337.
29. The New York Times, December 6, 1955.
30. Department of State, Press Release 683, December 8, 1955.

countries, such as represented by the Coal and Steel Community...
whereby the members would apply community principles. Such
European integration and the development of NATO are complementary and not mutually exclusive processes.'[31]

It is especially important to note, in this last sentence, the assumption that European unity and Atlantic cohesion were by nature
compatible. This assumption which developed into the idea of
Atlantic Partnership will be discussed in the concluding chapter of
this study.

On May 26, 1956, the President in an address at Baylor University said that 'with the prospect of the revival in Europe of the
concept of unification, a new sun of hope, security and confidence
would shine for Europe and for the rest of the world.'[32]

In 1957, the President mentioned the subject in his State of the
Union message.

'We welcome the efforts of a number of our European friends to
achieve an integrated community to develop a common market.
We likewise welcome their cooperative effort in the field of atomic
energy.'[33]

United States support was also mentioned[34] in all the Communi-

31. Department of State, *Bulletin,* April 30, 1956, pp. 706–710.
32. Department of State, *Bulletin,* June 4, 1956, p. 917.
33. *House Document I,* 85th Congr., 1st sess.
34. See for example:
    Joint Communiqué on Talks held between the Chancellor of the
    Federal Republic of Germany and the Secretary of State, Washington,
    June 13, 1956, Department of State, *Bulletin,* June 25, 1956, pp. 1047–1048.
    Joint Statement on Talks held between the President of the Council of
    Ministers of France and the President, Washington, February 28, 1957,
    Department of State, *Bulletin,* March 18, 1957, pp. 438–439.
    Joint Communiqué on Talks held between the Foreign Minister of the
    Federal Republic of Germany and the Secretary of State, Washington,
    March 5, 1957, Department of State, *Bulletin,* March 25, 1957,
    pp. 490–491.
    Communiqué and Declaration issued jointly by the Chancellor of the
    Federal Republic of Germany and the President, Washington, May 28,
    1957, Department of State, *Bulletin,* June 17, 1957, pp. 955–956.

qués of bilateral talks with European countries, especially with the French and the Germans.

On January 15, 1957, the Administration stated its views concerning the European Common Market and the Free Trade Area.[35] Strangely enough, it was a statement in which, on two points, there was a deviation from the real policy of the Administration. It placed much emphasis on the economic issues and far less on the political ones. And second, it treated the Free Trade Area as an equal structure to the Common Market. In real American policy, both issues were handled in a different way.

C. THE UNITED STATES AND EURATOM

The support of the United States for Euratom was more active than for the Common Market.

Its technical know-how and the possession of enriched uranium made its support nearly a condition for the success of the European initiatives in the field of nuclear power. The United States shared, at that time, the European concern about the threatening scarcity of non-atomic sources of energy. It had a great interest in the complicated issue of control of the uses to which atomic power might be put and it agreed to the notion that in this field quick results might be obtained because, compared to the common market structure, relatively few vested European interests existed in the atomic field.[36]

In a study about the American attitude towards Euratom H. L.

35. Department of State, *Bulletin*, February 4, 1957, p. 183.
36. Max Beloff, *op. cit.,* pp. 89–90.
     Arnold J. Zurcher *op. cit.,* pp. 144–145.
     Miriam Camps, *Britain and the European Community, op. cit.,* pp. 51–52.
     For an interesting discussion of the United States attitude towards Euratom see also: *Euratom and American Policy,* a Conference Report, by Klauss E. Knorr, Center of International Studies, Princeton University, 1956.

Nieburg gives a detailed account of American actions and motives.[37]

His main thesis is that, in this period, one can witness a brilliantly successful Anglo-American manoeuvre, aiming at excluding their continental partners from independent nuclear weapons production and co-equal strategic control of the alliance. There is no reason to share this view.

In the first place, as in other aspects of their attitude towards European integration, there was nothing like a common Anglo-American point of view with regard to Euratom. But more important is that Nieburg starts from the assumption that the six aimed, at that time, at a role in the nuclear field which would not be confined to a peaceful use of nuclear energy.

He writes:

'The most significant factor underlying these befurcated nuclear programs has been the policy adopted by the U.S. and Britain of excluding their continental NATO partners from independent nuclear-weapons production and co-equal strategy control of the alliance. Euratom was begun as an effort to create an independent capability task for electric power and for the production of weapons material.

... By means of U.S. loans, subsidies, technical aid, and equipment the Euratom program was redirected and controlled, depriving France or any other continental nuclear aspirant of the combined resources of Western Europe for producing weapons material.'

This is far from the truth.

The Messina concept and the Spaak Report explicitly confined the role of Euratom to the peaceful use of atomic energy.

The aims of Euratom were the development of research and production, the exchange of know-how and the facilitation of investments in the field of nuclear energy for peaceful purposes.

There was not only a complete absence, in the Report, of aspirations for nuclear weapon production, but one of the most complicated and time-consuming negotiations between the six took place on

37. H. L. Nieburg, 'Euratom, A Study in coalition politics', in *World Politics*, July, 1963, pp. 597–623.

the issue of combining the explicit wish of the negotiators to limit Euratom to peaceful use of atomic power with the desire of France to keep its weapon research program out of the control mechanism of Euratom. The ambiguous wording of article 84, section 3, is the result of these negotiations which ended by the resignation of the five partners to the possibility of a French weapon program.

In the American attitude toward Euratom, two aspects should be mentioned.

The first was that United States commercial interests were keen to sell their equipment to the new emerging entity. The United States, therefore, easily agreed with the distorted picture of the prospect of grave scarcity of non-nuclear sources of energy which prevailed in Europe, especially during and after the Suez crisis. Never had economic planners been so wrong as in this prognosis.

The second aspect was that of control. There was a strange analogy between the American attitude towards the control issue and its attitude towards the trade problem.

In both cases, there was the tension between two American trends of thought, the global approach and the regional one. While one trend supported the priority of a global control mechanism, the other trend preferred the regional system. In the American approach to Euratom, both tendencies were apparent.

In February 1957, the so called 'Three Wise Men', (Louis Armand, Franz Etzel and Francesco Giordani), appointed by the negotiating committee of Euratom, visited Washington.

Their visit was concluded by a communiqué [38] in which it was stated that the American Government welcomed the initiative taken in the Committee's proposal for a bold and imaginative application of nuclear energy and the American willingness to allocate to the new organization part of the 20,000 kilograms of U-235 which the President had made available in principle on February 22, 1956.[39]

38. Department of State, *Bulletin*, February 25, 1957, pp. 306–307.
39. Department of State, *Bulletin*, March 19, 1956, pp. 469–47.

On November 8, 1958, an important agreement was signed in Brussels between the United States and Euratom, in which the financial assistance, technical know-how, the sale of U-235 and the control issue were incorporated.

In a Message to Congress the President strongly recommended the approval of this agreement.[40]

The American diplomatic support for the new initiatives in Europe is not on record. Given the established policy of the American Administration under the direction of Dulles and the very close relationship between Monnet and the Secretary of State, an activity developed in which the United States diplomatic machinery was used to remove the many obstacles on the road to final and concrete results of the negotiations, leading to the Treaties of Rome. Monnet and his Action Committee were unofficially supervising the negotiations and as soon as obstacles appeared, the United States diplomatic machinery was alerted, mostly through Ambasssador Bruce and his successor Ambassador Butterworth, who had immediate access to the top echelon of the State Department where Robert Bowie of the Planning Staff and Under Secretary Dillon worked on this subject under the strong leadership of Dulles.

At that time, it was usual that if Monnet thought that a particular country made difficulties in the negotiations, the American diplomatic representative in that country approached the Foreign Ministry in order to communicate the opinion of the American Government which, in practically all cases, coincided with Monnet's point of view. Hardly ever, was there overt pressure, but there was no doubt where the United States stood on these issues.

On the one hand, this American diplomatic activity helped to bring the negotiations to a result. On the other hand, however, as was mentioned above in connection with the activities of Monnet's Action Committee, it led to a situation in which the United States

40. *House Document* 411, 85th Congr., 2nd sess.
     See for Euratom further: Jaroslav G. Polach, *Euratom,* (New York: Oceana Publications Inc., 1964).

had, in its desire to bring about concrete results, the tendency to support the point of view of the most difficult partner in the negotiations – France. This support of the French thesis occasionally led to a disregard of the legitimate interests of other countries.

In concluding an analysis of the United States attitude towards the Common Market and Euratom, mention should be made of the complete absence in American official thinking of the possibility that American and European interests might diverge.

Even such a staunch ally of the United States as Adenauer was at that time, said in a speech in Brussels, on September 25, 1956: 'The vital necessities of European countries need not always be identical with the vital interests of the United States and vice versa' and he called for some kind of confederation of European nations to re-establish Europe's shaken prestige and influence in world affairs.[41]

Dulles, however, refused to see an anti-American implication in the European developments and pointed out that the United States itself had long been the foremost advocate of European unity for the reasons already mentioned. [42]

The circumstances changed but the policy remained the same.

D. THE UNITED STATES AND THE FREE TRADE AREA NEGOTIATIONS

The years between 1956 and 1961 were a period in which the United States had to adjust its policies and to determine its attitude towards a European scene, dominated by the establishment of the Common Market and the growing tensions between this new, revolutionary creation and the other European members of OEEC.

41. 'New impetus for European idea'. Excerpts from a speech by Chancellor Adenauer, *The Bulletin,* issued by the Press and Information Office of the German Federal Government, October 4, 1956.
42. Richard P. Stebbins, *The United States in World Affairs, 1956,* Published for the Council on Foreign Relations, (New York: Harper & Brothers, 1957), pp. 288–289.

During this period its policy was increasingly influenced by its concern for its own economic interests and notably its deteriorating balance of payments position.

A growing tension between foreign policy considerations towards the problem of European integration and defense of United States legitimate economic interests became apparent.

In the preceding period, discrimination against United States exports, as a consequence of the development of and support for a regional European construction, was accepted by the United States without hesitation.

It was accepted on economic grounds mainly because of the all-important problem of Europe's dollar shortage. 'In the early post-war years, the United States acquiesced in a strictly intra-European attack on trade barriers, because the dollar shortage appeared to rule out a global attack.'[43]

It was accepted on political grounds for the various reasons stated before. The United States welcomed the creation of the supra-national Common Market, practically without second thoughts about discrimination.

In the later phases of the negotiations for a Free Trade Area, in the efforts to bring together the Europe of the six and the Europe of the seven and during the reconstitution of OEEC, the support for the six increasingly coincided with the American desire to avoid undue discrimination against its exports.

Those on the continent of Europe who for economic or political reasons, or both, were against all efforts to extend the integration process beyond the framework of the six, took full advantage of this American attitude and took great care to present their arguments, proposals and programs in such a way that they were in sympathy with the growing American concern for discrimination against its economic interests.[44]

43. Randall Hinshaw, *The European Community and American Trade*, Published for the Council on Foreign Relations, (New York: Praeger, 1964), p. 163.
44. See also Miriam Camps, *The European Common Market and Free Trade Area*, Center of International Studies, Princeton University, 1957, p. 30.

This led to the ironical situation that, in its struggle for more global solutions of trade problems, the United States found itself in alliance with the most protectionist tendencies in Europe against those in Europe who fundamentally shared the more liberal approach to economic problems.

The American policy in this period can best be demonstrated on three issues, first, its attitude towards the Free Trade Area negotiations, second, its policy towards the relation between the Common Market and the European Free Trade Association, initiated in Stockholm in November 1959, and finally its initiative for the remodelling of OEEC.

A full and accurate account of the Free Trade Area negotiations is given by Miriam Camps, Snoy and Kaiser.[45]

To put the American attitude in a true perspective, it is necessary to recall briefly the main facts and events of these confusing years.

At its meeting of July 1956, the Council of Ministers of OEEC decided to establish a special OEEC working party to study the possible forms and methods of association between the customs union of the six and the other OEEC countries and specifically, the possibility of a free trade area which would include the customs union of the six as one entity.[46]

This decision implied that the six, busily negotiating their own differences, were immediately faced with the problem of their relations with the outside world and notably their OEEC partners.

The special OEEC working party published its report in January 1957[47], and the Council of OEEC on ministerial level met in February. Before the Council meeting, the British Government circulated a memorandum containing its views on the report of the working

45. Karl Kaiser, *EWG und Freihandelszone, op. cit.*, pp. 92–227.
     Miriam Camps, *Britain and the European Community, op. cit.*, pp. 93–173.
     Baron Snoy et d'Oppuers, *Les Etapes de la Coopération Européenne et les Négotiations Relatives à une Zone de Libre Echange, op. cit.*, pp. 603–624.
46. OEEC Information Division, *Press Release*, A (56) 32.
47. OEEC, *Report on the Possibility of Creating a Free Trade Area in Europe*, Paris, January 1957.

party and proposed that the Council should approve the creation of a European Industrial Free Trade Area.[48]

It was to be expected that Britain was not able to obtain any commitment of its OEEC partners in the meeting of February and the Council fled, as usual in those circumstances, into a procedural arrangement. It decided to enter into negotiations in order to determine ways and means, on the basis of which there could be brought into being a European Free Trade Area which would, on a multilateral basis, associate the European Common Market with other member countries of the Organization.

The Chairman of the Council, Thorneycroft, was invited to organize the necessary working parties and in March 1957, the Council approved the establishment of Working Party no. 21, which was instructed to undertake negotiations in conformity with the Council decision of February 1957. Agriculture and arrangements for less developed countries should be examined by two other working parties.[49]

Strong pressure from the continent and the United States not to open negotiations before the French had ratified the Treaties of Rome in July 1957, led to a postponement of further discussion.

In October 1957, the OEEC Council met and while there was a wider cleavage between the British point of view and the consensus of opinion in the six than before, the October resolution was more positive than the February one.

The Council declared its determination to secure the establishment of a European Free Trade Area which would comprise all member countries of the Organization, which would associate, on a multilateral basis, the EEC with the other member countries and which, taking fully into consideration the objectives of the EEC,

48. *A European Free Trade Area,* United Kingdom Memorandum to the OEEC, (London: H.M.S.O., February 1957).
49. In January 1959, the British Government published a *Blue Book, Negotiations for a European Free Trade Area,* (London: H.M.S.O., January 1959), in which all the relevant documents relating to this period are collected.

would in practice take effect parallel with the Treaty of Rome.[50]

It also decided to establish an Intergovernmental Committee at ministerial level in which the negotiations could take place.

This British paper victory was won during a cabinet crisis in France. The Bourgès-Mannoury Government had fallen and the Gaillard Government had not yet succeeded.

The Intergovernmental Committee elected the British Paymaster-General Maudling as its chairman. The instrument for negotiations was created. The policies of the negotiators were, however, already from the beginning wide apart.

Many observers of the scene considered the British approach as a clever and purposeful exercise to torpedo the young Community of the six.

One can agree with Miriam Camps that the British motives were considerably purer than they were given credit for.[51]

For the British, the Free Trade Area proposals meant a reversal of their traditional OEEC policy that tariffs should be the subject of global agreements and should take place in the framework of GATT. They had to convince their public and parliamentary opinion of the wisdom of this new course which was by no means an accepted dogma in the United Kingdom. They were genuinely concerned about a course of events which they considered as a threat to the achievements of European cooperation since 1948.

It is, however, undeniable that they knew that their initiative would lead to a delay in the process of continental integration and could result in a system in which the Common Market concept would be superseded by a free trade area.

Their timing and their presentation was particularly unfortunate and showed an almost incredible lack of feeling for the forces at work on the continent of Europe and in the United States.

As to the timing, it forced the six to adopt a common front in the negotiations which tended to accentuate rather than to submerge national differences. Miriam Camps wrote:

50.   *Blue Book, op. cit.,* pp. 48–49.
51.   Miriam Camps, *op. cit.,* p. 119.

'It is an issue that focuses attention on fears and on contingencies that may never happen. Before the Six have had time to absorb the Treaty of Rome, to find out what in practice it will really mean... they embarked on another negotiation. But in the new negotiation the incentives to reach agreement appear much weaker at least to the crucial French, and the temptations to yield to domestic pressures are correspondingly greater.'[52]

This was exactly what Monnet and his Action Committee feared and their concern was shared by the central figure of the negotiations between the six, Spaak.

The Monnet Committee, in its September meeting of 1956, made it clear that it attached primary importance to quick agreements by the six governments.[53] This attitude of the founding fathers of the European Community was already enough to influence American policy into a negative attitude towards the free trade area concept.

But there were more motives which determined the hostility of American policy, even when this hostility was initially concealed behind the appearance of neutrality.

The United States supported regional economic arrangements in Europe and its resulting discriminating aspects as long as the dollar-shortage made this policy an obvious device to strengthen its European partners.

With the emergence of new economic strength in Europe, regionalism and discrimination was only accepted and even supported by the United States if this regionalism held promises for what it considered real integration in the economic and subsequently in the political field. Discrimination for purely commercial reasons was not acceptable anymore.

A further point was that the traditional United States resentment against the Commonwealth preferential system flared up again.

52. Miriam Camps, *The First Year of the European Community,* Center of International Studies, Princeton University, November 1958, pp. 15–16.
53. *Resolution of the Action Committee for a United States of Europe,* Third Session, Paris, September 19–20, 1956.

Since the early nineteen-thirties, the United States had fought against this system and during the foundation of GATT its victory on the issue of the acceptance of a non-discriminatory global and multilateral trade system, based on the most-favoured nation concept, had been only partial.[54] The Commonwealth preferences were maintained.

How much Britain underestimated these strong tendencies in the United States and how unfortunate its presentation was in the light of these tendencies may be proven by two official and important declarations.

The British memorandum of February 1957, stated emphatically: 'Her Majesty's Government's concept of the Free Trade Area differs in some important respects from that of the Customs and Economic Union now contemplated by the Messina Powers. The arrangements proposed for the Customs and Economic Union involve far-reaching provisions for economic integration and harmonisation of financial and social policies, and for mutual assistance in the financing of investment. These arrangements are to be effected within an appropriate institutional framework. Her Majesty's Government envisage the Free Trade Area on the other hand, as a concept primarily to the removal of restrictions on trade such as tariffs and quota's.'[55]

On the second issue of Commonwealth preferences, the Prime Minister in a speech before the House of Commons, on November 26, 1956, made it abundantly clear that the maintenance of Commonwealth preferences was not negotiable and the acceptance of a common outside tariff already for that reason out of the question.[56]

These statements might have had a good effect on British public opinion, to which they were primarily directed, but they certainly

54. For a detailed analysis of the British and the American approach to the problem of multilateral trade see
Richard N. Gardner, *Sterling-Dollar Diplomacy*, (Oxford: Clarendon Press, 1956).
55. *A European Free Trade Area, op. cit.,* par. 11.
56. *The Times,* November 27, 1956.

antagonized the American official position towards the free trade area concept even more than was already the case.

After the already mentioned declaration of January 15, 1957, the façade of American neutrality during the negotiations was maintained in a declaration which the American observer made at the meeting of the Maudling Committee of February 17, 1958. The United States Government expressed its hope that the negotiations would be successful and warned the Committee that a split between the European states would make the renewal of the Trade Agreement Act by Congress more difficult.[57]

There was only one more open American intervention. In a reaction to a French counter-proposal of a highly protectionist character, put forward during the negotiations, the United States officially transmitted its views to all participants in the beginning of April 1958.

It spelled out three points, all three symptomatic for the American attitude:

1. It stated that it would support the Free Trade Area only if it was compatible with the GATT and took the interest of third countries fully into account.

2. It was imperative that the negotiations on the Free Trade Area should not endanger the implementation of the Common Market Treaty because the Community of the six provided the starting point for a genuine political integration.

3. The United States feared that a breakdown of the negotiations might react unfavorably both in the situation on Europe and on NATO. It was therefore prepared to support the proposals of the Commission of the EEC for an interim solution, namely the extension to all members of GATT of the first round of tariff reductions under the treaty.[58]

57. Max Beloff, *op. cit.,* p. 93.
      Karl Kaiser, *op. cit.,* p. 164.
58. For the contents of the French proposal and the interim solution proposed by the EEC Commission, see
      Karl Kaiser, *op. cit.,* pp. 157–162 and pp. 170–172.

For the rest of the negotiations there was an absolute silence from
the American side as far as public declarations were concerned. At
the moment of the breakdown of the negotiations, in the meeting
of December 15, 1958, most participants hoped that the American
observer would act as mediator and pressed him to intervene in an
issue which was splitting America's partners in Europe. The observer refused, however, to comply and contributed to the general
frustration by complete silence.

There was, however, no passivity in the unofficial sphere. Drummond and Coblentz record the pressure of Dulles on the German
Minister of Economic Affairs, Erhard, in trying to persuade him to
drop his preference for the free trade area concept and they quote
Erhard as saying that the concept of the six was holy to Dulles.[59]

On every possible occasion, the American diplomatic representatives chose without hesitation for the forces who gave absolute
priority to the cohesion of the six over any compromise with the
British proposals.

For the member countries of the six, the negotiation of the Free
Trade Area was a permanent choice of loyalties. On the one hand,
there was the loyalty to the new community of the Rome Treaty.
On the other hand, there were especially with the Dutch, Belgians
and some Germans, strong loyalties to the liberal approach of the
Free Trade Area and the preservation of OEEC cooperation.

Monnet and the European Commission were compelled by their
concern for the cohesion of the six to align themselves with the
French attitude and concept. There is no doubt that by their own
conviction and through the influence of Monnet and his entourage,
the Americans were not at all neutral in the conflict but fully supported the thesis of the primacy of the six.

This point of view was also clearly set out by the American authors
who were close to this prevailing school of thought and policy.

Ben Moore wrote:

'In the question of membership we will undoubtedly continue to

59.   Drummond and Coblentz, op. cit., p. 198.

run up against the problems posed by the two differing concentring circles of the Six and the larger Europe. While our instinct for the widest possible participation is sound, it needs to be weighed against the deeper and more effective integration which a more limited and more united membership may make possible. Countries which are willing to accept the burdens and risks of a deeper integration in order to achieve the gains that go with it are entitled to receive special consideration in the framing of American policy.'[60]

In his philippic against British policy, Bowie described the Free Trade Area only in terms of its danger to the six.

'In 1956–1957 Britain greatly complicated the Common Market negotiations by her Free Trade Area proposals.'[61]

Robert Kleinman who finds himself also very close to the traditional State Department policy stated:

'Britain's reaction to the project for a Common Market from 1956–1958 threatened Europe's developing union more seriously. Britain was invited, but refused to join in drafting the Rome Treaty. For the next two and a half years, London pressed for a seventeen-nation Free Trade Area that would have destroyed the European Economic Community before it began to function.[62]

And in Europe, the President of the Commission of the EEC summarized his attitude which was also at the basis of American policy as follows: 'The first was the danger that within such a wider, looser and much more partial scheme, the Community itself might have dissolved, ceasing to be what was then a political entity, and becoming a mere commercial arrangement, indistinguishable from the free trade area, and thus incapable of giving it the continued political impetus necessary to achieve the benefits of free trade.'[63]

60. Ben T. Moore, op. cit., p. 244.
61. Robert R. Bowie, Shaping the Future, (Columbia University Press, 1964), p. 44.
62. Robert Kleinman, Atlantic Crisis, (New York: W. W. Norton & Cy., 1964), p. 82.
63. Walter Hallstein, op. cit., p. 73.

Beloff's admirable analysis of this period leaves still some doubt about the American attitude and its impact on the negotiations.[64]

In this study, however, the conclusion must be drawn that there was an outspoken hostility of the American Government towards the Free Trade Area concept and that its policy played a major role in the breakdown of the negotiations.

This American attitude was completely in line with the basic elements of its policy towards the problem of European integration. It had the strength of an imaginative and constructive approach. It had at the same time the weakness of rigidity.

In this specific case, the United States was right in its opinion that the Free Trade Area was primarily a commercial structure and lacked political overtones and perspectives. It underestimated, however, the fact that its breakdown was a political phenomenon of the first magnitude and not just the end of a commercial effort.

In the alliance against the Free Trade Area it accepted partners and ideas which to-day weaken the Atlantic Alliance.

In the period following the breakdown of the negotiations on a Free Trade Area in December 1958, the scene in Europe and the attitude of the United States towards the European developments were dominated by a few events which strengthened various tendencies, already mentioned in the preceding pages.

They were the move to convertibility of most European currencies, the deterioration of the United States balance of payments, the decision of Britain to form the European Free Trade Association and the policies of the Commission of the Common Market to prefer the global approach in its relations with the outside world to a specific European one.

The move to convertibility of the currencies of the principal European countries was taken in the closing days of 1958. These currencies would from now on be fully convertible into dollars by non-

64.   Max Beloff, *op. cit.,* pp. 93–96.

residents at offical rates of exchange. Furthermore, France announced the devaluation of the franc and the decision to liberalize ninety percent of its trade on an OEEC-wide basis.

Nearly four years earlier, this move was prepared by negotiations for the replacement of the European Payments Union and its substitution by the European Monetary Agreement.[65] From now on, Western European payments were placed on a hard-currency basis and the accounts of individual countries with each other were settled on exactly the same basis as their accounts with the United States.

'Viewed together with the convertibility measures, the end of the EPU reflects a general recognition that each OEEC country must focus its attention on its balance of payments over-all rather than regionally with the rest of the world.'[66]

This meant that the accepted rationale for the control of quota's for imports from outside the area, covered by the European Payments Union, was removed.

Immediately, the United States pointed out the implications of this event for what it considered the right trade policy. A joint United States–Canadian Communiqué of January 6, 1959, declared:

'Convertibility has removed the financial justification for discriminating against dollar suppliers, and should be followed by further moves... The United States and Canadian Governments will be watching with close and sympathetic interest the way in which the logic of the new situation is translated into action.'[67]

It would be beyond the scope of this study to deal extensively with the problem of the United States balance of payments. What is relevant is that the concern for its balance of payments emerged very clearly in the United States during the period under discussion.

The United States since 1950, practically always had a rather sub-

65. *Economic Expansion and its Problems,* Seventh Report of the Organisation for European Economic Cooperation, Paris, 1956, pp. 70–72.
66. Isaiah Frank, *op. cit.,* p. 265.
67. *Documents on American Foreign Relations 1959,* Published for the Council on Foreign Relations, (New York: Harper & Brothers, 1960), p. 517.

stantial balance of payments deficit. What was, however, particularly disturbing and strongly alarmed official and public opinion was the fact that the surplus of merchandise and services dropped from $5.72 billion in 1957 to $134 million in 1959 and the overall position from a surplus of $500 million in 1957 through a deficit of $3.52 billion in 1958 to $3.74 billion in 1959.[68]

The position of the United States balance of payments had and has to-day a great impact on American policy toward Europe and the problem of European integration. It symbolizes the shift of economic power from a monopoly of American strength in the first post-war decade to a more equal distribution of economic power in the Atlantic world.

68. From the mass of publications on the United States balance of payments problem I refer to:
Walter S. Salant *et al., The United States Balance of Payments in 1968,* (The Brookings Institution, 1963).
The International Position of the Dollar, A Statement on National Policy by the Research and Policy Committee of the Committee for Economic Development, 1961.
Henry G. Aubrey, *The Dollar in World Affairs,* (New York: Praeger, 1964).
The United States Balance of Payments, Report of the Joint Economic Committee, Senate Report 965, March 19, 1965.
Randall Hinshaw, *op. cit.,* pp. 57–65.
Prof. Dr. J. Kymmell, 'De Amerikaanse Betalingsbalans in 1963', in *Economisch Statistische Berichten,* November 4, 1964, pp. 1000–1004.
and by the same author, 'Het Amerikaanse betalingsbalans tekort', in *Het Financiële Dagblad,* November 5, 6, 7/9, 11, 1964.
Emile Benoit, *Europe at Sixes and Sevens, op. cit.,* pp. 123–137.
Don D. Humphrey, *The United States and the Common Market,* (New York: Praeger, 1962), pp. 98–123.
The Balance of Payments: Presidential Directive, November 16, 1960, Department of State, *Bulletin,* December 5, 1960, pp. 860–863.
The Balance of Payments and Gold Outflow from the United States: Message of President Kennedy to the Congress, February 6, 1961, *House Document 84,* 87th Congr., 1st sess.
The Balance of Payments: Message of President Kennedy to the Congress, July 18, 1963, *House Document 141,* 88th Congr., 1st sess.

After 1957, the balance of payments position influenced the American attitude towards a regional economic structure in Europe which would embrace the OEEC countries and which would discriminate against United States exports without the political appeal of the Common Market.

It was one of the determining factors in United States hostility towards the Free Trade Area concept, the European Free Trade Association and especially against the efforts to build a bridge between the Common Market and EFTA.

It had a major impact on the United States initiative to reconstitute OEEC and transform it into the Organization for Economic Co-operation and Development.

Finally, it formed one of the main economic motives for the concept of Atlantic Partnership, launched by President Kennedy in 1962.

The problem of the United States balance of payments is not only a currency problem in the traditional sense of the word, because it occurs in a country which is the leading nation of the Western alliance.

A preoccupation with its balance of payments problem might lead the United States to view its responsibilities in the world too much from the monetary angle and might therefore bring about a confusion of priorities and a distortion of the real issues. It was and still is tempting for the United States to solve its balance of payments problem by curtailing its political and military commitments in the world.

Furthermore, the position of leadership strongly limits the area of possible remedies.

For this position of leadership, without which the Atlantic world cannot survive, it is imperative that solutions be found for the American balance of payments difficulties which will neither lead the United States to curtail its commitments to the world nor to impose protectionist measures. Apart from the probable economic inadequacy of protectionist steps, they are not consonant with a position of political leadership. Greater internal monetary discipline in the United States and an open and imaginative attitude of its European partners are the means by which the problem can be solved without undue harm to the course of the Atlantic alliance.

E. THE UNITED STATES AND THE PROBLEM OF THE SIX AND THE SEVEN

The American attitude towards the Free Trade Area negotiations was mainly based on its concern to preserve the integrity of what it considered the most attractive form of European integration – the Common Market – and its reluctance to accept economic discrimination in Europe without the ultimate hope of a development in the direction of a political follow-up.

Britain formed the European Free Trade Association in the middle of 1959, to absorb the shock of the breakdown of its original attempt to form a link between the Common Market and the other OEEC countries in the form of a Free Trade Area. The United States opposition against what it considered as a purely commercial arrangement was intensified by the weakening of its balance of payments position.[69]

Furthermore, 'the seven proposal became active when the regional moves seemed a less appropriate and certainly less compelling means of contributing to world-wide objectives in international trade.'[70]

The United States from the beginning received the creation of EFTA with a 'coolness that for a time verged on hostility.'[71]

On every possible occasion, it made it clear that its preference in the struggle between the six and the seven was solidly for the Community of the six.[72]

69. Sydney Dell, *op. cit.,* pp. 126–127.
70. Isaiah Frank, *op. cit.,* p. 128.
71. Miriam Camps, *Britain and the European Community, op. cit.,* p. 236.
72. Michael Hanks and John Lambert, *Britain and the new Europe,* (London: Chatto and Windus, 1963), pp. 33–36.

Freymond concludes that if the United States supported the Europe of the six against the Europe of the seven, it was not because Jean Monnet's influence in Washington was so considerable, but rather because the United States approved of EEC's political objectives.[73] There is more reason to give to both elements equal weight.

In its official declarations, it was striking that in the Communiqué which was issued in Washington on June 12, 1959, after the visit of the Presidents of the three European Commissions, a visit which in itself had a highly political significance, not one word was said about the burning issue of the relations between the six and the seven.

'The President stated that the United States continues to support the objectives of the European Communities because of the significant promise they hold for enhancing the strength and well being not only of Europe but of the entire Free World... The Acting Secretary of State welcomed these statements. He pointed to the widespread interest in this country in the efforts of the communities to bring about European unity, to build a great single market among the six Member States and to contribute to international trade and development. He noted with satisfaction the close relations which have been established between the United States and the European Communities.'[74]

If coolness existed already toward EFTA as such, even stronger was American hostility against the efforts to build a bridge between the Common Market and EFTA.

For this aspect, it is necessary to analyze further the interrelation between the United States attitude and the activities of the Common Market and notably of its Executive Commission, for a global rather than a European approach to its external relations.

73. Jacques Freymond, *Western Europe since the War*,
(New York: Praeger, 1964), pp. 160–161.
74. Department of State, *Bulletin*, June 29, 1959, pp. 952–953.

In trying to find a solution for the tensions in the Community with regard to the relations with the other OEEC countries and, after the establishment of EFTA, with the so called outer seven, the Commission of the Common Market expressed its views in two Memoranda. These Memoranda were of great significance for the attitude of the United States.[75]

Both Miriam Camps and Karl Kaiser give an elaborate account of the contents of the two documents and the negotiations aiming at a consensus of opinion in the Community. The Memoranda were of a highly technical character but the main argument was that free trade was either a matter of a full economic union of the type of the Common Market or of a global problem, the tariff side of which should be dealt with in the framework of GATT. Special reference was made to the GATT negotiations (the so-called Dillon round) which the United States in an earlier phase had proposed to be held in the winter of 1960-61.

The motives for the attitude of the Commission were manifold.

The Commission was extremely worried about the tensions between the six governments with regard to the problem of the external relations of the Community with other European countries. These tensions first existed with regard to the Free Trade Area negotiations and later with regard to the relations with EFTA. The two extreme positions were taken by the French and the Dutch. The French simply did not want a European solution going beyond the framework of the six. For political reasons they rejected any compromise, because every accommodation with Great Britain would mean a watering down of their concept of the closed, continental form of integration in which they hoped to play a dominant role.

75. There is an English translation of these Memoranda but the original text can be better read in one of the languages of the Community. *Premier et Deuxième Mémorandum* de la Commission de la Communauté Economique Européenne au Conseil des Ministres de la Communauté 1959, Bruxelles, 26 février 1959 et 17 septembre 1959.

The economic motives of their attitude were mainly the same as those they skillfully defended in the negotiations for the Common Market Treaty. A common external tariff and the harmonization of economic and social policies were indispensable for the internal liberalization of trade. The exclusion of agriculture, which appeared in every British approach, strengthened their hostility.

The Dutch, without wanting to interfere with the accepted principles of the Rome Treaty, were willing to go very far in the attempt to find solutions for the broader European problem and to avoid a split in Europe which, both for economic and political reasons, they considered fatal for a sound development in Europe and in the Atlantic alliance. It was not only a clash between liberal and protectionist points of view. It was a clash between two concepts of the place of an integrated Europe in the Atlantic world.

The Germans were divided between the Adenauer and the Erhard school of thought. Ultimately and without exception, the Adenauer school prevailed. Belgium and Luxemburg were close to the Dutch on economic motives but politically they found themselves nearer to the French. The Italians were the great compromisers, which meant in the end always a tendency to agree with the French.

It was natural that the Commission not only assessed the forces in the Community, which on balance were unfavorable to a broader European solution, but added its own concern for the preservation of the 'purity' of the policy and institutions of the Rome Treaty.

Another powerful factor contributing to this development was the attitude of Monnet and his Action Committee. While at its sixth session in May 1959, the Committee had still endorsed the idea that a round-table conference should be held 'to define the bases of a multilateral negotiation on the European Economic Association',[76] in its November session of the same year, the Committee stressed the need to look at the problem not primarily

76. *Joint declaration of the Action Committee for the U.S. of Europe,* Sixth Session, May 11, 1959.

as a European problem but in a wider setting. It withdrew its original suggestion for a round-table conference between only European powers and now wanted the United States to take part.[77]

The Commission took great care in stressing the United States balance of payments problem and its full understanding for the American attitude that there were no reasons anymore to accept discrimination on purely commercial and non-political motives.

It wrote the two Memoranda skillfully and consciously for American eyes, because it knew that a combination of French and American support, to which the Monnet group was added, meant an alliance for victory. In the second Memorandum for example the Commission wrote: 'Not only has the United States made possible the reconstruction of Europe, thanks to substantial financial assistance, but taking into account the European balance of payments, it has for a period of years tolerated a significant discrimination against its own commerce, while its balance of payments is today radically changed.'

In the United States, this policy of the Commission was highly successful. 'When the discussions were resumed at the end of the summer (1959) it was clear that the general thesis of the Commission had not only become more generally accepted in Community circles but had attracted the support of a powerful ally – the United States.'[78] Even before the second Memorandum of the Commission was adopted, Dillon, the Under Secretary of State, threw his support behind the Commission's proposals at the Ministerial Meeting of the GATT in Tokyo, in October 1959.

'We have noted the recent proposals of the Commission of the European Economic Community designed to emphasize the liberal orientation of the Community's relations with the rest of the world.

77.   *Joint Declaration of the Action Committee for the U.S. of Europe,* Seventh Session, November, 19 and 20, 1959.
78.   Miriam Camps, *Britain and the European Community, op. cit.,* p. 191.

We welcome these proposals. We believe they should be supported by the Governments of the six countries.'[79]

At this place, it should be briefly noted that Dillon was a central figure in the determination of American foreign economic policy. First under Dulles, as Under Secretary of State for Economic Affairs and later under Herter as Under Secretary, he strongly influenced American policy on the lines of the Schuman-Monnet school of thought. By instinct and career inclined to be impressed by the French concept, he played a powerful role in the hostile attitude of the United States towards an accommodation between the six and the seven.[80]

Camps gives a judgment on this period when she writes: 'The Commission's desire to avoid intensifying, or even appearing to intensify, American difficulties was motivated in part by an appreciation of the willingness of the United States to accept and even to encourage discrimination against itself in the post-war period and in part by the recognition that it was to the interest of the rest of the world that the United States should be helped to meet its difficulties through expanding its exports rather than by cutting its foreign aid programmes or restricting its imports. But it is clear enough that political expediency played its part in the Commission's position as well, and one element in the Commission's solicitude was the hope that the United States would support the Com-

79. Statement by the Honourable Douglas Dillon, Under Secretary of State, at the Ministerial Meeting of the GATT, Tokyo, Japan, Department of State, *Press Release*, No. 755, October 26, 1959.
80. See further for the support of the Commission's point of view by the United States:
    Leon N. Lindberg, *The Policital Dynamics of European Economic Integration,* (Stanford University Press, 1963), p. 158.
    Nora Beloff, *The General says No,* (Penguin Books, 1963), pp. 85–86.
    Norbert Kohlhase, 'Die Europäische Wirtschaftsgemeinschaft in Amerikanischer Sicht', in *Europa Archiv,* Folge 22/1959, pp. 681–682.
    George Lichtheim, *op. cit.,* p. 56.

mission (and the French) in withstanding the pressure for a Europe-wide arrangement.'[81]

Especially for those who participated in the negotiations, the accent will be more on the element of political expediency.

When one has experienced the disdain with which the French met any reference to GATT during the negotiations of the Rome Treaty and then to find that they were solid supporters of the world-wide multilateral approach in 1959, one cannot escape the conclusion that their policy was in any case solely based on political expediency.

Frank concludes that 'apparently the French felt that the best way to counter pressure for the European Community to negotiate a broader agreement with the Seven was to embrace, as far as possible, the world-wide multilateral approach to trade problems, thereby minimizing the basis for complaint about the Common Market discrimination against outsiders, including the Seven.'[82]

The American attitude was a decisive factor in the impossibility of finding an accommodation between the six and the seven. Benoit rightly states: 'In the showdown, however, influence was put solidly behind the Community and its plans for European integration. Indeed our support at the strategic moment and our opposition to reciprocal concessions between the two groups on a bilateral basis gained for the Community a more decisive victory than might otherwise have been possible.'[83]

F. THE UNITED STATES AND THE RECONSTRUCTION OF OEEC

In the so-called Dillon initiative of December 1959, the United States took again an active part in European affairs. A meeting of

81.   Miriam Camps, *op. cit.,* p. 195.
82.   Isaiah Frank, *op. cit.,* p. 278.
83.   Benoit, *Europe at Sixes and Sevens, op. cit.,* p. 95.

a special Economic Conference was sponsored by the Western Summit Meeting in December 1959.[84]

The American initiative was motivated by many factors. There was at last a growing concern over the political consequences of the conflict in Europe between the six and the seven. In two important Congressional documents this concern was expressed.[85]

There was the growing concern for the United States balance of payments position and the fear that broader European solutions would imply a further discrimination against American exports.

84. Special Economic Communiqué issued by the Meeting of the Heads of State and Government of the United States, the United Kingdom, France and the Federal Republic of Germany, Paris, December 21, 1959. Department of State, *Bulletin,* January 11, 1960, p. 43.

For background of the Dillon initiative:

Cottrell and Dougherty, *The Politics of the Atlantic Alliance,* (New York: Praeger, 1964, pp. 152–156.

Kleiman, *op. cit.,* p. 116.

Howard Whidden, 'The changed American perspective on Western Europe', in *Western World,* Vol. 3, March 3, 1960, pp. 16–20.

Henry J. Tasca, 'Die Vereinigten Staaten, Westeuropa und die Entwicklungsländer', in *Europa Archiv,* Folge 5/1960, pp. 147–149.

Karl Kaiser, 'Strukturwandlungen in der atlantischen Zusammenarbeit', in *Europa Archiv,* Folge 23/1962, pp. 815–820.

Jean-Charles Snoy, 'La négociation européenne dans une nouvelle phase', in *Revue Générale Belge,* Février 1960.

For the main events during the meetings and conferences:

Miriam Camps, *Division in Europe,* P.E.P. Occasional Paper, no. 8, June 1960, and *Britain and the European Community, op. cit.,* pp. 244–273.

Richard Mayne, *op. cit.,* p. 145.

The official documents are published by OEEC in

The Organization for Economic Cooperation and Development, Paris, December 1960.

85. *United States Foreign Policy, Western Europe,* a study prepared at the request of the Committee on Foreign Relations U.S. Senate, No. 46478, October 15, 1959, p. 7.

A Study of European Economic Regionalism, Report of a Special Study Mission of the Sub Committee on Europe of the Committee on Foreign Affairs, House of Representatives, No. 48971, January 11, 1960, p. 7.

There was a desire to increase the role of European states in the field of assistance to developing countries.

There was the urge to create a forum to discuss common economic problems in a Western rather than in a purely European framework. All this was to be accomplished by the reorganization or, possibly, the replacement of OEEC, in which till now the United States and Canada only participated as associate members, by an organization in which the United States and Canada would become full members 'thus dramatizing the broadened scope of current Western economic preoccupations.'[86]

In his address to the Special Economic Committee on January 12, 1960, Dillon summarized the reasons for the initiative.

'The first of these questions relates to the commercial policies of the members of the European Economic Community and of the proposed European Free Trade Area with respect to trade with other countries, including their trade with each other.

The second is that of enlarging the flow of development capital from the industrialized free world to the less developed areas.

The third is the problem of finding the best mechanism for continuing international consultations on major economic problems, including the problem of development assistance.'[87]

The meeting was characterized by an almost complete identity of views between the six and the United States.

In the full conference, the least controversial issue was the question of aid.

A Development Assistance Group was set up consisting of Belgium, Canada, France, Germany, Italy, Portugal, the United Kingdom and the United States, which at their first meeting invited Japan to become a member.

In the discussions on the organizational questions, it became clear that the group of seven was reluctant to agree to the notion that

86. Richard P. Stebbins, *The U.S. in World Affairs 1960,* Published for the Council on Foreign Relations, (New York: Harper & Brothers, 1961), p. 121.
87. Department of State, *Bulletin,* February 1, 1960, pp. 140–144.

the OEEC had completed its task, thereby implying that there was no longer any special European trade problem. The United States and the six wanted a successor organization in which the United States and Canada would participate as full members.

Camps says:

'The United Kingdom and the rest of the Seven were, in contrast, determined to have the existence of a European loyalty and sense of mutual interest that ran beyond the Six fortified and acknowledged. It was not without a certain irony that the United Kingdom, which at various times in the past had sought to turn OEEC into a less European, more Atlantic organization, and the French who had, in the past, strongly rejected these attempts, now found their roles reversed.'[88]

It was finally agreed to appoint a group of four wise men to prepare a report on the reorganization of OEEC. This group of Four submitted its report on April 7, 1960.[89]

The conflict really flared up during the discussion on the resolution dealing with the trade problem. Although one of the motives of the United States in taking its new initiative was its concern over the intra-European trade conflict, in its attitude during the meeting there was no indication whatsoever that it had really changed its opinion about the undesirability of bringing together the two rival blocs in a special European framework.

The seven, on the other hand, wanted to treat the intra-European trade conflict as a matter of priority.

In the final resolution, there was a certain concession to this point of view in the preamble, but in the operative paragraph the point of view of the United States and the six prevailed.

It would go beyond the scope of this study to describe in detail the intricate and complex negotiations which ultimately led to the

88. Miriam Camps, *Britain and the European Community*, op. cit., p. 48.
89. *A Remodelled Economic Organization*, A Report by W. Randolph Burgess, Bernard Clappier, Sir Paul Gore-Booth, Xenophon Zolotas, Paris, April 1960.

signing of the Convention of the Organization for Economic Co-operation and Development on December 14, 1960. The result, however, was that the objectives of the United States and the EEC were achieved.

There was no longer an organization for cooperation on European problems. It was substituted by an organization dealing with economic problems affecting the relations between the Western countries and the relations of these countries with the third world.

In the fields of development assistance and in the field of economic coordination, the new organization would prove to be a useful instrument.

Especially, the confrontation of American economic policy on an equal footing with its European partners, constitutes a valuable tool of Atlantic cooperation.

In the field of trade, however, and especially in the solution of the intra-European trade dispute, its value was negligible. In this respect, brief mention should be made of the so-called acceleration proposals of the EEC, because they again demonstrated the affinity between the Common Market and the United States point of view and because they intensified the bitterness of the dispute in Europe.

In March 1960, the Commission published these proposals which were a combination of internal acceleration of the elimination of quota's and tariffs, external acceleration of the common tariff and certain reductions in the common tariff, which would be provisional until the GATT negotiations of 1960/1961 were completed.

The enthusiasm with which the United States welcomed these proposals, already the day after their publication,[90] was matched by the hostility of the EFTA countries who considered this plan as a deliberate move to terminate all efforts to find a broader European solution for the problems of trade under discussion.

Again the Commission succeeded in rallying the United States to its support. In a joint statement, after the meeting between Eisenhower and Adenauer on March 15, 1960, in Washington, it was

90. Department of State, *Press Release*, March 4, 1960.

declared that the two statesmen had discussed the recent trade proposals of the European Economic Commission and had noted that,
should these proposals be adopted, the result would be a major
contribution to a general lowering of world trade barriers.[91]

The Council of Ministers of the six adopted the proposals with
certain changes in May 1960.

A violent continental reaction to some press reports on the visit
of Prime Minister MacMillan to Washington in March 1960, added
to the growing bitterness between the two European groupings.

It became clear that a stronger impulse was required to improve a
situation, which underneath the technical and economic arguments,
had all the dangers of a clash between two political concepts with
grave consequences for the cohesion of the Atlantic world.

The emerging concept of Atlantic Partnership of which Britain's
decision to join the Common Market and the adoption of the Trade
Expansion Act were important elements, was going to dominate
the American approach to Europe and European integration in the
following years.

91. *The New York Times,* March 16, 1960.

CHAPTER VI

Atlantic Partnership
(1961–1965)

New concepts in the field of foreign policy do not appear suddenly. They are the result of a long process and they give concrete expression to something which has matured over a long period of time. As was the case in the emergence and formulation of the Marshall Plan, the concept of the Atlantic Partnership, formally launched by President Kennedy in July 1962, was an imaginative political effort to give concrete form to the necessity of finding a new relationship between the United States and Europe.

The Kennedy Administration, when it assumed office in January 1961, was confronted with a multitude of events and developments, in which it had to find its way and determine priorities and policies.

The Common Market had accelerated its program and while the new Organization for Economic Cooperation and Development provided a reasonable forum to discuss economic policies and to make a beginning of a more concerted action in the field of aid to developing countries, it proved incapable of finding a solution for the rift between EEC and EFTA. The situation of the United States balance of payments was a cause of growing concern. This contributed to a more pronounced feeling in the United States that it was necessary to find ways and means for a more equal sharing of the burden between the United States and its European partners with regard to the military burdens of the alliance and the global responsibilities of the United States, especially in relation to the developing countries.

There was also a growing preoccupation with the trading relations with the new European entity and the necessity to protect and advance American interests in a market which took approximately one fifth of its exports.

The policy of General de Gaulle added another element to the complexity of the situation. It confronted the United States for the first time with a concept which did not accept the integration of Europe along the Schuman-Monnet lines, both in its internal structure and its external relations.

In the military field the American desire for a more equal sharing of the burden took the form of insistence on a larger European contribution to the conventional forces, which most European countries not only resented for economic reasons but which also gave rise to a highly sensitive controversy over the whole strategic concept of the Alliance.

It is not possible, within the scope of this study, to give a detailed and complete analysis of all elements which determined American policy. It is, however, possible to illustrate the evolution of this policy by the American attitude towards a few major problems, among which rank the military developments which had taken place, the issue of the relationship of the United Kingdom with the Common Market and finally the Trade Expansion Act.

A. MILITARY DEVELOPMENTS

It is ironical that in the relationship between the United States and its European partners, the military element has become one of the greatest sources of discord.

American policy has preserved the integrity of Western Europe through the commitment of its military power to NATO; six divisions and a huge arsenal of American weapons are still in Europe, twenty years after the termination of the Second World War; Europe has rebuilt its political stability and economic prosperity under the protection of American nuclear power. In short,

NATO which basically is the expression of the commitment of the military force of the United States to the defense of Europe, has met with an unusual degree of success in reaching the objectives for which it was created in 1949. In order to clarify why the Kennedy Administration was so strongly preoccupied with the military element in its relation to Europe, it is necessary to analyze briefly the main elements of the situation.

In general, the growing economic strength of Western Europe and its progressing political weight in world affairs exposed, more clearly than before, how completely it was dependent on the United States in the military field. Seen from the United States, the question arose whether Western Europe's prosperity did not require a fairer sharing of the defense burden in the Atlantic alliance.

There were, however, also some more specific problems. When NATO was conceived in 1949, the United States possessed the monopoly of nuclear weapons. NATO strategy was based on the possibility of a massive attack of Soviet conventional forces which would be met by a build-up of conventional forces, 'the shield', but completely relying on the 'sword' of American strategic nuclear weapons.

Particularly, the Eisenhower Administration based its military policy towards NATO on the assumption that there would be a permanent inferiority of NATO conventional forces compared to those of the Soviet bloc. This gap could only be bridged by complete dependence on American nuclear forces. It was assumed that any attack on Europe would involve general nuclear war.

In this concept, there was no real and meaningful place for large European conventional forces but the Western European countries considered their contribution primarily as a premium for American nuclear protection and as an inducement to the maintenance of substantial United States military forces in Europe.

During these years, the American monopoly of nuclear weapons disappeared with the emergence of the Soviet Union as a nuclear power of the first magnitude. Great Britain possessed a nuclear capability of its own and France was on the way of developing one.

Furthermore, tactical nuclear weapons were now a regular part of the armament of NATO forces in Europe, although they could not be brought into use without the consent of the United States.

In the first period of the Kennedy Administration a strategic concept was developed which was best expressed in the speeches of Secretary of Defense McNamara in February and June 1962.[1]

The main elements of this new concept were:

a. The so-called flexible response. Instead of relying on a single all-out response to a Soviet attack, a strategy to which the European countries got accustomed in the preceding years, the Kennedy Administration based its military policy on the necessity of a variety of alternative options.

b. These alternative options required a greater reliance on conventional forces and renewed pressure on the European allies to strengthen these forces.

Instead of the doctrine that NATO conventional forces could never match the superiority of the Soviet bloc in this field, it became the policy of the United States to aim at a build-up of conventional forces to the point at which they could safely resist all forms of non-nuclear aggression.

c. The concept of flexible response assumed the existence of a completely centralized system of command and control of nuclear weapons. This, besides many other arguments, implied a rejection of any profileration of nuclear weapons in the alliance and a reluctance to accept the existing ones.

1. Address before the Fellows of the American Bar Foundation, Chicago, February 17, 1962, Department of Defense, *News Release,* No. 239–262, February 17, 1962, pp. 6–7.
    Address at the Commencement Excercises, University of Michigan, Ann Arbor, June 16, 1962, Department of Defense, *News Release,* No. 980–62, June 16, 1962, pp. 9–11.
    William W. Kaufmann, *The McNamara Strategy,* (New York: Harper & Row, 1964), pp. 114–121.

The reaction to this new doctrine in Europe was mainly that the feeling of reliance on an automatic American nuclear response to a Soviet attack was weakened and the urge to a greater share in the strategic planning and in the control of the use of nuclear power was enhanced. The Europeans were reluctant to accept the American pressure for a greater European defense effort, the more so because they felt that their increased effort would have to take place in a field which they did not consider relevant to the actual military situation.

There was also a growing concern over the sudden changes in American strategic doctrine without adequate and previous consultation with the other NATO allies.

Apart from all other political and psychological problems the theory of flexible response brought the problem of a new relationship in the control of nuclear strategy to the forefront, stronger than ever before.

The search for a new pattern of United States–European relations cannot be understood without this evolution in the military field.[2]

2. Out of the countless studies about this problem reference is made to: Richard P. Stebbins, *The United States in World Affairs 1962,* Published for the Council on Foreign Relations, (New York: Harper & Row, 1962), pp. 114–155.
Alastair Buchan, 'Partners and Allies', in *Foreign Affairs,* July, 1963, pp. 621–638.
Alastair Buchan and Philip Windsor, *Arms & Stability in Europe,* The Institute for Strategic Studies, London, 1963.
Robert R. Bowie, 'Strategy and the Atlantic Alliance', in *International Organization,* Summer 1963, pp. 709–733.
Frank Munk, *Atlantic Dilemma,* (New York: Ocean Publications, 1964), pp. 91–111.
Henry A. Kissinger, 'The Search for Stability', in *Foreign Affairs,* July, 1959, pp. 537–561;
'The Unsolved Problems of European Defense', in *Foreign Affairs,* July, 1962, pp. 515–542;
'Strains on the Alliance', in *Foreign Affairs,* January, 1963, pp. 261–286;
'NATO's Nuclear Dilemma', in *National Security,* (New York: Praeger, 1963), pp. 293–317; (Footnote continued overleaf)

B. BRITAIN'S APPLICATION FOR MEMBERSHIP
OF THE EEC

The United States attitude towards European integration has been one of the controlling factors in the decision of Britain to apply for membership of the Common Market.

Support for the Common Market, as was analyzed in the preceding chapters, was a generally accepted policy in the United States. It was not challenged and only a very few dissenting voices questioned the wisdom of this unqualified support.

One of these was Lincoln Gordon who in an article which appeared in the first month of the Kennedy Administration analyzed American policy in an unorthodox and penetrating way.[3]

This remarkable article is quoted, not only because it deviated from the general trend of American policy, but mainly because the problems it raised are still relevant to the situation of to-day.

Gordon objects to the exclusive support for the continental form of integration and pleads for American support for an all-European solution.

'The basic reason for this conclusion is that all-European integration, even if less intensive in scope than might be achieved by six-nation integration, promises over the long run to act as a force in the world more closely allied with basic American objectives than does a new political unit limited to the continental Six. And in the perilous situation which threatens to confront us in this decade, it

'Coalition Diplomacy in a Nuclear Age', in *Foreign Affairs,* July 1964, pp. 525–546;
The Troubled Partnership, (New York: McGraw-Hill Book Company, 1965), pp. 91–117.
Leonard Beaton, *The Western Alliance and the McNamara Doctrine,* Adelphi Papers, No. 11, August, 1964, The Institute for Strategic Studies, London.
Robert E. Osgood, *Nuclear Control in NATO,* The Washington Center of Foreign Policy Research, 1962.
3.   Lincoln Gordon; 'Economic Regionalism Reconsidered', in *World Politics,* January 1961, pp. 231–253.

is essential that Western Europe, which is the other major free world center of advanced production, technology and leadership in ideas, be fully on our side – not a would-be 'third force'...

From the viewpoint of assured identification with long run American foreign policy objectives, the basic internal social and political forces in Britain, Scandinavia, Switzerland and the Netherlands give much greater assurance of common outlook than do the corresponding forces in Italy, France and Germany...

We do of course, also need – and need desperately – Germany, Italy and France as allies. But they are much more likely to be reliable allies if their integration includes Britain and the smaller stable democracies than if it is limited to the present grouping of the Six alone.'

There was more awareness in the new Kennedy Administration of the importance of the stabilizing influence of British foreign policy for the process of European integration.

'At the same time, President Kennedy's distrust of German and French views on foreign policy have made him much more anxious than his predecessor to have Britain inside the Community.'[4]

Miriam Camps states that one of the reasons of the support of the United States for the United Kingdom joining the Common Market was that 'the addition of the United Kingdom would increase the political stability of the Six and would tend to strengthen the commitment to NATO.'[5]

And Herter in explaining the support of the United States for British membership considers 'this support entirely logical if one favors a closer relationship among the nations of the Atlantic Community since the British are clearly a major link between the two sides of the Atlantic.'[6]

But where the new Administration continued exactly the policy

4. Shanks and Lambert, *op. cit.*, p. 235.
5. Miriam Camps, *Four Approaches to the European Problem*, Occasional Paper, no. 12, P.E.P., March 1961, p. 18.
6. Christian A. Herter, *Toward an Atlantic Community*, Published for the Council on Foreign Relations, (New York: Harper & Row, 1963), p. 26.

of the former one, was in its conviction that there was only one way for Britain to use its beneficial influence, notably by full membership of the Common Market and by nothing short of that.

In the policy of Great Britain, concerning its relations with the process of European integration, the question of its relations with the United States played a major role. In general, one can say that, apart from the instinctive reluctance against joining a new structure in which the question of loss of certain elements of sovereignty was involved, Britain's attitude was determined by its concern over its position as the center of the Commonwealth and its special relationship with the United States.[7]

The whole history of Anglo-American relations[8] proves that this special relationship is a major element in British diplomacy and was inevitably enforced by the close and intimate relationship during the Second World War. It would be wrong to disregard this special

7. Under Labour Governments in Britain one should add the fear of interference in domestic economic planning.
8. For an analysis of Anglo-American relations and apart from the studies referred to, see:
Denis Healey, 'Britain's attitude towards European integration', in *The United States and the Western Community* (ed. by H. Field Havilland, Jr.), Haverford, 1957.
H. C. Allen, *The Anglo American Predicament,* (London: MacMillan Cy., 1960).
Lionel Gelber, *America in Britain's place,* (New York: Praeger, 1961).
R. W. G. Mackay, *Towards a United States of Europe,* (London: Hutchison, 1961).
Bruce M. Russett, *Community and Contention, Britain and America in the Twentieth Century,* (Cambridge: The M.I.T. Press, 1963).
John Mander, *Great Britain or Little England,* (London: Secker & Warburg, 1963).
Coral Bell, *The Debatable Alliance,* Chatham House Essays 3, London, 1964.
Kenneth Younger, *Changing Perspectives in British Foreign Policy,* Chatham House Essays 7, London, 1964.
Max Beloff, 'Britain, Europe and the Atlantic Community', in *International Organization,* Vol. XVII, no. 3, 1963.

bond which is not only based on racial and linguistic affinities but on many other tangible and intangible elements.

Under the Eisenhower Administration and especially in 1960, the British became convinced that the unqualified support of the United States for the continental European integration implied that in the framework of the Atlantic alliance the American Administration would focus its policy on the closely-knit European Community. Consequently, the special relationship with the United Kingdom was in the process of being substituted by an even more special relationship with that community.

It was logical, however, that no definite British decision was taken before the policies of the Kennedy Administration became known. There was a hope in Britain that what they considered as the dogmatic line of the Eisenhower period, would change into a more sophisticated approach in which the special link with Britain and the dangers of the rift between the six and seven would be more prominent elements in the formulation of American policy.

As was described above, there was in the Kennedy Administration a keener awareness of the importance of British influence on the process of European integration but this did not affect at all the conviction of the new Administration that this influence could and should be exerted by British membership of the Common Market.

This could not be more clearly demonstrated than by some of the key appointments of the President. Dillon became Secretary of the Treasury and George Ball Under Secretary of State for Economic Affairs and ten months later, Under Secretary.[9]

The former had been instrumental, especially after Dulles' death, in the formulation of American policy towards the problem of European integration. The latter had been the closest American associate of Jean Monnet and legal representative of the Coal and Steel Comminuty and the new Brussels institutions.

9. For the choice of the President's advisors and their collaborators see Joseph Kraft, *The Grand Design,* (New York: Harper & Brothers, 1962), pp. 16–43.

Both men were convinced that Britain would only join the Common Market if no other options were open for it. Only then, Britain would accept the *fait-accompli* and take its decision. The *fait-accompli* was there, but it was principally in the power of the United States Government to close the road to other options and compromise solutions.

This was also Monnet's policy. In its July session of 1960, his Action Committee adopted a resolution, which stated:

'Now that the Common Market is becoming irreversible and profitable in the eyes of all, the conditions exist for the creation of new links between the European Community and the United Kingdom and the other European countries. Today, it is possible to envisage the participation of all in the common task of unifying Europe. Accordingly the Action Committee, echoing the wishes of the vast majority of citizens in our country, earnestly hopes that the United Kingdom and the other European countries will simultaneously become members of the Coal and Steel Community, Euratom and the Common Market...'[10]

In March 1961, during a visit to London, Under Secretary Ball was supported in his policies by the impression he gained that the British Government seriously considered an application to join the Communities.[11]

The crucial confrontation with the policies of the new Administration, however, took place during the visit of Prime Minister MacMillan to Washington in the beginning of April 1961.

There, the Prime Minister wanted to find out what exactly the United States's attitude towards the problem was.[12]

'The most formidable problem that faced the Prime Minister and his government in deciding whether or not to approach the Community was whether the intimate relationship between the

10. *Joint declaration by the Action Committee for a United States of Europe,* Eighth Session, July 11, 1960.
11. Miriam Camps, *Britain and the European Community, op. cit.,* p. 336.
12. Uwe Kitzinger, *The Challenge of the Common Market, op. cit.,* p. 187.

United States and the United Kingdom would survive Britain's entry.'

All evidence points to an attitude of President Kennedy which made it clear that Britain's joining the Community might lead to a much closer and more far-reaching relationship between the two countries than had been the case in the last years.

The United States was ready to support this move and accept the eventual economic disadvantages for itself on the condition that Britain's attitude would be unequivocal. *The Economist* wrote:

'Britain must join without reservations of any sort; only then would the United States undertake to try to induce General de Gaulle to make concessions on such obstacles as agriculture, the Commonwealth or the European Free Trade Association.'[13]

The Communiqué of the conversations only mentioned that the President and the Prime Minister recognized both the urgency and the importance of further steps toward the economic and political unity of Europe.[14]

The British decision to apply for membership of the Common Market, made public by the Prime Minister in the House of Commons on July 31, 1961, was a result of a multitude of considerations. Miriam Camps rightly states that 'the controlling consideration was the belief that Britain would have more influence – in Europe, with the United States and in the world generally – as a member of the European Community than it would alone.'[15]

This was not an abdication from the wish to have a special relationship with the United States.

Bowie[16] goes too far when he says: 'In taking it, the British have decided to abandon the European Free Trade Area (EFTA) and to turn from the Commonwealth and from the hoped-for special

---

13.   *The Economist,* April 15, 1961, p. 219.
14.   Department of State, *Bulletin,* April 24, 1961, p. 579.
15.   Miriam Camps, *op. cit.,* p. 513.
16.   Robert R. Bowie and Theodore Geiger, *The European Economic Community and the United States,* 87th Congr., 1st sess., No. 76810, p. 9.

relationship with the United States', a point of view which he repeated in 1962.[17]

This underestimates the special affinities between the two countries which exist on both sides of the Ocean.

The issue was not whether a special relationship existed, but in what way this relationship could have the most beneficial impact on the Atlantic alliance.

Meanwhile, the American Administration continued its support for the continental European integration in every way possible.

The Communiqués issued after the series of bilateral discussions were significant in that respect.

When Adenauer visited Washington on April 13, 1961, right after the MacMillan visit, the Communiqué stated: 'The important role of the European Economic Community as a powerful and cohesive force in the core of the Atlantic Community was stressed. The dynamic political and institutional potential of the EEC was agreed to be an important element of present strength for the Atlantic Community.'[18]

On the second visit of Adenauer on November 22, 1961, it was declared that:

'The President reaffirmed the strong support of the United States for the movement toward European unity through the European Economic Community, the European Coal and Steel Community, and Euratom. The President and the Chancellor agreed on the important role that the development of the European Communities can play in further strengthening and complementing the entire Atlantic Community. They agreed particularly on the importance and significance of proposals now being considered for a European Political Union pursuant to the Bonn Declaration of July 1961.'[19]

17. Robert R. Bowie, 'Prospects for Atlantic Community', in *The Harvard Review,* Vol. I, No. 1, Fall 1962, p. 11.
18. Department of State, *Bulletin,* May 1, 1961, p. 622.
19. Department of State, *Bulletin,* December 11, 1961, pp. 967–968.

This statement was made after the negotiations between the United Kingdom and the Six had already started. It is probable that no mention was made nor any hope for successful conclusion of the negotiations was expressed because the German Chancellor was not a warm supporter of the extension of the Common Market and was far more inclined to consolidate the economic structures by a move to political unification, rather than by admitting new members. The United States Government either did not recognize or did not take seriously this feature of Adenauer's policy. Moreover, American-German relations were strained because of Adenauer's distrust of the German policy of the Kennedy Administration.

On the other hand, the President welcomed the British decision in a special statement on August 10, 1961,[20] and in a joint Anglo-American Communiqué after the Bermuda Conference of December 22, 1961. 'The President and the Prime Minister took note of progress in the negotiations between the United Kingdom and the European Economic Community and expressed the hope that these would be brought to a successful conclusion.'[21]

As soon as Britain had declared its decision to apply for membership of the Common Market and the negotiations in Brussels had started, United States policy took the successful outcome of the negotiations practically for granted. Britain's entry into Europe had become a major element in the emergence of the Atlantic Partnership concept. The almost religious fervour with which this concept was pursued left no room for doubts about the success of one of its important elements. It is not unusual in the conduct of American foreign policy that there is confusion between what is desirable and what is obtainable. A clear expression of that state of mind can be found in a staff study prepared for the Committee on Foreign Relations of the Senate. 'American policy admits no alternative to eventual British membership in the EEC – so apparent is the inevit-

20. Department of State, *Bulletin*, August 28, 1961, p. 361.
21. Department of State, *Bulletin*, January 15, 1962, p. 95.

ability of the move – and Atlantic Partnership in that context.'[22] But whether American policy admitted alternatives was not the relevant question. Much more relevant was the question whether the right assessment of forces on the continent justified the American optimism and the wisdom of conceiving the new Atlantic Partnership on the explicit assumption that Britain would be a member of the European Community.

The conclusion must be that the assessment was too optimistic and therefore inadequate. The political foundation of the process of European integration was no longer only that of Schuman and Monnet. The Franco-German rapprochement was not led by Schuman and Adenauer of 1950, but by de Gaulle and Adenauer of 1960. It was this difference that was not taken into account in the policies of the Kennedy Administration.

Walter Lippmann was a very lonely voice when he expressed his grave doubts regarding the successful conclusion of the negotiations between Britain and the Common Market. 'The issue is deep, momentous and highly charged with sentiment. No solution of it is in sight at this writing. To find a solution, the Continentals will have to move into a much more generous and flexible position than General de Gaulle and Dr. Adenauer now occupy. The British are not so hard pressed that they can be brought to a kind of unconditional surrender to Paris and Bonn. Thus the immediate fate of the grand project depends primarily on Paris and Bonn.'[23]

C. THE TRADE EXPANSION ACT

The interdependence and interaction between Britain's application for the Common Market, the introduction of the Trade Ex-

---

22. *Problems and Trends in Atlantic Partnership I,* Senate Document, No. 132, 87th Congr., 2nd sess., September 14, 1962, p. 190.
23. Walter Lippmann, *Western Unity and the Common Market,* (London: Hamish Hamilton, 1962), p. 17.

pansion Act and the concept of Atlantic Partnership was extremely strong.

Britain's application confronted the United States more than ever with the necessity to reappraise its relations with the strong and seemingly expanding entity on the other side of the Ocean. The Trade Expansion Act, as a new instrument for American trade policy, had its roots in the purely economic chain of events, which was started in 1958, when Dillon called for the 'Dillon round' of tariff reductions and the transformation of OEEC in 1960.[24] The success of its presentation and acceptance by American public and Congressional opinion depended, however, on the possibility of putting it in the framework of a broader concept, also conditioned by other than purely economic factors.

In describing the internal process inside the Administration Kraft concludes:

'At that point the stage was set for the Grand Design. On the one hand, Atlantic Partnership held out the kind of broad, general appeal necessary to push renewal of the Trade Act through the Congress. On the other hand, the Act was a means of dropping Atlantic Partnership into the hopper of interest politics. In the last week of October 1961, by a process difficult to trace but familiar in government, the logic of the merger suddenly asserted itself. In many minds, in many places, the Trade Act was fused with Atlantic Partnership. The merger expressed itself in a sustained, and many-sided, stretch drive to put Atlantic Partnership across.'[25]

This close interdependence between Britain's entry, the new Trade legislation and the concept of Atlantic Partnership is analyzed in many studies on the subject.[26]

24. Uwe Kitzinger, *The Challenge of the Common Market, op. cit.,* pp. 234–235.
25. Joseph Kraft, *op. cit.,* p. 36.
26. See among others:
    J. William Fulbright, *Prospects for the West,* (Harvard University Press, 1963), pp. 58–68.
    Randall Hinshaw, *op. cit.,* p. 164. (Footnote continued overleaf)

Before analyzing the efforts to put the proposal for new Trade legislation into a political framework, one particularly close link between Britain's application for the Common Market and the Trade Expansion Act should be mentioned.

There was an outspoken concern in some Administration circles that an introduction of such far-reaching new possibilities in the field of trade liberalization might prejudice Britain's willingness to pursue its negotiations in Brussels. It could have opened other options for Britain which the United States Administration wanted to exclude.

It seriously considered for this reason the possibility to let the existing Trade Act expire and to submit a new Bill only in 1963, at which time it thought that the negotiations would be concluded.[27]

Reuss is highly critical of that attitude and writes that Senator Douglas and he 'were not inclined to entrust our trading future to Britain's chances of entry.'

Karl Kaiser, *EWG und Freihandelszone, op. cit.*, p. 234:
'Nachdem im Winter 1961 die Verhandlungen über den Beitritt Englands zur EWG aufgenommen worden waren, verstärkten die U.S.A. ihre Bemühungen, den Einigungsprozess in Europa in die Bildung neuer Formen der atlantischen Zusammenarbeit einzubetten. Anfangs 1962 brachte Kennedy die Trade Expansion Act ein, der das Fernziel zu Grunde lag die Atlantische Region zum Zentrum einer Neuordnung der Wirtschaftsbeziehungen der nicht-Kommunistischen Welt zu machen. Der Beitritt Gross Britanniens zur EWG sollte die Voraussetzungen für eine 'Partnerschaft' zwischen Nord-Amerika und Europa schaffen, bei der die grossen Aufgaben der Gegenwart gemeinsam angepackt werden konnten.'

Karl Kaiser, 'Strukturwandlungen in der Atlantischen Zusammenarbeit', in *Europa Archiv,* Folge 23, 1962, pp. 824-829.

Richard P. Stebbins, *The United States in World Affairs 1962,* Published for the Council on Foreign Relations, (New York: Harper & Brothers, 1963), p. 129.

Jaques Freymond, *op. cit.,* pp. 203-205.

Henry A. Kissinger, 'The Essentials of Solidarity in the Western Alliance', in *The Conservative Papers,* (New York: Doubleday's Cy., 1964), pp. 18-19.

27.   Joseph Kraft, *op. cit.,* p. 35.

They proposed an amendment to the Bill which would have given the United States 'down to zero' bargaining power on the twenty-six major groups of commodities (a power which could according to the Bill only be used in the event that the United States and the EEC together accounted for 80 percent or more of world trade in a representative period), whether or not Britain and other countries joined the Common Market.

In his effort to stop the adoption of this amendment, Under Secretary Ball testified for the Senate Finance Committee as follows: 'We would be injecting ourselves into the U.K.-EEC negotiations...Opponents of the entry of Britain into the Common Market could say that there was an alternative presented to Britain which had not been available before. They would say the United States had given up hope that Great Britain was going to enter the Common Market and therefore that it was a hopeless enterprise. I think that this politically would be a highly undesirable action for the United States to take.'[28] The Senate adopted the amendment but it was removed in conference between the House and the Senate.[29]

All public statements regarding the new trade legislation and its wider implications stressed the link between the economic and political aspects of the new relationship with Western Europe.

The Congressional reports emphasized strongly the economic necessities for a new approach but never neglected the political framework.[30]

28. Senate Finance Committee, *Hearings on the Proposed Amendment to the Trade Expansion Act of 1962*, August 16, 1962, p. 2261.
29. See for a detailed account Reuss, *op. cit.*, pp. 43–46.
30. See among others:
    The task for 1962: A Free World Community, by Henry S. Reuss, Joint Committee Print, 87th Congr., 1st sess., 1961, no. 76494.
    United States Commercial Policy, A Program for the 1960's, by Peter B. Kenen, Joint Committee Print, 87th Congr., 1st sess., 1961, no. 77115.
    The European Community and the United States, by Robert Bowie, and Theodore Geiger, Joint Committee Print, 87th Congr., 1st sess., 1964, no. 76810. (Footnote continued overleaf)

Clayton and Herter in their report went so far as to suggest something approaching full American membership of the Common Market. This, however, was not regarded by the Administration as a feasible policy within the foreseeable future.

The strongest expression of the political aims of the new trade legislation in Congressional reports can be found in the staff study on Problems and Trends in Atlantic Partnership:

'From the spreading basis of this mutually beneficial trade, the two great communities on either side of the Atlantic should be able to perform a number of tasks that have become indivisible to reach major goals that neither could reach alone.'[31]

The launching of the concept of Atlantic Partnership, and within this concept the new trade legislation was, from the Administration's side handled as a concerted action, comparable only to the introduction of the Truman Doctrine and the Marshall Plan. The response and activities, however, of the non-public sector were stronger in the years 1947 and 1948, than now.

One of the first major and significant outlines of the new concept was contained in a speech of one of the President's closest advisers, McGeorge Bundy, on December 6, 1961.[32]

'But my own belief is that the most productive way of conceiving the political future of the Atlantic Community is to think in terms of a partnership between the United States, on the one hand and a great European power, on the other.'

Foreign Economic Policy for the 1960's, Joint Committee Print, 87th Congr., 2nd sess., 1962, no. 78532.

A New Look at Foreign Economic Policy, by Chr. A. Herter and William L. Clayton, Joint Committee Print, 87th Congr., 1st sess., no. 76372.

31. *Problems and Trends in Atlantic Partnership I, op. cit.,* p. 30.

32. Address to the Economic Club of Detroit, December 6, 1961, quoted in Jaques Freymond, *op. cit.,* pp. 203–204.

See also for Bundy's speech:

Kurt Birrenbach, 'Europa und Amerika in der Welt von Morgen', in *Politik,* Schriftenreihe zu grundsätzlichen und aktuellen Fragen, Freiburg, 1964, pp. 29–31.

For the first time the partnership in terms of a bond between equals was launched, long before the solemn proclamation of this concept by the President in July 1962.

In his State of the Union Message the President said:

'The emergence of the new Europe is being matched by the emergence of new ties across the Atlantic... The greatest challenge of all is posed by the growth of the European Common Market. Assuming the accession of the United Kingdom, there will arise across the Atlantic a trading partner behind a single external tariff similar to ours with an economy which nearly equals our own.'[33]

On January 25, 1962, the President sent the proposals for new trade legislation to Congress with a message which contained the outline of the political framework in which the Trade Expansion Act[34] was placed by the Administration.[35]

It was the policy of the Administration to present the Act as an important element in a truly 'grand design'.

'Its enactment could well affect the unity of the West, the course of the cold war, and the growth of our nation for a generation or more to come...

For the first time, as the world's greatest trading nation, we can welcome a single partner whose trade is even larger than our own – a partner no longer divided and dependent, but strong enough to share with us the responsibilities and initiatives of the free world...

It is now time to write a new chapter in the evolution of the Atlantic Community... An integrated Western Europe, joined in trading partnership with the United States, will further shift the world balance of power to the side of freedom.

33. *House Document* 251, 87th Congr., 2nd sess.
34. Text of the Trade Expansion Act (Public Law 87–794, approved October 11, 1962), in Department of State, *Bulletin,* October 29, 1962, pp. 656–660.
35. *House Document* 314, 87th Congr., 2nd sess.

We will have our greatest opportunity since the Marshall Plan to demonstrate the vitality of free choice.'

The Act was a complicated piece of legislation. Its main provision gave the Administration authority to

a. reduce existing tariffs by 50 % on a reciprocal basis with any other country,

b. eliminate tariffs on products in which the United States and the Common Market conduct 80 % of the world trade,

c. reduce or eliminate all tariffs against agricultural commodities produced by the underdeveloped countries,

d. negotiate across the board reductions instead of on an item-by-item basis,

e. establish an Adjustment Assistance Program domestically.[36]

The Act passed the House on June 28, 1962, by a bipartisan majority of 298–125 and the Senate on September 19, 1962, by the even more decisive vote of 78–8.

During the first months of 1962, there was a concerted action from the side of the Administration to acquaint public opinion with the features and significance of the new concept of which the Trade Expansion Act was the first concrete expression.

Under Secretary for Political Affairs George McGhee said: 'The real challenge of the Trade Program lies in the fact that it provides the keystone to our whole forward national strategy.'[37]

Secretary of State Rusk in an address in Davidson said on February 22, 1962: 'We aim to develop a new partnership with Europe

36. Out of the many comments on the Trade Expansion Act, reference is made to:
Howard C. Petersen, 'The U.S. invitation to Europe', in *European Atlantic Review*, March–April 1962, pp. 9–12.
Don D. Humphrey, *The U.S. and the Common Market*, op. cit., pp. 164–170.
A rather critical analysis is:
Oscar Gass, 'The Crusade for Trade' (I and II), in *The New Republic*, March 19, 1962, pp. 9–14, and March 26, 1962, pp. 17–22.
37. Department of State, *Bulletin*, February 19, 1962, p. 289.

in all the dimensions that responsibility as a great power in the 1960's requires ... It is in this large perspective that the President has asked Congress for new trade legislation.'[38]

Of particular importance in this respect were the public statements of Under Secretary Ball who in the Administration was and is today one of the central figures in the formulation and conduct of American foreign policy towards Europe and one of the main architects of the concept of Atlantic Partnership. Two of his many speeches and statements are singled out.

The first is an address before the World Affairs Council in Philadelphia on February 16, 1962,[39] the second an address to the German Society for Foreign Affairs in Bonn on April 2, 1962[40]. In these speeches the whole philosophy, underlying the declaration of President Kennedy in July 1962, was exposed and analyzed.

The notion that a partnership was only possible between equals was stressed. In Philadelphia he said: 'Yet a strong partnership must by definition mean a collaboration of equals. When one partner possesses over 50 per cent of the resources of a firm and the balance is distributed among 16 or 17 others the relationship is unlikely to work very well. And so long as Europe remained fragmented, so long as it consisted merely of nations small by modern standards, the potentials for true partnership were always limited.'

He then rejected the danger of Europe as a possible third force out of hand. 'Such a prediction, I am persuaded, misconceives the nature of the forces at work.' He proceeded, after having assumed that the negotiations between Britain and the Common Market would lead to 'the creation of a potential partner commanding resources not incommensurate with those which we ourselves command' by placing the Trade Expansion Bill in this concept of equal partnership: 'It will enable the President to give a new dimension

38. Department of State, *Bulletin,* March 19, 1962, pp. 448–454.
39. Text in *Release* of United States Information Service, American Embassy, London, February 19, 1962.
40. Department of State, *Bulletin,* April 23, 1962, pp. 666–673.

to this Atlantic Partnership in the area of international trade...

I cannot emphasize enough to you that the Trade Expansion Bill is not merely a grant of new authority to the President to assist him in commercial relations; it has a larger meaning as providing a new field of action for the Atlantic Partnership.'

In his speech in Bonn, he conditioned Atlantic Partnership on the creation of a united Europe.

'We regard a united Europe as a condition to the development of an effective partnership...

To our minds – and I am sure to your minds as well – a strong partnership must always by definition mean a collaboration of equals.'

In the crowning proclamation of this concept the President stated at Independence Hall, Philadelphia on July 4, 1962:[41]

'We would see in such a Europe a partner with whom we could deal on a basis of full equality in all the great burdensome tasks of building and defending a community of free nations.

It would be premature at this time to do more than to indicate the high regard with which we view the formation of this partnership. The first order of business is for our European friends to go forward in forming the more perfect union which will some day make this partnership possible.'

The President then made his 'Declaration of Interdependence', leading to a concrete Atlantic Partnership between equals – 'the new union now emerging in Europe and the old American union founded here 175 years ago.'

The concept of Atlantic Partnership, as described above, would dominate the relations between the United States and Europe for the next years and at the time of the conclusion of this study it still is an important factor in American policy towards Europe and the Atlantic alliance.

41. Text in Department of State, *Bulletin,* July 23, 1962, pp. 131–133.

In America and on the European side of the Atlantic, there was in general a warm welcome to the new American ideas.[42]

From the European side it was especially important that Monnet's Action Committee fully endorsed the idea in its meeting of June 26, 1962.

'The economic and political unity of Europe, including England, and the establishment of European-American relations as between equal partners will alone permit the consolidation of the West, and thus, the creation of the conditions for peace between East and West.'[43]

The European Movement formulated its support during its Congress in Rome in November 1963.

The concept became the cornerstone of the policies of practically all those in Europe who had stood in the forefront of the struggle for European integration along the Schuman-Monnet lines.[44]

42. In the United States, outside the Administration circles, the concept of equal partnership was supported in the clearest and purest form in the writings of Robert R. Bowie, especially in his:
Shaping the Future, (Columbia University Press, 1964), and further in 'Tensions within the Alliance', in Foreign Affairs, October 1963, Vol. 42, No. 1, pp. 49–70, and 'Strategy and the Atlantic Alliance', in International Organization, Summer 1963, Vol. XVII, No. 3, pp. 709–732.

43. Comité d'Action pour les Etats Unis d'Europe, Déclaration Commune du 26 juin 1962; English text in Jaques Freymond, op. cit., p. 205.

44. See among many other publications:
Walter Hallstein, United Europe, Challenge and Opportunity, (Harvard University Press, 1962).
Kurt Birrenbach, The future of the Atlantic Community, (New York: Praeger, 1963).
Pierre Uri, Partnership for Progress, Published for the Atlantic Institute, (New York: Harper & Row, 1963).
John Pinder, Europe against de Gaulle, (London: Pall Mall Press, 1963).
Max Kohnstamm, The European Community and its Role in the World, (University of Missouri Press, 1964).

D. DE GAULLE'S PRESS CONFERENCE OF JANUARY 1963

The concept was, however, basically challenged by the policies of De Gaulle.

His press conference on January 14, 1963,[45] which is known for the veto it contained against Britain's entry into the Common Market, was a frontal attack on the concept of Atlantic Partnership as conceived by the Kennedy Administration and understood in a great part of Europe.

The first question which arises is whether this policy of De Gaulle, apart from the method of unilateral action while the negotiations in Brussels were in progress, could be expected.

For those who read and analyzed his writings and speeches, the veto to Britain's entry not only could be expected but was an inevitable consequence of the Gaullist concept.

De Gaulle has always been clear in what he thought about the Schuman-Monnet construction of Europe.

'The States are, in truth, certainly very different from one another, each of which has its own spirit, its own history, its own language, its own misfortunes, glories and ambitions; but these States are the only entities that have the right to order and the authority to act.'[46]

He has been equally clear about the position of leadership, he claimed for France on the continent of Europe and the role this continent should play between the United States and Soviet Union.[47]

Furthermore, he left no doubt about his opinion that integration of defense efforts, a basic notion in the life of NATO, was un-

---

45. *Major Addresses, Statements and Press Conferences of General Charles de Gaulle, May 19, 1958–January 31, 1964,* French Embassy, Press and Information Division, New York, 1964, pp. 216–220.

46. See among many other expressions, Charles de Gaulle, *op. cit.,* Press Conference, May 15, 1962, p. 176.

47. See among many other expressions, Charles de Gaulle, *War Memoirs, Vol. III, Salvation 1944–1946* (London: 1960), pp. 175–180, and the first ten pages of Vol. I of his *War Memoirs, The Call to Honour.*

acceptable to him and that military independence for France was vitally important. 'It is intolerable for a great State to leave its destiny up to the decisions of another State, however friendly it may be.'[48]

The optimism of the United States and most European countries about the outcome of the negotiations between the Community in Brussels and the United Kingdom was unfounded. The contents of the press conference of January 1963, were not new. They were a strictly logical consequence of everything De Gaulle had written or said in the previous years.

It was and is to-day equally unfounded to try to rationalize De Gaulle's policy as a reaction to policies or events from outside France.

There is a flood of political science studies and analyses trying to explain present French policy by shortcomings of the policy followed primarily by the United States and the United Kingdom, during the Second World War and in the post-war era.

Of course the French President uses policies, and especially weak spots in those policies of others, to demonstrate the rightness of his own policy and of specific French objectives. But basically De Gaulle's policies and concepts are not a reaction. They spring from an almost mythological belief in the genius of France and the role it should play in the world.

The ten first pages of his War Memoirs are already sufficient to understand this phenomenon.

It would not be the first time in European history that so much harm was done by not reading and believing what statesmen in power had written or said in all clarity.

The concept of Atlantic Partnership was based on a few fundamental political convictions and objectives.

48. See among many other expressions Charles de Gaulle, *Major Addresses, Statements and Press Conferences, op. cit.,* Press Conference on April 11, 1961, p. 124, and Press Conference on May 15, 1962, pp. 180–181.

1. Europe could only be a valuable partner if it were united and organized along the Schuman-Monnet lines and if Britain would join.

2. With this Europe the United States could deal in the economic field on the assumption that Europe's economic regime would be liberal toward the outside world. The Trade Expansion Act was conceived under this assumption.

3. With this Europe, the United States would form a partnership, economically and politically, and share the burdens which fell upon the Atlantic group in the fulfilment of the tasks toward the developing world.

4. In the military field the United States would contribute to the Atlantic Partnership a centrally controlled nuclear deterrent, while the European partner would increase its conventional contribution to NATO, thereby providing the conventional option in a strategy of flexible response.

De Gaulle, in his press conference of January 14, 1963, made it clear that he did not consider Britain eligible for entry into the Common Market and described in precise terms on the one hand, the natural affinity which, according to his concept, existed between the six countries and on the other hand the fundamentally different political and economic structure of Great Britain. Coupled with his previous statements, it became again clear that he considered Britain as a rival, not as a partner. He underlined his rejection of the supranational construction of Europe by paying a compliment to the work of the European Commission but stressing that 'all the decisions were taken by the Governments, for nowhere else is there any authority or responsibility.'

Especially in the agricultural field, he stressed the protectionist character and policies which he thought would be the logical consequence of a common agricultural policy. He made it further clear that he rejected British entry primarily because of the latter's close ties with the United States and dealt with the concept of Atlantic Partnership by describing it as 'a colossal Atlantic Community under American leadership which would soon completely swallow up the European Community,...not at all what France has wanted.' Finally, he claimed the right for France to develop its own nuclear arsenal. 'For us integration in this field is something that is unimaginable.'

With these words he rejected the four main elements of the Atlantic Parnership concept.

To-day, the policies of the United States toward the process of European integration and the problems of European and Atlantic cooperation still find themselves in the aftermath of the shock produced by the press conference of January 1963. While it seemed that the post-war development in American-European relations was well on its way to a crowning achievement, practically every basic assumption of that era was challenged. The result was a sudden halt to a development which responsible opinion in the United States and in Europe considered as constructive and beneficial.

The result was also that some complex and difficult problems in the relationship between the United States and Europe, which were not fully recognized and analyzed in the conduct and formulation of American foreign policy, came to the forefront.[49]

49. For the impact of De Gaulle's press conference of January 1963, see further:

Nora Beloff, *op. cit.*

Miriam Camps, *Britain and the European Community, op. cit.,* pp. 455–507.

Richard P. Stebbins, *The U.S. in World Affairs 1963,* Published for the Council on Foreign Relations, (New York: Harper & Row, 1964), pp. 94–141.

Henry A. Kissinger, *The Troubled Alliance,* (New York: McGraw-Hill, 1965), pp. 41–65.

Paul Henri Spaak, 'Hold Fast', in *Foreign Affairs,* July 1963, Vol. 41, No. 4, pp. 611–621.

Jean Charles Snoy, 'The Crisis of Europe', in *Atlantic Community,* Summer 1963, pp. 131–143.

Stewart Alsop, 'The Collapse of Kennedy's Grand Design', in *The Saturday Evening Post,* April 6, 1963.

E. AMERICAN POLICY AFTER THE PRESS CONFERENCE

In the relationship between the United States and the process of European integration, the years after January 1963, were characterized by the gap between the concept of Atlantic Partnership and the impossibility to translate this concept into an operational policy.

The United States continued to present the concept as if circumstances still existed in which the achievement of its policy were feasible. In doing so, it created a certain amount of confusion in its own ranks and also in the minds of its European allies.

In this context it was significant that President Kennedy in his State of the Union Message on January 14, 1963, said: 'No doubt differences of opinion will continue to get more attention than agreements on action, as Europe moves from dependence to more formal interdependence. But these are honorable differences among honorable associates – more real and frequent in fact, among our West European Allies, than between them and the United States. ...The basic agreement of this alliance on fundamental issues continues.'[50]

These words were spoken before the text of De Gaulle's press conference was known. They betray, however, an underestimation both of the gravity of the conflict and of the extent of American involvement.

In statements on January 24, 1963, and February 7, 1963,[51] the President expressed strong disappointment about the exclusion of Great Britain from the process of European integration and in a review of United States foreign policy on February 13, 1963, Secretary Rusk repeated the concern of the United States about this fact and about the political philosophy underlying French motives.[52]

Both, however, made it clear that there was only question of a

50. *House Document I*, 88th Congr., 1st sess.
51. Department of State, *Bulletin*, February 11, 1963, p. 197.
52. Department of State, *Bulletin*, March 4, 1963, pp. 311–316.

temporary halt. Both warned against the notion that something fundamental had happened.

'But it has not, as some commentators have dramatically asserted, left our Atlantic policy in shambles. On the contrary, the main lines of that policy have become more than ever valid and urgent.'[53]

Two statements spell out very clearly what United States policy toward Europe would be in the aftermath of January 1963. One is a letter from Under Secretary of State Ball to Senator Paul H. Douglas on February 15, 1963.[54]

The other was the address by President Kennedy during his German visit on June 25, 1963, in the Paulskirche at Frankfurt am Main.[55]

After having restated the general lines of post-war United States policy toward the process of European integration and the main elements of the concept of Atlantic Partnership, based on equality between the United States and a united Europe, Ball continued by mentioning the French veto against Britain's entry into the Common Market.

'In our opinion the action of the French Government must be regarded as motivated primarily by political reasons. It is still too early to know what the French Government's veto may imply for future French policy.'

One would expect that this opinion implied a certain reluctance to restate United States policy in exactly the same terms as before January 1963, or at least the desire to have some time for reflection to determine the impact of the new events on the concept of Atlantic Partnership, as it was launched in 1962.

Ball, however, continued by stating: 'It seems clear enough, however, that this action has not changed the underlying facts that have dictated the need for greater European unity or effective Atlantic

53. Secretary Rusk in his address before the Regional Foreign Policy Conference in Los Angelos on Februarn 13, 1963.
54. Department of State, *Bulletin,* March 18, 1963, pp. 412–415.
55. Department of State, *Bulletin,* July 22, 1963, pp. 118–123.

cooperation...The existence of these facts, it seems to us, deter-
mines the broad policy lines that we intend to pursue.'

He then spelled out the program for American policy. In dealing
with the impact on American policy of the veto against Britain, Ball
stated: 'While we continue to regard the ultimate accession of Great
Britain to the Rome Treaty as an objective to be encouraged, we
recognize that it is unlikely to occur for some time. Meanwhile,
recent events do not appear to have destroyed the vitality of the
strong drive toward unity nor seriously impaired the value of the
integration so far achieved through the EEC. Obviously, it is in
the interest of the whole free world that the EEC develop in an
outward-looking manner and that it not acquire autarchic characteristics.'

He further restated the intention to utilize to the fullest the powers
granted to the President under the Trade Expansion Act, the basic
philosopy on NATO implying the strengthening of conventional
forces, the opposition against proliferation of national nuclear
deterrents, the recognition of the desire of Europeans to play a full
role in their own nuclear defense and the proposal to create within
NATO a multilateral nuclear force.

He terminated by saying that 'the veto of British accession to the
EEC is not an insuperable obstacle to our policies. In 1954, the
French Assembly turned down the European Defense Community
Treaty, but the next few years were years of unprecedented prog-
ress towards European integration along other lines. The basic
soundness of United States policy was not affected.'

In his speech in Frankfurt, Kennedy, apart from a penetrating analysis of American policy toward Europe, stressed three points.

One was the thesis that the United States could only constructively
deal with a united Europe.

'It is only a fully cohesive Europe that can protect us all against
fragmentation of the alliance. Only such a Europe will permit full
reciprocity of treatment across the Ocean, in facing the Atlantic
agenda. With only such a Europe can we have a full give-and-take

between equals, an equal sharing of responsibilities, and an equal level of sacrifice.'

The second was the notion that how Europe was organized was a matter to be decided by the Europeans.

'It is Europeans who are building Europe...I repeat again–so that there may be no misunderstanding–the choice of paths to the unity of Europe is a choice, which Europe must make.'

The third was the heavy emphasis on the round of tariff negotiations following the Trade Expansion Act.

'Another great economic challenge is the coming round of trade negotiations...In short, these negotiations are a test of our unity.'

These two statements contained the main elements of American policy toward Europe since January 1963.

They expose both the strength and the weakness of this policy.

The strength lies in the permanence of the foreign policy line of the United States, started in 1947, the weakness lies in the confusion between a concept and an operational policy, between what is desirable and what is obtainable.

In stating that the French veto against the United Kingdom, based on a concept which was in total opposition to the American one, had no basic consequences for the pursuance of American policy objectives, the United States was compelled to present a distorted view of the actual situation. The American concept was perhaps not affected. But giving concrete form to that concept was made impossible.

Ball's comparison with the situation of 1954, was symptomatic. In 1954, there was no challenge of a concept. There was only the refusal of France to accept German rearmament by the specific means of the European Defense Community. But in January 1963, the whole concept of European integration and Atlantic cooperation was challenged.

In stressing the fact that the United States could only form a meaningful partnership with a united Europe, a situation was created in which every form of European unity seemed to be better for Atlantic cooperation, than a temporary continuance of the existing forms of NATO cooperation, especially in the fields of foreign and military policy.

This danger was strengthened by the statement that the organization of Europe was a matter to be decided by the Europeans. This was not according to the real political facts. A Gaullist Europe would not be an acceptable partner for the United States even if it was united. It would not even be a partner at all.

A further weakness was the fact that the confusion between the concept and the operational policy led to a situation of overstressing the importance of the only field left for practical policy – the Kennedy round of tariffs.

Tariff negotiations by nature are not and should not be a test of unity between countries or groups of countries. First, because this gives an undue importance to the role of tariffs in international economic intercourse. Second, because tariff negotiations are highly technical time-consuming affairs, which are not suited to be considered as the touchstone of political relations between countries.

American diplomacy continued to stress the theme of Atlantic Partnership based upon equality. An analysis of the official declarations and speeches since January 1963 shows a great consistency on this point.

On May 9, 1964, Secretary Rusk[56] said in Brussels: 'First, we

56. Department of State, *Press Release*, May 8, 1964, no. 2, and further speeches by W. W. Rostow, Counselor and Chairman of the Policy Planning Council, Department of State, on
May 9, 1963, Dep. of State, *Press Release*, May 9, 1963, No. 256;
Sept. 18, 1963, Dep. of State, *Press Release*, May 17, 1963, No. 475;
March 16, 1964, Dep. of State, *Press Release*, May 13, 1964, No. 110;
June 23, 1964, U.S. Information Service, *Press Release*, The Hague, June 25, 1964,
and a speech by Secretary Rusk on March 6, 1965, Dep. of State, *Press Release*, March 6, 1965, No. 39.
Edward R. Murrow, Director of U.S. Information Agency, 'The Community of the West', and W. W. Rostow, 'The Integration of the Atlantic Community', both in *The Atlantic Future*, ed. by H. V. Hodson, (London: Longmans & Green, 1964), pp. 1-17 and pp. 72-83.

Americans wish you well in your continued quest for European economic and political unity. You have had our support from the beginnings in 1950; you have it now. But this is a European task and it must continue to be led and carried out by Europeans.'

And in his first Presidential Message to the NATO Council in December 1963, President Johnson said:

'To this end we welcome the emergence of a Europe growing in unity and strength. For we know that only a uniting Europe can be a strong Europe and only a strong Europe will be an effective partner.'[57]

F. THE MULTILATERAL FORCE

In analyzing the main events in American-European relations since January 1963, some attention should be given to the problem of the organization and control of nuclear weapons in the alliance. No single subject has dominated this relationship so much as the discussion about the multilaterally owned force of nuclear weapons, the so-called MLF.

It would go far beyond the scope of this study to describe this discussion, its background and its political and strategic consequences, in detail.

In the paralysis of the Western alliance since the beginning of 1963, the MLF proposal, however, constituted the most serious effort of the United States to exert its leadership in the alliance and to make a meaningful contribution to the changing relationship between itself and its European partners.

A multitude of factors has led to the debate as to whether and how the European allies should share with the United States the responsibilities for strategic decisions whose implementation depended almost totally on American owned weapons.

Among them are the growing strength and unification of Western

57. Department of State, *Bulletin*, January 6, 1964, pp. 29-30.

Europe, the danger of proliferation of nuclear weapons in Europe and especially the consequences for Germany of the pursuance of national nuclear capabilities by the United Kingdom and France, the question of the confidence in the American nuclear commitment to NATO in view of her own vulnerability to Soviet strategic nuclear forces, the military requirements to offset by some means the Soviet missile threat to Europe and the growing need to share more equally the burdens of strategic deterrence between the United States and the other partners in NATO.[58]

Around 1960, between the two extreme possibilities of a complete American monopoly and a multitude of national nuclear capabilities, three possible courses emerged.

The first course was the so-called multinational one, based on the concept that essentially NATO is a coalition of sovereign states with an international command system for certain forces in which major political and military decisions cannot be delegated to a central system.

In this alternative, however, much could be done to improve the system of consultation and coordination, among other things with the aim to give the European partners a greater influence on American strategic thinking and planning.

The second course was the emergence of a European strategic nuclear force under the control of a political European authority, working in full coordination with the American force.

Nobody envisaged that such a force could be comparable to the American nuclear capability, but it could be developed to the extent that it would enable Europe to have its own strategic concept, coordinated with the United States on, what Buchan calls, 'the basis of right rather than of grace'.

The third alternative course was to create within the alliance a new force owned, operated and controlled jointly by nuclear and non-nuclear powers – the so called multilateral solution.

58. Alastair Buchan, *The Multilateral Force: an Historical Perspective,* Adelphi Papers, No. 13, October 1964, The Institute for Strategic Studies, London, p. 3.

It was this last solution which became the object of American foreign policy and was presented with the full force of American diplomacy.

In the concept of partnership based on equality, it would have been more logical that the United States would have supported the second course.

One of the weaknesses of the thesis that partnership is only and exclusively possible between equals, is that it leads to unforeseen and undesired consequences or might be understood by others in a way which was not consonant with the purpose of its originators.

No American Administration, rightly, has ever meant to extend the notion of equal partnership to the nuclear relations in the Atlantic Alliance. But nobody can blame others, that such a heavy underlining of the concept that a constructive partnership implies equality, might lead to misunderstandings and ambitions in this field.

The idea of a so-called NATO deterrent was first formally launched by Secretary Herter at the NATO Ministerial Meeting of December 1960. It contained proposals for a force, assigned to SACEUR, of Polaris missiles installed on submarines. These ships were to be jointly owned, operated and financed by the participants. Each participant was to have a veto. Its origin was mainly military and stood in relation to the threat of Soviet medium-range ballistic missiles aimed at Europe.

The new Kennedy Administration, however, after a study of its NATO policy came to the conclusion that this policy should be based on a strengthening of the conventional forces by the European partners in NATO and on a centralized system of control over nuclear weapons, exercised by the United States.

In this concept there was no room for a high priority for a NATO nuclear force.

The Administration did not reject the idea but it conditioned the emergence of a new force on two developments. One was the achievement of the NATO conventional force goals, the second was some measure of agreement between the European countries about a control plan.[59]

For more than a year the NATO nuclear force practically disappeared from the priority list of NATO.

The nuclear problem in NATO was rather discussed in terms of a greater insight of the NATO-partners in Anglo-American and specially American nuclear targeting and planning.

Gradually, however, a multitude of developments led to a revival of the idea. The German interest in some multilaterally controlled NATO force increased with its anxiety about the new strategy of flexible response and the resulting doubts about an automatic American nuclear protection.

In the United States, there was a growing fear that the justification for a British deterrent and even more the constant French justification for its own and independent nuclear potential, might lead to a general spread of distrust in the American commitment, especially in Germany.

In the American Administration, there were forces at work which were strongly committed to the multilateral approach to the nuclear problem in NATO and not for the first time, they worked in close harmony with the Monnet group in Europe which for several reasons had embraced the multilateral solution.

It saw in this force a possibility for Britain to enter into the process of European unification, a prevention against a further spread of nuclear forces which would at a certain moment reach Germany and an eventual forerunner of a European force which would consolidate the process of European unification in the military and political field.

While these developments took place, not much was achieved in NATO which could open a new perspective for a strengthening of the multinational machinery of consultation and coordination.

In a news conference on December 10, 1962, Secretary Rusk still took a fair degree of distance from an eventual multilateral project.

59. J. F. Kennedy, Speech in Ottawa, May 17, 1961, Department of State, *Bulletin,* June 5, 1961, p. 841.

'We have not ourselves put forward a precise plan in this regard. This is something that our friends across the Atlantic would presumably wish to do if they conclude what it is they would like to propose in this field'.[60]

At the NATO meeting of December 1962, no initiative was taken with regard to a multilateral force. But in the so called Nassau Agreement there appeared a sentence about agreement between the United States and the United Kingdom with respect to the provision of Polaris missiles in connection with the development of a multilateral NATO nuclear force.[61]

This Agreement, caused by the United States cancellation of the Skybolt missile, led to differences in interpretation between the United States and Britain.

The first saw in it a commitment to the multilateral formula, while the latter interpreted the agreement in the direction of assignment of national forces to NATO.

The real impetus for stronger and more purposeful American action was, however, provided by the press conference of De Gaulle in January 1963. De Gaulle rejected the offer of Polaris missiles, clarified and underlined France's decision to develop a wholly independent nuclear force and placed his whole concept of European and Atlantic cooperation in direct opposition to the American one. He did not elaborate on any subtle difference between multinational or multilateral solutions of the nuclear problem. For him only a national solution was feasible.

From this moment the American drive behind the idea of the MLF was primarily based on the German issue. The press conference of January 1963, and the Franco-German Treaty had shocked the United States and the possibility of a Franco-German nuclear cooperation, with grave consequences for the cohesion of the Atlantic alliance and the concept of an Atlantic Partnership, required the offer of a constructive alternative to Germany.

60. Dean Rusk, News Conference on December 10, 1962, Department of State, *Bulletin,* December 31, 1962, p. 995.
61. Department of State, *Bulletin,* January 14, 1963, p. 44.

In March 1963, this alternative proposal was offered and after initial discussions its main contents became the following:

The MLF was to be composed of twenty-five surface ships, each carrying eight Polaris missiles. The ships would be manned by crews, drawn from at least three nationalities. No nation should contribute more than forty percent of the financial costs and the command of the ships was to be in proportion to the financial contribution. The control system would be decided later but it was assumed that, initially, all participants would be represented in the executive body, which would take decisions by unanimity.

The force would be jointly owned, financed and controlled. Some of the most important consequences of the adoption of the plan would be that the withdrawal of nuclear warheads would only be possible by the consent of all the participants and would involve the United States in a more binding association than under the existing bilateral arrangements.

Germany would be linked to the nuclear effort on a non-discriminatory basis and, certainly in the event of Britain joining the force, it would mean a turn in the tide of the spread of national nuclear deterrents.

In the following months, the effort to get European support for the MLF became the central theme of American policy toward Europe.

After the blow to the American concept of Atlantic Partnership at the press conference of January 1963, the MLF became, as it were, the symbol for the opposition of American policy against the Gaullist theses.

Roughly speaking, the idea was supported in Europe by a substantial part of the protagonists of the partnership concept in American-European relations.

There were, however, strong sources of opposition mainly in military circles and among those who rejected basically any alternative to the exclusive control of nuclear strategic forces by the President of the United States.

The latter were alarmed by the possibility that the MLF might leave open an option for a later development into a European nuclear force.

This option was, however, the reason why the proposal was supported by a substantial part of the orthodox European integrationalists.

Many prominent Americans underlined this ultimate possibility of a European nuclear force in which an American veto would not be operative anymore.[62]

It was not always made clear that such a force could only operate on the basis of a degree of European political unification which was completely out of the question for a time period, relevant to the problem under discussion.

From the left the MLF was attacked by a combination of anti-American, anti-German and anti-nuclear sentiments and from a part of the right, primarily by Gaullist and pseudo-Gaullist opinion in Europe. There is no question that the heavy American pressure led to a bitter controversy in Europe, comparable to the situation during the discussion on the European Defense Community in the years 1950–1954.

At the end of 1964, a situation was created in which the success or failure of the MLF became closely linked with the attitude of the new British Government.

The Labour Party in its election campaign had declared itself in opposition to the American proposals which they considered military unnecessary and politically dangerous.

62. See among others:
    Robert R. Bowie, 'Strategy and the Atlantic Alliance', in *International Organization*, Vol. XVII, No. 3, 1963, pp. 709–733.
    McGeorge Bundy, 'Building the Atlantic Partnership: Some lessons from the past', Speech on September 27, 1962, Department of State, *Bulletin*, October 22, 1962, pp. 604–605.
    J. Robert Schaetzel, 'The Nuclear Problem and Atlantic Interdependence', in *Atlantic Community*, Vol. I, No. 4, p. 567.

Labour based itself on a concept in which there would be no room for an independent British nuclear contribution; it adhered to the exclusive possession and control of the nuclear element in NATO by the United States; it rejected any possibility of a European nuclear formation and it claimed a greater role in the planning and targeting of American nuclear forces.

The decision of the Labour Government to abolish Britain's purely national nuclear role could have been a major contribution to the solution of the Atlantic nuclear problem, if this would have been combined with the acceptance of the main lines of the MLF proposal, notably a substantial element of mixed manning of the ships of which the force would be composed and a non-discriminatory attitude towards the German contribution. Whether this could be achieved depended mainly on the first meeting between President Johnson and the new British Prime Minister in December 1964.

Wilson came to Washington with new British proposals which on important points differed from the American concept. It seems that President Johnson was not prepared to put heavy pressure on the British to accept the main elements of the MLF. One can understand that the President was reluctant to force a project on his British visitor, the more so because there was, apart from the German Government, not enough open European support in order to induce him to fight an ultimate battle over the American concept with the French President.

Nevertheless, one cannot escape the conclusion that his decision to take away the pressure and the time limit of the project was regrettable. Part of the blame, undoubtedly, falls on the reluctance of many European governments to be more positive and constructive in their reactions to the American plan. But the American decision suddenly to change the priority it had given to the MLF, left the protagonists in Europe in an awkward position. This certainly is true with regard to the German Government which had exposed itself so completely in support of this concept.

The decision also proved that, in the present circumstances, leaving solutions of this kind to intra-European discussions without strong leadership of the United States, creates a vacuum in which no positive and constructive action is possible.

The MLF was not an ideal or even near-perfect solution. It was, however, a constructive effort to open a new perspective for a nuclear relationship in NATO. Projected against other alternatives, it was at the same time a certain safeguard against further proliferation of nuclear weapons in Europe, an opening of a new avenue of Atlantic cooperation and the offer of an honorable place for Germany in the most sensitive field of American-European relations.[63]

G. CONCLUSION

Since 1947, the constant element in United States foreign policy has been to consider European cooperation and integration as a vital contribution to the strength of the Atlantic world and the interests of the United States.

American support for European integration in general was based on the conviction that the medium-size nation-state in Europe was obsolete in relation to the solution of basic political, military and economic problems.

It was inspired by the genuine and almost missionary belief that the United States should use its power to transplant the blessings of its own federal system and of its own continental size to the countries in Europe, with which it felt itself so emotionally linked.

It was also motivated by its strong desire to simplify its relations in the political, military and economic field with the great number of European partners.

63. In the mass of literature on this subject, see for a penetrating analysis of the arguments against the MLF: Henry A. Kissinger, *The Troubled Partnership, op. cit.* pp. 127–159,
and in defense of the MLF: E. Osgood, *The Case for the M.L.F., A Critical Evaluation,* (The Washington Center of Foreign Policy Research, 1964).

Apart from these general motives, the more specific reasons for its support for European integration changed in emphasis according to the circumstances of the various post-war periods.

In the first years after 1947, its support was specifically based on its conviction that the European nations should be economically assisted in order to prevent them from becoming an easy prey of communism. Reconstruction of their dislocated economies was necessary in order to make them politically invulnerable to the communist threat. This reconstruction, in American eyes, could best be achieved through cooperative and unifying efforts and not on a purely national basis.

Economic cooperation and integration, in American eyes, were a precondition for economic strength and the only way in which Europe could become independent of American assistance.

Around 1950, a new period began in the concern of the United States for European integration.

NATO was established as a military alliance and the United States became convinced that the solution of the German problem in general and the German contribution to the defense of the West in particular could only be achieved through a specific form of European integration along the lines of the Schuman Plan.

The Schuman initiative of May 1950, met all the main hopes and aspirations of United States policy toward the European problem.

The Schuman-Monnet concept of European integration would bring about, at the same time, the establishment of a continental market, the federal structure of the European continent, the simplification of relations between the United States and its European partners and the re-establishment of Germany in a framework which would guarantee its full contribution to Western strength and avoid the dangers of its nationalism.

In the decade between 1950 till 1960, this specific form of European integration became almost the exclusive object of American policy toward Europe. In American eyes this was a natural and self-evident process. The failure of the European Defense Community was considered as a temporary deviation in a development in which there was no conflict between what was desirable and what could be obtained. The conflicts in Europe and notably the split between the Communities of the six continental powers and the other Western European countries, were not completely disregarded but never considered as potentially dangerous for the cohesion of the Atlantic world.

Around 1960, and more specifically in the first year of the Kennedy Administration, the justification for American support for the process of European integration concentrated on the concept of partnership between the two equal pillars of the Atlantic world, the United States and a unified Europe.

Only a united Europe could be strong, only a strong Europe could be an equal partner and only equal partners could form a meaningful partnership.

The re-emergence of a strong economic grouping in Europe, the relative weakening of the American economic position which found its expression in the deterioration of the United States balance of payments and the dilemma of the nuclear relationship in NATO brought the United States to a concept in which the relations inside the Atlantic world and an effective policy of the Western nations towards the outside world could only be solved on the basis of an equal partnership.

Only in such a partnership could the burdens which had so heavily fallen on the United States be more equally shared.

This development of American policy towards the problem of European integration was based on a few assumptions:

1. European unity was *per se* a contributing and even an indispensable factor for Atlantic strength and in the best interest of the United States.

2. The German problem could only be solved in a European framework along the lines of the Schuman-Monnet concept.

3. The economic integration of Europe would automatically lead to political integration and the emergence of a United States of Europe.

4. The United Kingdom would be a part of the united Europe.

5. Atlantic defense was indivisible and there would be no real challenge to the nuclear hegemony of the United States.

When the idea of Atlantic Partnership was launched by the Kennedy Administration, it looked to the United States as if these assumptions, broadly speaking, were realistic and politically valid.

The idea of an Atlantic partnership based on equality was the logical consequence of United States policy towards the problem of European integration, followed since 1947.

Therefore, this concept should be analyzed in the conclusion of this study and the question should be answered, whether it should still constitute the exclusive approach to United States–European relations in the foreseeable future.

It is not possible to state with certainty, whether the Kennedy concept of Atlantic Partnership was the expression of an ultimate long-term objective, an imaginative goal for the future relationship in the Atlantic world or whether it was meant to be an exclusive and operational policy for the very near future. It is also not clear whether the concept was so much motivated by economic circumstances that its consequences in the political and military field were simply not thought through.

Duchêne and Kaiser are convinced that it was meant as a very long term promise.[64]

Their arguments are strengthened by the fact that one of the two required pillars on which the partnership should be based was not yet established and that therefore, necessarily, the idea was launched as an ultimate and long-term objective.

Relevant is, however, that there was at least widespread confusion about its exact meaning for actual policy and it certainly created the

64. Francois Duchêne, *Beyond Alliance,* The Atlantic Papers, NATO Series 1, (Paris: The Atlantic Institute, 1965), pp. 33–34.
Karl Kaiser, 'Die Amerikanische Aussenpolitik im Wandel. Die Vereinigten Staaten und Europa in der Westlichen Allianz', in *Europa Archiv,* 25–12–1964, p. 913.

feeling that nothing constructive could be achieved in Atlantic relations without the realization of equality between the United States
and Europe.

Many declarations from the United States policy-makers, even if
not aimed at that conclusion, contributed to that confusion.

Duchêne considers the 'theoretically lamentable vagueness of the
concept...as perhaps its greatest virtue'. In any case, it brought
about strong expressions of adhesion from groups which were
fundamentally antagonistic on basic problems of the alliance and on
the problem of the desirable relation between the United States and
Europe.

In the study made for the Atlantic Institute by Pierre Uri, the
generally warm welcome to the idea of equal partnership is demonstrated by four quotations of Kennedy, Hallstein, MacMillan and
De Gaulle.[65]

There is no better proof of the confusion about the concept.

It might be argued that in spite of rather important nuances between their different approaches, there existed a measure of agreement on basic issues between Kennedy, Hallstein and MacMillan.
It cannot be argued that their convictions were shared by the
French President in spite of the words quoted in Uri's study. It was
at the same time the strength and the weakness of the concept that
it rallied around it so many different groups and policies.

The orthodox partisans of the Schuman-Monnet concept in
Europe saw in Atlantic Partnership, based on equality, an additional
instrument to obtain their objectives of integration. They argued
that the United States had made it clear beyond doubt that it could
only deal with a united Europe as a partner in a meaningful
Atlantic relationship.

Those who aimed at an independent role for Europe embraced the
idea of equality and forgot the element of interdependence with the
United States.

And while the Americans did not, most probably, have in mind

65.   Pierre Uri, *op. cit.,* pp. XXIX–XXX.

that the notion of equality implied that Europe should extend the structure of the Common Market to the fields of foreign and military policy, the presentation of their concept strengthened many Europeans in their aim of a superstate which would assume all the powers of the traditional nation-state.

Stanley is right when he says:

'The concept of an Atlantic Partnership has become everybody's favorite refuge, for it is broad enough to cover views as divergent as those of De Gaulle's and the late President Kennedy.'[66]

A further analysis of the concept of Atlantic Partnership is necessary in order to reach a conclusion as to its validity. First, the question should be answered whether the thesis that a meaningful partnership is only possible between equals is acceptable in the more general sense. There are never complete parallels in history, but it can be stated that in the past there is no example of a partnership between equals which has really worked.

In the years between the two World Wars, France and Britain were the leading partners of approximately equal size, responsible for the state of European affairs. The Soviet Union was weak and the United States had withdrawn to the other side of the Ocean.

This partnership did not work and because it did not work the disaster of 1940, could not be prevented. The partnership between Syria and Egypt is neither a happy omen, nor is the intended partnership between the Soviet Union and China a classical example of perfect harmony.

If partnership is only possible between equals, what is the United States going to say to Canada, to Mexico, to Brazil and to Japan? Would it exclude all these countries from a meaningful partnership with the United States because they are not equal? Does this concept not result in the fallacious notion that only equals qualify for partnership and others will be satellites? This could be the fatal

66. Timothy W. Stanley, *NATO in Transition: The Future of the Atlantic Alliance,* Published for the Council on Foreign Relations, (New York: Praeger, 1965), p. 68.

consequence of a too rigid interpretation of what the United States has said but probably not really meant.

Second, it is contrary to the facts of international relations, that solutions can more easily be found between two major parties than between a larger number.

Livingston Hartley is right in stating: 'Two nations lack the capacity a larger group has of providing a majority in support of one view which may bring a consensus.'[67]

And Stanley points out that bilateral confrontations sometimes make it harder to compromise, than negotiations where there are many and each knows it must yield in some measure.[68]

In history, countries of equal size have more often been enemies than partners. A partnership is either necessary in front of a common foe, or to embark upon a new joint venture. In neither case equality is required.

Less academic than the question whether in general the thesis that partnership is only possible between equals is valid, is the problem whether real equality between the United States and Europe exists or will exist in the foreseeable future.

Mainly because some parts of European opinion, in their confusion between prosperity and power, overlook the enormous difference in strength between the United States and a united Europe, it is of some importance to compare the strength and power of the United States with that of Europe in certain respects.

For two reasons it is logical to begin with a comparison in economic strength, first, because only in the economic field can one speak about a European partner, and second, because this is the field where the notion of equality is the least remote from reality.

The gross national product in actual prices in 1964, was for the Common Market countries $271 billion against $622 billion for the United States.

67. Livingston Hartley, *Atlantic Challenge,* (New York: Oceana Publications, 1965), p. 43.
68. Stanley, *op. cit.,* p. 73.

Per capita this means roughly $1500 for the Common Market and $3250 for the United States.

Total domestic investments in 1964, amounted to $63.7 billion for the Common Market and $99.5 billion for the United States.

In 1963, the Common Market countries spent $2.3 billion for research and development in the public sector and $1.4 billion in the private sector. The comparable figures for the United States were $11.4 billion and $5 billion.

It is difficult to get a reliable picture about another indicator of economic strength, notably investments made in third countries. It can be estimated, however, that these investments for the Common Market in 1964, amounted to approximately $2.5 billion and for the United States to approximately double that amount.

Only in two important aspects of economic life has the Common Market surpassed the United States. The foreign trade of the Common Market in 1964, amounted to roughly $50 billion and that of the United States to roughly $45 billion.

The combined gold and foreign exchange reserves of the Common Market were $19.8 billion at the end of 1964, while those of the United States amounted to $15.9 billion.

It is not very probable that the still existing great discrepancies in economic strength between the United States and Europe will substantially narrow in the foreseeable future. Studies about the Gross National Product in 1970 reveal that based on 1955 prices this product for the United States in 1970 will be $650 billion while for all European members of NATO together the estimate is $300 billion.[69]

While there could still be an argument to treat Europe and the United States as near-equals in the economic field because the Common Market is already an economic unit and has comparable strength in some important sectors of economic life, there is and will be a glaring discrepancy between their military power.

69.   Stanley, *op. cit.,* p. 24.

The fact that the United States disposes of approximately ninety-seven percent of the nuclear power in the NATO alliance precludes already that all the European NATO partners, even if they were united, could join the United States and the Soviet Union as a third power in the coming decades.

Another striking example of the absurdity of treating Europe and the United States as equal or potentially equal in the military field is the comparison of defense expenditure.

In the year 1964, the United States spent more than $54 billion on defense, the six countries of the Common Market nearly $12 billion and all European NATO partners almost $20 billion.[70]

Even among those in Europe, who aim at equality with the United States, there is not the slightest inclination to accept the economic and social consequences of an increase in defense expenditure.

On the contrary, it rather looks as if the discrepancy in expenditure for defense between the United States and Europe will increase.

All this implies that not only there is no equality between the United States and Europe in the military field but total and utter dependence of Europe on the military power of the American ally.

Equality in foreign policy cannot be treated as a quantitative problem. What can be done, however, is to state that military power is a prerequisite for the conduct of foreign policy or at least for a foreign policy which is relevant for the balance of power in the present world.

Furthermore, politically and militarily Europe cannot function as an equal partner until it has developed a governmental structure sufficiently integrated to conduct a single foreign and military policy. Whether such a single policy would be a desirable objective is open to serious doubt. But there is no chance, and today perhaps

---

70. *The Military Balance 1963–1964* and *The Military Balance 1964–1965*, published by the Institute for Strategic Studies, London.
     F. D. Gregh, 'Some Economic and Financial Aspects of the NATO Alliance', in *NATO's Fifteen Nations*, Vol. 8, Number 2, April–May 1963, pp. 82–90.

less than two or three years ago, that such a governmental structure will be established in the foreseeable future.

Finally, consideration should be given to the question what kind of Europe the United States had in mind when it launched the idea that the Atlantic Alliance could only function when it was based on two pillars, the United States and a unified Europe. It seems reasonable to suggest that what it had in mind was an Atlantic-minded Europe, which would include the United Kingdom and other democratic countries not belonging to the Common Market; a Europe which would be liberal in economic outlook and which would feel the interdependence with the United States as logical and self-evident; a Europe which would know its limitations in the field of military and foreign policy; a Europe structured on the lines of the Schuman–Monnet concept in which the obsolescense of the nation-state was recognized and which would develop into a federal entity, democratic in structure and liberal in policy.

The United States never made it clear, however, that not every kind of Europe and not every kind of European unity qualified for being the equal and exclusive partner of the United States.

The United States has never made it clear that Gaullist policies and the exclusion of the United Kingdom had affected the concept it had launched in 1962, and pursued, practically without qualification, since.

The United States has officially supported the idea of a political union between the Common Market countries in 1964. Has it sufficiently realized that such a Europe would be in danger of becoming an instrument of French anti-Atlantic policies?

Has it sufficiently realized that such a Europe would probably be dominated far more by champions of independence from the United States than by champions of supranational institutions and Atlantic Partnership?

Has it sufficiently realized that a Europe of national states, generated by the French under the banner of European nationalism, and Atlantic interdependence are mutually exclusive?

Has it sufficiently analyzed that while there never can be a guarantee that a united Europe will automatically be a loyal partner of the United States in the framework of the Atlantic Alliance, at least the components of that United Europe should be such that stability, restraint and democratic convictions have a fair chance?

Has it given enough attention to the fact that the history of Germany, France and Italy do not provide shining examples of these requirements and that therefore a Europe which will be Atlantic-minded and a loyal partner has by necessity to include more countries, whose history has shown less instability and more democracy than is present in the framework of the Common Market?

Has it recognized that a partnership with any united Europe can be more dangerous than a relationship with individual countries?[71]

Has it, as Stanley puts it, without dictating the details of intra-European relationships exerted its leadership in such a way, that it has insisted that these arrangements would not produce the type of Europe which would jeopardize the interest of the United States in European security, seek to become a third force and become inward-looking and protectionist?[72]

If the United States has recognized these potential dangers it certainly has not made this clear to the outside world and it has by the pursuance of a policy which could have been feasible in 1962, but not afterwards, contributed to the confusion in the Atlantic alliance.

All this does not imply that the concept of partnership, as it was launched in 1962, is not valid.

On the contrary, everything which has happened after the Second World War points in the direction of a structure of the Atlantic world which ultimately must be based on a relation between the United States and its European partners in which, as Duchêne says, there will be more equality in the 'process of mutual persuasion'.[73]

The concept of Atlantic Partnership is constructive and imagina-

71. J. L. Heldring, 'Atlantic Partnership: European Unity', in Survival, Jan.–Febr., 1965, Vol. 7, Number 1, pp. 30–38.
72. Stanley, op. cit., p. 74.
73. Duchêne, op. cit., p. 28.

tive if it is understood in this way and if it is the ultimate goal of a process of working relationships inside the Alliance in which the development of European unity has its legitimate place.

The strengthening of Atlantic relations cannot and should not, however, be preconditioned by the uncertain process of European unification and the notion of equality should be qualified and better presented as to its contents as well as to the kind of Europe to which it applies.

It is quite natural that the concept of equal Atlantic Partnership was the subject of numerous non-official studies and publications and was criticized from many different angles and approaches.

There are those who accept the basic Atlantic policies but reproach the Administration that not enough account is taken of the growing strength of Europe and the notion of a European identity, also in the military field. In this group Henry Kissinger and Stanley Hoffmann are prominent.[74]

Others, often for different reasons, question the alliance-system, as such, in the present state of international relations and are doubtful about the wisdom of fostering a new center of force in Europe.[75]

74. See Henry Kissinger, 'The Unsolved Problem of European Defense', 'Strains on the Alliance' and 'Coalition Diplomacy in a Nuclear Age', in *Foreign Affairs*, July, 1962, pp. 515–542, January, 1963, pp. 261–286 and July, 1964, pp. 525–546, 'NATO's Nuclear Dilemma', in *National Security*, (New York: Praeger, 1963), pp. 293–317, and his *The Troubled Partnership, op. cit.*
Stanley Hoffmann, 'Cursing De Gaulle is not a Policy', in *The Reporter*, January 30, 1964, 'Discord in Community: The North Atlantic Area as a Partial International System', in *International Organization*, No. 3, 1963, pp. 521–550, 'De Gaulle, Europe and the Atlantic Alliance', in *International Organization*, No. 1, 1964, pp. 1–29, and 'Europe's Identy Crisis', in *Daedalus*, Fall 1964, pp. 1244–1297.
75. See among others:
George Kennan, 'Polycentrism and Western Policy', in *Foreign Affairs*, January 1964, pp. 171–184.
Ronald Steel, *The End of Alliance*, (London: André Deutsch, 1964).
Edmund Stillman and William Pfaff, *The New Politics*, (New York: Harper & Row, 1961).

The basic question, whether it was right on the part of the different United States Administrations to consider European unity per definition as a contribution to Atlantic cohesion and hence in the interest of the United States is posed in two publications which are, next to the already mentioned analyses of Lincoln Gordon, the most important contributions from the American side to the clarification of this vital issue.

One is a pamphlet published by the Critical Issues Council of the Republican Citizens Committee of the United States and prepared by a task force under the chairmanship of General Lauris Norstadt.[76] The other is an article by Livingston T. Merchant, who served as United States Ambassador and as Under Secretary of State for Political Affairs.[77]

The Norstadt paper states: 'It can no longer be taken for granted that what is good for the narrow circle of countries seeking a powerful political merger will necessarily serve the purposes of those other allies with whom they are aligned in the crucial task of collective Atlantic defense... We must now reappraise our view of European unity... in terms of America's own interest...

Greater unity in Europe is desirable, insofar as it strengthens the Atlantic Community; developments in Europe that weaken Atlantic unity are undesirable. This must be our guiding standard...

The term "partnership"...is useful, if it is not made to suggest a partnership of equal powers, or one necessarily limited to two partners only.'

And Merchant writes: 'There was always an inarticulate premise to our support for European unity – that such unity or integration was desirable from our point of view only in the framework of an Atlantic Community to which we belonged. The new Europe we urged and hoped for was to be eventually a partner with Canada

76. *The Atlantic Alliance and United States Security,* Paper no. 3 of the Critical Issues Council, 1964.
77. Livingston T. Merchant, 'Evolving United States Relations with the Atlantic Community', in *International Organization,* Summer 1963, pp. 610–629.

and the United States, not an economic or political rival. Whether this important premise was adequately examined or discussed with our European friends is another matter. The fact is that it has always been there…Developments in Europe during 1962, and early 1963, should give pause to those who have automatically assumed that any form of European integration was good in itself and in our own interest.' Had Merchant written his article in 1965, the events of 1963 and 1964, could only have strengthened his remarkable analysis.

It is significant and gratifying that these voices are now heard in the United States and that they come from men, whose loyalty to the cause of Atlantic cohesion and European intregation cannot be questioned.

The two great achievements in the Western world since 1945, are the commitment of the United States to European strength and security, symbolized in NATO, and the process of European integration started in 1950, when the Schuman plan was launched. The first is the result of American foreign policy decisions, the second has been constantly and generously supported by the United States.

This is a great tribute to the wisdom and the permanence of American foreign policy. There is no example in history to be found where a great power not only supports the reconstruction of its allies, but aims at the emergence of a new powerful center of force in the world.

There is no example in history where 'divide et impera' in the policy of a major power was replaced by the determined desire to help create a strong partner. In American opinion, this policy served the best interest of the United States. This interest was, however, interpreted in the most enlightened and imaginative way.

On balance, the record of United States policy towards Europe and specifically towards the problem of European integration is remarkably constructive, generous and steady. The only criticism which should be made is that it has shown from time to time too much rigidity and too great an attachment to exclusive solutions.

A certain dogmatism, especially in the higher echelons of the Department of State, has led from time to time to a confusion between ends and means and a reluctance to adapt policies to changing circumstances.

But these are marginal errors when compared to the overall scope and *grandeur* of the policy.

It is inconceivable that the countries of the Western world could not mobilize enough mental and political forces to overcome the frustration of to-day.

France should wake up at a certain day and realize what the real source of its greatness is and what the real limitations of its position are.

The United Kingdom should learn that its place is in the process of European integration and that there are no alternatives in special relations with the United States and the Commonwealth, or in bridge-building between the two parts of Europe, if it wants to cure its economic ills and play its indispensable role in the alliance and in the world.

The five partners of France in the revolutionary process of European integration should recognize that development of economic integration cannot and should not be bought by concessions to the principles of the Treaty of Rome nor by acceptance of unrealistic and dangerous adventures in the field of military and foreign policy which would estrange them from the United States. They should also recognize that the ultimate aim of the integration of Europe is not the emergence of a superstate with all the powers of the traditional nation-state.

As to Germany, one should have confidence in its democratic development in the framework of the Atlantic alliance. Germany's allies should realize that the eventual reemergence of a dangerous German nationalism cannot be absorbed in the Europe of the Common Market, as was assumed in the period of the Schuman Plan, but only in the larger framework of NATO and in the presence of the United States in Europe.

The United States should recognize, as it has always done, that Europe is totally dependent on the willingness of the United States to guarantee its freedom, but that the United States without Europe would find itself in frightening isolation.

And as Europe should overcome its unrealistic ambitions, because it often confuses prosperity and power, the United States should, in exerting a new leadership of the alliance, realize that this new leadership might imply an infraction of its own sovereignty.

These hopes for developments are preconditions for a structure of the Atlantic world, which takes into account the changes and the evolutions since the creation of NATO and the tasks for the future.

They are, however, not enough for even the broadest outline of how American-European relations in the framework of an Atlantic world should be structured.

Even apart from the fact that in 1969, the NATO Treaty can be denounced by any party,[78] there is a widespread feeling that the organization of Atlantic cooperation should be rethought and renewed.

In terms of NATO, this implies that NATO should evolve from a security pact to the center of the Atlantic world, no longer primarily preoccupied with internal problems but directed towards external tasks.

There are no exclusive and clear-cut solutions for this transition, but a few basic points should be kept in mind.

While the possibility of a Soviet attack on Western Europe is much less plausible now than in any period since the creation of NATO – a proof of its success and at the same time a reason for its declining cohesion – there is no ground to suppose that this is caused by a basic and permanent change in the communist philosophy.

But even if there is more stability in the East-West relations in Europe, this certainly is not true with regard to the situation in the 'third' world.

78.   The Treaty does not expire in 1969.

There, the Communist challenge, both in its military and economic aspects, is constantly present.

Both tasks, the maintenance of security in the Atlantic area and the maintenance of economic and political order in the outside world, require a maximum of cohesion between the United States and Europe.

Neither task could be adequately performed without an Atlantic partnership in which America and the European countries, individually or collectively, play their full role. To suppose that these tasks can be fulfilled by separate entities working in their own sphere of influence, even when they are so large and powerful as the United States or an eventually united Europe, implies a grave underestimation of the scope of the task and the required resources to fulfil it.

A second basic point for a better organization of the Atlantic world is the necessity to recognize that this improvement cannot await the creation of the single European partner of Kennedy's grand design.

Many activities will, in the foreseeable future, be based on the relation of the United States with individual and smaller partners.

The process of growing Atlantic cohesion and a more important role of the European countries in Atlantic cooperation cannot be made dependent on the emergence of a strong European entity. This, in present circumstances, would mean an irresponsible delay.

On the other hand, however, all the means to improve Atlantic cooperation must leave room for the development and consolidation of European integration and must be structured in such a way that in important fields of activity, the role of individual European countries can, in a later phase, be taken over by a European collectivity and by European institutions.

The third assumption should be especially stressed in Europe.

Europe's role in the world should not be based on a concept that ultimately it must assume all the powers of the traditional nation-state. Europe should realize that it is already, to-day, closely connected with important tasks in the world which can only be performed by larger entities than the European one.

When a real European unity emerges, it will spring from the conviction of the inadequacy of the nation-state for certain important functions. There are functions to be performed by the Western world for which Europe, even if it is united, is not adequate.

One of these is the military one. In recognizing the necessity for a gradual change in Atlantic cooperation it is evident that a solution must be found for military cooperation and the nuclear defense within NATO.

When an American nuclear monopoly is not acceptable, a further proliferation of nuclear weapons in Europe is undesirable and a European nuclear structure is unattainable and in contradiction to the indivisible character of nuclear defense of the West, then a revival of the multilateral force or some other form of Atlantic nuclear force is imperative.

The nuclear problem of NATO to-day is, rightly or wrongly, a source of discord which should be taken away.

A nuclear force, jointly owned, manned, controlled and financed could well meet all the necessary requirements for a more cohesive Atlantic organization.

Its precise form should be elaborated but it should include Germany on a non-discriminatory basis; it should give expression to a greater voice of the European countries in the nuclear affairs of the alliance and it should imply a greater European technical and financial contribution; it should decrease complete American freedom of action and it should leave open the possibility of an evolution in the relations between the European members.

There will never be an ideal solution for a problem which, by its nature, does not lend itself to clear-cut solutions, but it might constitute an example of Atlantic cooperation with beneficial consequences for other fields of activity.

Another aspect of a possible improvement in Atlantic cooperation is the relation between NATO and OECD. These two organizations are the instruments which the Atlantic world has at its disposal.

It is important that their activities should be streamlined and brought together.

The fact that the membership of both organizations is different should not stand in the way of a closer cooperation and an eventual merger.

The situation of the European neutrals and Japan should be considered and eventually solved through special relationships for specific activities.

A real improvement in Atlantic institutions is, however, too important to be stopped by the self-chosen neutrality of Sweden and Switzerland or the specific position of Austria, for which a solution should be found.

As to Japan, its cooperation in economic matters and problems of assistance to developing countries is very valuable, but this should not prevent the United States and its European partners from improving their instruments of cooperation. Serious thought should be given to the creation of a political body which would cover the activities of NATO and OECD and which would direct and control their secretariats and staffs.

This Atlantic body could meet at ministerial level with a variable composition, changing with the subjects under discussion and it could have one council on a permanent basis.

An evolution in that direction would have several advantages.

It would above all bring about a greater emphasis on the external problems of the alliance. OECD already deals with the problem of assistance to the 'third' world. It is necessary, however, that also in the military and political field the emphasis shifts to cooperation in areas and problems outside the Atlantic world.

One of the defects of NATO, at present, is its preoccupation with internal developments, while the more burning problems happen in the outside world and gravely affect the security and the well-being of every member of NATO.

An Atlantic cooperation of this kind should be flexible enough to enable European countries to act as an entity in so far as such action is justified by the process of European integration. In important economic matters, the Common Market could act as one element, preferably represented by its common institutions.

As long ast he unfortunate split between EEC and EFTA exists and is not solved by an enlargement of the Common Market, there also should be a possibility for EFTA to act collectively in a wider framework.

Problems relating to the international monetary system and aid policies to developing countries will probably be dealt with in a European, an Atlantic and a worldwide framework.

The Atlantic framework is indispensable, because some major aspects of these problems require a cohesive Atlantic point of view.

In talking about the new forms of Atlantic cooperation it is not possible to refrain from mentioning the institutional aspects.

In itself, institutional constructions do not solve problems of policy, but it is equally true that no common or concerted policy can be pursued without a minimum of institutional provisions.

This is not a field in which detailed suggestions can be made, acceptable to the major partners in the Atlantic world at this time.

Only a few general points should be mentioned.

If the scope of Atlantic cooperation is widened and deepened, the institutional system should be such, that it differs from an orthodox coalition of completely sovereign states and it should be flexible enough to leave room for further developments, either between some partners or between all partners.

More delegation to limited groups and stronger executive responsibilities seem to be required.

A real partnership, confronted with the enormous tasks of the Atlantic world, cannot function without certain limitations of sovereignty and without a gradual process towards common responsibility for common problems.

Apart from present France, the issue of limitation of sovereignty is the most sensitive in relation to the United States.

The United States, at present, bears an unusual degree of responsibility for the stability and peace in the world. Most other countries are not willing to share these responsibilities, mainly because they do not want to share the burden and the sacrifices and, only to a very small degree, because they are hardly consulted in the policy-making process of the United States.

As long as this is the case, it is logical that the United States demands a maximum freedom of action.

A solution of this dilemma is only possible, when the European countries share more equally the burdens of the Atlantic world, primarily in connection with the non-Atlantic responsibilities of the United States.

The United States for its part, should then recognize that a more equal sharing of the burden implies limitations of sovereign and independent action.

'No taxation without representation' is equally fundamental as 'no representation without taxation'.

The precise elaboration of these general principles is a matter of time and prevailing circumstances.

Without them, however, it seems doubtful whether a viable Atlantic Partnership can be created.

In looking at the future of Atlantic cooperation, one matter should be mentioned which might seem trivial but which has some importance for the smooth and constructive working of Atlantic institutions.

Both OECD and NATO are located in Paris.

There are two reasons to consider seriously whether this should remain so in future.

The first is the intangible question of atmosphere. In a country in which the Atlantic spirit is probably the least developed, compared to all other NATO partners, the institutions work and the representatives meet in an unfriendly, uninspiring and isolated atmosphere.

The second is that the best way to understand and influence decisions and policies of the most powerful partner in the Atlantic Partnership is to be as near as possible to the center where these decisions are made and the policies are formulated.

This does not mean a plea for the transfer of all instruments of Atlantic cooperation to the United States, but it implies more activity for the future Atlantic institutions in the country where 'the greatest number of different interests bisect.'[79]

There are no easy solutions for the problems of American-European relations, nor for the organization of an Atlantic cooperation which could constructively and imaginatively fulfill its task in the years to come.

Those who work at possible solutions should know, however, that what is at stake, is the survival of a society of free men.

79.   Alastair Buchan, 'The Atlantic Debate', in *Foreign Affairs*, July 1965, p. 586.

Reference and
Background Material

A. BOOKS

G. H. J. Abeln, *De Vrijhandelszone als Economische Integratievorm voor West-Europa,* (Leiden: H. E. Stenfert Kroese N.V., 1958).

Dean Acheson, *A Democrat Looks at his Party,* (New York: Harper & Brothers, 1955).

—, *Power and Diplomacy,* (Cambridge, Mass.: Harvard University Press, 1958).

—, *Sketches From Life of Men I Have Known,* (New York: Harper & Brothers, 1961).

Selig Adler, *Isolationist Impulse, Its Twentieth Century Reaction,* (New York: Collier Books, 1961).

René Albrecht-Carrié, *One Europe, The Historical Background of European Unity,* (Garden City, N.Y.: Doubleday & Company, 1965).

H. C. Allen, *The Anglo-American Predicament, The British Commonwealth, The United States and European Unity,* (London: Macmillan Co. Ltd., 1960).

—, *The United States of America,* (London: Ernest Benn Limited, 1964).

Gabriël A. Almond, *The American People and Foreign Policy,* (New York: Frederick A. Praeger, 1960).

F. A. M. Alting van Geusau, *European Organizations and Foreign Relations of States,* (Leiden: A. W. Sythoff, 1964).

Hamilton Fish Armstrong, *The Calculated Risk,* (New York: The Macmillan Company, 1947).

— (ed.), *The Foreign Affairs Reader,* (New York: Published for the Council on Foreign Relations by Harper & Brothers, 1947).

Raymond Aron, *Le Grand Débat, Initiation à la Stratégie Atomique,* (Paris: Calman-Lévy, 1963).

Raymond Aron et Daniel Lerner, *La Querelle de la C.E.D.,* (Paris: Librairie Armand Colin, 1956).

Atlantica e.v. (Herausgeber), *Europa und Amerika in der Welt von Morgen,* (Freiburg: Verlag Rombach, 1964).

Louis F. Aubert, *Securité de l'Occident, Ruhr-Rhin,* (Paris: Librairie Armand Colin, 1946).

Louis F. Aubert etc., *Contrôle de l'Allemagne,* (Paris: Librairie Marcel Rivière et Cie., 1949).

Henry G. Aubrey, *The Dollar in World Affairs: An Essay in International Financial Policy,* (New York: Published for the Council on Foreign Relations by Frederick A. Praeger, 1964).

The Earl of Avon, *The Eden Memoirs,* 3 Volumes: Facing the Dictators, The Reckoning, Full Circle, (London: Cassell, 1960, 1962, 1965).

Ray Stannard Baker and William E. Dodd (ed.), *The New Democracy, The Public Papers of Woodrow Wilson,* Vol. I and Vol. II, (New York: Harper & Brothers, 1926).

Bela Balassa, *The Theory of Economic Integration,* (Homewood, Ill.: Richard D. Irwin, Inc., 1961).

M. Margaret Ball, *NATO and the European Union Movement,* (London: Stevens & Sons Ltd., 1959).

Arnold B. Barach, *The New Europe and its Economic Future,* (New York: The Macmillan Company, 1964).

Hollis W. Barber, *The United States in World Affairs, 1955,* (New York: Published for the Council on Foreign Relations by Harper & Brothers, 1956).

Bernard Baudry, *Euro-America,* (Paris: Librairie Plon, 1962).

Charles A. Beard and Mary R. Beard, *A Basic History of the United States,* (Philadelphia: The New Home Library, 1944).

Coral Bell, *The Debatable Alliance, An Essay in Anglo-American Relations,* (London: Oxford University Press, 1964).

Max Beloff, *Foreign Policy and The Democratic Process,* (Baltimore: The Johns Hopkins Press, 1955).

—, *Europe and the Europeans,* (London: Chatto & Windus, 1957).

—, *The American Federal Government,* (London: Oxford University Press, 1959).

—, *New Dimensions in Foreign Policy,* (London: George Allen & Unwin Ltd., 1961).

—, *The United States and the Unity of Europe,* (Washington, D.C.: The Brookings Institution, 1963).

Nora Beloff, *The General Says No, Britain's Exclusion From Europe,* (Penguin Books, 1963).

Emile Benoit, *Europe at Sixes and Sevens, The Common Market, The Free*

Trade Association and The United States, (New York: Columbia University Press, 1961).

Waldemar Besson, *Von Roosevelt bis Kennedy, Grundzüge der amerikanischen Aussenpolitik 1933–1963,* (Frankfurt a.M.: Fischer Bücherei, 1964).

Hubert Beuve-Méry, *Réflexions Politiques 1932–1952,* (Paris: Editions du Seuil, 1951).

Percy W. Bidwell etc., *Le Rôle de l'Allemagne dans l'Economie Européenne,* (Paris: Librairie Marcel Rivière et Cie, 1949).

Kurt Birrenbach, *Die Zukunft der atlantischen Gemeinschaft,* (Freiburg: Verlag Rombach, 1962).

Robert R. Bowie, *Shaping the Future, Foreign Policy in an Age of Transition,* (New York: Columbia University Press, 1964).

D. W. Brogan, *The American Problem,* (London: Hamish Hamilton, 1944).

The Brookings Institution, *Major Problems of United States Foreign Policy,* 7 Volumes, 1947, 1948–1949, 1949–1950, 1950–1951, 1951–1952, 1952–1953, 1954, (Washington, D.C.: The Brookings Institution).

William Adams Brown, Jr. and Redvers Opie, *American Foreign Assistance,* (Washington, D.C.: The Brookings Institution, 1953).

Alastair Buchan, *NATO in the 1960's, The Implications of Interdependence,* (New York: Frederick A. Praeger, 1963).

Alastair Buchan and Philip Windsor, *Arms and Stability in Europe,* (London: Published for the Institute for Strategic Studies by Chatto & Windus, 1963).

Vannevar Bush, *Modern Arms and Free Men,* (New York: Simon and Schuster, 1949).

James F. Byrnes, *Speaking Frankly,* (New York: Harper & Brothers, 1947).

John C. Campbell, *The United States in World Affairs,* Volumes 1945–1947, 1947–1948, 1948–1949, (New York: Published for the Council on Foreign Relations by Harper & Brothers).

Miriam Camps, *Britain and the European Community 1955–1963,* (London: Oxford University Press, 1964).

—, *What Kind of Europe, The Community since De Gaulle's Veto,* (London: Oxford University Press, 1965).

Holbert M. Carroll, *The House of Representatives and Foreign Affairs,* (Pittsburgh: University of Pittsburgh Press, 1958).

Daniel S. Cheever and H. Field Haviland, Jr., *American Foreign Policy and the Separation of Powers,* (Cambridge, Mass.: Harvard University Press, 1952).

Charles L. Clapp, *The Congressman, His Work As He Sees It,* (Washington, D.C.: The Brookings Institution, 1963).

Henry Steele Commager (ed.), *America in Perspective, The United States Through Foreign Eyes*, (New York: Mentor Books, 1947).

John O. Coppock, *North Atlantic Policy – The Agricultural Gap*, (New York: The Twentieth Century Fund, 1963).

Edward S. Corwin, *The President: Office and Powers*, (New York: New York University Press, 1948).

Alvin Cottrel and James E. Dougherty, *The Politics of The Atlantic Alliance*, (New York: Frederick A. Praeger, 1964).

René Courtin, *L'Europe de l'Atlantique à l'Oural*, (Paris: Editions l'Esprit Nouveau, 1963).

Robert A. Dahl, *Congress and Foreign Policy*, (New York: Harcourt, Brace and Company, 1950).

Vera Micheles Dean, *Europe, and the United States*, (New York: Alfred A. Knopf, 1950).

Sidney Dell, *Trade Blocks and Common Markets*, (London: Constable & Co. Ltd., 1963).

J. F. Deniau, *The Common Market*, (London: Barrie and Rockliff, 1960).

William Diebold, Jr., *Trade and Payments in Western Europe, A Study in Economic Cooperation 1947–1951*, (New York: Published for the Council on Foreign Relations by Harper & Brothers, 1952).

—, *The Schuman Plan, A Study in Economic Cooperation 1950–1959*, (New York: Published for the Council on Foreign Relations by Frederick A. Praeger, 1959).

Roscoe Drummond and Gaston Coblentz, *Duel at the Brink, John Foster Dulles' Command of American Power*, (Garden City, N.Y.: Doubleday & Company, Inc., 1960).

John Foster Dulles, *War and Peace*, (New York: The Macmillan Company, 1950).

Foster Rhea Dulles, *America's Rise to World Power 1898–1959*, (New York: Harper & Brothers, 1954).

William Y. Elliott and Associates, *The Political Economy of American Foreign Policy*, Report of a Study Group Sponsored by the Woodrow Wilson Foundation and the National Planning Association, (New York: Henry Holt and Company, 1955).

Howard S. Ellis, *The Economics of Freedom, The Progress and Future of Aid to Europe*, (New York: Published for the Council on Foreign Relations by Harper & Brothers, 1950).

Amitai Etzioni, *Political Unification, A Comparative Study of Leaders and Forces*, (New York: Holt, Rinehart and Winston, Inc., 1965).

Europeus, *La Crise de la Zone de Libre Echange,* (Paris: Librairie Plon, 1959).

Thomas K. Finletter, *Foreign Policy: The Next Phase, The 1960's,* (New York: Frederick A. Praeger, 1960).

Michael T. Florinsky, *Integrated Europe,* (New York: The Macmillan Company, 1955).

W. C. Ford (ed.), *The Writings of George Washington,* Vol. IX, (New York: 1889–1893).

Isaiah Frank, *The European Common Market, An Analysis of Commercial Policy,* (New York: Frederick A. Praeger, 1961).

Oliver S. Franks, *Britain and the Tide of World Affairs,* (London: Oxford University Press, 1955).

Jaques Freymond, *Western Europe Since the War, A Short Political History,* (New York: Frederick A. Praeger, 1964).

J. William Fulbright, *Prospects for the West,* (Cambridge, Mass.: Harvard University Press, 1963).

Lewis Galantière (ed.), *America and the Mind of Europe,* (London: Hamish Hamilton, 1951).

Richard N. Gardner, *Sterling-Dollar Diplomacy, Anglo-American Collaboration in the Reconstruction of Multilateral Trade,* (Oxford: Clarendon Press, 1956).

Ellen Clayton Garwood, *Will Clayton, A Short Biography,* (Austin: University of Texas Press, 1958).

Charles de Gaulle, *Mémoires de Guerre, L'Appel 1940–1942, L'Unité 1942–1944, Le Salut 1944–1946,* (Paris: Librairie Plon, 1954, 1956, 1959).

Lionel Gelber, *America in Britain's Place, The Leadership of the West and Anglo-American Unity,* (New York: Frederick A. Praeger, 1961).

Richard Goold-Adams, *The Time of Power, A Reappraisal of John Foster Dulles,* (London: Weidenfeld and Nicolson, 1962).

Norman A. Graebner (ed.), *An Uncertain Tradition, American Secretaries of State in the Twentieth Century,* (New York: McGraw-Hill Book Company, 1961).

Stichting Grotius Seminarium, *Limits and Problems of European Integration,* (The Hague: Martinus Nyhoff, 1963).

Ernst B. Haas, *The Uniting of Europe, Political, Social and Economic Forces 1950–1957,* (London: Stevens & Sons Limited, 1958).

—, *Beyond the Nation-State, Functionalism and International Organization,* (Stanford, Calif.: Stanford University Press, 1964).

C. Grove Haines, (ed.), *European Integration,* (Baltimore: The Johns Hopkins Press, 1957).

Walter Hallstein, *United Europe, Challenge and Opportunity,* (Cambridge, Mass.: Harvard University Press, 1962).

Oscar Handlin, *The Americans, A New History of the People of the United States,* (Boston: Little, Brown and Company, 1963).

Seymour E. Harris, *The European Recovery Program,* (Cambridge, Mass.: Harvard University Press, 1948).

— (ed.) *Foreign Economic Policy for the United States,* (Cambridge, Mass.: Harvard University Press, 1948).

— (ed.), *The Dollar in Crisis,* (New York: Harcourt, Brace & World, Inc., 1961).

Livingston Hartley, *Atlantic Challenge,* (New York: Oceana Publications, 1965).

H. Field Haviland, Jr. (ed.), *The United States and the Western Community,* (Haverford, Penn.: Haverford College Press, 1957).

H. J. Heiser, *British Policy With Regard To The Unification Efforts On The European Continent,* (Leyden: A. W. Sythoff, 1959).

Burton J. Hendrick, *Bulwark of the Republic, A Biography of the Constitution,* (Boston: Little, Brown and Company, 1937).

Christian A. Herter, *Toward an Atlantic Community,* (New York: Published for the Council on Foreign Relations by Harper & Row, 1963).

Randall Hinshaw, *The European Community and American Trade, A Study in Atlantic Economics and Policy,* (New York: Published for the Council on Foreign Relations by Frederick A. Praeger, 1964).

H. V. Hodson (ed.), *The Atlantic Future,* (London: Longmans, Green and Co., Ltd., 1964).

Paul G. Hoffman, *Peace Can Be Won,* (Garden City, N.Y.: Doubleday & Cy., 1951).

Stanley Hoffman and Associates, *In Search of France,* (Cambridge, Mass.: Harvard University Press, 1963).

P-H. J. M. Houben, *De Raad van Ministers in de Europese Gemeenschappen,* ('s-Gravenhage: Europe Printing, 1963).

Emmet John Hughes, *The Ordeal of Power, A Political Memoir of the Eisenhower Years,* (New York: Atheneum, 1963).

Don D. Humphrey, *The United States and the Common Market,* (New York: Frederick A. Praeger, 1962).

Joseph M. Jones, *The Fifteen Weeks, (Febr. 21-June 5, 1947),* (New York: The Viking Press, 1955).

Karl Kaiser, *EWG und Freihandelszone*, (Leiden: A. W. Sythoff, 1963).

William W. Kaufmann, *The McNamara Strategy*, (New York: Harper & Row, 1964).

George F. Kennan, *American Diplomacy 1900–1950*, (Chicago: The University of Chicago Press, 1951).

—, *Realities of American Foreign Policy*, (Princeton, N.J.: Princeton University Press, 1954).

—, *Russia, the Atom and the West*, (New York: Harper & Brothers, 1957).

John Maynard Keynes, *The Economic Consequences of the Peace*, (London: Macmillan and Co. Limited, 1919).

Henry A. Kissinger, *Nuclear Weapons and Foreign Policy*, (New York: Published for the Council on Foreign Relations by Harper & Brothers, 1957).

—, *The Necessity for Choice, Prospects of American Foreign Policy*, (New York: Harper & Brothers, 1960).

—, *The Troubled Partnership, A Reappraisal of the Atlantic Alliance*, (New York: Published for the Council on Foreign Relations by McGraw-Hill Book Company, 1965).

Uwe Kitzinger, *The Challenge of the Common Market*, (Oxford: Basil Blackwell, 1962).

—, *Britain, Europe and Beyond, Essays in European Politics*, (Leiden: A. W. Sythoff, 1964).

Robert Kleiman, *Atlantic Crisis, American Diplomacy Confronts a Resurgent Europe*, (New York: W. W. Norton & Company, Inc., 1964).

Klaus Knorr (ed.), *NATO and American Security*, (Princeton, N. J.: Princeton University Press, 1959).

Max Kohnstamm, *The European Community and Its Role In The World*, (Columbia: University of Missouri Press, 1964).

Joseph Kraft, *The Grand Design, From Common Market to Atlantic Partnership*, (New York: Harper & Brothers, 1962).

Harold J. Laski, *The American Democracy, A Commentary and an Interpretation*, (New York: The Viking Press, 1948).

Ernest W. Lefever, (ed.), *Arms and Arms Control*, (New York: Published for The Washington Center of Foreign Policy Research by Frederick A. Praeger, 1962).

George Lichtheim, *The New Europe, Today and Tomorrow*, (New York: Frederick A. Praeger, 1963).

Leon N. Lindberg, *The Political Dynamics of European Economic Integration*, (Stanford, Calif.: Stanford University Press, 1963).

J. Linthorst Homan, *Europese Integratie*, (Den Haag: Martinus Nyhoff, 1955).

Walter Lippmann, *U.S. Foreign Policy: Shield of the Republic,* (Boston: Little, Brown and Cy., 1943).

—, *U.S. Foreign Policy and U.S. War Aims,* (New York: Overseas Editions, Inc., 1943).

—, *The Cold War: A Study in U.S. Foreign Policy,* (New York: Harper & Brothers, 1947).

—, *The Public Philosophy,* (London: Hamish Hamilton, 1955).

— , *Western Unity and the Common Market,* (Boston: Little, Brown and Cy., 1962).

George Liska, *Europe Ascendant, The International Politics of Unification,* (Baltimore: The Johns Hopkins Press, 1964).

R. W. G. Mackay, *Towards a United States of Europe,* (London: Hutchinson, 1961).

Salvador de Madariaga, *Portrait of Europe,* (London: Hollis & Carter, 1952).

John Mander, *Great Britain or Little England,* (London: Secker & Warburg, 1963).

Golo Mann, *Vom Geist Amerikas,* (Stuttgart: W. Kohlhammer Verlag, 1954).

Robert Marjolin, *Europe and the United States in the World Economy,* (Durham, N.C.: Duke University Press, 1953).

Jesse W. Markham, C. E. Fiero and Howard S. Piquet, *The Common Market: Friend or Competitor,* (New York: New York University Press, 1964).

Roger Massip, *De Gaulle et l'Europe,* (Paris: Flammarion, 1963).

Richard Mayne, *The Community of Europe,* (New York: W. W. Norton & Company, Inc., 1963).

John J. McCloy, *The Challenge to American Foreign Policy,* (Cambridge, Mass.: Harvard University Press, 1953).

E. W. Meier, *De Europese Economische Integratie,* (Leiden: E. H. Stenfert Kroese N.V., 1958).

Drew Middleton, *The Supreme Choice, Britain and the European Community,* (London: Secker & Warburg, 1963).

Walter Millis (ed.), *The Forrestal Diaries,* (New York: The Viking Press, 1951).

Ben T. Moore, *NATO and the Future of Europe,* (New York: Published for the Council on Foreign Relations by Harper & Brothers, 1958).

S. E. Morison, *The Oxford History of the United States 1783–1917,* Vol. I and Vol. II, (London: Oxford University Press, Humphrey Milford, 1927).

Frank Munk, *Atlantic Dilemma, Partnership or Community,* (New York: Oceana Publications, 1964).

Richard E. Neustadt, *Presidential Power, The Politics of Leadership,* (New York: John Wiley & Sons, Inc., 1960).

Reinhold Niebuhr, *The Irony of American History,* (New York: Charles Scribner's Sons, 1952).

F. S. C. Northrop, *European Union and United States Foreign Policy, A Study in Sociological Jurisprudence,* (New York: The Macmillan Company, 1954).

Anthony Nutting, *Europe Will Not Wait, A Warning and a Way Out,* (London: Hollis & Carter, 1960).

Robert Endicott Osgood, *Ideals and Self-Interest in America's Foreign Relations,* (Chicago: The University of Chicago Press, 1953).

—, *NATO The Entangling Alliance,* (Chicago: The University of Chicago Press, 1962).

Gardner Patterson, *Survey of United States International Finance,* (Princeton, N.J., Princeton University Press, 1950).

Dexter Perkins, *The American Approach to Foreign Policy,* (Cambridge, Mass.: Harvard University Press, 1962).

John Pinder, *Europe Against De Gaulle,* (London: Pall Mall Press, 1963).

Jaroslav G. Polack, *Euratom, Its Background, Issues and Economic Implications,* (New York: Oceana Publications, Inc., 1964).

Political and Economic Planning, *European Organisations,* (London: George Allen & Unwin Ltd., 1959).

Julius W. Pratt, *Cordell Hull,* Volume I and II, (New York: Cooper Square Publishers, Inc., 1964).

Harry Bayard Price, *The Marshall Plan and Its Meaning,* (Ithaca, N.Y.: Cornell University Press, 1955).

Roy Price, *The Political Future of the European Community,* (London: John Marshbank Limited, 1962).

Henry S. Reuss, *The Critical Decade, An Economic Policy for America and the Free World,* (New York: McGraw-Hill Book Company, 1964).

A. H. Robertson, *European Institutions, Cooperation: Integration: Unification,* (London: Stevens & Sons Limited, 1959).

W. W. Rostow, *The United States in the World Arena, an Essay in Recent History,* (New York: Harper & Row, 1960).

Bruce M. Russett, *Community and Contention, Britain and America in the Twentieth Century,* (Cambridge, Mass.: The M.I.T. Press, 1963).

Walter S. Salant and Associates, *The United States Balance of Payments in 1968,* (Washington, D.C.: The Brookings Institution, 1963).

Rolf Sannwald and Jaques Stohler, *Economic Integration*, (Princeton, N.J.: Princeton University Press, 1959).

Arthur M. Schlesinger, Jr. and Morton White (ed.), *Paths of American Thought*, (London: Chatto & Windus, 1964).

Hans A. Schmitt, *The Path to European Union, From the Marshall Plan to the Common Market*, (Baton Rouge: Louisiana State University Press, 1962).

Michael Shanks and John Lambert, *Britain and the New Europe, The Future of the Common Market*, (London: Chatto & Windus, 1962).

Marshal D. Shulman, *Stalin's Foreign Policy Reappraised*, (Cambridge, Mass.: Harvard University Press, 1963).

André Siegfried, *Les Etats-Unis d'Aujourd'hui*, (Paris: Librairie Armand Colin, 1928).

George Soule, *America's Stake in Britain's Future*, (New York: The Viking Press, 1945).

John W. Spanier, *American Foreign Policy Since World War II*, (New York: Frederick A. Praeger, 1960).

Timothy W. Stanley, *NATO in Transition, The Future of the Atlantic Alliance*, (New York: Published for the Council on Foreign Relations by Frederick A. Praeger, 1965).

Richard P. Stebbins, *The United States in World Affairs*, Volumes 1949, 1950, 1951, 1952, 1953, 1954, 1956, 1957, 1958, 1959, 1960, 1961, 1962, 1963, (New York: Published for the Council on Foreign Relations by Harper & Brothers).

Ronald Steel, *The End of Alliance: America and the Future of Europe*, (London: Andre Deutsch, 1964).

Edward R. Stettinius, Jr., *Lend-Lease, Weapon for Victory*, (New York: The Macmillan Company, 1944).

Adlai E. Stevenson, *Call to Greatness*, (London: Rupert Hart-Davis, 1954).

Edmund Stillman and William Pfaff, *The New Politics, America and the End of the Postwar World*, (New York: Harper Colophon Books, 1961).

Robert Strausz-Hupé, James E. Dougherty and William R. Kintner, *Building the Atlantic World*, (New York: Harper & Row, 1963).

Paul Streeten, *Economic Integration, Aspects and Problems*, (Leyden: A. W. Sythoff, 1964).

Cushing Strout, *The American Image of the Old World*, (New York: Harper & Row, 1963).

Kennedy W. Thompson, *Political Realism and The Crisis of World Politics, An American Approach to Foreign Policy*, (Princeton, N.J.: Princeton University Press, 1960).

Alexis de Tocqueville, *De la Démocratie en Amérique,* Tome Premier et Second, (Paris: Librairie Medicis, 1951).

Harry S. Truman, *Year of Decisions, Vol. I of the Memoirs of Harry S. Truman,* (Garden City, N.Y.: Doubleday & Company, Inc., 1955).

--, *Years of Trial and Hope, Vol. II of The Memoirs of Harry S. Truman,* (Garden City, N.Y.: Doubleday & Company, Inc., 1956).

Frank Tannenbaum, *The American Tradition in Foreign Policy,* (Norman: University of Oklahoma Press, 1955).

Pierre Uri, *Partnership for Progress, A Program for Transatlantic Action,* (New York: Published for the Atlantic Institute by Harper & Row, 1963).

Richard W. Van Alstyne, *American Crisis Diplomacy, The Quest for Collective Security 1918–1952,* (Stanford, Calif.: Stanford University Press, 1952).

Arthur H. Vandenberg, Jr. (ed.), *The Private Papers of Senator Vandenberg,* (Boston: Houghton Mifflin Cy., 1952).

Barbara Ward, *The West at Bay,* (New York: W. W. Norton & Company, Inc., 1948).

—, *Policy for the West,* (New York: W. W. Norton & Company, 1951).

—, *The Interplay of East and West, Elements of Contrast and Cooperation,* (London: George Allen & Unwin Ltd., 1957).

Sumner Welles, *The Time for Decision,* (London: Hamish Hamilton, 1944).

—, *Where Are We Heading,* (New York: Harper & Brothers, 1946).

D. C. Watt, *Britain Looks To Germany, British Opinion and Policy Towards Germany Since 1945,* (London: Oswald Wolff, 1965).

Theodore H. White, *Fire in the Ashes, Europe in Mid-Century,* (New York: William Sloane Associates, 1953).

—, *The Making of the President 1960,* (New York: Atheneum Publishers, 1961).

David Wightman, *Economic Cooperation in Europe,* (New York: Frederick A. Praeger, 1956).

Arnold Wolfers (ed.), *Alliance Policy in the Cold War,* (Baltimore: The Johns Hopkins Press, 1959).

Quincy Wright (ed.), *A Foreign Policy for the United States,* (Chicago: The University of Chicago Press, 1947).

Kenneth Younger, *Changing Perspectives in British Foreign Policy,* (London: Oxford University Press, 1964).

Arnold J. Zurcher, *The Struggle to United Europe 1940–1958,* (New York: New York University Press, 1958).

B. ARTICLES, DOCUMENTS, MEMORANDA,
PAMPHLETS, PAPERS AND REPORTS *

Dean Acheson, 'The Dilemmas of our Times', in *The Atlantic Community Quarterly,* Winter, 1963–1964.

H. C. Allen, 'An Ever Closer Union', in *The Spectator,* October 5, 1962.

Stewart Alsop, 'The Collapse of Kennedy's Grand Design', in *The Saturday Evening Post,* April 6, 1963.

F. A. M. Alting van Geusau, 'Europe beyond the Six', in *International Spectator,* Jaargang XIX, Nr. 7, 1965.

Karl Arnold, *Deutsche Beitrage zur Verwirklichung der Europa Idee,* (Bonn: Politeia, Bonner Universitätsreden zu öffentlichen Fragen, 1948).

Raymon Aron, 'Old Nations, New Europe', in *Daedalus,* Winter, 1964.

Walter Bauer, 'Die EWG nach dem Abbruch der Brüsseler Verhandlungen', in *Europa Archiv,* 18. Jahr, 6. Folge, 1963.

—, 'Weitere Schritten zur Europäischen Einigung', in *Europa Archiv,* 18. Jahr, 19. Folge, 1963.

Max Beloff, 'American Attitudes', in *The Spectator,* October 5, 1962.

—, 'Britain, Europe and the Atlantic Community', in *International Organization,* Summer, 1963.

David Bendall, 'Verdeling van de NAVO-defensielasten', in *NAVO Maandblad,* September, 1963.

Emile Benoit, 'The United States and a United Europe', in *Current History,* March, 1962.

—, 'Rüstungsbeschränkung und europäische Integration', in *Europa Archiv,* 19. Jahr, 10. Folge, 1964.

Godfried Benthem van den Bergh, 'Hedendaags nationalisme in de oude Staten', in *Oost-West,* June, 1965.

E. H. van der Beugel, 'De Samenwerking met de Amerikanen', in *Herwonnen Welvaart,* ('s-Gravenhage: Ministerie van Buitenlandse Zaken, 1954).

—, 'De ontwikkeling van Europa tot een Eenheid, Economische Aspecten', in *Vier Maal Europa,* (Alphen a/d Rijn: N. Samsom N.V., 1959).

---

* Unsigned articles, newspaper articles and publications like the Bulletin of the Department of State, O.E.E.C. Documents, the Congressional Record, Congressional Hearings, Declarations of the Action Committee for a United States of Europe etc. are not mentioned.

E. H. van der Beugel, 'Hans Max Hirschfeld, Staatsman en Econoom', in *Economisch-Historisch Jaarboek*, ('s-Gravenhage: Martinus Nyhoff, 1963).

—, 'Europese Politieke Unie en Atlantische Samenwerking', in *Socialisme en Democratie*, December, 1964.

—, 'The Clash in Europe', in *European Review*, Winter, 1964–1965.

—, 'The United States and European Unity', in *Internationale Spectator*, Jaargang XIX, Nr. 7, 1965.

Kurt Birrenbach, 'Grossbritannien und die Montanunion', in *Europa Archiv*, 18. Jahr, 3. Folge, 1963.

—, 'Die Erhaltung der Dynamik der EWG', in *Europa Archiv*, 18. Jahr, 11. Folge, 1963.

—, 'Partnership and Consultation in NATO', in *The Atlantic Community Quarterly*, Spring, 1964.

P. A. Blaisse, 'Het Examen in de O.E.E.S.', in *Herwonnen Welvaart*, ('s-Gravenhage: Ministerie van Buitenlandse Zaken, 1959).

Robert R. Bowie, 'Prospects for Atlantic Community', in *The Harvard Review*, Fall, 1962.

—, 'Strategy and the Atlantic Alliance', in *International Organization*, Summer, 1963.

—, 'Tensions within the Alliance', in *Foreign Affairs*, October, 1963.

Heinrich von Brentano, 'Kontinuität und Dissonanzen der deutschen Politik', in *Europa Archiv*, 18. Jahr, 4. Folge, 1963.

Bernard Brodie, 'Conventional Capabilities in Europe', in *The Reporter*, May 23, 1963.

The Brookings Institution, *Governmental Mechanism for the Conduct of United States Foreign Relations*, (Washington, D.C.: 1949).

Zbigniew Brzezinkski, *Peaceful Engagement in Europe's Future*, (New York: School of International Affairs, Columbia University, 1965).

Alastair Buchan, 'Partners and Allies', in *Foreign Affairs*, July, 1963.

—, 'The Changed Setting of the Atlantic Debate', in *Foreign Affairs*, July, 1965.

Miriam Camps, *The European Common Market and American Policy*, (Princeton University, Center of International Studies, 1956).

—, *The European Common Market and Free Trade Area*, (Princeton University, Center of International Studies, 1957).

—, *The First Year of the European Economic Community*, (Princeton University, Center of International Studies, 1958).

—, *Division in Europe*, P.E.P. Occasional Paper No. 8, June, 1960.

—, *Four Approaches to the European Problem*, P.E.P. Occasional Paper No. 12, March 27, 1961.

—, 'The Six and Political Union', in *The World Today*, November, 1964.

Central Office of Information, *Western Cooperation,* A Reference Handbook, (London: 1955).

Wilhelm Cornides, 'Die Bundesrepublik vor der Ratifizierung des deutsch-französischen Vertrages', in *Europa Archiv,* 18. Jahr, 7. Folge, 1963.

Committee for Economic Development, *The European Common Market, Its Meaning to the United States,* (New York: 1959).

—, *The International Position of the Dollar,* A Statement on National Policy by the Research and Policy Committee, 1961.

Committee of European Economic Cooperation, *General Report,* Vol. I, and *Technical Reports,* Vol. II, (London: H.M.S.O., 1947).

L. Cornil, 'Les Etats-Unis d'Amérique et la reconstruction économique de l'Europe occidentale', in *Publications des Annales de Sciences Economiques Appliquées,* (Louvain, 1948).

Council on Foreign Relations, *Foreign Aid and the National Interest,* A Report on the Views of Leading Citizens in Twenty-Five Cities, 1952.

—, *Documents on American Foreign Relations,* 1953 and 1954, edited by Peter V. Curl, (New York: Harper & Brothers, 1954, 1955).

—, *Documents on American Foreign Relations,* 1955, 1956, 1957, 1958, 1959, edited by Paul E. Zinner, (New York: Harper & Brothers, 1956, 1957, 1958, 1959, 1960).

—, *Documents on American Foreign Relations,* 1960, 1961, 1962, 1963, edited by Richard P. Stebbins, (New York: Harper & Brothers, 1961, 1962, 1963, 1964).

—, *Atlantic Unity and the American Interest,* A Report on the Views of Leading Citizens in Thirty-Two Cities, 1963.

The Department of State, *Germany 1947–1949, The Story in Documents,* (Washington, D.C.: 1950).

—, *In Quest of Security,* Selected Documents on American Foreign Policy 1941–1951, (Washington, D.C.: 1951).

—, *The Scope and Distribution of United States Military and Economic Assistance Programs,* Report to the President from the Committee to Strengthen the Security of the Free World, (Washington, D.C.: March, 1963).

William Diebold, Jr., 'Imponderables of the Schuman Plan', in *Foreign Affairs,* October 1950.

—, 'The Process of European Integration', in *Current History,* March, 1962.

—, 'Economic Aspects of an Atlantic Community', in *International Organization,* Summer 1963.

François Duchêne, *Beyond Alliance,* The Atlantic Papers, NATO Series I, (Paris: The Atlantic Institute, 1965).

Jean-Baptiste Duroselle, 'La Tradition Isolationiste de la Politique Etrangère Américaine', in *The American Review*, September 1961.

Economic Cooperation Administration, *Quarterly Reports to Congress*, covering the period April 1948 to and including March 1951, Washington, D.C.

Fritz Erler, 'Die deutsche Aussenpolitik nach dem Abkommen von Nassau', in *Europa Archiv*, 18. Jahr, 5. Folge, 1963.

—, 'The Basis of Partnership', in *Foreign Affairs*, October 1963.

—, 'Westeuropa und die Vereinigten Staaten in der strategischen Weltsituation', in *Europa Archiv*, 18. Jahr, 24. Folge, 1963.

—, 'The Alliance and the Future of Germany', in *Foreign Affairs*, April 1965.

European Customs Union Group, *First Report*, (Brussels: 1948).

André Fontaine, 'Die Entwickelung der französisch-britischen Beziehungen', in *Europa Archiv*, 20. Jahr, 6. Folge, 1965.

Lord Franks, 'Cooperation is not Enough', in *Foreign Affairs*, October 1962.

Oliver Franks, 'Britain and Europe', in *Daedalus*, Winter 1964.

Carl J. Friedrich, 'Panhumanismus: Die kommende Weltordnung und die Einigung Europas', in *Europa Archiv*, 19. Jahr, 23. Folge, 1964.

Oscar Gass, 'The Crusade for Trade', in *The New Republic*, March 19 and March 26, 1962.

Charles De Gaulle, *Major Addresses, Statements, and Press Conferences of General Charles De Gaulle, May 19, 1958–January 31, 1964*, (New York: French Embassy, Press and Information Division, 1964).

Theodore Geiger and H. van B. Cleveland, *Making Western Europe Defensible*, (National Planning Association, Pamphlet No. 74, August 1951).

Pierre Gerbet, 'La Genèse du Plan Schuman des origines à la déclaration du 9 mai 1950', in *Revue Française de Science Politique*, Vol. VI, 1956.

Lord Gladwyn, *Prospects for a European Political Community*, Europe House Paper 8, 1962.

—, 'The Place of a United Western Europe in the Atlantic Community', in *The American Review*, December 1962.

—, 'Atlantic Dreams and Realities', in *Encounter*, December 1963.

—, 'Europe mit oder ohne Grossbritannien', in *Europa Archiv*, 19. Jahr, 15. Folge, 1964.

Elliot R. Goodman, 'Five Nuclear Options for the West', in *Forensic Quarterly*, August 1964.

Lincoln Gordon, 'Myth and Reality of European Integration', in *Yale Review*, September 1950.

Lincoln Gordon, 'The Organization for European Economic Cooperation', in *International Organization*, February 1956.

—, 'Economic Regionalism Reconsidered', in *World Politics,* January 1961.

Stephen Graubard, 'A New Europe', in *Daedalus,* Winter 1964.

F. D. Gregh, 'Some Economic and Financial Aspects of the NATO Alliance', in *NATO's Fifteen Nations*, April–May 1963.

Ernest S. Griffith, 'The Place of Congress in Foreign Relations', in *Annals of the American Academy of Political and Social Science,* Vol. 289, September 1963.

Alfred Grosser, 'France and Germany in the Atlantic Community', in *International Organization,* Summer 1963.

Ernst B. Haas, 'Persistent Themes in Atlantic and European Unity', in *World Politics,* July 1958.

Walter Hallstein, 'The European Community and Atlantic Partnership', in *International Organization,* Summer 1963.

Anthony Hartley, 'The British Bomb', in *Encounter,* May 1964.

Livingston Hartley, 'On the Political Integration of the Atlantic Community', in *Orbis,* Winter 1963.

Kai-Uwe von Hassel, 'Organizing Western Defense', in *Foreign Affairs,* January 1965.

H. Field Haviland, Jr., 'Building a Political Community', in *International Organization,* Summer 1963.

J. L. Heldring, 'Atlantisch deelgenootschap en Europese eenheid', in *Internationale Spectator,* Jaargang XVIII, Nr. 13, 1964.

—, 'Europe: a greater Holland?', in *Internationale Spectator,* Jaargang XIX, Nr. 7, 1965.

Christian A. Herter, 'Atlantica', in *Foreign Affairs,* January 1963.

H. M. Hirschfeld, 'Idee en ontstaan van het Marshall Plan', in *Herwonnen Welvaart,* ('s-Gravenhage: Ministerie van Buitenlandse Zaken, 1954).

—, '10 jaar Europese Integratie', in *Herstelbank 1945–1955,* ('s-Gravenhage: Martinus Nyhoff, 1955).

Stanley Hoffmann, 'Problems of Atlantic Partnership', in *The Harvard Review,* Fall, 1962.

—, 'Discord in Community: The North Atlantic Area as a Partial International System', in *International Organization,* Summer 1963.

—, 'De Gaulle, Europe and the Atlantic Alliance', in *International Organization,* January 1964.

—, 'Cursing De Gaulle is not a Policy', in *The Reporter,* January 30, 1964.

—, 'Europe's Identity Crisis', in *Daedalus,* Fall, 1964.

John W. Holmes, 'Political Implications of the European Economic Community', in *Queen's Quarterly*, Spring 1962.
—, 'The Atlantic Community – Unity and Reality', in *The Atlantic Community Quarterly*, Winter 1964–1965.
J. H. Huizinga, Eight articles on American-European relations in *Nieuwe Rotterdamse Courant*, March 30, 31, April 2, 3, 5, 9, 13, 15, 1965.
—, 'Which Way Europe', in *Foreign Affairs*, April 1965.

Fred Charles Iklé, 'Der westliche und der sowjetischer Verhandlungsstil', in *Europa Archiv*, 19. Jahr, 22. Folge, 1964.
The Institute for Strategic Studies, *The Communist Bloc and the Western Alliances, The Military Balance 1962–1963*, (London: 1962).
—, *The Control of Western Strategy*, Adelphi Paper, Number Three, April 1963.
—, *The Defense of Western Europe*, Adelphi Paper, Number Four, May 1963.
—, *The Evolution of NATO*, Adelphi Paper, Number Five, October 1963.
—, *The Military Balance 1963–1964*, (London: 1964).
—, *The Western Alliance and the McNamara Doctrine*, Adelphi Paper, Number Eleven, by Leonard Beaton, August 1964.
—, *The Multilateral Force: An Historical Perspective*, Adelphi Paper, Number Thirteen, by Alastair Buchan, October 1964.
—, *The Military Balance 1964–1965*, (London: 1965).

C. D. Jackson, 'The American Dilemma', in *Think*, February 1963.
Edmond Jouve, 'Die Europa-Politik Frankreichs unter de Gaulle', in *Europa Archiv*, 20. Jahr, 7. Folge, 1965.

Karl Kaiser, 'Strukturwandlungen in der atlantischen Zusammen-Arbeit', in *Europa Archiv*, 17. Jahr, 5. Folge, 1962.
—, 'Die amerikanische Aussenpolitik im Wandel. Die Vereinigten Staaten und Europa in der westliche Allianz', in *Europa Archiv*, 19. Jahr, 24. Folge, 1964.
—, 'L'Europe des Savants', in *Journal of Common Market Studies*, Spring 1965.
George F. Kennan, 'Polycentrism and Western Policy', in *Foreign Affairs*, January 1964.
Nicolas de Kerchove, 'De Gaulle et les mirages de la Grandeur', in *Revue Générale Belge*, avril 1965.
Ch. P. Kindleberger, 'La fin du rôle dominant des Etats-Unis et l'avenir d'une politique économique mondiale', in *Cahiers de l'Institut de Science Economique Appliquée*, (Paris: mai 1961).

Henry A. Kissinger, 'Missiles and the Western Alliance', in *Foreign Affairs*, April 1958.

—, 'The Search for Stability', in *Foreign Affairs*, July 1959.

—, 'The Unsolved Problems of European Defense', in *Foreign Affairs*, July 1962.

—, 'NATO's Nuclear Dilemma', in *National Security: Political, Military and Economic Strategies in the Decade Ahead*, (New York: Frederick A. Praeger, 1963).

—, 'Strains on the Alliance', in *Foreign Affairs*, January 1963.

—, 'Coalition Diplomacy in a Nuclear Age', in *Foreign Affairs*, July 1964.

—, 'The Essentials of Solidarity in the Western Alliance', in *The Conservative Papers*, (New York: Doubleday & Cy., 1964).

—, 'The Illusionist: Why we Misread De Gaulle', in *Harper's Magazine*, March 1965.

—, 'The Price of German Unity', in *The Reporter*, April 22, 1965.

Uwe Kitzinger, 'Europe: The Six and the Seven', in *International Organization*, January 1960.

Klaus E. Knorr, *Union of Western Europe: A Third Center of Power?*, (New Haven, Conn.: Yale Institute of International Studies, 1948).

—, *Euratom and American Policy*, (Princeton University, Center of International Studies, 1956).

Norbert Kohlhase, 'Die Europäische Wirtschaftsgemeinschaft in amerikanischer Sicht', in *Europa Archiv*, 14. Jahr, 22. Folge, 1959.

Ernst Kobbert, 'Der politische Kern der EWG-Krise', in *Europa Archiv*, 20. Jahr, 14. Folge, 1965.

Max Kohnstamm, 'The European Tide', in *Daedalus*, Winter 1964.

Heinz L. Krekeler, 'The European Community as a Pillar of the Atlantic Partnership', in *The American Review*, December 1962.

J. Kymmell, 'Het Amerikaanse Betalingsbalans tekort', in *Het Financiële Dagblad*, 5, 6, 7/9, 11 November, 1964.

—, 'De Amerikaanse Betalingsbalans in 1963', in *Economisch Statistische Berichten*, 9 November, 1964.

—, 'European economic integration and atlantic cooperation', in *Internationale Spectator*, Jaargang XIX, Nr. 7, 1965.

Halvard Lange, 'European Integration and Atlantic Partnership', in *The Atlantic Community Quarterly*, Winter 1963–1964.

Eric Larrabee, 'Transcripts of a Transatlantic Dialogue', in *Daedalus*, Winter 1964.

Nathan Leites and Christian de la Malène, *Paris from EDC to WEU*, Research Memorandum RM-1668-RC of The Rand Corporation, March 1956.

Daniel Lerner, 'Will European Union Bring about Merged National Goals', in *The Annals of the American Academy of Political and Social Science,* July 1963.

Daniel Lerner and Morton Gorden, *European Community and Atlantic Security in the World Arena,* (Cambridge, Mass.: Center for International Studies, Massachusetts Institute of Technology, 1961).

Jean de Lipkowski, 'Das deutsch-französische Gespräch über die Zukunft der EWG', in *Europa Archiv,* 18. Jahr, 12. Folge, 1963.

Leslie Lipson, 'Independent or Interdependent', in *The Spectator,* October 5, 1962.

Fred Luchsinger, 'Deutsche Politik im Rückblick', in *Europa Archiv,* 19. Jahr, 8. Folge, 1964.

J. M. A. H. Luns, 'Independence or Interdependence', in *International Affairs,* January 1964.

Herbert Lüthy, 'De Gaulle: Pose and Policy', in *Foreign Affairs,* July 1965.

M. C. J. Baronesse Mackay, 'De koncepties van John Fitzgerald Kennedy', in *Internationale Spectator,* Jaargang XVIII, Nr. 19, 1964.

Robert Marjolin, 'The Common Market: Inward or Outward?', in *The Atlantic Community Quarterly,* Summer 1964.

Richard Mayne, 'Economic Integration in the New Europe: A Statistical Approach', in *Daedalus,* Winter 1964.

Livingston T. Merchant, 'Evolving United States Relations with the Atlantic Community', in *International Organization,* Summer 1963.

—, 'North America and The Atlantic Community', in *The Atlantic Community Quarterly,* Winter 1964–1965.

Hans-Joachim von Merkatz, 'Politische Aktionseinheit', in *Europa Archiv,* 20. Jahr, 7. Folge, 1965.

Leonard Miall, 'How the Marshall Plan Started', in *The Listener,* May 4, 1961.

Ministère des Affaires Etrangères, *Documents de la Conférence des Ministres des Affaires Etrangères de la France, du Royaume Uni et de l'URRS, tenue à Paris du 27 juin au 3 juillet 1947,* (Paris: 1947).

Frank Munk, 'The Atlantic Community and World Community', in *The Atlantic Community Quarterly,* Spring 1964.

Netherlands Information Bureau, *The Netherlands Government's Plan of Action for European Integration,* (New York: 1950).

Netherlands Ministry of Foreign Affairs, *Quarterly Reports by the Government of the Netherlands on the Operations and Progress under the Economic Aid Program,* covering the period April, 1948 to and including June 1953, (The Hague: Ministry of Foreign Affairs).

H. L. Nieburg, 'Euratom, A Study in Coalition Politics', in *World Politics,*
   July 1963.
Lauris Norstad, 'The Longer Second Look', in *The Atlantic Community
   Quarterly,* March 1963.
—, 'The Future of the Atlantic Community', in *International Organization,*
   Summer 1963.

Organization for European Economic Cooperation, *Report to the Economic
   Cooperation Administration on the First Annual Program, July 1st, 1948–June
   30th, 1949,* (Paris: October 1948).
—, *Interim Report on the European Recovery Program,* Vol. I and II, (Paris:
   December 1948).
—, *Report to the Economic Cooperation Administration on the 1949–1950
   Programme,* Vol. I and II, (Paris: January 1949).
—, *European Recovery Programme, Second Report of the O.E.E.C.,* (Paris:
   February 1950).
—, *Financial Stability and the Fight against Inflation,* (Paris: 1951).
—, *Economic Progress and Problems of Western Europe,* (Paris: June 1951).
—, *Europe – the Way Ahead,* (Paris: December 1952).
—, *The Internal Financial Situation in Member and Associated Countries,* (Paris:
   1952).
—, *Progress and Problems of the European Economy,* (Paris: January 1954).
—, *From Recovery towards Economic Strength,* Vol. I and II, (Paris: March
   1955).
—, *Economic Expansion and its Problems,* (Paris: February 1956).
—, *Europe To-day and in 1960,* Vol. I and II, (Paris: April 1957).
—, *A Decade of Cooperation, Achievements and Perspectives,* (Paris: April 1958).
—, *Policies for Sound Economic Growth,* (Paris: March 1959).
—-, *Europe and the World Economy,* (Paris: April 1960).
—, *A Remodelled Economic Organization, A Report by the Group of Four,*
   (Paris: April 1960).
—, *Twelfth Annual Economic Review,* (Paris: September 1961).
Robert E. Osgood, *Nuclear Control in NATO,* (Washington, D.C.: The
   Washington Center of Foreign Policy Research, 1962).
—, *The Case for the M.L.F., A Critical Evaluation,* (Washington, D.C.: The
   Washington Center of Foreign Policy Research, 1964).
Henry Owen, 'NATO Strategy: What is Past is Prologue', in *Foreign
   Affairs,* July 1965.

C. L. Patijn, 'Germany and the European Future', in *Internationale Spectator,*
   Jaargang XIX, Nr. 7, 1965.

Howard C. Petersen, 'The U.S. invitation to Europe', in *European Atlantic Review,* March-April 1962.
Political and Economic Planning, *France and the European Community,* Occasional Paper No. 11, January 1961.
—, *The Negotiations on Political Union,* October 1962.
S. Posthuma, 'Amerikaanse hulp en inter-Europees betalingsverkeer', in *Herwonnen Welvaart,* ('s-Gravenhage: Ministerie van Buitenlandse Zaken, 1954).

Republican Citizens Committee, *The Atlantic Alliance and United States Security,* Paper No. 3 of the Critical Issues Council, 1964.
Eric Roll, 'The OEEC', in *Lloyds Bank Review,* April 1958.
François de Rose, 'Nuclear Weapons and the Alliance', in *Foreign Affairs,* April 1963.
Eugene W. Rostow, 'Prospects for the Alliance', in *The Atlantic Community Quarterly,* Spring 1965.
Royal Institute of International Affairs, *Documents on European Recovery and Defense, March 1947–April 1949,* (London: 1949).

I. Samkalden, 'A Dutch retrospective view on European and Atlantic cooperation', in *Internationale Spectator,* Jaargang XIX, Nr. 7, 1965.
C. T. Saunders, *The Kennedy Trade Plan,* Europe House Paper 9, 1962.
J. Robert Schaetzel, 'The Nuclear Problem and Atlantic Interdependence', in *The Atlantic Community Quarterly,* Winter 1963–1964.
Ulrich Scheuner, 'Gegensätze der deutschen und der französischen Europa-Politik', in *Europa Archiv,* 20. Jahr, 1. Folge, 1965.
Johanna Schomerus, 'De Gaulles Europa-Konzeption im Spiegel seiner Memoiren und Reden', in *Europa Archiv,* 18. Jahr, 9. Folge, 1963.
Andrew Shonfield, 'After Brussels', in *Foreign Affairs,* July 1963.
—, 'Transatlantic Differences', in *Encounter,* September 1963.
Sir John Slessor, 'Multilateral or Multinational, an Alternative to the M.L.F.', in *The Atlantic Community Quarterly,* Summer 1964.
Jean-Charles Snoy et d'Oppuers, *Les Etapes de la Cooperation Européenne et les Négociations Relatives à une zone de Libre Echange,* (Bruxelles: Institut Royal des Relations Internationales, 1959).
—, 'La négociation européenne dans une nouvelle phase', in *Revue Générale Belge,* février 1960.
—, 'La Crise de l'Europe', in *Revue Générale Belge,* mars 1963.
Theo Sommer, 'For An Atlantic Future', in *Foreign Affairs,* October 1964.
Paul-Henri Spaak, 'Hold Fast', in *Foreign Affairs,* July 1963.
—, 'A New Effort to Build Europe', in *Foreign Affairs,* January 1965.

Altiero Spinelli, 'Europe and the Nuclear Monopoly', in *The Atlantic Community Quarterly,* Winter 1964–1965.

Hans-Jürgen Stieringer, 'Die Auslandshilfegesetzgebung des amerikanischen Kongresses und die europäische Integration', in *Europa Archiv,* 9. Jahr, 6. Folge, 1954.

Dirk U. Stikker, 'The Functional Approach to European Integration', in *Foreign Affairs,* April 1951.

—, 'De O.E.E.S. als instrument van Europese samenwerking', in *Herwonnen Welvaart,* ('s-Gravenhage: Ministerie van Buitenlandse Zaken, 1954).

—, 'NATO – The Shifting Alliance', in *The Atlantic Community Quarterly,* Spring 1965.

Henry Tasca, 'Die Vereinigten Staaten, Westeuropa und die Entwickelungsländer', in *Europa Archiv,* 15. Jahr, 5. Folge, 1960.

United Kingdom Government, *Blue Book, Negotiations for a European Free Trade Area,* (London: H.M.S.O., 1959).

United States Congress, *Outline of European Recovery Program,* 80th Congr., 1st sess., 1947.

—, *Final Report on Foreign Aid,* by Select Committee on Foreign Aid, House of Representatives, 80th Congr., 2nd sess., 1948.

—, *What Western Europe can do for itself,* Preliminary Report No. 14 of the Select Committee on Foreign Aid, House of Representatives, 80th Congr., 2nd sess., 1948.

—, *The European Recovery Program,* Report of the Senate Committee on Foreign Relations, No. 935, 80th Congr., 2nd sess., 1948.

—, *North Atlantic Treaty,* A Report of the U.S. Senate Committee on Foreign Relations, 81st Congr., 1st sess., 1949.

—, *A Decade of American Foreign Policy,* Basic Documents, 1941–1949, prepared for the Senate Committee on Foreign Relations by the Staff of the Committee and the Department of State, 81st Congr., 1st sess., 1950.

—, *The Union of Europe; its Progress, Problems, Prospects and Place in the Western World,* Senate Document No. 90, 82nd Congr., 2nd sess., 1952.

—, *United States Foreign Policy: Western Europe,* A Study prepared at the request of the Committee on Foreign Relations, U.S. Senate by the Foreign Policy Research Institute of Pennsylvania, 86th Congr., 1st sess., October 1959.

—, *United States Foreign Policy, Basic Aims of United States Foreign Policy,* Study for the Senate Committee on Foreign Relations by the Council on Foreign Relations, 86th Congr., 1st sess., 1959.

United States Congress, *Legislation on Foreign Relations* with explanatory notes, Senate Committee on Foreign Relations, 86th Congr., 1st sess., 1959.

—, *U.S. Foreign Aid, Its Purpose, Scope, Administration and Related Information,* prepared by the Library of Congress, 86th Congr., 1st sess., 1959.

—, *United States Foreign Policy, The Operational Aspects of United States Foreign Policy,* Study for the Senate Committee on Foreign Relations by Maxwell Graduate School of Citizenship and Public Affairs, Syracuse University, 86th Congr., 1st sess., 1959.

—, *United States Foreign Policy, The Formulation and Administration of United States Foreign Policy,* Study for the Senate Committee on Foreign Relations by The Brookings Institution, 86th Congr., 2nd sess., 1960.

—, *United States Foreign Policy, Ideology and Foreign Affairs,* Study for the Senate Committee on Foreign Relations by Center for International Affairs, Harvard University, 86th Congr., 2nd sess., 1960.

—, *A Study of Economic Regionalism. A new Era in Free World Economic Politics,* Report of a Special Study Mission of the Subcommittee on Europe of the Committee on Foreign Affairs, House of Representatives, 86th Congr., 2nd sess., 1960.

—, *Trade Adjustment in Theory and Practice,* Subcommittee on Foreign Economic Policy of the Joint Economic Committee, 87th Congr., 1st sess., 1961.

—, *Background Documents Relating to the Organization for Economic Cooperation and Development,* Senate Committee on Foreign Relations, 87th Congr., 1st sess., 1961.

—, *Documents on Germany, 1944–1961,* Senate Committee on Foreign Relations, 87th Congr., 1st sess., 1961.

—, *The Task for 1962: A Free World Community,* Study Paper by Henry S. Reuss for the Subcommittee on Foreign Economic Policy of the Joint Economic Committee, 87th Congr., 1st sess., 1961.

—, *United States Commercial Policy, A Program for the 1960's,* Study Paper by Peter B. Kenen for the Subcommittee on Foreign Economic Policy of the Joint Economic Committee, 87th Congr., 1st sess., 1961.

—, *The European Economic Community and the United States,* Study Paper by Robert R. Bowie and Theodore Geiger for the Subcommittee on Foreign Economic Policy of the Joint Economic Committee, 87th Congr., 1st sess., 1961.

—, *A New Look at Foreign Economic Policy,* by Christian A. Herter and William L. Clayton, Subcommittee on Foreign Economic Policy of the Joint Economic Committee, 87th Congr., 1st sess., 1961.

United States Congress, *Problems and Trends in Atlantic Partnership I, Some Comments on the European Economic Community and NATO*, Staff Study for the Senate Committee on Foreign Relations, 87th Congr., 2nd sess., 1962.

—, *Foreign Economic Policy for the 1960's*, Report of the Joint Economic Committee, 87th Congr., 2nd sess., 1962.

—, *A Compilation of Material Relating to United States Defense Policies in 1962*, prepared by the Library of Congress, 88th Congr., 1st sess., 1963.

—, *Problems and Trends in Atlantic Partnership II*, Staff Study for the Senate Committee on Foreign Relations, 88th Congr., 1st sess., 1963.

—, *The United States Balance of Payments – Perspectives and Policies*, Joint Economic Committee, 88th Congr., 1st sess., 1963.

—, *The United States Balance of Payments*, Report by the Joint Economic Committee, 88th Congr., 2nd sess., 1964.

United States Government, *National Resources and Foreign Aid*, (Washington, D.C.: 1947).

—, *European Recovery and American Aid*, A Report by the President's Committee on Foreign Aid, (Washington, D.C.: 1947).

—, *The Impact of Foreign Aid upon the Domestic Economy*, A Report to the President by the Council of Economic Advisors, (Washington, D.C.: 1947).

Jaques Vernant, 'Paris, Bonn und Europa', in *Europa Archiv*, 20. Jahr, 1. Folge, 1965.

Raymond Vernon, 'Die Vereinigten Staaten und die europäischen Handelsblöcke', in *Europa Archiv*, 15. Jahr, 17. Folge, 1960.

Wolfgang Wagner, 'De Gaulle drängt zur Entscheidung', in *Europa Archiv*, 19. Jahr, 17. Folge, 1964.

Barbara Ward, *Future Policies for the West – A Reappraisal*, Europe House, Paper 10, 1963.

Howard Whidden, 'The Changed American Perspective on Western Europe', in *Western World*, March 1960.

Joachim Willmann, 'Europa-Partner der Vereinigten Staaten', in *Europa Archiv*, 18. Jahr, 8. Folge, 1963.

—, 'Die Kennedy-Runde im Spannungsfeld amerikanischer und europäischer Interessen', in *Europa Archiv*, 19. Jahr, 18. Folge, 1964.

Albert Wohlstetter, 'Nuclear Sharing: NATO and the N + I Country', in *Foreign Affairs*, April 1961.

Arnold Wolfers, 'Integration in the West: The Conflict of Perspectives', in *International Organization*, Summer 1963.

World Peace Foundation, *Documents on American Foreign Relations,* Vol. VIII, IX, X, XI, and XII, edited by Raymond Dennett and Robert K. Turner, (Princeton, N.J.: Princeton University Press, 1948, 1949, 1950, 1950, 1951).

Willy Zeller, 'Die Niederlande als "Neinsager" der Europa Politik?', in *Europa Archiv,* 20. Jahr, 6. Folge, 1965.

Gilbert Ziebura, 'Ideologische Grundlagen der Aussenpolitik de Gaulles', in *Europa Archiv,* 20. Jahr, 8. Folge, 1965.

Index

A

B

C

D

E

I

J

K

L

P

S